T4-ADQ-852

Innovations of Knowledge Management

Bonnie Montano
Georgetown University, USA

IRM Press

Publisher of innovative scholarly and professional information technology titles in the cyberage

Hershey • London • Melbourne • Singapore

Acquisitions Editor:	Mehdi Khosrow-Pour
Senior Managing Editor:	Jan Travers
Managing Editor:	Amanda Appicello
Development Editor:	Michele Rossi
Copy Editor:	Ingrid Widitz
Typesetter:	Amanda Appicello
Cover Design:	Lisa Tosheff
Printed at:	Integrated Book Technology

Published in the United States of America by
IRM Press (an imprint of Idea Group Inc.)
701 E. Chocolate Avenue, Suite 200
Hershey PA 17033-1240
Tel: 717-533-8845
Fax: 717-533-8661
E-mail: cust@idea-group.com
Web site: http://www.irm-press.com

and in the United Kingdom by
IRM Press (an imprint of Idea Group Inc.)
3 Henrietta Street
Covent Garden
London WC2E 8LU
Tel: 44 20 7240 0856
Fax: 44 20 7379 3313
Web site: http://www.eurospan.co.uk

Copyright © 2005 by IRM Press. All rights reserved. No part of this book may be reproduced in any form or by any means, electronic or mechanical, including photocopying, without written permission from the publisher.

Library of Congress Cataloging-in-Publication Data

Innovations of knowledge management / Bonnie Montano, editor.
p. cm.
Includes bibliographical references and index.
ISBN 1-59140-229-8 (pbk.) -- ISBN 1-59140-281-6 (hardcover) -- ISBN 1-59140-230-1 (ebook)
1. Knowledge management. I. Montano, Bonnie.
HD30.2.I536 2005
658.4'038--dc22
2004003765

British Cataloguing in Publication Data
A Cataloguing in Publication record for this book is available from the British Library.

All work contributed to this book is new, previously-unpublished material. The views expressed in this book are those of the authors, but not necessarily of the publisher.

Innovations of Knowledge Management

Table of Contents

Preface vi
Bonnie Montano, Georgetown University, USA

Section I: Knowledge Management Methods

Chapter I
The Impact of Informal Networks on Knowledge Management Strategy 1
Tony Jewels, Queensland University of Technology, Australia
Alan Underwood, Queensland University of Technology, Australia

Chapter II
Knowledge Capture Between Consultancies and Freelance Subcontractors: A Model and Empirical Evidence 22
W. A. Taylor, University of Bradford, UK
N. A. Boraie, House of Egypt Consultants, Egypt and Triple Line Consulting, UK

Chapter III
Awareness Matters in Virtual Communities: An Awareness Ontology 51
Farhad Daneshgar, The University of New South Wales, Australia

Chapter IV
Corporate Memories: Tombs or Wellsprings of Knowledge? 69
Meliha Handzic, The University of New South Wales, Australia
Glenn Bewsell, The University of New South Wales, Australia

Chapter V
Knowledge Discovery Process and Introduction of Domain Knowledge 86
Katsutoshi Yada, Kansai University, Japan

Chapter VI
The Organizational Characteristics of Knowledge-Centricity 99
Jonathan Pemberton, Northumbria University, UK
George Stonehouse, Northumbria University, UK

Section II: Knowledge Management Tools

Chapter VII
Making Knowledge Management System an Effective Tool for Learning and Training 124
Albert C. K. Leung, Lingnan University, Hong Kong

Chapter VIII
Web Service Modeling Framework for the Enhanced Data Warehouse 149
Krzysztof Wecel, The Poznan University of Economics, Poland
Pawel Jan Kalczynski, University of Toledo, USA
Witold Abramowicz, The Poznan University of Economics, Poland

Chapter IX
Enterprise Portals and Knowledge Management Processes 175
Abdus Sattar Chaudhry, Nanyang Technological University, Singapore

Chapter X
Amalgamating Ontological Modeling with Bluetooth Service Discovery 200
Maria Ruey-Yuan Lee, Shih Chien University, Taiwan
Ching Lee, Hyper Taiwan Technology Inc., Taiwan

Chapter XI
Effective Integration of Computer-Supported Collaborative Learning into Knowledge Management Structures: A Model and an Evaluation Framework **215**
Francisco Milton Mendes Neto, Federal University of Campina Grande, Brazil and Serpro – Federal Service of Data Processing, Brazil
Francisco Vilar Brasileiro, Federal University of Campina Grande, Brazil

Section III: Knowledge Management for Attaining Strategic Advantage

Chapter XII
The European Challenge of KM and Innovation: A Skills and Competence Portfolio for the Knowledge Worker in SME's **252**
Ana Maria R. Correia, Universidade Nova de Lisboa, Portugal
Anabela Sarmento, Instituto Politécnico Porto, Portugal and University of Minho, Portugal

Chapter XIII
The Role of Knowledge Creation in Competitive Advantage **285**
Patricia C. Miller, University at Albany, USA

Chapter XIV
Promoting Organizational Knowledge Sharing **300**
Jack S. Cook, Rochester Institute of Technology, USA
Laura Cook, State University of New York at Geneseo, USA

Chapter XV
Value Creation through Customer Derived Revenue **322**
Michael Hall, Nakamura Gakuen University, Japan

About the Editor **336**

About the Authors **337**

Index **345**

Preface

The importance of organizational knowledge has been recognized for over fifty years. In recent years, organizations worldwide have embraced formal knowledge management initiatives as a way to create value from their intangible assets. Knowledge has proven so vital to organizational success that a new organizational form – knowledge-based firms – has emerged. With a slowdown in the world economy, the bursting of the technology bubble, and tighter budgets, the importance of leveraging existing knowledge and expertise has reached new highs. Knowledge management will remain a critical success factor for organizations as the economy recovers.

The purpose of this book is to survey some of the newest trends and findings in knowledge management. The series of chapters included in the book show the wide variety of directions in which knowledge management has evolved and illustrates the wide-ranging impact that knowledge management can effect for organizational success, thus emphasizing the continued importance of knowledge management for organizational success. Each chapter offers a discussion of some unique innovation, but common themes emerge as well. The themes center on methodologies and models, and tools for enhanced knowledge management as well as the competitive advantage that can be achieved by implementing knowledge management.

The chapters in this book are divided into three sections, one per theme. The first section, "Knowledge Management Methodologies," presents work on innovative approaches and methodologies for undertaking knowledge management. Each chapter highlights a particular aspect of knowledge management and provides a way to improve upon it. The first section contains six chapters.

In Chapter 1, Jewels and Underwood recognize the importance of not only formal knowledge management initiatives, but also the informal knowledge networks that already exist in organizations. They suggest that organizations must consider the impact of these informal knowledge networks when constructing formal knowledge management policies, procedures, and behaviors.

In Chapter 2, Taylor and Boraie examine knowledge capture from subcontractors by their sponsor organizations. Their study identifies cultural sensitivity and the process of knowledge capture to be the most important variables for successful knowledge capture. The lack of formal methods for capture and management of knowledge from subcontractors led the authors to develop a "Revolving Door" model for knowledge management.

In Chapter 3, Daneshgar studies knowledge sharing, which is arguably the cornerstone of knowledge management. Specifically, Daneshgar presents a methodology for sharing contextual knowledge in virtual communities.

In Chapter 4, Handzic and Bewsell explore the use of corporate memories in enhancing individual working knowledge and performance. They find that approximately one-third of knowledge stored in corporate memories is left untapped. This suggests much room for improvement in the leveraging of knowledge encoded in corporate memories. Quantity, quality, and diversity of the knowledge in the repositories are found to be directly related to their effectiveness.

In Chapter 5, Yada presents a framework for knowledge acquisition. The framework consists of a two-dimensional matrix whose dimensions are (1) consideration of time series data and (2) level of analysis. Yada uses knowledge discovery from sales data to understand how the knowledge discovery process proceeds from purchase history. By understanding how knowledge is discovered, the processes can be further enhanced for organizational gain.

In Chapter 6, Pemberton and Stonehouse conclude the section of the book on methodologies. Their chapter presents a matrix for gauging an organization's knowledge-centricity. The matrix emphasizes organizational characteristics necessary for success in a knowledge-centric business.

The second section of the book, "Knowledge Management Tools," presents some of the newest tools for carrying out knowledge management. These can be thought of as the instruments that enable organizations to conduct knowledge management as prescribed in the methodologies of the first six chapters of the book. The second section consists of five chapters.

In Chapter 7, Leung focuses on knowledge management for learning and training. Six major design factors for knowledge management systems are presented. These include media of representation, multiple perspectives, complexity, user control, online support, and navigation aids. By incorporating these features in knowledge management systems, the systems become potent tools for carrying out organizational knowledge management.

In Chapter 8, Wecel, Kalczynski, and Abramowicz present an open Web-services based system called the enhanced Knowledge Warehouse (eKW). The open and flexible system is extended from a pre-existing one by leveraging the system architecture. The authors discuss the role of eKW in the Semantic Web and how it fits within the broader context of knowledge management.

In Chapter 9, Chaudhry examines the ability of enterprise portals to support organizational knowledge management. The author finds that portals cannot adequately support all aspects of knowledge management, contrary to the marketing claims of many portal product companies. In response to the current shortcomings of portals, Chaudhry suggests several capabilities for future development – ability to handle multimedia, incorporate metadata or taxonomy into their content, and provide tools for data mining and workflow. Despite their shortcomings, portals remain the most promising tool for supporting knowledge management.

In Chapter 10, Lee and Lee discuss Bluetooth wireless networks and present a new approach for finding service capabilities. Because the system is wireless, the environment is dynamic, which raises interesting challenges for discovering and matching services as requested by devices. The trend towards wireless technology continues to grow on a global scale, suggesting that knowledge management via wireless networks can benefit from Lee and Lee's research.

In Chapter 11, Neto and Brasileiro conclude the second section of the text by examining the use of computer-supported collaborative learning tools in conjunction with other knowledge management tools (e.g., mapping tools, repositories). They find that computer-supported collaborative learning supports both knowledge creation and transfer, but that it is not exploited to its full potential. The problem is incomplete integration with other knowledge management tools. Neto and Brasileiro describe an approach to successfully employing computer-supported collaborative learning tools.

The third section of the book, "Knowledge Management for Attaining Strategic Advantage," presents a series of chapters on how innovative knowledge management can help organizations achieve strategic or competitive advantages over their competition. While the first sections of the book focused on specific methods or tools for "doing" knowledge management, this final section presents a broader overview of how value-added is provided to organizations through knowledge management. This section consists of four chapters.

In Chapter 12, Correia and Sarmento draw broad strokes showing how small and medium sized organizations can use knowledge management strategically. The authors use the Portuguese strategy for evolving a knowledge-based society as a case example and develop a list of critical areas of study and practice necessary for successfully leveraging knowledge management.

In Chapter 13, Miller investigates the relationship between an organization's character and its ability to create knowledge, which ultimately impacts the organization's competitive advantage. Miller draws on the Core Competency Model and the concept of Intellectual Bandwidth for knowledge creation to support his arguments.

In Chapter 14, Cook and Cook examine what organizations can do to promote knowledge sharing in order to gain a competitive advantage. They recognize the importance of knowledge sharing as vital to organizational success in the modern economy.

In the final chapter of the book, Hall explores an increasingly important knowledge asset, that of customer knowledge. Historically, knowledge management has focused on employee or organizational knowledge. The author extends the view of organizational knowledge assets to include those of the customer. By exploiting customer knowledge, organizations find another way to leverage knowledge for advantage above their competitors.

Knowledge management is a vast and dynamic field. To attempt to capture every concept of importance in a single book would be futile. However, I believe this book can serve as a colorful snapshot of the most recent innovations in knowledge management. There is thorough discussion of several knowledge management methodologies as well as specific tools for carrying out knowledge management initiatives. The international flavor of this book also suggests it should have wide appeal to academicians and practitioners around the globe.

Section I

Knowledge Management Methods

Chapter I

The Impact of Informal Networks on Knowledge Management Strategy

Tony Jewels
Queensland University of Technology, Australia

Alan Underwood
Queensland University of Technology, Australia

Knowledge Management *- the collection and processing of disparate knowledge in order to affect mutual performance.*

Abstract

The application of a knowledge management strategy does not take place in a vacuum. Successfully meeting objectives of a knowledge management strategy may depend not only on the efficacy of the strategy itself or of the team that is responsible for its implementation, but also on the environment into which it is being introduced. Research carried out with an application service provider (ASP) indicates that existing informal communication networks will continue to operate independently of any formal strategy

Copyright © 2004, Idea Group Inc. Copying or distributing in print or electronic forms without written permission of Idea Group Inc. is prohibited.

introduced. The significance of informal knowledge sharing activity may be in its incompatibility, or possible conflict, with any formal structures that are introduced. The success of any formally instigated knowledge management strategy might therefore depend on an understanding of the existence and nature of already active informal knowledge sharing structures. It is important for management to recognise the existence of such informal networks and to understand how they might affect the success of any formally introduced knowledge management strategy. In this paper the existence and reasons for informal networks and their subsequent effects on formal knowledge management policy are examined.

Introduction

In 1998 an application service provider (ASP), with the assistance of a major international consultancy company acting as its implementation partner, had coordinated the simultaneous implementation of SAP R/3 across five government agencies. Three years later, this ASP, like several other organizations following the spate of Enterprise Systems (ES) implementations prior to the turn of the century, was facing its first major upgrade. The ASP General Manager (GM) appreciated the need to recall the lessons and practices from these initial projects as the extent and cost of these major upgrades were likely to match or exceed those of the initial implementation. The GM had long recognised the importance of knowledge capture, access, sharing and re-use, both for the current upgrade process and for future upgrades, and university researchers had already been engaged with the ASP in a number of research projects in the area of knowledge management within an ES environment (Chan & Rosemann, 2000; Chang, Gable, Smythe & Timbrell, 2000; Timbrell & Gable, 2001).

Knowledge of the forthcoming upgrade and the awareness of a newly published paper, "Theory of Knowledge Reuse: Types of Knowledge Reuse Situations and Factors in Reuse Success" (Markus, 2001) provided an opportunity to test the validity of the paper's typology of knowledge reuse and to concurrently provide research data that might assist the ASP in providing conditions under which successful knowledge reuse was likely to occur. An original study conducted by Timbrell & Jewels (2002) tested Markus's theory by matching the expected and actual responses to a set of predetermined questions linked

Copyright © 2004, Idea Group Inc. Copying or distributing in print or electronic forms without written permission of Idea Group Inc. is prohibited.

to that theory. This study concluded by generally supporting the theory of knowledge reuse, whilst also indicating the pervasiveness of informal knowledge sharing networks within the organization. An initial review of the published literature on informal networks provided prima facie evidence that the type of informal knowledge sharing activities that had been identified in the research is likely to influence the ultimate effectiveness of any formal knowledge management strategy.

Responses from the original study were then carefully re-examined, specifically from an informal network knowledge sharing perspective, and subsequently compared to the current literature. This chapter examines informal network knowledge sharing behaviour identified in the research and compares and contrasts that behaviour with the existing literature.

Objectives

This research forms part of an exploratory stage of an investigation into knowledge management practices within knowledge intensive organizations and evaluates the nature of informal knowledge sharing practices within the organization, a rationale for its existence and its possible effect on the operation of the organization's formal knowledge management policy. In seeking to better understand the dynamics of informal knowledge sharing practices, our objective is to inform academe and practitioners on ways of improving the effectiveness of knowledge management strategy.

Research Process

Using a questionnaire derived from the Markus model, semi-structured interviews were conducted over a period of six days with all 28 employees within the ASP. The interviews were taped for later transcriptions and relevant notes taken to highlight key issues. Interviews held in an office provided specifically for the purpose by management were planned for 30 minutes duration, commencing at 0830 and finishing at 1700 each working day until completion.

The interview technique used was a combination of the standardized, otherwise known as structured, interview (Fontana & Frey, 1998, p. 47) and guided

Copyright © 2004, Idea Group Inc. Copying or distributing in print or electronic forms without written permission of Idea Group Inc. is prohibited.

interviews. The research team prepared a semi-standardized set of questions that would take about three quarters of the interview time and the remainder of the scheduled time was used to revisit issues that had arisen during the more structured questioning, by referring to the question topic guide. The interviewer's technique was based on the styles described by Fontana and Frey (1998, pp. 52-53) as "balanced rapport" and "interested listening," meaning that a casual yet impersonal attitude that neither evaluated nor judged the interviewees' responses was maintained.

An assurance that responses would be kept confidential may have contributed to the candid nature of responses. To ensure that it was not possible for individuals or definable groups to be identified by the published data, identification numbers were allocated to each interviewee, which were used for report analysis rather than names. Names with matching identification numbers were kept in a separate database table and were kept strictly confidential, available only to the researchers.

The actual questions used in the interviews were primarily designed to identify how closely each interviewee aligned to Markus' theory of knowledge re-use, and were segmented to achieve various objectives linked to her taxonomy. In attempting to identify how closely interviewees' responses compared with Markus' taxonomy of knowledge re-use there was a need to match characteristics of the employee with his or her knowledge re-use practices, and the interviews set out to:

- Capture the demographics of employees, their experiences and work backgrounds.
- Identify both the knowledge repositories used and the different types of knowledge re-use situations.

The interviews included questions designed to identify:

- The purposes of knowledge reuse.
- What users need to know, know and do not know.
- Challenges re-users experience (and strategies used) when defining a search question.
- Location of experts or knowledge expertise.

Copyright © 2004, Idea Group Inc. Copying or distributing in print or electronic forms without written permission of Idea Group Inc. is prohibited.

- How experts or expertise were selected.
- How the knowledge was applied.
- Their recommendations for promoting successful reuse.

Some examples of the actual types of questions asked were:

- Where do you acquire new knowledge that others have generated?
- How do you get advice about how to handle a particularly challenging or unusual situation that is new to your team?
- Do you store context information (i.e., metadata) with all repositories to facilitate reuse?
- Would you normally (within a team) keep good records about what you did as a by-product of the work?
- Do you have suitable criteria for judging the quality of experts/expertise?

In testing the validity of the Markus model using the questionnaire developed for this purpose, it was thought appropriate to investigate other variables relating to our wider study objectives. The use of a predominantly deductive approach (the inference of particular instances by reference to a general law or principle (Reader's Digest, 2001)) was combined with an inductive approach (the inference of a general law from particular instances (*Reader's Digest*, 2001)) by embedding in the interview process open-ended questions aimed at identifying particular knowledge sharing activities of the individual interviewee. The combining of these approaches is discussed by Perry and Jensen (2002), who cite Miles and Huberman (1994) as concluding that induction and deduction are linked research approaches, with Parkhe (1993, pp. 253, 256) arguing that "both extremes are untenable and unnecessary" and that the process of ongoing theory advancement requires "continuous interplay" between the two.

Using this approach, it was possible to test both an existing theory and still identify characteristics that had no direct relationship to the theory being studied.

Copyright © 2004, Idea Group Inc. Copying or distributing in print or electronic forms without written permission of Idea Group Inc. is prohibited.

Background

A considerable amount of literature is now available relating to principles of knowledge management, yet there appears to still be relatively little relating to the application of those principles. The literature selected relates specifically to the subject of the effects of informal networks on formal knowledge management strategies and covers three key areas: stakeholders, knowledge requirements and the nature of informal networks.

Stakeholders

For the purposes of examining knowledge dynamics within an organization it is important to understand the roles and interactions played by each of the types referred to by Frame (1999) in contributing to competence: the individual, the team and the organization.

The Individual

The traditional and popular view is that it is the individuals within organizations, and not the organizations themselves that learn (Simon, 1976; Weick, 1978). Although new knowledge is developed by individuals, organizations do play a critical role in articulating and amplifying that knowledge (Nonaka, 1994).

The role that individual-level processes play in organizational learning is examined by Andrews and Delahaye (2000) in terms of how knowledge inputs and outputs are mediated by individuals. Knowledge inputs are discussed in terms of the individuals' social confidence and their perception of the credibility of the knowledge source. Knowledge outputs are discussed in terms of what knowledge would be shared with whom, determined by the perceived trustworthiness of the recipient. The term "psychosocial filter" is used to describe the cluster of factors that influence knowledge sharing processes, and is described as working at the "micro-level".

The Team

The literature is increasingly discussing the use of "teams" and "communities" according to Ferrán-Urdaneta (1999), who discusses the differences between

Copyright © 2004, Idea Group Inc. Copying or distributing in print or electronic forms without written permission of Idea Group Inc. is prohibited.

these two types of groups. From an organizational learning perspective, Andrews and Delahaye (2000) also add the group level to that of the individual and the organization. We may, for the purpose of this study, define a team (or community) simply as more than one individual collaborating together. It might however be more contentious to suggest that for knowledge sharing purposes a team need not necessarily be part of the same organization.

The Organization

Achieving any quality product or service requires that knowledge workers share data, information and experiences, and in order to optimize knowledge sharing, as well as have a supportive culture, an organization must possess a suitable infrastructure (Gross, 2001).

Successful knowledge sharing practices according to Dixon (2000) require a complete solution that does not merely provide access to information technology and repositories. Because of the high cost of establishing effective knowledge sharing strategies the organization must pay careful attention to:

- The design of incentives for contributing to and using repositories.
- The roles of intermediaries in developing and maintaining repositories in order to facilitate the process.

Formal organization charts have little relevance to the true sources of power in the high-value enterprise, according to Reich (1991, p. 99): "Power depends not on formal authority or rank, (as it did in the high-volume enterprise), but on the capacity to add value to enterprise webs".

Knowledge Required

According to Chan (1999) and Chan and Rosemann (2000), ES implementations require a wide range of knowledge, including project knowledge, technical knowledge, product knowledge, business knowledge and company-specific knowledge.

In explaining the knowledge required in a project, Frame (1999) suggests a three-stage approach by asking:

Copyright © 2004, Idea Group Inc. Copying or distributing in print or electronic forms without written permission of Idea Group Inc. is prohibited.

- What skills should we possess in order to do the job?
- Do we have them?
- How can we acquire them?

Where an organization believes that it does not have the requisite expertise, it will seek knowledge-based resources from third-party providers such as consulting firms (knowledge vendors), which act in the capacity of implementation partner (Timbrell & Gable, 2001).

Informal Networks

Failing to take account of the powerful internal forces within organizations, according to Cook (1999), is a fundamental weakness in many knowledge management implementation processes. Insights can be gained into what Levinson (1999, p. 19) describes as "mutual utility" and Capron and Kuiper refer to (1998) as a shared spirit of community.

Informal networks are important devices for promoting communication within and between organizations, which are viewed by Jones, Conway and Steward (2002) as structures that supplement, complement and add value to the formal organization. In sometimes bypassing the formal organization's system of communication, Rachman and Mescon (1985) suggest that such structures strongly influence the distribution of power, and while the formal organization spells out who should have power, it is the informal organization that sometimes reveals who actually has it.

Whereas formal organizational structures are able to handle easily anticipated problems, when unexpected problems arise, Krackhardt and Hanson (1993) suggest that an informal organization kicks in. The phenomenon is also discussed by Bhatt (2002), who states that employees often form their own informal communities of expertise from which they can get necessary pieces of knowledge. Often, in the type of work that "symbolic analysts" perform, frequent and informal conversations are used, as neither problems nor solutions can be defined in advance (Reich, 1991). Informal organizations are described by Krackhardt and Hanson (1993) as being highly adaptive, moving diagonally and elliptically, skipping entire functions to get work done, and by Stacey (1996) as the mechanism that people employ to deal with the highly complex, the ambiguous, the unpredictable, the inconsistent, the conflicting, the frustrating, and the alienating.

Copyright © 2004, Idea Group Inc. Copying or distributing in print or electronic forms without written permission of Idea Group Inc. is prohibited.

It should be emphasised that the informal structures that are being referred to in this chapter do not directly relate to the informal transfers of tacit knowledge described by Nonaka (1994) occurring between employees (although this type of informal transfer might still occur within an informal structure). Informal networks are relationships developed between individuals independently of any formal structure (although an informal structure might occur within a formal structure), and are not the chance meetings at the water cooler or cafeteria that Davenport and Prusak (1998) discuss, but carefully conceived personal 'networks of knowing,' built up over time and used as complementary knowledge sharing alternatives to an organization's formal strategy. In describing "the network of social interactions that are not specified by the formal organization, but that develop on a personal level among workers in a company," Wells and Spinks (1994, p. 24) use the term "grapevine". They describe the ubiquitous grapevine as humanly permanent, extremely fast, and highly accurate, providing qualified answers and usually bad news. Although obviously also an existing communication network, it is also, like the chance meetings at the water cooler, not directly related to the informal structures discussed here, but belonging to what might be more accurately described as an unofficial structure.

There are according to BizMove.com (2002, p. 2), three basic channels of organizational communication:

> "*Formal* – Communication within the formal organizational structure that transmits goals, policies, procedures and directions.
>
> *Informal* – The communication outside the formal organizational structure that fills the organizational gaps, maintains the linkages, and handles the one-time situations.
>
> *Unofficial* – The interpersonal communication within, (or among), the social structure of the organization that serves as a vehicle for casual interpersonal exchanges, and transmittal of unofficial communications."

In using the term *quasi-formal* structure, an additional level between the formal and informal structures that is sanctioned by the organization is identified by Schoonhoven and Jelinek (1990).

Although these communication channels operate seamlessly in most organizations and each is likely to affect the impact of the others, it is the interaction between the informal and formal channels that is to be examined in this chapter.

Copyright © 2004, Idea Group Inc. Copying or distributing in print or electronic forms without written permission of Idea Group Inc. is prohibited.

Factors Influencing the Prominence of Informal Networks

The prominence of informal organizations, according to Stacey (1996), is caused by two factors:

- The subordination of individuality related to the alienating and de-motivating nature of bureaucracies.
- The inability of bureaucracies to handle environmental ambiguity and uncertainty.

In exploring attitudes towards organizational versus individual ownership of information, Jarvenpaa and Staples (2001) discuss the propensity to share information/knowledge in terms of organizational culture. Culture, according to McDermott and O'Dell (2001), is often seen as a key inhibitor of effective knowledge sharing.

Organizational Culture

A wide body of evidence exists to indicate that organizational or corporate culture is critical to the success of most, if not all, enterprise systems implementations. There are four hypothesized categories of organizational obstacles in information systems development, according to Jin (1993), namely:

- Bureaucratic complexity,
- Personality conflict,
- Technical complexity, and
- Acute resource scarcity.

The effect that organizational culture has on knowledge management strategies is being increasingly recognised as a major barrier to leveraging intellectual assets, according to De Long and Fahey (2000), who consider four ways in which culture influences the behaviour central to knowledge creation, sharing and use:

Copyright © 2004, Idea Group Inc. Copying or distributing in print or electronic forms without written permission of Idea Group Inc. is prohibited.

- Culture, and particularly subcultures, shape assumptions about what knowledge is and which knowledge is worth managing.
- Culture defines the relationships between individual and organizational knowledge, determining who is expected to control specific knowledge, as well as who must share it and who can hoard it.
- Culture creates the context for social interaction that determines how knowledge will be used in particular situations.
- Culture shapes the processes by which new knowledge, with its accompanying uncertainties, is created, legitimated and distributed in organizations.

Certain types of identifiable culture have the potential to affect an ERP environment according to Stewart, Milford, Jewels, Hunter and Hunter (2000). Although these culture states can affect different types of organizations in different ways and each can be more prevalent in certain types of organization, they may best be identified by comparing how closely the organization meets the following principles:

- Genuine user empowerment that produces internal as well as external commitment.
- Acceptance of "risk-taking" as a necessary factor in planning, which does not punish failure, and the move away from non-competitive or even anti-competitive cultures to true market competitive cultures.

Bliss (1999) reminds us that a desired organization culture and an actual organization culture are often worlds apart, and it is important to understand how each are playing out in the workplace. He states that it is imperative to know the company culture and assess new employees' belief systems against the organizational culture.

Employee Empowerment and Risk Orientation

Decision-making processes in organizations are, according to Allison (1971), performed by individuals from three different perspectives:

Copyright © 2004, Idea Group Inc. Copying or distributing in print or electronic forms without written permission of Idea Group Inc. is prohibited.

- The rational actor model, where individuals weigh up alternatives and select the one that makes most sense to them.
- The operational procedures model, where the decision-making process is driven principally by the organizations' standard operating procedures (SOPs).
- The political model, where perceived self-interest dominates the decision-making process.

The objective of empowerment is to assure individual member success within the framework of the organization's mission, vision, and strategy (Galbraith, Lawler et al., 1993). If this is to be accomplished, the organizational environment must support the following three practices:

- Freedom to act.
- Commitment by individual members of their responsibility for the consequences of their own behaviour.
- Collaboration by simultaneous involvement of individual members in the process of their own and others' success.

Empowerment, however, remains very much like the emperor's new clothes: it is praised loudly in public, but privately we ask ourselves why we cannot see it. True empowerment results in internal as well as external commitment by employees, yet despite all the rhetoric and the change programs, empowerment, Argyris (1998) believes, is still mostly an illusion.

Managerial behaviour is often directed toward preventing employees from making mistakes (Pope, 1996). Organizations use administrative systems (rules and roles) to reduce the probability of human error, and to reduce the variability of human behaviour. Such systems now typically remove an individual's ability to make decisions in a work situation. This philosophical orientation has the outcome of preventing failure and provides a psychological safety net to individuals in the organization. Specifically, organizations act to restrict the necessity for individual decisions by:

- pre-defining multiple independent tasks,
- pre-determining organizational decision points, and
- pre-assigning scarce or valuable resources.

Copyright © 2004, Idea Group Inc. Copying or distributing in print or electronic forms without written permission of Idea Group Inc. is prohibited.

To successfully manage complex projects, Breen (1995) suggests that an initiative must be taken in educating, actually encouraging and empowering project teams to cut across organizational barriers, allowing organizations to overcome natural barriers to successful project management.

Findings

The small sample size of 28, further reduced by the unusability of two of the interviews, obviously limits the validity of the findings. On the other hand, open access to a whole department, from general manager through to the most junior staff member, provided an opportunity to snapshot the activities of individuals, teams and the organization in which they worked more holistically than may have been possible with a larger but non-universal sample.

Knowledge Required

Based partly on its experiences with the original implementation partner, for its forthcoming upgrade, the ASP had decided to "go it alone," choosing to employ just a few key individual contractors to work with its internal staff. The GM believed that his organization was already experienced enough in all the identified knowledge areas to execute the upgrade without the assistance of an implementation partner. The key contractors consisted mainly of individuals who had worked for the organization at the time of the original implementation but had since left to pursue alternative employment.

Informal Networks

It was apparent from the responses in the interviews that knowledge sharing was occurring in at least two identifiable modes. Management had introduced a range of formal knowledge-sharing initiatives that could be considered as a top-down approach. It was, however, clearly evident that employees were using an alternative method of knowledge sharing to the one created by management. Individuals had formed their own personal networks and had developed their own "communities of interest" in what could be considered as an informal bottom-up approach.

Copyright © 2004, Idea Group Inc. Copying or distributing in print or electronic forms without written permission of Idea Group Inc. is prohibited.

What was particularly interesting in our findings was that although management executives themselves had indicated that they were using their own informal knowledge sharing structures, they still did not fully appreciate that similar practices operated extensively at other levels within their organization. Although recognising the existence of the "grapevine" type social network, management had little idea of the extent and frequency of use of the same type of informal networks that they themselves were using and had had no direct role in either creating or nurturing them.

The following examples were typical of the responses:

> *"Who I use (as experts) and the people on the formal experts list are different."*
>
> *"I network with people that I have worked with in the past."*
>
> *"I use my personal network of contacts if I can't readily find appropriate documentation."*
>
> *"I have an extensive personal collection of books that I use."*

Factors Influencing the Prominence of Informal Networks

Although evidence of all four categories of organizational obstacle referred to earlier by Jin (1993) was identified in the research, it appeared that when confronted with these obstacles employees would merely find an alternative way to reach their objectives. There was a general feeling that these organizational obstacles, although considered annoying, could be bypassed whenever necessary. One of the common methods employees used to circumvent organizational obstacles was to marshal their own informal structures.

However, the barriers that De Long and Fahey (2000) refer to are not as easily bypassed. These are the ones that appear able to be controlled only by organizational initiatives. The barriers referred to by Stewart et al. (2000) are either similarly organizationally controlled or are deeply personalised in the individual.

System security appeared to be an issue that was affecting knowledge-sharing activities. One contractor admitted:

> *"I don't know of any contractors that have had direct access to the knowledge database."*

Copyright © 2004, Idea Group Inc. Copying or distributing in print or electronic forms without written permission of Idea Group Inc. is prohibited.

while one relatively new full-time employee commented:

"I wasn't even told about the existence of the knowledge data base."

There was a policy that employees should only be given access to the specific areas that they were working in, and subsequently lessons learnt from one part of the system could seldom be formally shared with those that did not have access to that part. Remarks such as:

"No-one would be interested in what I am doing."
"I only bother formally documenting for myself because I am the only person who would need to use this type of information."

indicated a general under-utilisation of formal knowledge-sharing practices.

Formal Knowledge Management Strategies

The importance of formal team building and creating a sense of shared purpose as described by Senge (1992) was clearly evident to management, as they had embarked on a range of formal initiatives to harness its potential.

By his introduction of such initiatives as a free text knowledge database and the championing of specific knowledge transfer sessions, the GM appeared typical of the sort of individual that Skyrme (1999) and Health Canada (2000) refer to when they suggest that the appointment of a senior executive responsible for knowledge initiatives appeared to be a prerequisite to a successful KM strategy.

Yet the formal knowledge transfer sessions were not well regarded, with comments such as:

"Skill transfer sessions were not popular, they were seen as a waste of time and irrelevant."

Although it was evident that management understood the rationale for these sessions it was uncertain whether there was an understanding by employees of

Copyright © 2004, Idea Group Inc. Copying or distributing in print or electronic forms without written permission of Idea Group Inc. is prohibited.

their raison d'être. Even though some individuals clearly supported the concept of formally sharing knowledge, the knowledge transfer sessions were not considered to be the most appropriate process. Furthermore, although management had allocated time to attend the knowledge transfer sessions, they had not formally allocated equivalent times for employees to update the free text database.

The term "key people" who, as one interviewee suggested:

> *"... make themselves visible in all projects"*

was frequently used. It was implied that these so-called key people were in fact in such great demand, and their workloads at critical times so heavy that they could clearly not find the time to properly document what they were doing or share the lessons learnt with others.

It was also made evident that these people were not being retained by the organization, with comments such as:

> *"Although management assumed that the implementation partner had transferred knowledge, most people who had actually benefited from this knowledge transfer have moved on [left the organization]."*
>
> *"Most of the 'real' experts have moved on."*
>
> *"We have allowed our own experts and expertise to slip through our hands, like sand through our fingers, because their importance was not valued."*

What was made unambiguously clear in the interviews was that the knowledge sharing that was intended to take place with the original implementation partner (IP) did not occur properly. Comments such as:

> *"[The IP] knew very little regarding SAP and the Government's business rules."*
>
> *"[The IP] kept public servants at 'arm's length' or possibly didn't have the required knowledge themselves."*

indicated a lack of trust and confidence in the IP. It was, however, never ascertained what contractual arrangements the IP may have entered into with the ASP regarding knowledge sharing activities.

Copyright © 2004, Idea Group Inc. Copying or distributing in print or electronic forms without written permission of Idea Group Inc. is prohibited.

Conclusion

There was a clear indication that not only was informal knowledge sharing taking place throughout the organization, but that it was the preferred strategy. It was evident that many individuals within these informal structures had maintained their links after job changes, or even after leaving the organization in which the original structure was formed, suggesting that the organization itself may have had little impact on how informal knowledge sharing structures were formed or operated.

No pattern was evident to suggest that these knowledge sharing structures were anything but randomly 'user formed,' although many of the individuals who were more actively involved in informal knowledge-sharing groups were those people who had been with the organization (or ones similar to it) the longest.

There was evidence to suggest that wherever there was a perceived failure to provide a process for adequate individual or organizational learning, individual knowledge workers engaged automatically in alternative strategies to ensure that they would be able to do their work. One of the main strategies used was that of engaging their informal networks, appearing to confirm the independence and self-motivation of knowledge workers, described by Drucker (1999) in their willingness to 'get the job done' by whatever means available to them. Even when appropriate supportive organizational cultures and formal infrastructures are not in place, knowledge workers appear to create their own informal systems and still remain highly task or output motivated.

The use of existing 'user controlled' knowledge-sharing networks appeared in this research to be affecting the proper utilisation of management's formally introduced knowledge management strategies.

It would appear to indicate that the prevalence and strength of an informal network would impact the internal acceptance of any newly introduced formal knowledge management strategy. Evidence of robust informal network activity within the subject organization would at least partly explain the relatively unenthusiastic acceptance by staff of formally introduced knowledge management initiatives.

Knowledge workers' acceptance of, and commitment to, any formally introduced knowledge management initiative appears to be influenced by whatever knowledge management practices are already being employed by them. Even though management may have had no involvement in the creation and operation

Copyright © 2004, Idea Group Inc. Copying or distributing in print or electronic forms without written permission of Idea Group Inc. is prohibited.

of informal knowledge sharing practices, their impacts, as well as the reasons for their existence, should be taken into consideration prior to the introduction of any formal management strategy. Any formally introduced knowledge management initiative, in order to gain acceptance by users, might require the perception by users that it is likely to be at least as relevant and effective as the strategy that they currently use.

Further research relating to knowledge sharing is currently being undertaken within one private sector organization and a local government body. A comparison of differences between the effects of informal knowledge sharing on formal knowledge strategies in public and private sector organizations may provide additional evidence on how management might increase the likelihood of success of any formally introduced knowledge management strategy.

References

Allison, G.T. (1971). *The essence of decision: Explaining the Cuban Missile Crisis.* Boston: Little Brown.

Andrews, K.M., & Delahaye, B.L. (2000). Influences on knowledge processes in organizational learning: The psychosocial filter. *Journal of Management Studies, 37*(6), 797-810.

Argyris, C. (1998). Empowerment: The emperor's new clothes. *Harvard Business Review, 76*(3).

Bhatt, G.D. (2002). Management strategies for individual knowledge and organizational knowledge. *Journal of Knowledge Management, 6*(1), 31-39.

BizMove.com. (2002). Communicating within the organization [URL]. *BizMove.com - The Small Business Knowledge Base.* Retrieved November 4, 2002, from *http://www.bizmove.com/skills/m8m.htm*

Bliss, W.G. (1999, February). Why is corporate culture important? *Workforce.*

Breen, T.A. (1995). Project management: Developing the right "culture" can make a world of difference. *Plant Engineering, 49.*

Capron, B., & Kuiper, D. (1998, April). Corporate culture—The seeds of failure. *Manufacturing Systems (Supplement): A Manager's Guide to Application Systems.*

Copyright © 2004, Idea Group Inc. Copying or distributing in print or electronic forms without written permission of Idea Group Inc. is prohibited.

Chan, R. (1999, November 1-2). *Knowledge management for implementing ERP in SMEs.* Paper presented at the 3rd Annual SAP Asia Pacific SAPPHIRE 1999, Singapore.

Chan, R., & Rosemann, M. (2000, August 3-5). *Managing knowledge in enterprise systems.* Paper presented at the Americas Conference of Information Systems, Boston, USA.

Chang, S.-I., Gable, G.G., Smythe, E., & Timbrell, G.T. (2000, December 10-13). *A Delphi examination of public sector ERP implementation issues.* Paper presented at the International Conference of Information Systems, Brisbane, Australia.

Cook, P. (1999). I heard it through the grapevine: Making knowledge management work by learning to share knowledge, skills and experience. *Industrial and Commercial Training, 31*(3), 101-105.

Davenport, T.H., & Prusak, L. (1998). *Working knowledge: How organizations manage what they know.* Boston: Harvard Business School Press.

De Long, D.W., & Fahey, L. (2000). Diagnosing cultural barriers to knowledge management. *Academy of Management Executive, 14*(4), 113-127.

Dixon, N.M. (2000). *Common knowledge: How companies thrive by sharing what they know.* Boston: Harvard Business School Press.

Drucker, P.F. (1999). Knowledge-worker productivity: The biggest challenge. *California Management Review, 41*(2), 79-94.

Ferrán-Urdaneta, C. (1999). *Teams or communities? Organizational structures for knowledge management.* Paper presented at the SIGCPR '99, New Orleans.

Fontana, A., & Frey, J. (1998). Collecting and interpreting qualitative materials. In N. Denzin & Y. Lincoln (Eds.), *Interviewing: The art of science* (pp. 47-78). Thousand Oaks, CA: Sage.

Frame, J.D. (1999). *Project management competence.* USA: Jossey-Bass.

Galbraith, J., Lawler, E. and Associates. (1993). *Organizing for the future: The new logic for managing complex organizations.* San Francisco: Jossey-Bass.

Gross, A.E. (2001). *Knowledge sharing—The crux of quality.* Paper presented at the Annual Quality Congress Proceedings, Milwaukee.

Copyright © 2004, Idea Group Inc. Copying or distributing in print or electronic forms without written permission of Idea Group Inc. is prohibited.

Health Canada. (2000). *Vision and strategy for knowledge management and IM/IT for Health Canada.* Health Canada. Retrieved November 22, 2001, from http://www.hc-sc.gc.ca/iacb-dgiac/km-gs/english/vsmenu2_e.htm

Jarvenpaa, S.L., & Staples, S. (2001). Exploring perceptions of organizational ownership of information and expertise. *Journal of Management Information Systems, 18*(1), 151-183.

Jin, K.G. (1993). Overcoming organizational barriers to system development: An action strategy framework. *Journal of Systems Management, 44*(5), 28-33.

Jones, O., Conway, S., & Steward, F. (2002). *Social interaction and organizational change: Aston perspectives on innovation networks.* River Edge, NJ: ICP.

Krackhardt, D., & Hanson, J.R. (1993, July-August). Informal networks: The company behind the chart. *Harvard Business Review.*

Levinson, W.A. (1999). Mutual commitment. *Executive Excellence, 16*(6).

Markus, M.L. (2001). Toward a theory of knowledge reuse: Types of knowledge reuse situations and factors in reuse success. *Journal of Management Information Systems, 18*(1), 57-93.

McDermott, R., & O'Dell, C. (2001). Overcoming cultural barriers to sharing knowledge. *Journal of Knowledge Management, 5*(1), 76-85.

Miles, M.B., & Huberman, A.M. (1994). *Qualitative data analysis - An expanded sourcebook.* Newbury Park: Sage.

Nonaka, I. (1994). A dynamic theory of organizational knowledge creation. *Organizational Science, 5*(1).

Parkhe, A. (1993). 'Messy' research, methodological predispositions and theory development in international joint ventures. *Academy of Management Review, 18*(2), 227-268.

Perry, C., & Jensen, O. (2002). *Approaches to combining induction and deduction in one research study.* Tweed Heads: Southern Cross University.

Pope, S. (1996). The power of guidelines, structure and clear goals. *Journal for Quality and Participation, 19*(7), 56-60.

Rachman, D.J., & Mescon, M.H. (1985). *Business Today* (4th ed.). New York: Random.

Copyright © 2004, Idea Group Inc. Copying or distributing in print or electronic forms without written permission of Idea Group Inc. is prohibited.

Reader's Digest. (2001). *Reader's Digest Wordpower Dictionary.* Turnhout, Belgium: Reader's Digest Association.

Reich, R.B. (1991). *The work of nations.* USA: Vintage Books.

Schoonhoven, C., & Jelinek, M. (1990). Dynamic tensions in innovative firms: Managing rapid technological change through organizational structure. In M. von Glinow & A. Mohrman (Eds.), *Managing complexity in high technology organizations.* New York: University Press.

Senge, P.M. (1992). *The fifth discipline: The art and practice of the learning organization.* Adelaide, Australia: Random House.

Simon, H.A. (1976). *Administrative behaviour: A study of decision making processes in administrative organization* (3rd ed.). New York: Free Press.

Skyrme, D.J. (1999, April 20). *Knowledge management: Making it work.* David Skyrme Associates. Retrieved November 22, 2001, from http://www.skyrme.com/pubs/lawlib99.htm

Stacey, R. (1996). *Strategic management and organizational dynamics* (2nd ed.). London: Pitman Publishing.

Stewart, G., Milford, M., Jewels, T., Hunter, T., & Hunter, B. (2000, August). *Organizational readiness for ERP implementation.* Paper presented at the AMCIS 2000, Long Beach, CA.

Timbrell, G., & Jewels, T. (2002, May 19-22). *Knowledge re-use situations in an enterprise systems context.* Paper presented at the 13th Information Resources Management Association Conference, Seattle, Washington.

Timbrell, G.T., & Gable, G.G. (2001, May 20-23). *The SAP ecosystem: A knowledge perspective.* Paper presented at the Information Resources Management Association International Conference, Toronto, Canada.

Weick, K.E. (1978). *The social psychology of organizing.* Reading, MA: Addison-Wesley.

Wells, B., & Spinks, N. (1994). Managing your grapevine: A key to quality productivity. *Executive Development, 7*(2), 24-27.

Copyright © 2004, Idea Group Inc. Copying or distributing in print or electronic forms without written permission of Idea Group Inc. is prohibited.

Chapter II

Knowledge Capture Between Consultancies and Freelance Subcontractors: A Model and Empirical Evidence

W. A. Taylor
University of Bradford, UK

N. A. Boraie
House of Egypt Consultants, Egypt and Triple Line Consulting, UK

Abstract

This chapter focuses on a perceived knowledge gap created whenever consultancy organizations sub-contract work to freelance consultants in the field. These field consultants often gain valuable knowledge from sub-contracted assignments, but this is not subsequently captured by their sponsors. From the perspective of any consultancy organization, the

Copyright © 2004, Idea Group Inc. Copying or distributing in print or electronic forms without written permission of Idea Group Inc. is prohibited.

knowledge process to capture such local knowledge is vital. Our exploratory research addresses three questions:

- Are management consulting firms aware of the importance of local knowledge possessed by freelance sub-contractors?
- Do they perceive any value in capturing this knowledge?
- To what extent do they currently capture such localized knowledge from sub-contractors and what methods do they use to do so?

The focus of the chapter is on smaller European consultancy practices operating in Egypt, many of which do not have the dedicated knowledge management departments and infrastructure of their larger competitors. We present results of two studies of European consultancy organizations that were active in developing countries in general and Egypt in particular. The first study (n = 48) was used as a pilot, since knowledge sharing between freelance consultants and their principal sponsors is relatively under-researched. Based on these preliminary findings and our review of the extant literature, we identified four dimensions that seemed to be particularly important for capturing knowledge in this context, namely (i) appreciating the value of local knowledge, (ii) building relationships with freelance consultants, (iii) sensitivity to national culture differences and (iv) the knowledge capture process itself. The second study (n = 170) developed a survey instrument based on these four dimensions. Through factor analysis, we produced robust support for all four constructs. Further, using self-reported measures of success with knowledge capture, we show that the knowledge capture process and cultural sensitivity are the most significant predictors of the dependent variable, with the remaining two dimensions also being significant. Finally, since we found that most of the respondents did not have formal systems for the capture and management of knowledge from their sub-contractors, we propose a "Revolving Door" model of knowledge capture, based on our findings. This model may alleviate the knowledge gap between consultancies and their sub-contracted agents in the field, and is a practical tool that is suitable for smaller consultancy practices who are less likely to have the resources to invest in technology-based knowledge management infrastructures.

Copyright © 2004, Idea Group Inc. Copying or distributing in print or electronic forms without written permission of Idea Group Inc. is prohibited.

Introduction

The European Commission finances many projects directed at developing countries to facilitate knowledge transfer and infrastructure development. For example, since 1999 the European Commission's Information Society and Technologies (IST) Program (EC, 2002) has co-funded research and development projects in knowledge management and organizational innovation, including the "Knowledge Management Made in Europe" initiative. Expending such large amounts of public money has a social dimension (through a contribution to the growth of developing nations), but there is also an implicit agenda to increase the capability of sponsored firms to compete in global markets.

European Union (EU) funding initiatives are channeled through European consulting organizations who act as knowledge brokers, and are often project members or leaders of particular projects. In the conduct of these projects they sub-contract assignments to freelance consultants. From our involvement in several EU financed Technical Assistance Projects, we have observed that while there are project reviews, final reports, monitoring and evaluation activities and audits, what is often missed is the capture of the knowledge gained by consultants "on the ground". Indeed we have also found low levels of awareness of knowledge management in this consulting community.

When operating in developing countries, local knowledge can be valuable to understand the local business culture and to adapt best international consulting practices in that context. It is also important to understand local business practices that depend heavily upon trust and personal relationships. Moreover, in many developing countries, business practices are quite different from that found in Northern Europe. For example, clients may have more than one set of accounts. Local knowledge can therefore be vital to appreciate the local business environment and avoid loss of credibility and even ridicule. This applies not only during the conduct of assignments but also when prospecting for engagements and writing and presenting client proposals. The central issue is whether the sponsoring consultancies capture this localized knowledge from freelance agents, so that they may enhance their capability to undertake future assignments. There are two questions that arise. First, do the consulting firms recognize this need, and second, what are they doing to address the problem?

The rest of the chapter is organized as follows: In the next section we review some of the pertinent literature. We then outline the methodology and present

Copyright © 2004, Idea Group Inc. Copying or distributing in print or electronic forms without written permission of Idea Group Inc. is prohibited.

results from our two surveys among European consulting firms currently undertaking assignments in Egypt. We find that the majority show little concern for capturing localized consulting knowledge from freelance consultants; consequently only a minority have formal systems in place to make this happen. We therefore propose a practical model that may help to overcome the problem. The final section concludes with implications of our findings for future research and management practice.

Background

Knowledge Infrastructures

There is a considerable body of research that examines the transfer of knowledge among strategic alliance partners (Grant & Baden-Fuller, 1995; Inkpen, 1998; Inkpen & Dinur, 1998) or between organizational units at the firm level (Davenport, DeLong & Beers, 1998; Huber, 2001; Szulanski, 1996). One sector that has been at the forefront of knowledge management practice is management consulting, but while many researchers have investigated knowledge transfer and sharing in this context (Apostolou & Mentzas, 1999; Hansen, Nohria & Tierney, 1999; Lapause, 2003a), we know of none that have examined the specific issue of knowledge transfer between freelance consultants and their sponsoring firms.

There is general agreement that knowledge is the lifeblood of consulting firms. There are at least two key concerns for consulting firms regarding the capture and exploitation of knowledge. The first is to provide field consultants with a knowledge infrastructure (Lapause, 2003b), such that "when one of our consultants shows up, the client gets the best of the firm, not just the best of that consultant" (Stewart, Godsey & Dunlap, 1995, p. 209). The second is to ensure that locally derived knowledge from assignments is absorbed back into the practice so that in-house staff upgrade their skills, avoiding the problem that "too often, when the consultant's job is finished, they take with them all of the knowledge of how to do that job" (Kerr, 1998, p. 20). It is this second issue that forms the primary focus of our chapter.

While several studies have focused on the ways in which large consulting firms capture and share knowledge (Hansen et al., 1999; Sarvary, 1999; Weiss,

Copyright © 2004, Idea Group Inc. Copying or distributing in print or electronic forms without written permission of Idea Group Inc. is prohibited.

1999) there has been little exploration of smaller consulting organizations and particularly how they manage their reliance on sub-contracted freelance personnel. Many smaller consulting firms do not have the resources to invest in and maintain technically advanced knowledge management systems and rely instead on their personal networks to assemble project teams for assignments. Studies of consulting firms support this viewpoint. For example, Reimus found that of 82 U.S. based consulting firms, 60% maintained no active best practices databases, 33% did not use groupware and less than 25% utilized the Internet to support internal activities (Reimus, 1997). Similarly, Raz reported that 64% of consulting firms did not take advantage of electronic tools for managing knowledge (Raz, 2001).

Psychological Contracts Between Freelance Consultants and Sponsors

Smaller consulting firms depend upon their capacity to develop networks of consultants based on their ability to determine *what* knowledge is required for specific projects and *where* this may be found. Developing such partnerships or alliances can be a key capability in the smaller consulting practice. Where these alliances or networks involve freelance consultants, there should be recognition of the importance of the psychological contract (Rousseau, 1995), with consequent implications for trust, loyalty and security of employment. The term "psychological contract" was defined some 40 years ago by Argyris as "the perceptions of both parties to the employment relationship and the obligations implicit in the arrangement. Psychological contracting is the social process by which these perceptions are arrived at" (Argyris, 1960). With the advent of outsourcing and the upsurge of interest in knowledge management, the psychological contract has assumed greater importance for knowledge transfer and innovation (Flood, Turner, Ramamoorthy & Pearson, 2001; Lee, 2001; Roehling, 1996) such that "firms that replace employment security with employability without the requisite complement of accumulating, linking and bonding mechanisms are likely to lose more human and social capital than they accumulate" (Ghoshal & Moran, 1997, p. 7).

The changing nature of the psychological contract is not unique to consulting firms but it does assume particular importance given the centrality of knowledge to their competitive advantage. Wherever firms move toward shorter-term contracts, there is a tendency for long-term employer loyalty to be replaced by

Copyright © 2004, Idea Group Inc. Copying or distributing in print or electronic forms without written permission of Idea Group Inc. is prohibited.

the demands of having a flexible workforce that can adjust quickly to market needs, "regardless of who needs to be hired, terminated or changed" (Lee, 2001, p. 3). As a consequence, there is an erosion of employee perceptions of mutual loyalty, whereby short-term contracts encourage employees to take responsibility for their own career development without regard for their obligations to any one organization (Hardijzer, 2000). This transition from long-term relational contracts (Milward & Hopkins, 1998) to short-term transactional arrangements can erode employee commitment (Westwood, Sparrow & Leung, 2001) and employee loyalty (Turnley & Feldman, 1999), and these in turn will reduce the willingness of employees to voluntarily share their knowledge (Flood et al., 2001).

Therefore, our argument is that while it may be commercially beneficial for small consulting firms to rely upon freelance consultants, this has implications for the knowledge transfer process. On the one hand, freelance consultants possess valuable local knowledge that can determine assignment success in the field, while on the other hand they may have little incentive to share their knowledge with the main contractor. To retain their knowledge will likely result in repeat engagements (Lahti & Beyerlein, 2000), yet the main contractor needs to capture and share this knowledge internally to enhance future capability. Thus the role of freelance consultant is changing to one of coach and mentor, not only within the client organization, but more significantly within the consulting network (Ingleson, 2000). The consultant is now required to share knowledge twice: once to the client and once to the sponsoring company. Whether or not this happens in practice depends upon the ability of the sponsor to maintain a balance between the relational and transactional dimensions of the contract with freelance knowledge workers, and upon the extent to which this need is recognized.

The management of knowledge must also take account of the type of knowledge. For example, there has been much discussion of the trade-offs between codified and personalized knowledge management approaches, echoing Nonaka and Takeuchi's distinctions between the socialized transfer of tacit knowledge and system-based transfer of explicit knowledge (Nonaka & Takeuchi, 1995). Equally, there are many classifications of knowledge type (Tsoukas & Vladimirou, 2001) using phrases such as know-how, know-why, care-why (Garud, 1996; Quinn, Anderson, & Finkelstein, 1996) and so forth. While we do not wish to extend this debate about knowledge types and taxonomies, we believe that most have not recognized the importance of situated knowledge (Billett, 1996). What we mean by this statement is that we need to consider all knowledge

Copyright © 2004, Idea Group Inc. Copying or distributing in print or electronic forms without written permission of Idea Group Inc. is prohibited.

management activities in context (Coakes, 2003) to understand what type of local knowledge should be captured from freelance agents and what significance this knowledge could have for the sponsoring firm.

Transferability of Management Practices

In this chapter our focus is on European consulting firms involved with projects in developing countries to facilitate knowledge transfer and infrastructure development. We have selected Egypt because there is an acknowledged lack of research into management practices in Arab countries generally and in Egypt in particular (Atiyya, 1992; Parnell & Hatem, 1999). There is some empirical work that suggests that the transfer of Western management models to Arab cultures can be problematic because of the complex differences in cultural values, language, verbal and non-verbal cues (Feghali, 1997), insensitivity to local customs (Harari, 1990), and inability to read political dynamics (Seefeldt, 1985). Notwithstanding these differences, "the hypothesis of cultural transferability still underpins much of the 'aid' provided by the developed world to poorer countries" (Brown & Humphreys, 1995, p. 5), often culminating in Western partners adopting superior attitudes (Liu & Vince, 1999) and displaying more concern for satisfying the donor countries' politicians and citizens regardless of whether these values are shared at the receiving end (Hofstede, 1991).

Differences in National Cultures

Hofstede's seminal work is often used to develop the discussion of national culture differences (Hofstede, 1980, 1991) using four orthogonal dimensions, namely individualism versus collectivism, masculinity versus femininity, uncertainty avoidance and power distance. Based on these bipolar constructs, Arab countries are often clustered together as displaying preferences for collective, masculine cultures that more readily tolerate unequal distribution of power (high power distance) and that avoid feeling threatened by ambiguity (high uncertainty avoidance) when compared to Western cultures (Brown & Humphreys, 1995). However, these generalized stereotypes may not always hold. For example, there are many differences among Western countries in Hofstede's analysis. Moreover, as Feghali observes, in Hofstede's work, "the data of respondents from five Arab countries was eliminated from analysis, due to

Copyright © 2004, Idea Group Inc. Copying or distributing in print or electronic forms without written permission of Idea Group Inc. is prohibited.

insufficient sample size" and that "Arab countries are frequently cited as collective, based on descriptions which may not realistically reflect dynamic societal change in certain areas of the region" (Feghali, 1997, p. 355). Further, several Arab countries including Egypt have large Christian populations, such that the notion of "an Arab country" is far from a homogeneous concept. Despite these points, and more recent criticisms of Hofstede's cultural typology (Fernandez, Carlson, Stepina & Nicholson, 1997; Myers & Tan, 2002), it is still widely believed that national cultural differences are an important factor in many aspects of information systems research (Singh, Zhao & Hu, 2003).

It is precisely for these reasons that freelance consultants assume such importance for European consulting firms. With local knowledge, they can introduce Western management practices in ways that are appropriate to the cultural beliefs, values and expectations of Egyptian managers and that understand the differences in thought processes associated with different national cultures (Abramson, Keating & Lane, 1996). While consultants of Western origin might theoretically be able to understand many of the cultural differences associated with dealing with Egyptian managers, it is unlikely that they will be as adept in appreciating the nuances and complexities as local freelance consultants. For our empirical investigations we wished to establish the extent to which European consulting firms were aware of the potential value of local knowledge from their freelance sub-contractors, and what their perceived benefits of capturing it were. We also examined the methods they currently used to capture such localized knowledge. In the next section we outline our research methods to address these objectives.

Research Design and Methods

Since knowledge sharing between freelance consultants and their principal sponsors is relatively under-researched, we conducted our investigation in two stages. The first stage was an exploratory survey of the issues, based on our literature review. From this we formulated a causal model, which was used in stage two to develop a fuller survey instrument, administered to a larger sample of respondents. We now report the method and results of these two stages in sequence.

Copyright © 2004, Idea Group Inc. Copying or distributing in print or electronic forms without written permission of Idea Group Inc. is prohibited.

(a) Exploratory Study

Sample Selection

Some 138 European consultancies active in the Middle East/Egypt were selected from a database compiled by the authors. Egypt was chosen as the research focus because it is one of the largest recipients of aid and technical assistance, and it is relatively close to Europe, yet culturally distinct. From this sample, 10 firms were selected for preliminary interviews to explore the issues identified in the literature review. A questionnaire was then designed based on these interviews and pilot tested before distribution. The questionnaire was sent to named individuals in each company. A cover letter explained the purpose of the survey and its perceived importance.

Survey Instrument

The questionnaire was in five sections:

- ***Section 1*** asked for the profile of each respondent's organization, including the percentage of business conducted in the Middle East, and Egypt in particular.
- ***Section 2*** explored the importance assigned to having previous experience in the region for business development, commercial prospecting and proposal writing, together with the proportion of assignments that had been won where the consultants had local country experience.
- ***Section 3*** investigated the use of local consultants and localized experience, using open questions to identify typical recurrent problems and practical anecdotes.
- ***Section 4*** addressed the use of knowledge capture systems and the methods used to transfer knowledge between project groups. This section also explored the extent to which knowledge from subcontractors was captured formally or informally and the methods that were employed to this end.
- ***Section 5*** gauged the perceptions of respondents as to the importance of capturing localized knowledge, and the benefits that they believed would

Copyright © 2004, Idea Group Inc. Copying or distributing in print or electronic forms without written permission of Idea Group Inc. is prohibited.

accrue from so doing. Finally, it ascertained whether or not practical models were needed to facilitate this process.

Exploratory Findings

For this exploratory pilot study we obtained a response rate of 34% (see Table 1).

Table 1. Respondent profile.

Country	Total Sent Questionnaires	Responses			%
		Questionnaire /Interview	General responses	Declined	
Belgium	11 (8%)	1	0	1	1 (1%)
Denmark	13 (9%)	2	2	1	5 (4%)
France	10 (7%)	2	2	0	4 (3%)
Germany	23 (17%)	0	1	2	3 (2%)
Greece	8 (6%)	1	1	0	2 (1%)
Ireland	6 (3%)	3	0	0	3 (2%)
Italy	8 (6%)	0	3	0	3 (2%)
Luxembourg	1 (1%)	0	1	0	1 (1%)
Netherlands	9 (7%)	3	0	3	6 (4%)
UK	40 (29%)	14	3	1	18 (13%)
Others	9 (7%)	0	0	1	1 (1%)
TOTAL	**138 (100%)**	**26 (19%)**	**13 (9%)**	**9 (6%)**	**34%**
		48 responses or 34%			

The sample size is statistically small, but nevertheless significant, as the research elicits first-hand experience from practitioners. Some 80% of respondents had between 80-100% of their business in developing countries with an average of 40% of business conducted directly in Egypt.

Importance of Local Experience

Some 75% considered localized regional experience very important for business development and commercial prospecting, as well as for proposal writing (88%). From the open questions, one issue that arose several times was that it was probably better to hire local counterparts than to attempt to "act" local, which can often be offensive. One respondent commented that:

Copyright © 2004, Idea Group Inc. Copying or distributing in print or electronic forms without written permission of Idea Group Inc. is prohibited.

> *"Egyptians are deferential towards foreign consultants, especially Northern Europeans. They often know when the Europeans are wrong, lazy or useless but never say so."*

while another added that:

> *"Often consultants treat the client in the developing country as if they were less intelligent."*

The majority of respondents (81%) intended to maintain a presence in the Middle East region and in Egypt in particular. However, there was little perceived motivation to capture local experience because they had won business without it, and thus the focus was on forging local alliances. All respondents used local partners when operating in the Middle East, with, on average, 30% of the work being assigned to the sub-contracted parties. This represents a high level of reliance on local counterparts. One respondent observed that:

> *"The importance of intuition, knowledge, perception of body language and voice intonation and mannerisms in connection with local culture is underrated, as is the manner and delivery of questions."*

Knowledge Capture Systems

Only 38% of respondents had formal knowledge capture/management systems and processes, and of those only half were computer-based systems. All used informal systems such as networking and face-to-face meetings with knowledge workers. One respondent commented:

> *"Like most consultancies of our size, knowledge management relies on 'water-cooler' exchange, based on case stories and experiences."*

However, this can be difficult when people are always on the move, and are geographically separated by hundreds or thousands of miles. Most indicated that knowing *where* to find knowledge was the key issue, rather than capturing

Copyright © 2004, Idea Group Inc. Copying or distributing in print or electronic forms without written permission of Idea Group Inc. is prohibited.

and storing it. Mentoring, coaching and debriefing were highlighted as essential, and this is consistent with changing industry practices as mentioned earlier. Some 88% of respondents said they considered it important to capture knowledge from sub-contracted consultants, and 81% said they already did so, although not in a formal and systematic way. One sample comment supports this view:

> *"Personally I have never thought of it as knowledge management, but more as a common sense approach to developing one's consultancy skills."*

The majority (90%) stressed that maintaining good personal relationships with sub-contractors based on mutual trust and respect was also significant.

Criteria for Implementing a Knowledge Management System

The most important criterion (86%) for implementing a knowledge management system was considered to be the value of the knowledge captured to winning future business (see Table 2), confirming that there must be a business reason for doing so. Not surprisingly, resource and cost constraints (64%) were the next most important criteria. Securing repeat assignments scored low (36%); the reason given was that successful project teams get repeat assignments without much difficulty, and thus there is no concern to capture local knowledge as freelancers can be re-contracted – "you can always hire them again".

Table 2. Criteria for implementing a knowledge capture system (n = 48).

Ranking	Criterion	Importance
1	Capturing valuable knowledge to win new business	86%
2	Resources constraints	64%
3	Cost constraints	64%
4	To access new ideas and boost intellectual capital	50%
5	Time constraints and to shorten the learning curve	43%
6	To secure repeat assignments	36%
7	To raise our corporate profile	7%

Copyright © 2004, Idea Group Inc. Copying or distributing in print or electronic forms without written permission of Idea Group Inc. is prohibited.

Perceptions of the Need to Capture Knowledge

Respondents were divided in their opinions about the business need to capture knowledge, particularly from subcontractors. Many felt that it should be a natural process, based on personal chemistry, rather than a system. Conversely some thought that:

> *"All consulting companies should make it a specific contractual requirement that all output, or knowledge gained from a project is provided electronically to the main contractor."*

For others, there were less positive reactions, for example:

> *"Not in my company - management time is scarce. It's the usual excuse - too busy looking for work or else doing it."*

Another respondent added:

> *"I doubt it for consultancies, but maybe for multinationals with large projects. This is something for academics like Peters, Handy and Hofstede to do case material for MBA students to chew over."*

Based on these preliminary findings and the literature review, four dimensions seemed to be particularly important for the process of capturing the local knowledge of freelance consultants.

- First, the sponsoring employer needs to understand the value of local knowledge when operating in countries like Egypt, especially for winning new business and for bringing project assignments to successful completion. Several respondents also mentioned the stimulus of such local knowledge for generating new and useful ideas, which in many cases led to modification of their proposal writing and project management methods.
- Second, it is important to build effective relationships with freelance consultants, so that they feel sufficiently committed to share their knowledge voluntarily. Without such relationships, the commitment of freelance

Copyright © 2004, Idea Group Inc. Copying or distributing in print or electronic forms without written permission of Idea Group Inc. is prohibited.

contractors will be attenuated. Conversely, many principals thought that reliance on the initial freelance contract was sufficient to ensure adequate knowledge sharing. The short-term nature of such contracts has been used by some firms as an implicit form of incentive and reward, whereby freelance consultants who share freely are given further assignments; those who do not share endure the sanction of no further work.

- Third, firms need to understand the business culture, customs, values and expectations of clients in Arab countries. This may also entail a willingness to modify products and services that are based on Western management models, and to acknowledge the possibility that cultural transferability may not be a straightforward process.
- Finally, transmutation of the accumulated local knowledge of freelance field consultants into a corporate asset (Stewart et al., 1995) requires an effective process of project management and review.

We postulated that these four dimensions would be positively and significantly associated with the effectiveness with which consulting firms were able to capture local knowledge from their freelance agents, as shown in Figure 1.

To test our model, we conducted a second study, as outlined in the following section.

Figure 1. Model of influences on effective knowledge capture.

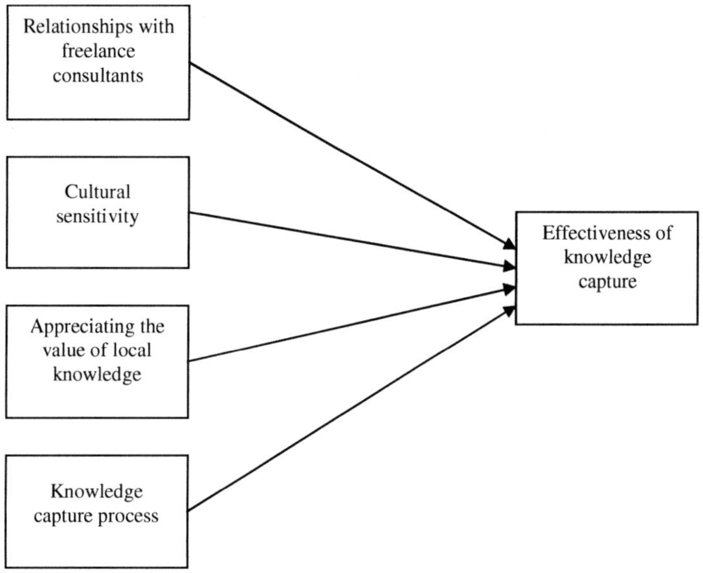

Copyright © 2004, Idea Group Inc. Copying or distributing in print or electronic forms without written permission of Idea Group Inc. is prohibited.

(b) Main Study

Survey Instrument

For this main survey, we developed 31 item statements that, from the literature and our initial findings, were representative of the four hypothesized influences on knowledge capture in this context. These were discussed with 12 practitioners who had consulting experience in Egypt to refine the wording. Respondents were asked to answer each question on a five-point Likert scale, anchored by 1 = strongly disagree and 5 = strongly agree. To measure the effectiveness of knowledge sharing, we developed six statements also using the same scaling.

Sample Selection

We expanded our database of European consulting firms, using referrals from existing contacts, and secondary sources, including European Community databases and publications. This yielded 219 potential respondents to whom the survey instrument was sent. Two follow-up letters with a copy of the questionnaire were sent, three weeks and six weeks after the initial mail-shot, resulting in a response of 170 completed questionnaires (77.6%). This was a much higher response rate than in our pilot study, probably due to the increased focus on follow-up of non-responses. Non-response bias was assessed by comparing the correlations between waves of respondents, based on the initial mail-shot and two follow-up phases. No significant differences were found.

Data Analysis Procedures

The larger sample size permitted more robust statistical analysis of the data. First we used factor analysis to categorize the items into theoretically meaningful constructs. Reverse scoring was applied to some variables to prevent a canceling-out of items with positive and negative valences. The 31 independent variables were subjected to exploratory factor analysis using Principal Components Analysis as the extraction method and Varimax rotation with Kaiser normalization. We used the twin criteria of factors with eigenvalues greater than 1.0 (Kaiser, 1970) and the elbow of the scree test (Cattel, 1978) to determine

Copyright © 2004, Idea Group Inc. Copying or distributing in print or electronic forms without written permission of Idea Group Inc. is prohibited.

the number of factors. The case-to-variable ratio was above the recommended minimum of 5:1 (Hair, Anderson, Tatham & Black, 1998). The critical assumptions underlying factor analysis were tested using the Bartlett test of sphericity (significant at the 0.001 level) and the Kaiser-Meyer-Olkin measure of sampling adequacy (KMO=0.867).

Factor loadings were evaluated on two criteria: the significance of the loadings and the simplicity of the factor structure. Items were deleted from the analysis according to guidelines developed by Churchill (1979) and Kim and Mueller (1978), namely: loadings of less than 0.35, or cross-loadings greater than 0.35 on two or more factors. On this basis, after the first factor analysis, three items were deleted. A second iteration resulted in two more items being deleted. This iterative process is recommended as an effective way of deriving a stable factor structure (Rai, Borah & Ramaprasad, 1996; Sethi & King, 1991). After two iterations, all remaining 26 variables loaded satisfactorily onto four latent factors. The factor analysis was also examined to ensure acceptable levels of variable communality and multicollinearity.

We then used multiple regression with the four composite independent factors, expressed as factor scores calculated from the item responses, regressed with the composite mean of all six performance variables.

Results

Table 3 reports the descriptive statistics and bi-variate correlations for the four extracted latent constructs.

Table 3. Descriptive statistics and bi-variate correlation matrix for latent constructs.

	Mean	s.d.	F1	F2	F3
F1. Knowledge capture process	2.07	.784			
F2. Relationships with consultants	2.49	.677	.220**		
F3. Cultural sensitivity	2.63	.792	.154*	.030	
F4. Appreciating the value of local knowledge	3.43	.682	.288**	.134	.051

** Correlation is significant at the 0.01 level   1 = strongly disagree   5 = strongly agree
* Correlation is significant at the 0.05 level

Copyright © 2004, Idea Group Inc. Copying or distributing in print or electronic forms without written permission of Idea Group Inc. is prohibited.

Table 4 shows the construct reliabilities for the four latent factors extracted from the 26 variables, and the loadings for the principal factor to which each variable contributes. Item statements with reversed valences are indicated "R".

Table 5 presents the details of the composite measure of the dependent variable, effective knowledge capture.

Table 4. Factor analysis.

ITEMS	FACTOR 1	2	3	4
F1. Knowledge capture process $\alpha = 0.9406$				
We document knowledge captured during the conduct of projects	.907			
We analyze the knowledge captured during the conduct of projects	.887			
KM documents and lessons learned are reviewed at corporate level as well as project level	.876			
Prior to assignments we formally establish the expectations of the assignment team	.874			
Lessons learned are captured throughout a project	.770			
Projects are also reviewed immediately after project execution	.769			
Project reviews are supported by trained facilitators	.733			
Our review procedure involves a minimum of bureaucracy	.713			
The method of recording is simple for communication purposes	.710			
Review participants (especially freelance contractors) are able to discuss mistakes without fear of negative consequences	.688			
F2. Relationships with freelance consultants $\alpha = 0.9653$				
Forging strong relationships with freelance consultants is vital for us		.971		
We treat our freelance consultants as partners		.965		
Our freelance consultants are extremely committed when working for us in Egypt		.955		
Freelance knowledge sharing will happen if it is mandated by the initial contract [R]		.954		
We provide incentives to our freelance consultants to share their knowledge with us		.917		
We reward our freelance consultants for sharing knowledge with us		.733		
F3. Cultural sensitivity $\alpha = 0.9040$				
It is vital to understand the local business culture			.901	
We underestimate the importance of understanding Egyptian business culture			.866	
We know as much as we need to know about Egyptian business culture [R]			.853	
Our standards, products and services must be modified for use by Egyptian clients			.847	
We always take account of national cultures when delivering our services in Egypt			.762	
F4. Appreciating the value of local knowledge $\alpha = 0.7941$				
Local knowledge is a key factor in winning contracts in Egypt				.825
For us, local knowledge is a key factor in completion of successful projects in Egypt				.773
Local knowledge from freelance consultants is a valuable source of new ideas				.721
We must do a lot more to capture local knowledge from our freelance consultants				.686
We win enough business without capturing local knowledge from freelance consultants [R]				.672
Eigenvalues	7.89	4.58	3.68	2.40
% of variance explained	30.4	17.6	14.2	9.2
Cumulative % of variance explained	30.4	48.0	62.2	71.4
Bartlett's test of sphericity χ^2=4428.47, df=325, p<0.0001				
KMO Measure of sampling adequacy = 0.867				

Copyright © 2004, Idea Group Inc. Copying or distributing in print or electronic forms without written permission of Idea Group Inc. is prohibited.

Table 5. Composite measure of effective knowledge capture.

ITEMS	Loadings
Effective knowledge capture $\alpha = 0.9804$	
We regularly capture local knowledge from freelance consultants	.989
We have a formal process for capturing local knowledge from freelance consultants	.983
We do not have time to capture local knowledge from freelance consultants [R]	.973
We are very clear how to set about capturing knowledge from freelance consultants	.941
There is a lot of local knowledge we do not get back	.938
We are good at capturing local knowledge	.905

In Table 6 the regression of the dependent variable, effective knowledge capture, and the four predictor variables is quite strong ($R^2 = 0.503$), with the two most significant predictors ($p<0.01$) of knowledge capture being the process employed and sensitivity to local cultural differences.

Table 6. Regression results.

Factor	Beta	T	Significance
F1. Knowledge capture process	0.665	12.117	0.000
F3. Cultural sensitivity	0.171	3.122	0.002
F2. Relationships with consultants	0.140	2.556	0.012
F4. Appreciating the value of local knowledge	0.111	2.031	0.044

Model Summary	**R**	**R^2**	**Adjusted R^2**	**Std error of estimate**	
	0.709	0.503	0.491	0.56	
Analysis of Variance					
	Sum of squares	Df	Mean Square	F	Significance
Regression	52.231	4	13.058	41.805	0.000
Residual	51.537	165	0.312		
Total	103.768	169			
Dependent variable: Effective knowledge capture					

Copyright © 2004, Idea Group Inc. Copying or distributing in print or electronic forms without written permission of Idea Group Inc. is prohibited.

Discussion

We set out to investigate three questions. First, for European consulting firms with operations in Egypt, is there an awareness of the importance of local knowledge possessed by their freelance sub-contractors? Second, do they perceive any value in capturing this local knowledge? Third, to what extent do these consulting firms currently capture such localized knowledge from sub-contractors and what methods do they use to do so? Since this aspect of knowledge sharing (between freelance consultants and their focal sponsors) has been relatively under-researched, we employed a two-stage methodology.

In stage one, we used a survey (n = 48) developed from the extant literature and 10 interviews to delineate the issues. This pilot study identified four main points:

1. There was a high level of awareness of the importance of local knowledge for proposal writing and commercial prospecting but much less motivation to capture such local knowledge and make it part of the structural capital of the sponsor's firm, because more than enough business was won without it, and freelance consultants could always be re-hired. We observe that this is a shortsighted view that overlooks the value of such local knowledge for stimulation of learning and generation of new ideas in the focal consulting practice. Moreover, given that the majority of respondents intended to maintain a presence in the Middle East region and Egypt in particular, the lack of capture of local knowledge implied a continuing reliance on local freelance consultants. While this is a satisfactory situation for the freelance agents, it does little to build the consulting capability of the respondents' firms and could be a threat to their competitive position.
2. As a consequence of this lack of will to capture such local knowledge, there was little use of formal knowledge management systems and processes. Most respondents relied upon informal "water-cooler" exchanges for knowledge capture, which, although appropriate for smaller organizations (Davenport & Prusak, 1998), proved difficult when freelance consultants were geographically isolated from their sponsoring firms.
3. Local knowledge was recognized as especially valuable in order to deal sensitively with the complexities of Arab business cultures, and to adapt Western management practices to localized contexts, with differing customs, values and political dynamics.

Copyright © 2004, Idea Group Inc. Copying or distributing in print or electronic forms without written permission of Idea Group Inc. is prohibited.

4. The nature of the relationship with freelance consultants poses unique challenges for knowledge acquisition. Freelance consultants are usually employed on short-term contracts, on the basis that they possess knowledge and skills that are valuable to the sponsor. Consequently, they have little incentive to share their knowledge with the sponsor, since it would erode the preservation of their livelihood (Wang & Rubenstein-Montano, 2003). Short-term transactional arrangements are also known to undermine employee loyalty and commitment and reduce the willingness of individuals to share knowledge voluntarily. Moreover, freelance consultants are not subject to the culture, norms, infrastructure and reward systems of the sponsoring firm (Davenport & Prusak, 1997) and not inculcated into the socialization processes (Nonaka & Takeuchi, 1995) that would normally facilitate tacit knowledge sharing. The challenge is therefore to develop relationships with freelance consultants that go beyond the "arms-length" arrangements of transactional contracts.

While the pilot study indicated some views of what was happening "on the ground," the small sample size and the lack of follow-up procedures for non-respondents could mean that the reported percentages are not truly representative. We therefore conducted a second study, informed by our pilot investigations.

The second study (n = 170) formulated a model of the factors that influence the effectiveness of the knowledge capture process between freelance consultants and their sponsors. The model postulated that the four main factors from the pilot study would be positively and significantly associated with the efficacy of knowledge capture. Our results strongly support this proposition. From our exploratory interviews and the review of the literature we developed 31 item statements to characterize the four factors. Through factor analysis, we have produced a survey instrument with robust reliability. Further, our six-item measure of the effectiveness of knowledge capture also has high reliability.

Inspection of the descriptive statistics of each factor reveals a reasonably high level of awareness of the value of local knowledge (mean = 3.43), but much lower levels of appreciation of the need for cultural sensitivity (mean = 2.63) and for building relationships with freelance consultants (mean = 2.49). Consistent with the results from our pilot study, there is also much less activity to capture freelance consultants' knowledge through formal processes (mean = 2.07). Subsequent regression analysis showed the relative influence of each factor on the dependent variable, with *knowledge capture processes* and

Copyright © 2004, Idea Group Inc. Copying or distributing in print or electronic forms without written permission of Idea Group Inc. is prohibited.

cultural sensitivity having the most significant predictive capacity ($p<0.01$). The remaining two factors in our model, *relationships with consultants* and *appreciating the value of local knowledge* were also significant ($p<0.05$).

It might be tempting to simply close the discussion at this point, having highlighted some challenges within this group of firms, foremost of which is a need to develop knowledge capture processes. However, we propose a potential and practical solution to address these issues. We have drawn on our consulting experiences in developing countries, and on the results from these studies, to suggest a model that we refer to as the "revolving door procedure".

The Revolving Door Procedure

The model is based on four stages as represented in Figure 2.

These four stages are:

- Pre-action review (PAR)
- Knowledge capture (KC)
- Knowledge management (KM)
- After action review (AAR)

Figure 2. Revolving door model.

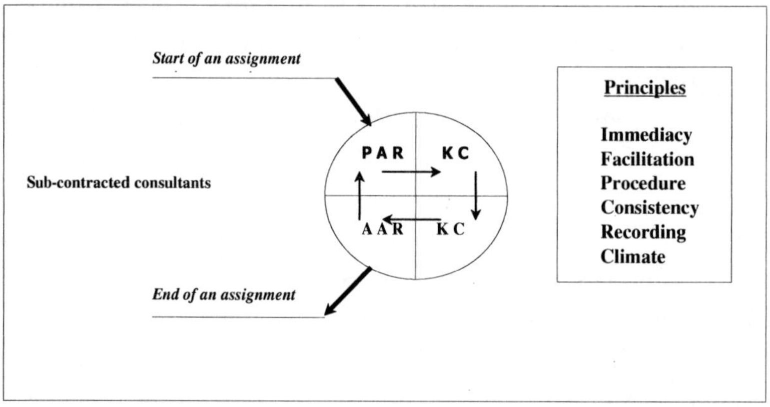

Copyright © 2004, Idea Group Inc. Copying or distributing in print or electronic forms without written permission of Idea Group Inc. is prohibited.

The model may appear to be a simple approach, but as Andrew McMahon, a Lotus veteran and a senior director of product marketing at Groove Networks observed, “To really make knowledge sharing work, you have to find a way to connect people with each other that doesn’t require unnecessarily technical overhead” (Roberts-Witt, 2002, p. 87). The model was inspired by the after action review similar to that developed by the U.S. Army (Meliza, 1995). In essence the concept is to assess what was intended to be achieved during consulting assignments, what actually was achieved, and why there was a difference.

- ***Stage 1*** is to conduct a pre-action review to capture expectations and concepts, and to derive a performance standard to measure against. Thus the consulting team should be interviewed before the commencement of an assignment using a standardized questionnaire.
- ***Stage 2*** involves an on-going process throughout the duration of a project to capture knowledge on an immediate basis, rather than waiting for the formal end of the project before reviewing and capturing lessons learned, which is the norm in many projects.
- ***Stage 3***, knowledge management, needs to be done at both the project and corporate levels. This involves the documentation, analysis and updating of the knowledge captured in the previous stage. At the project level, this is to ensure speedy identification of difficulties and problems in the project implementation and to enable corrective action. At the corporate level, these issues can then be used to address broader policy issues to address underlying causes.
- ***Stage 4***, the after action review, should adopt the principles advocated by Garvin (1996); that is:

  Immediacy - the review should take place immediately after project execution so that the knowledge is still fresh in the minds of the consultants and while they are still in the mindset of behaving as a team.

  Facilitation - the review should be supported by trained facilitators who have good understanding and intuition. The value of the knowledge captured will depend on asking the right questions.

  Procedure - the review procedure should be simple and direct with a minimum of bureaucracy, such that the paperwork does not impede the free interchange of views and ideas.

Copyright © 2004, Idea Group Inc. Copying or distributing in print or electronic forms without written permission of Idea Group Inc. is prohibited.

Consistency - the procedure must be applied across all components of a project and become a standardized framework that becomes embedded and internalized into working practice.

Recording - the method of recording the knowledge captured should be simple so that it can be communicated upwards from the project to the corporate level, and desirably between co-operating partners in other organizations.

Climate - perhaps most importantly of all, the main contractor needs to cultivate a climate of openness and frank dialogue so that participants feel able to discuss mistakes without fear of negative consequences. This is particularly important for the freelance participants who must be assured that this will not have any implications for future assignments.

This is a simple tool designed to enable the capture of freelance consultants' knowledge in operational settings. While it was developed expressly for situations where main contractors seek to gather knowledge from sub-contractors in the field, we see no reason why it could not be implemented in many other organizations too.

Conclusions and Future Directions

We conclude that these consultancies are aware of the potential loss of knowledge from sub-contractors, but are not particularly concerned about it, largely due to their current success at gaining new business. While they perceive some value in capturing this sub-contractor knowledge, the methods employed are still unsystematic and informal. Our interviews and open-question responses highlighted many reasons why local knowledge is necessary when operating in developing countries such as Egypt. Given that most of our respondents planned to maintain a presence in this market, the data suggests that they ought to pay more attention to capturing sub-contractor knowledge, and to understand more fully the nature of the psychological contracts that they should be developing.

We claim a contribution to knowledge, in that the literature has yet to address this particular dimension of knowledge management, which is significant for

Copyright © 2004, Idea Group Inc. Copying or distributing in print or electronic forms without written permission of Idea Group Inc. is prohibited.

many smaller consulting organizations. We encourage researchers to look beyond the study of knowledge management practice in large consulting firms and to explore these issues in other developing countries. The focus of our study was European consulting firms, largely because our funding was linked to a European Community initiative. Yet there is nothing inherently European about this phenomenon, and it would be interesting to investigate the same issues in consulting firms in other continents, such as North America. We have only examined this issue from the perspective of the sponsoring consulting firms; it would be useful to also canvass the views of freelance consultants.

We believe our work also contributes to management consulting practice, highlighting the importance of local knowledge and the factors that influence knowledge capture from freelance consultants. We also offer the revolving door model as a practical manifestation of our findings. Our results suggest that the model of knowledge capture will work effectively only when supported by the other three factor constructs we have identified. The survey instrument can be used to assess the extent to which these supportive factors are present in any consulting firm, and to identify which of them require improvement. The instrument can also be used to assess the effectiveness of the knowledge capture process itself. For freelance consultants, the revolving door model should be "sold" to them as a benefit that will accelerate and enhance their personal worth, to overcome the perception that they will be giving away their priceless knowledge. In fact, it could become an additional selection factor for freelance consultants that the best contributors to these review procedures will be most likely to be given future assignments.

References

Abramson, N.R., Keating, R.J., & Lane, H.W. (1996). Cross-national cognitive process differences. *Management International Review, 36*(2), 123-148.

Apostolou, D., & Mentzas, G. (1999). Managing corporate knowledge: A comparative analysis of experience in consulting firms. *Knowledge and Process Management, 6*(3), 128-138.

Argyris, C. (1960). *Understanding organizational behavior.* Homewood, IL: Dorsey Press.

Copyright © 2004, Idea Group Inc. Copying or distributing in print or electronic forms without written permission of Idea Group Inc. is prohibited.

Atiyya, H.S. (1992). Research into Arab countries. *Organisation Studies, 13*(1), 105-112.

Billett, S. (1996). Situated learning: Bridging sociocultural and cognitive theorising. *Learning and Instruction, 6*(3), 263-280.

Brown, A.D., & Humphreys, M. (1995). International cultural differences in public sector management: Lessons from a survey of British and Egyptian technical education managers. *International Journal of Public Sector Management, 8*(3), 5-23.

Cattel, R.B. (1978). *The scientific use of factor analysis.* New York: Premium Press.

Churchill, G.A. (1979). A paradigm for developing better measures of marketing constructs. *Journal of Marketing Research, 16*, 64-73.

Coakes, E. (2003). Preface. In E. Coakes (Ed.), *Knowledge management: Current issues and challenges.* Hershey, PA: IRM Press.

Davenport, T., & Prusak, L. (1998). *Working knowledge.* Cambridge, MA: Harvard University Press.

Davenport, T., DeLong, D., & Beers, M. (1998). Successful knowledge management projects. *Sloan Management Review, 39*, 43-57.

Davenport, T.H., & Prusak, L. (1997). *Information ecology: Mastering the information and knowledge environment.* New York: Oxford University Press.

European Commission. (2002). Information Society Technologies (IST) Programme (1999-2002). *Terms of reference: Study on market prospects, business needs and technological trends for business knowledge management.* Retrieved from http://europa.eu.int/comm/research/nfp.html

Feghali, E. (1997). Arab cultural communications patterns. *International Journal of Intercultural Relations, 21*(3), 345-378.

Fernandez, D., Carlson, D.S., Stepina, L.S., & Nicholson, J.D. (1997). Hofstede's country classification 25 years later. *Journal of Social Psychology, 137*(1), 43-54.

Flood, P.C., Turner, T., Ramamoorthy, N., & Pearson, J. (2001). Causes and consequences of psychological contracts among knowledge workers in the high technology and financial services industries. *International Journal of Human Resource Management, 12*(7), 1152-1165.

Copyright © 2004, Idea Group Inc. Copying or distributing in print or electronic forms without written permission of Idea Group Inc. is prohibited.

Garud, R. (1996). *On the distinction between know-how, know-what and know-why.* Paper presented at the Annual Conference of the American Academy of Management.

Garvin, D.A. (1996). *Putting the learning organization to work.* Boston: Harvard Business School Publishing.

Ghoshal, S., & Moran, P. (1997). *Employment security, employability and sustainable competitive advantage.* Working Papers 97/20SM. Fontainbleau, France: INSEAD.

Grant, R.M., & Baden-Fuller, C. (1995). *A knowledge-based theory of inter-firm collaboration.* Paper presented at the Annual Conference of the Academy of Management, Vancouver, Canada.

Hair, J.F., Anderson, R.E., Tatham, R.L., & Black, W.C. (1998). *Multivariate data analysis.* New Jersey: Prentice-Hall.

Hansen, M., Nohria, N., & Tierney, T. (1999, March-April). What's your strategy for managing knowledge? *Harvard Business Review,* 106-116.

Harari, D. (1990). *The role of the technical assistance expert.* Paris: The Development Centre for the Organization for Economic Cooperation and Development.

Hardijzer, C. (2000, February). Forging new careers in the changing world of work. *People Dynamics,* 36-40.

Hofstede, G. (1980). *Culture's consequences: International differences in work-related values.* London: Sage.

Hofstede, G. (1991). *Cultures and organizations: Software of the mind.* London: McGraw-Hill.

Huber, G.P. (2001). Transfer of knowledge in knowledge management systems: Unexplored issues and suggested studies. *European Journal of Information Systems, 10*(2), 72-79.

Ingleson, M. (2000). *Background to knowledge management as a business issue.* Cambridge, England: Cambridge Market Intelligence Limited.

Inkpen, A.C. (1998). Learning, knowledge acquisition and strategic alliances: Alliancing skills and the role of alliance structure and systems. *European Management Journal, 16*(2), 223-229.

Inkpen, A.C., & Dinur, A. (1998). Knowledge management processes and international joint ventures. *Organization Science, 9*(4), 454-468.

Copyright © 2004, Idea Group Inc. Copying or distributing in print or electronic forms without written permission of Idea Group Inc. is prohibited.

Kaiser, H.F. (1970). The varimax criterion for analytical rotation in factor analysis. *Psychometrika, 23,* 187-200.

Kerr, J. (1998). What consultants should leave behind. *Software Magazine, 18,* 20-21.

Kim, J., & Mueller, C.W. (1978). *Factor analysis: Statistical methods and practical issues.* Beverly Hills, CA: Sage.

Lahti, R.K., & Beyerlein, M.M. (2000). Knowledge transfer and management consulting: A look at the firm. *Business Horizons,* 65-74.

Lapause, R. (2003a). The process of converting consultants' tacit knowledge to organisational explicit knowledge. In E. Coakes (Ed.), *Knowledge management: Current issues and challenges* (pp. 212-225). Hershey, PA: IRM Press.

Lapause, R. (2003b). Tacit knowledge sharing in management consulting firms. In E. Coakes (Ed.), *Knowledge management: Current issues and challenges* (pp. 92-103). Hershey, PA: IRM Press.

Lee, G. (2001). Towards a contingent model of key staff retention: The new psychological contract reconsidered. *South African Journal of Business Management, 32*(1), 1-9.

Liu, S., & Vince, R. (1999). The cultural context of learning in international joint ventures. *The Journal of Management Development, 18*(8), 666-675.

Meliza, L.L. (1995). *ATAFS: A first generation 'smart' AAR system.* US Army Research Institute for the Behavioral and Social Sciences. Retrieved from http://www-ari.army.mil/atafs.htm

Milward, L.J., & Hopkins, L.J. (1998). Psychological contracts: Organizational and job commitment. *Journal of Applied Social Psychology, 28*(16), 1530-1556.

Myers, M.D., & Tan, F.B. (2002). Beyond models of national culture in information systems research. *Journal of Global Information Management, 10*(2), 24-32.

Nonaka, I., & Takeuchi, H. (1995). *The knowledge creating company: How Japanese companies create the dynamics of innovation.* Oxford, England: Oxford University Press.

Parnell, J.A., & Hatem, T. (1999). Cultural antecedents of behavioural differences between American and Egyptian managers. *Journal of Management Studies, 36*(3), 399-419.

Copyright © 2004, Idea Group Inc. Copying or distributing in print or electronic forms without written permission of Idea Group Inc. is prohibited.

Quinn, J.B., Anderson, P., & Finkelstein, S. (1996). Managing professional intellect: Making the most of the best. *Harvard Business Review, 72*(2), 71-80.

Rai, A., Borah, S., & Ramaprasad, A. (1996). Critical success factors for strategic alliances in the information technology industry: An empirical study. *Decision Sciences, 27*(1), 141-155.

Raz, T. (2001). *Wishing up on knowledge management,* Retrieved from www.myprimetime.com

Reimus, B. (1997). *Knowledge sharing within management consulting firms (Reports on how U.S.-based management consultancies deploy technology, use groupware and facilitate collaboration).* Kennedy Information Inc.

Roberts-Witt, S. (2002, March). Know thyself. *PC Magazine, 21,* 87.

Roehling, M.V. (1996). *The origins and development of the psychological contract construct.* Paper presented at the Annual Conference of the Academy of Management, pp. 202-206, ISBN: 08967911.

Rousseau, D.M. (1995). *Psychological contracts in organizations.* Thousand Oaks, CA: Sage.

Sarvary, M. (1999). Knowledge management and competition in the consulting industry. *California Management Review, 41*(2), 95-107.

Seefeldt, F.M. (1985). Cultural considerations for evaluation consulting in the Egyptian context. In M.Q. Patton (Ed.), *Culture and evaluation: New directions for program evaluation.* San Francisco: Jossey-Bass.

Sethi, V., & King, W.R. (1991). Construct measurement in information systems research: An illustration in strategic systems. *Decision Sciences, 22*, 455-472.

Singh, N., Zhao, H., & Hu, X. (2003). Cultural adaptation on the Web: A study of American companies' domestic and Chinese Websites. *Journal of Global Information Management, 11*(3), 63-80.

Stewart, T.A., Godsey, K., & Dunlap, K. (1995). Mapping corporate brainpower. *Fortune, 132,* 209-211.

Szulanski, G. (1996). Exploring internal stickiness: Impediments to the transfer of best practice within the firm. *Strategic Management Journal, 17*, 27-43.

Tsoukas, H., & Vladimirou, E. (2001). What is organizational knowledge? *Journal of Management Studies, 38*(7), 973-993.

Copyright © 2004, Idea Group Inc. Copying or distributing in print or electronic forms without written permission of Idea Group Inc. is prohibited.

Turnley, W.H., & Feldman, D.C. (1999). The impact of psychological contract violations on exit, voice, loyalty and neglect. *Human Relations, 52*(7), 895-911.

Wang, R., & Rubenstein-Montano, B. (2003). The value of trust in knowledge sharing. In E. Coakes (Ed.), *Knowledge management: Current issues and challenges* (pp. 116-130). Hershey, PA: IRM Press.

Weiss, L. (1999). Collection and connection: The anatomy of knowledge sharing in professional service firms. *Organizational Development Journal, 17*(4), 61-77.

Westwood, R., Sparrow, P., & Leung, A. (2001). Challenges to the psychological contract in Hong Kong. *International Journal of Human Resource Management, 12*(4), 621-651.

Copyright © 2004, Idea Group Inc. Copying or distributing in print or electronic forms without written permission of Idea Group Inc. is prohibited.

Chapter III

Awareness Matters in Virtual Communities: An Awareness Ontology

Farhad Daneshgar
The University of New South Wales, Australia

Abstract

A methodology is introduced in this chapter for sharing the contextual knowledge in virtual communities. Context is represented by a set of semantic concepts and their relationships that form specific collaborative business processes within the virtual community. Two sets of objects/concepts are identified: (i) objects that make up a community member's actual contextual knowledge, *and (ii) objects that make up the* contextual knowledge *expected from a community member, by a specific task object that the member performs within the community, that are sufficient to enable the member to perform the task and/or to participate in relevant interactions. The excess of the objects in (ii) compared to the objects in (i) is identified. These objects need to be put within the focus of the community member in order to enable him/her to successfully get involved in various tasks within the community.*

Copyright © 2004, Idea Group Inc. Copying or distributing in print or electronic forms without written permission of Idea Group Inc. is prohibited.

Introduction

With few exceptions, *awareness* has been regarded by CSCW (Computer-Supported Cooperative Work) researchers as a "kind of information that is highly relevant to a specific actor/role and situation of a process participant" (Baker et al., 2002, pp. 145-173). It involves information that is localised to, and has value in, a specific context. In milestone research Dourish et al. noted the importance of awareness in the shared workspace (1992). Some other earlier examples include *peripheral awareness,* that is, an awareness that is specific to co-located work, and is gained by implicit monitoring of the local work environment (Robinson, 1993). Also, Bentley (1995) notes the importance of a standardized display of the airspace to support air traffic controllers gaining *at-a-glance awareness* of the airspace others are controlling. More recent studies include *collaborative process awareness* (Daneshgar, 2000b) and focused awareness, customised awareness, temporarily constrained awareness and external awareness (Baker et al., 2002).

It is argued in this chapter that (i) there is a strong relationship between the awareness of people in virtual communities (VCs) and the concepts of focus and nimbus; and (ii) that people in VCs require a certain level of awareness about various channels of collaboration (referred to as a class of *contextual knowledge*) through which knowledge flows within the VC. Such contextual knowledge is a pre-requisite for the members' effective involvements in various interactions/tasks within the VC. This approach to knowledge sharing is consistent with the growing view shared by many in the community of knowledge management that demands clear separation of context, narrative and content management with the aim of enhancing collaboration and self-organising capabilities of the communities (Snowden, 2002).

In this chapter the writer's previously developed primitives, the *awareness net* and *awareness model,* that were originally developed for enterprise environments, are adjusted to meet collaboration requirements of people in virtual work environments.

Previous Work

In an effort to enhance collaboration in enterprise environments the writer has introduced a *process awareness framework* with the two components:

Copyright © 2004, Idea Group Inc. Copying or distributing in print or electronic forms without written permission of Idea Group Inc. is prohibited.

awareness net and *awareness model*. The *awareness net* is a representation of the collaborative business process that facilitates visualisation, storage and re-use of awareness of the actors within collaborative business processes (see example in Figure 2). The awareness levels themselves are defined by various sets of components of the *awareness net.* This framework was initially used for identifying awareness requirements of the actors in collaborative business processes (Daneshgar, 1997a). Later on, it led to development of a specialised knowledge-base system that maintains records of collaboration and knowledge-sharing in business processes (Daneshgar, 1999). An expert system is currently under development that consists of two major components: (i) an inference engine that stores a set of generic rules, definitions, and relationships regarding awareness requirements of the actors that apply to any collaborative business process; and (ii) a knowledge-base component that holds domain-specific knowledge, and initially is empty. As a result of separation of the above two components, the expert system can then be reused for various applications. The main expertise of this expert system is to identify *awareness gaps* for the actors, and to remove these gaps by bringing within the *focus* of the actors relevant required objects.

A Methodology for Enhancing Knowledge Sharing in Virtual Communities

A Historical Background

The main motivation for this research is to extend an existing awareness framework for enhancing knowledge sharing in generic business processes to the VCs by explicitly incorporating notions of *focus* and *nimbus,* concepts that are quite relevant to VCs. According to the *interactionist* school in social psychology, awareness is maintained if each person *actively* provides a kind of *nimbus* by which s/he selectively exposes some of his/her properties (that is, their activities, etc.) to others. According to this school, pairwise interactions between people occur either by *nimbus* (an object's presence), or by *focus* (its attention); the more an object is within one's focus, the more aware the person is of it. Also, the more an object provides a nimbus the more aware others will be of it (Benford et al., 1995).

Copyright © 2004, Idea Group Inc. Copying or distributing in print or electronic forms without written permission of Idea Group Inc. is prohibited.

In the past, and at least within the field of knowledge management, the concept of *nimbus* has not been given explicit attention in actual implementations of systems that support collaboration and knowledge-sharing. In VCs, however, issues related to nimbus such as shyness (desire to hide, and yet to participate effectively within the community), presence (e.g., this "icon" or that "private_work_space" represents me), and so on become quite relevant.

Knowledge in VCs requires a space before it can be shared. Designers of the groupware systems usually allocate a shared space in their applications' user interface where people exchange their knowledge (e.g., chat room, shared documents, and shared applications). Clear separation of content and context as mentioned before will have a particular implication in VCs. Contents of knowledge is more absolute and fixed than the context or (human) channels through which the contents are shared. In other words, the absolute/fixed knowledge exists within people, whereas how much they are willing to share in VCs, among other things, is highly dependent on the person who has the knowledge; hence a need for clear separation of context management and content management. As a result, the same context can be seen by different people differently, depending on a combination of the degree of willingness of the object to expose itself (nimbus) as well as the eyesight of the viewers (focus).

The proposed methodology is closely related to an analytical tool called the *awareness net* that represents awareness levels of actors in collaborative business processes, and is explained in the following section.

An Awareness Framework for VCs

As mentioned before, the proposed framework/methodology consists of two components. These components are discussed below in detail.

Awareness Net

Awareness net is a representation of collaborative business process within the VC, and consists of a collection of collaborative semantic concepts and their relationships for the purpose of defining and measuring the awareness requirements of the actors within the VC. Generally speaking, one distinctive factor that separates process models from other types of models in computer science is that humans rather than machines must enact many of the phenomena

Copyright © 2004, Idea Group Inc. Copying or distributing in print or electronic forms without written permission of Idea Group Inc. is prohibited.

modelled. As a result, a good collaborative process model must not focus solely on the actors' behaviour at the interface or the flow and transformation of data within the system but also focus on the communication, cooperation and coordination (3Cs) among the actors. This is particularly true for VCs where people's interactions can take many forms, depending on the purpose of the interaction or the tasks the actors perform within the VC. Many collaborative process models have already been developed that provide a common representation format that facilitate human understanding and communication, and at the same time support and automate collaborative process management (Baker et al., 2002; Farquhar et al., 2003; Lee et al., 2000; Nabuco et al., 2001). From a philosophical perspective the awareness net has its roots in the *actant network theory* which in turn has its origin in studies of the networks of interdependent social practices that constitute work in science and technology. An *actant network* is the acts that are linked together with all of their influencing factors producing a network (Latour, 1996).

In the following paragraphs some of the objectives and relevant unique attributes of the awareness net are discussed:

1. *Providing a combined and integrated 3C perspectives as well as functional, behavioural and organisational perspectives for analysis of knowledge sharing requirements of actors in VCs:* Generally speaking, the perspectives that a process model is able to present are bounded by the constructs of the language (textual, graphic, objects, etc.) used for modelling. The object-orientation of the constructs of the proposed language facilitates interleaving of all these perspectives, resulting in a comprehensive analysis of the knowledge sharing requirements of the actors in collaborative business processes.
2. *Providing a unified analysis of both the knowledge-sharing requirements as well as the collaborative business process:* Generally speaking, this requirement will be met if the same analytical tools are used for representation of both the awareness and the collaborative process. This means that there should be no need to have separate models, one for the collaborative process and one for the knowledge sharing requirements. A special type of connected graph called *awareness net* is used for representation of the collaborative business process by which the knowledge-sharing requirements of the actors can also be identified in terms of the collaborative semantic concepts used to construct this net. This will result in a unified analysis of the knowledge-sharing requirements of the

Copyright © 2004, Idea Group Inc. Copying or distributing in print or electronic forms without written permission of Idea Group Inc. is prohibited.

actors in collaborative business processes. In order to provide such unified analytical approach, a rule-based model was developed by the author that guides the representation of both the process structure as well as the relationships among the language constructs in a way that knowledge sharing requirements of the actors can be defined in term of the process elements.

A connected graph is used to represent the collaborative processes. The awareness net consists of the following collaborative semantic concepts:

1. A non-empty set of *role* vertices and *simple task* (or, *task*) vertices (as opposed to *collaborative task*). A *collaborative task* is a pair of *simple tasks,* each performed by a separate (collaborating) *role,* where these roles use a common artefact called *task artefact* for their collaboration (see below). Also, despite the fact that *role* and *actor* are not the same (*actors* are human agents that assume one or more *roles* within the process) but since the representation tool does not provide any representation for the *actor,* we may therefore assume that the role also represents the actor. After all, "behind each role there is an actor".
2. A set of edges or arcs that connect above vertices together and represents various artefacts used by *roles* in order to execute their tasks. Connectedness of the graph implies the interrelationships among various semantic concepts of the process that was referred to before as the relevant portion of the VC.

The edges in the graph represent artefacts that are used by actors when performing various tasks. A separation is made between the two kinds of artefacts. One is called the *role artefact* and has a role and a simple task as its endpoints. This artefact, among other things, encapsulates personal knowledge/resources the actor would use to execute the task successfully. Some examples of the role artefact include: technical skills, personal databases, spreadsheets, previous experience in other (similar) jobs, and so forth.

The other kind of artefact is called *task artefact,* which has two simple tasks as its endpoints. These two simple tasks together constitute a collaborative task. Two collaborating actors, that is, actors with a common task artefact, use/exchange/act-upon their task artefact in order to collaborate. Examples of the

Copyright © 2004, Idea Group Inc. Copying or distributing in print or electronic forms without written permission of Idea Group Inc. is prohibited.

Figure 1. An awareness net with four roles and 14 tasks.

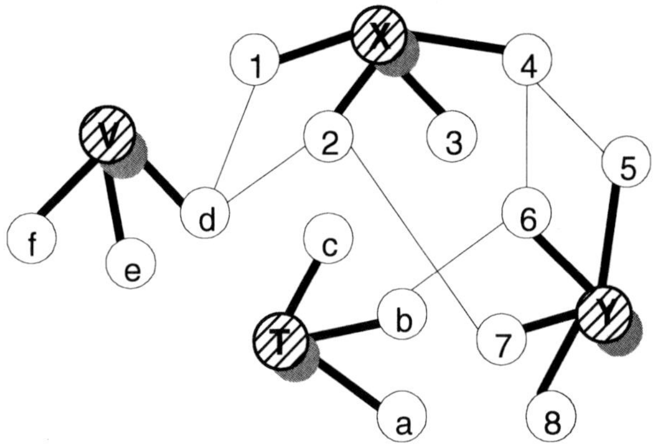

task artefact include e-mail, project plan, students' exam paper, and so forth. Task artefacts tend to be more institutionalised than the role artefacts.

Figure 1 is a representation of a hypothetical VC with four roles X, Y, T and V represented by the filled circles, and many plain circles representing tasks that each role performs. Thick lines represent role artefacts and narrow lines represent task artefacts.

An Example of Awareness Net in Australian Health Insurance Sector (AHIS):

The following real-life self-explanatory scenario (Figure 2) represents a health insurance claim process within the Australian health insurance sector (Daneshgar & Lee, 2003). In this figure the roles are shown by dark circles, tasks are shown by light circles, role artefacts are shown by straight lines and the task artefacts are shown by broken lines.

Figure 3 shows an emerging and more collaborative scenario of the simplified process of Figure 2. This scenario is representative of nearly 20% of total claims where the medical providers, utilising an electronic facility representative of business process outsourcing (BPO), process claims with insurance companies without the onus of the claiming process being left to the patient.

From the identification of roles participating in the AHIS and the discussion of the related task artefacts, current AHIS collaboration challenges have been

Copyright © 2004, Idea Group Inc. Copying or distributing in print or electronic forms without written permission of Idea Group Inc. is prohibited.

Figure 2. An awareness net for Australian Health insurance sector.

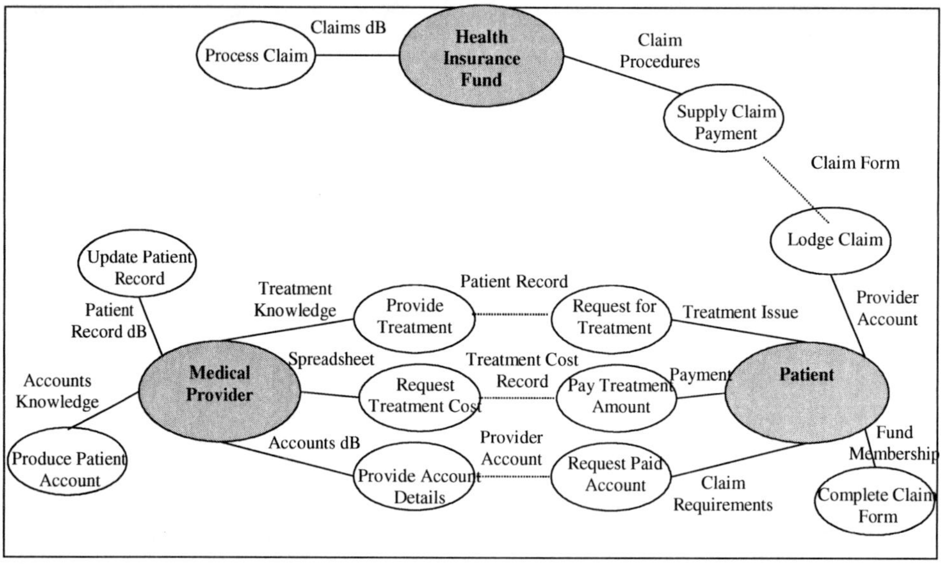

identified. From the data collected from the respondents there is clear empirical evidence that the major process challenges occur during collaboration between the roles. The following section discusses these process challenges and identifies some key areas requiring process improvement.

Currently, the electronic BPO claims that are rejected by the system are either resubmitted in hardcopy by the medical provider, or the patient is required to make a paper based claim. Errors in electronic files or incomplete paper based claims tend to create spurious output from the various fund systems, as there is currently no unified approach. A characteristic survey response sums up the current approach to systems error handling: "If an error exists in an electronic file we are alerted either with a 'graceful' warning or by program 'abort'. As a result the file is either corrected by hand or a new file is requested from the supplier." Errors detected in the paper forms are queried with the supplier and corrected or re-sent; this process can involve multiple phone calls, faxes and e-mails, representing a major opportunity for improvement and time saving. Errors from claims assessing, if identified, are reviewed when assessed incorrectly. If not enough information is supplied on the account when received by the health insurance fund the medical provider is contacted to verify the information. Funds return documentation if correct information is not supplied or further information is required. Another aspect is the tracking and delivery

Copyright © 2004, Idea Group Inc. Copying or distributing in print or electronic forms without written permission of Idea Group Inc. is prohibited.

of certificates for the treatments provided that may be required to process the claim. Funds also report if there are instances where overpayment of a claim can occur. Some examples of the identified situations where multiple processing attempts may occur include: medical provider incorrectly itemises an account, duplication of services, and error in transmitting the item numbers to the fund or fund assessing error.

Therefore the challenges identified were:

- Better handling of claims with errors. An obvious lack of focus and nimbus for the actors is evident in this case.
- Paper based claims should not be the default way to process claims; instead, an online community of actors with appropriate levels of awareness will be able to deal with the situation much more effectively.
- Too many formats exist for claims and their processes, for example, telephone, fax, e-mail and paper based. There is no formal procedure for the choice of the format. One alternative is to leave the decision to be made

Figure 3. AHIS awareness net BPO facilitator.

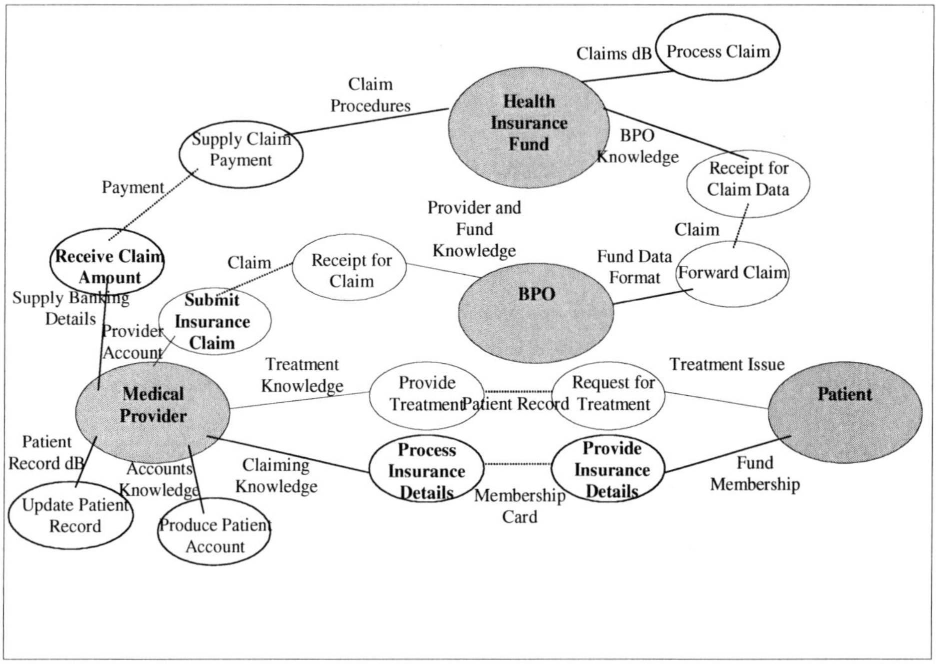

Copyright © 2004, Idea Group Inc. Copying or distributing in print or electronic forms without written permission of Idea Group Inc. is prohibited.

collaboratively by the relevant members of the online community based on their levels of process awareness.

- Incomplete forms being filed for claiming.
- Person submitting claim may not be aware of certificate requirements for the claim. A classic example of "awareness gap" as mentioned later in this chapter.
- Overpayment of claim.

Process Awareness Model in Virtual Communities

Sharing of the contextual knowledge in VCs occurs at various levels depending on both focus and nimbus related to various semantic concepts involved. Five levels are identified in this chapter and are discussed in the following:

Level-0 Context-Sharing (or Awareness):

An actor is at level-0 if s/he possesses contextual knowledge about the objects that lead the actor to an understanding of the tasks that the actor performs within the VC. This knowledge is the sum of the actor's *focus* (his or her visibility and eyesight) as well as the tasks' *nimbus* (how clearly the tasks are presented to, and then conceived by, the actor). In Figure 2 examples of nimbus for the level-0 awareness for "patient" include clarity of treatment procedures provided by the MD, and a clear address/map of the MD's location. Similarly examples of nimbus for the MD include the evidence that patient provides as proof of identity.

In Figure 1, level-0 awareness for the role X is a sub-graph that can be shown by the following set of objects (for simplicity, mathematical set notations have been used to show a sub-graph):

$$A0\,(\text{'X'}) = \{\{X, 1\}, 1, \{X, 2\}, 2, \{X, 3\}, 3, \{X, 4\}, 4\}$$

Similarly, in Figure 2, level-0 awareness for the health insurance fund (HIF) is:

A0 ('HIF) = {Claims dB, Process Claim, Claim Procedures, Supplying Claim Payment}

Copyright © 2004, Idea Group Inc. Copying or distributing in print or electronic forms without written permission of Idea Group Inc. is prohibited.

The above statement means that the awareness level-0 for the role "X" is the sum of the four *role artefacts* shown by the lines (X,1), (X,2), (X,3) and (X,4), as well as four task vertices, 1, 2, 3 and 4. And for HIF the awareness level-0 is the sum of two role artefacts and two tasks.

Level-0 awareness does not provide the actors with adequate awareness to enable them to get involved in any kind of context-sharing transactions with others, as it does not include objects beyond the actor's perception of his/her own personal "tasks" within the process.

Level-1 Context-Sharing/Awareness:

Level-0 awareness is a pre-requisite for the next level up. An actor that reaches level-1 awareness will possess a specialised knowledge about all the objects that leads the actor to awareness about some of the actors within the VC. These are the actors with whom the actor has a direct task dependency. In Figure 1 level-1 awareness for the actor V is the path that links vertex "V" to all other related role vertices. In this example role "V" happens to have task dependency with one other role, that is, role "X". In this particular case, there are two alternatives/paths for the V's level-1 awareness because there are two separate between V and X. The mathematical representation for these alternatives are:

Alternative_1_A1 ('V') = {A0 {'V'}, {d, 1}, 1, {1, X}, X}
Alternative_2_A1 ('V') = {A0 {'V'}, {d, 2}, 2, {2, X}, X}

Where:

Each of {d,1}, (1,X}, {d,2} and {2,X} represent four different arcs; and each of 1, 2 and X represent one node.

Level-2 Awareness:

An actor at level-2 awareness will have a knowledge about the objects that leads the actor towards an understanding of every (other) role within the VC. Level-2 awareness for the role "V" is the path that links V to all other role vertices within the process. There are many alternatives for the V's level-2. The mathematical representation of one of these alternatives is:

Copyright © 2004, Idea Group Inc. Copying or distributing in print or electronic forms without written permission of Idea Group Inc. is prohibited.

Alternative_1_A2 ('V') = {A1 ('V'), {X,4} , 4 , {4 , 5}, 5 , {5, Y}, Y, {Y , 6}, 6 , {6 , b}, b , {b , T}, T}

Level-3 Awareness:

An actor at level-3 awareness has the knowledge about the objects that leads that actor towards an understanding of all interactions that occur between any pair of roles within the VC. Attaining level-3 awareness enables an actor to initiate level-3 context-sharing transactions within the VC. The mathematical representation of this level for the alternative 1 of the level-2 awareness for the role V is:

A3 ('V') = {alternative_1_A2 ('V'), {4 ,6}, {7 , 2}}

Notice that {4, 6} and {7 , 2} are the only two other task artefacts that were not included in the alternative_1_A2('V').

Level-4 Awareness:

An actor at level-4 awareness has a specialised knowledge about the objects that leads that actor to an understanding of all the objects within the VC. Graphically, this level can be represented by the whole of the awareness net. At this level the actor has adequate contextual knowledge about what everyone does with the VC and how they perform their tasks (that is, the sum of everybody's level-0 awarenesses), who directly collaborates with whom and how (sum of everybody's level-1 awarenesses), and who directly or indirectly collaborates with whom and how (sum of all the level-2 awarenesses), and finally, how other actors collaborate with one another (sum of all the level-3 awarenesses). The mathematical representation of this level can be shown by the following sets of equations:

A4 (X) = A4 (Y) = A4 (T) = A4 (V)

A4(X) = {A3(X), {V, e}, {V, f}, e, f, {T, c}, {T, a}, c, a, {Y, 8}, 8}

A4(Y) = {A3 (Y), {V, e}, e, {V, f}, f, {X, 3}, 3, {T, c}, c, {T, a}, a}

A4(T) = {A3 (T), {V, e}, {V, f}, e, f, {Y, 8}, 8, {X, 3}, 3}

A4 (V) = {A3 (V), {X,3}, 3, {T, c}, c, {T, a}, a, {Y, 8}, 8, {X, 3}, 3}

Copyright © 2004, Idea Group Inc. Copying or distributing in print or electronic forms without written permission of Idea Group Inc. is prohibited.

In short, the level-4 awareness is the sum of all the roles' level-3 awareness, plus the sum of all the roles' single tasks and corresponding role artefacts. Awareness at this level is highest as the actor will know not only how everybody interacts with others, but also how each role performs its own very personal task(s).

Steps of the Methodology

Introduction

In order to explicitly incorporate nimbus within the above awareness framework the writer provides the following proposition:

> With the exception of the task artefact each other object within the awareness net, say Object X, (that is, either of role, role artefact, or task objects) will have an additional array of attributes. The size of the array is the total number of roles within the awareness net, minus 1. Each element of this array consists of the following fields:
>
> 1. A reference to another role; that is, a role other than the one that is related to the Object X, and
> 2. An indication of the nimbus according to which the Object X would decide how much of itself needs to be revealed to the other role(s).

Under this arrangement each of the role, role artefact and task objects will reveal desired attributes of themselves to other roles. The task artefact object is a shared object and requires a negotiation between the two roles concerned before values for the above array are determined. With this proposition in mind, the following section describes a revised methodology for enhancing collaboration and knowledge sharing in VCs.

Enhancing Collaboration in VCs

The following two additional concepts need to be explained at this stage:

Copyright © 2004, Idea Group Inc. Copying or distributing in print or electronic forms without written permission of Idea Group Inc. is prohibited.

Actual Level of Awareness: an attribute of the actor who assumes a role within the process. It represents the awareness that the actor actually possesses, and is independent from the required level of awareness (below).

Required Level of Awareness: an attribute of the task, and represents the expected awareness from the actor who performs this task.

The main objective of this methodology is to identify potential areas that could enhance knowledge sharing within VCs. This means identification of the objects that need to be put within the focus of an actor in order to raise his/her actual level of awareness and knowledge sharing to its ideal level. The latter is determined by cultural and social factors that fall outside the scope of this chapter and are external to the framework. It was due to these factors that Section 5 was designed. This methodology is explained in the following four steps.

- **Step One:** Construct an awareness net for the VC. The awareness net is a visualisation tool that graphically shows various levels of awareness for different roles. Obviously, the role(s) who is (are) assigned to the task of constructing this awareness net must themselves be at level-4 awareness before they can build this network.
- **Step Two:** determine the actual levels of awareness for each actor. Several methods can be used in order to determine these actual levels. One method is to use software developed by the writer called "Aware-Ware Template" or AWT (Daneshgar, 1999, 2000b). Actors in VCs interact with this software and express their awareness (Yes/No) with regards to the objects that exist on the awareness net. The algorithm of this software is capable of parsing the awareness net, which has already been mapped into a Lotus-Notes database, in order to identify various objects that make up various awareness levels for each actor, based on their responses. Another method for determining the actual level of awareness (obviously, in small processes) is the interview method. Both of these methods have already been used and appropriate results were produced.
- **Step Three:** define a desired/ideal level of awareness for each role in relation to each task that the actor performs within the process. It is assumed in this chapter that such a level of awareness is directly related to both the nature of the task as well as to the community culture. For example, a trainee programmer who works in the Army (a closed culture)

Copyright © 2004, Idea Group Inc. Copying or distributing in print or electronic forms without written permission of Idea Group Inc. is prohibited.

may not need more than level-1 awareness whereas the same programmer in a Telecom organization (assuming to have a more open culture) must ideally possess level-3 awareness. In either culture, a trainee programmer does not need a higher level of awareness than his/her supervisor. Again, the AWT software can be used to identify objects that constitute various levels of awareness that are required from the actors within the community. In the absence of the AWT software, this can be done either by interviewing the actors, or by manually tracing the awareness net and recording the objects (that is, nodes and vertices) that constitute various levels of awareness for each actor.

- **Step Four:** for each actor, if the ideal level of awareness is higher than the actual level of awareness, that is, if there is an *awareness gap,* then there is potential for enhancing collaboration and knowledge sharing space within the community. This can be done by exposing the actor to the relevant objects within the awareness net that are currently outside the focus of the actor. Alternatively, another actor can be assigned to this role that possesses a higher actual level of visibility.

Concluding Remarks and Future Work

This chapter introduced a framework for knowledge sharing of knowledge workers in VCs. It was shown that knowledge space could be expanded by identifying the awareness gaps for various actors within the community. It was further suggested that these objects be put within the focus of the actors. Some classic originations from a CSCW (computer-supported cooperative work) perspective include "encouraging the *articulation work*" (Gerson, 1986), "explicification of *situated actions*" (Allen, 1984), "identification of *mutual* influence" (Robinson, 1991a), "facilitation of *shared views/shared materials*" (Robinson, 1991b), and "provision of a *double-level language* that allows both ambiguity and clarity" (Robinson, 1991a). These concepts have been selected and their historic development is under investigation by the authors for addressing the process of effective knowledge sharing for VCs.

Copyright © 2004, Idea Group Inc. Copying or distributing in print or electronic forms without written permission of Idea Group Inc. is prohibited.

References

Allen, T.J. (1984). *Managing the flow of technology.* Cambridge: MIT Press.

Baker, D., Georgakopoulos, D., Schuster, H., & Cichocki, A. (2002). Awareness provisioning in collaboration management. *International Journal of Cooperative Information Systems (World Scientific Publishing Company), 11*(1/2) 145-173.

Barker, D., Georgakopoulos, D., Schuster, H., & Cichoki, A. (2002). Awareness provisioning in collaboration management. *International Journal of Cooperative Information Systems, 11*(1/ 2), 145-173.

Bentley, R., & Dourish, P. (1995, September 10-14). Medium versus mechanisms: Supporting collaboration through customisation. *Proceedings of the Fourth European Conference on CSCW,* Stockholm, Sweden.

Constantine, L.L. (1995, January). Leading your team - wherever they go: Leadership models for software development. *Software Development.*

Constantine, L.L., & Lockwood, L.A.D. (1994, December). Fitting practices to the people. *American Programmer.*

Daneshgar, F. (1997a). A CSCW approach for: Enhancing collaboration in enterprise environments. *Proceedings of CAiSE'97 DC* (Consortium on Advanced Information Systems Engineering), Barcelona, Spain.

Daneshgar, F. (1999). A methodology for planning, analysis, design and implementation of collaborative databases: Introducing AWT software. *Proceedings of the 2nd International Symposium on Cooperative Database Systems for Advanced Applications,* Wollongong, Australia.

Daneshgar, F. (2000b). *An awareness framework for business processes.* PhD Thesis, University of Technology, Sydney, Australia.

Daneshgar, F. (2001a). *A methodology for redesigning collaborative processes with undesirable multi-way task dependencies.* 15th International Conference on Information Networking, Beppu City, Japan.

Daneshgar, F. (2001b). An object-oriented awareness-based methodology for enterprise resource planning. In L. Hossain & J. Patrick (Eds.), *Enterprise resource planning: Opportunities and challenge.* Hershey, PA: Idea Group Inc.

Copyright © 2004, Idea Group Inc. Copying or distributing in print or electronic forms without written permission of Idea Group Inc. is prohibited.

Daneshgar, F., & Lee, K.M. (2003). Enhancing collaboration in the Australian Health Insurance Sector. *Proceedings of KMAC'2003,* Aston University, UK.

Daneshgar, F., & Ray, P. (1997b). Management based on awareness modelling. *Proceedings of the 8th IEEE/IFIP International Workshop on Distributed Systems Operations and Management* (DSOM'97), Sydney, Australia.

Daneshgar, F., & Ray, P. (2000a). Cooperative management based on awareness modelling: A formalised model. *Proceedings of the 7th International Conference on Parallel and Distributed Systems* (ICPADS'00), Morioka, Japan.

Dourish, P., & Bellotti, V. (1992). Awareness and coordination in shared workspaces. *Rank Xerox EuroPARC, CSCW 92 Proceedings.*

Farquhar, A., & Rice, J. (2003). *The Ontolingua Server: A tool for collaborative ontology construction.* Stanford's Knowledge Systems Laboratory, Stanford University, USA (*http://ontolingua.stanford.edu*).

Gerson, E., & Star, S. (1986). Analysing due process in the workplace. ACM *Transactions on Office Information Systems, 4*(3).

Hawrysszkiewycz, I. (1997). *Designing the networked enterprise.* Norwood, MA: Archer House Inc.

Latour, B. (1996). *Aramis or the love of technology.* ISBN 0-674-04323-5. Harvard University Press.

Lee, J.D., Hickey, A.A., Zhang, D., Santanen, E., & Zhou, L. (2000). *ColD SPA: A tool for collaborative process model development.* 33rd Hawaii International Conference on System Sciences, Hawaii, USA.

Nabuco, O., Drira, K., & Dantas, E. (2001). *A layered design model for knowledge and information sharing cooperative systems.* IEEE 10th International Workshop on Enabling Technologies, Cambridge, MA, USA.

Nonaka, I. (1991, November-December). The knowledge-creating company. *Harvard Business Review,* 96-104.

Robinson, M. (1991a). Double level languages and cooperative working. *AI & Society, 5,* 34-60.

Robinson, M. (1991b). Computer supported cooperative work: Cases and concepts. *Proceedings of Groupware 91,* SERC, Utrecht, the Netherlands.

Copyright © 2004, Idea Group Inc. Copying or distributing in print or electronic forms without written permission of Idea Group Inc. is prohibited.

Snowden, D. (2002, May). Complex acts of knowledge: Paradox and descriptive self-awareness. *Special Issue of the Journal of Knowledge Management, 6*(2).

Copyright © 2004, Idea Group Inc. Copying or distributing in print or electronic forms without written permission of Idea Group Inc. is prohibited.

Chapter IV

Corporate Memories: Tombs or Wellsprings of Knowledge?

Meliha Handzic
The University of New South Wales, Australia

Glenn Bewsell
The University of New South Wales, Australia

Abstract

This chapter explores the nature of corporate memories in enhancing individual working knowledge and performance in a decision-making context. Our findings from a series of experiments indicate that people tended to use effectively up to two-thirds of the encoded knowledge, missing at least one-third of its maximum potential. Our findings also indicate that the effectiveness of knowledge repositories was highly contingent upon quantity, quality and diversity of their knowledge content. Finally, our study suggests that individuals can potentially benefit from additional knowledge management initiatives such as analytical and procedural knowledge, learning histories, guidance or interactive social environments. Future research may look at the impact of these initiatives independently, or at the possibility of a synergistic effect when combined and integrated.

Copyright © 2004, Idea Group Inc. Copying or distributing in print or electronic forms without written permission of Idea Group Inc. is prohibited.

Introduction

Human society is experiencing a major transformation from an industry-based society to a knowledge-based society. With this transition comes a growing recognition among researchers and practitioners alike for the need to better understand the value of knowledge, what knowledge is, and how it should be managed. In general, the knowledge management literature indicates a widespread recognition of the importance of knowledge with respect to the struggle for economic success (Devlin, 1999; Drucker, 1993; Stewart, 1997), but little shared understanding of the construct itself (Davenport & Prusak, 1998; Devlin, 1999; Grayson & Dell, 1998). There are also differences among researchers in what constitutes useful knowledge and the ways in which it is created. A recent review of the knowledge management literature (Baxter & Chua, 1999) identifies two major strategies: *codification* and *personalisation.* The proponents of codification show a central preoccupation with organisational databases and *explicit* knowledge. On the other hand, proponents of personalisation seem to be more interested in *tacit* knowledge sharing.

As organisations become more knowledge-based their success will depend on how successfully knowledge workers are applying knowledge productively and efficiently. The central task of those concerned with organisational knowledge management is to determine ways to better cultivate, nurture and exploit knowledge at different levels and in different contexts. Knowledge management is seen as central to process and product improvement, to executive decision making, and to organisational adaptation and renewal (Earl, 2001). This opens up new opportunities for research and practice in behavioural decision making.

A knowledge management systems framework (Hahn & Subramani, 2000) suggests that the availability of a KM system such as codified repository should lead to an increase in individual knowledge and result in improved performance. Other frameworks (e.g., Handzic, 2003) propose that KM technology should have an enabling or facilitating effect on managing knowledge processes. Reliable empirical evidence to support these propositions is largely missing (Alavi & Leidner, 2001). The existing KM research is mainly limited to anecdotal stories and descriptive case studies. Therefore, it is necessary to recognise the importance and the need for better understanding of this issue. The main purpose of this chapter is to provide a deeper insight into potential and limitations of codified repositories of business artefacts in enhancing individual working knowledge and performance in the context of decision making.

Copyright © 2004, Idea Group Inc. Copying or distributing in print or electronic forms without written permission of Idea Group Inc. is prohibited.

Managerial decision making can be viewed as a knowledge intensive activity. Decision makers often obtain explicit knowledge from the stores of business intelligence available in organisations and gain tacit know-how in response to the demands of their work. It is implicitly assumed that the availability of such stores should lead to an increase in their working knowledge, resulting in improved job performance. However, little is known about the actual success of these initiatives and returns resulting from them.

With the growing abundance of business artefacts enabled by modern technology, it is of particular interest to this study to examine whether and how knowledge captured in computerised organisational stores affects individual decision makers' working knowledge, and what impact this may have on the quality of their subsequent decisions. The authors conducted a series of laboratory experiments to address this issue. The next sections report on prior research on the issue, present the results of the authors' own studies and suggest some possible directions for future research.

Review of Prior Related Research

Corporate Memory

Corporate memory can be viewed as the set of repositories of knowledge that organisations acquire and retain, and then bring from the past to bear on their present activities with the goal of avoiding mistakes (Jennex & Olfman, 2002). The concept can be studied from two perspectives. The content perspective focuses on the knowledge that is captured and the context in which it is used. The repository perspective focuses on how knowledge is stored and retrieved. Both perspectives are relevant to this chapter. Different abstract and concrete memory forms may serve different representational and interpretational functions by presenting the knowledge for a given context, and providing frames of reference as a means to synthesise past knowledge for application to new situations.

It is generally anticipated that applying corporate memories will result in improved organisational effectiveness. Jennex and Olfman (2002) put forward a number of propositions to define the beneficial outcomes of the use of organisational memories. These range from improved decisions, through reduced decision resistance, to more successful change efforts. However,

Copyright © 2004, Idea Group Inc. Copying or distributing in print or electronic forms without written permission of Idea Group Inc. is prohibited.

these may or may not happen. Some researchers (O'Leary, 2002) argue that while knowledge may be gathered, created and converted, if it is not assimilated, the organisations will not be able to take action on that knowledge or actualise its potential value. As a result, corporate memories will have only limited impact on an organisation. Other researchers (Fayyad & Uthurusamy, 2002) warn that the increasing ability to capture and store data may produce a phenomenon called the data tombs. These are effectively write-only stores where knowledge artifacts are deposited to merely rest in peace, never to be accessed again. Such stores represent missed opportunities to support exploration in a scientific activity or commercial exploitation by a business organisation.

If knowledge captured in organisational stores stays unused, most opportunities to discover, profit, improve service or optimise will be lost. Despite this recognition, much of the previous research on knowledge management has ignored the issues associated with extraction and internalisation of knowledge from corporate stores. As a result, this chapter has particularly focused on factors that inhibit/promote effective use of corporate memories in order to demonstrate the promise and the benefit of these systems. The challenge is to find ways to turn corporate memories into wellsprings of knowledge.

Business Intelligence and Decision Making

Theoretically, the availability of environment and organisation specific knowledge, as well as a variety of cause-effect relationships, can play an important role in improving decision quality. The value of such contextual knowledge may be seen primarily in its ability to explain past and anticipate future changes in the behaviour of any particular variable of interest and enabling the decision maker to deal more competently with his or her decision task. In the case of production planning, for example, product and industry knowledge should help the decision maker to make more accurate estimates of future sales, translate these estimates into more suitable production plans, and minimise losses due to overproduction or missed sales opportunities. The provision of valid contextual knowledge in codified organisational databases should increase the decision maker's working knowledge base and consequently improve an individual's decision performance.

Past empirical studies indicate mixed and inconclusive findings. Several studies using real world settings support the notion that contextual knowledge improves the quality of human judgment. Edmundson et al. (1988) found that

Copyright © 2004, Idea Group Inc. Copying or distributing in print or electronic forms without written permission of Idea Group Inc. is prohibited.

business practitioners who possessed considerable experiential knowledge of the specific products being forecast made more accurate sales predictions than students with no such contextual knowledge. This finding was also supported by Sanders and Ritzman (1992). Comparative analysis showed that the difference in the accuracy of forecasts generated with and without contextual knowledge was particularly significant under conditions of high variability of time series data. In addition, human judgment with contextual knowledge was found to lead to improved forecast accuracy over statistical models (Edmundson et al., 1988; Fildes, 1991). In the judgmental adjustment context, non-time series contextual knowledge was also found to be beneficial. Mathews and Diamantopoulos (1986, 1989) reported that managers who possessed considerable product knowledge were able to successfully adjust exponential smoothing forecasts. Similarly, Wolfe and Flores (1990) showed that the accuracy of a statistical forecast could be improved when judgmentally adjusted in the light of contextual knowledge when the statistical forecast was of low quality and the time series involved contained a high level of variability.

In contrast, a more recent field study of sales forecasting by Lawrence et al. (1995) revealed that bias and inefficiency could mask any contribution of seemingly helpful contextual knowledge to the accuracy of judgmental forecasts. This study compared the accuracy of judgmentally produced monthly product forecasts with naive forecasts of 13 companies. Contrary to expectations, the company forecasts were more accurate than the naive forecasts in only four of the companies, while the naive forecast was more accurate than the company forecasts in two companies. In the remaining seven companies, the difference was insignificant.

Empirical evidence from a number of laboratory studies also casts doubt on people's ability to effectively process contextual/causal knowledge. In a study comparing the accuracy of judgmental causal forecasting with judgmental extrapolation, Andreassen (1991) showed that the causal group, provided with current situational diagnostic variables, significantly underperformed the extrapolation group. Similarly, Harvey et al. (1994) found that cross-series forecasts of train passengers made from correlated train criminals series were less accurate than the corresponding within-series forecasts made from the past passengers series only. However, it is possible that these causal variables had poor predictive validity. Finally, in a series of judgmental adjustment studies, Lim and O'Connor (1995, 1996a) found that people had difficulty in placing adequate weight on the reliable causal factors and did not learn to modify this behaviour over time. When the environment was multivariate, people were

Copyright © 2004, Idea Group Inc. Copying or distributing in print or electronic forms without written permission of Idea Group Inc. is prohibited.

found to have problems in both evaluating and using the explicit contextual knowledge available (Lim & O'Connor, 1996b). Task complexity may be one of the potential contributing factors to the reported inefficiency (Beach & Mitchell, 1978; Payne, 1982; Wood, 1986).

Research Questions

In view of inconsistent prior findings and concerns expressed, it is of particular interest to this research to examine the situation in which decision makers are provided with codified repositories of decision relevant contextual knowledge of varying quantity, quality and diversity. It is argued that such situations represent the complexities of real-world corporate memories. The research questions of interest are: (i) whether and how well individual decision makers can make sense of what is available in such knowledge repositories and enhance their working knowledge, and (ii) whether and what impact the application of that knowledge may have on their subsequent decision performance.

Description and Results of Our Empirical Study

Research Method

A series of experiments were conducted in controlled laboratory settings using graduate students as voluntary subjects. For the purpose of the investigation, a common experimental task was designed in which subjects assumed the role of production manager for a fictitious firm selling fresh ice cream from its beach outlet. All subjects were novices to the task and were required to predict daily sales of ice cream and make corresponding production decisions over a period of 30 consecutive days. Each subject had access to a computerised repository that provided decision relevant facts and figures regarding the past product sales, as well as contextual factors such as the daily temperature, visitor numbers and sunshine conditions expected on the beach.

Different groups of subjects were provided with codified knowledge of varying quantity, quality and diversity. This was achieved by changing the number of

Copyright © 2004, Idea Group Inc. Copying or distributing in print or electronic forms without written permission of Idea Group Inc. is prohibited.

contextual artefacts and correlation coefficients (r) between contextual and predicted variables provided to each group. Group 1 was provided with one piece of moderately predictive artefact (r_1=0.8). Group 2 was provided with two pieces of similarly relevant artefacts ($r_{1,2}$=.8) and group 3 was provided with three such pieces ($r_{1,2,3}$=.8). In group 4 subjects were given a mix of three artefacts of different predictive ability (r_1=.9; $r_{2,3}$=.3), while group 5 was offered all three highly predictive artefacts ($r_{1,2,3}$=.95). All artefacts were presented in the form of line graphs and were accessible on request one at a time by a simple mouse click on a corresponding icon.

Subjects' performance was evaluated in terms of decision accuracy. It was operationalised by *symmetric absolute percentage error* (SAPE), chosen because it controls for scale and computational bias of MAPE. SAPE was obtained by dividing the absolute difference between subject-estimated and actually demanded units of product by an average of the two values and multiplying by 100% (Makridakis, 1993). In addition, the corresponding errors of nominal naive and nominal optimal decision makers were calculated. These are the error scores that would have been obtained by people who produced their decisions by using naive (random walk) and optimal strategies. Optimal strategies were obtained by regression analysis consistent with Brunswik's (1956) lens model. Naive SAPE was set to 20.67 and optimal SAPE to 8.30, 6.28, 5.13, 4.69 and 2.63 for groups 1-5 respectively. These scores were used to assess how much of the full potential of the available artefacts to improve performance was used/unused by the actual subjects.

The difference between naive and actual subject SAPE indicated the amount of achieved improvement due to used knowledge, while the difference between actual and optimal subject SAPE indicated the amount of unrealised potential improvement due to unused knowledge. The collected data were analysed statistically using one-way ANOVAs followed by multiple comparison tests (Scheffe rule) to compare actual subjects' performance with that of their nominal naive and optimal counterparts. All results were significant at $p<0.05$.

Results

The analyses performed found significant differences in error scores between actual subjects and nominal naive decision makers in all groups. As shown in Figure 1, actual subjects tended to make smaller decision errors than their nominal naive counterparts irrespective of the experimental treatment (14.41, 11.59, 11.37, 12.21, 10.47<20.67). The results of the analyses also revealed

Copyright © 2004, Idea Group Inc. Copying or distributing in print or electronic forms without written permission of Idea Group Inc. is prohibited.

significant differences in error scores between actual subjects and nominal optimal decision makers. Figure 1 shows that actual subjects tended to make greater decision errors than their simulated counterparts applying optimal artifact-weighting strategy on the task, regardless of the experimental treatment (14.41>8.30, 11.59>6.28, 11.27>5.13, 12.21>4.69, 10.46>2.63).

Finally, a cross-group analysis discovered significant differences in subjects' performance due to varying quantity, quality and diversity of the repository content. Figure 1 shows that achieved improvement was generally consistent with the overall task predictability due to increased quantity and quality of the available artefacts, but not diversity. The difference between naive and actual subject SAPE increased from 6.26 through 9.08, 9.30, 8.46 to 10.20 for groups 1-5 respectively.

Figure 1 also shows that the amount of unused knowledge and subsequent unrealised improvement grew with increased artefact quantity, quality and diversity. In real terms, the difference between actual and optimal subject SAPE increased from 5.31 to 6.24 with increased quantity (groups 2 & 3);

Figure 1. Mean error scores (SAPE) of actual and notional subjects by group.

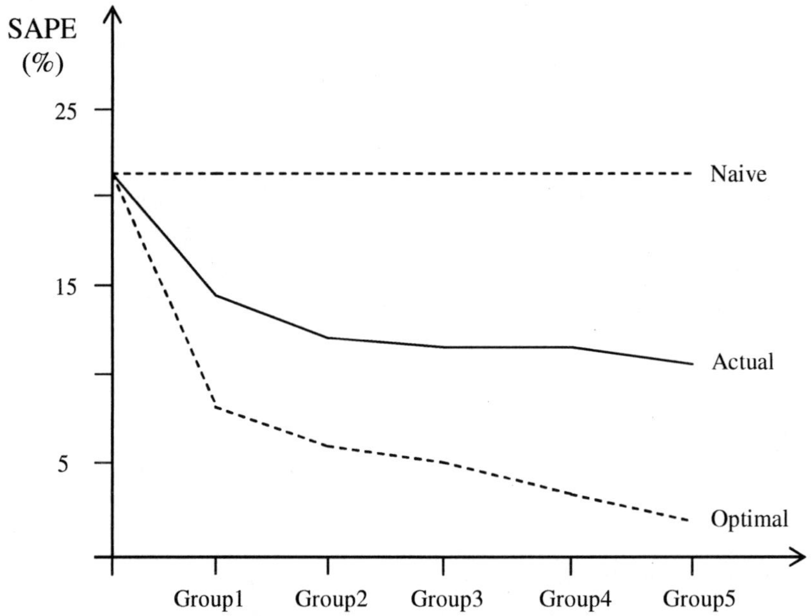

Copyright © 2004, Idea Group Inc. Copying or distributing in print or electronic forms without written permission of Idea Group Inc. is prohibited.

from 6.24 to 7.84 with increased quality (groups 3 & 5); and from 6.24 to 7.52 with increased diversity (groups 3 & 4) of the available artefacts. One notable exception to this general trend was a decrease from 6.11 to 5.31 in the difference score with an initial increase in artefact quantity (groups 1 & 2). The nature of the results across different groups enables drawing of a number of conclusions and provides a basis for possible directions for future research.

Discussion of Main Findings and Future Research Directions

Main Findings

In summary, the main findings of the series of empirical tests presented in this paper indicate that the provision of codified knowledge repositories containing task relevant artefacts was useful, but insufficient *alone* to enable individual decision makers to achieve optimal performance. The findings also reveal a highly contingent nature of the impact of these repositories, being dependent upon the quantity, quality and diversity of their available content.

The fact that subjects tended to make substantially smaller than naive strategy decision errors suggests that they were able to make use of some of the potential of their available artefacts, and as a result, improve their subsequent performance. On average, error scores dropped by 30-49% compared to naive errors. These findings give a more optimistic picture of human judgment than earlier MCPL research (Brehmer, 1980). One potential explanation for the difference may be in the characteristics of the decision task. Participants in the current study were provided with: a meaningful task context, sequential history of task relevant variables that provided some clues to causal relationships, and forecast values of contextual variables to suggest future behaviour. It is also possible that a graphical form of presentation facilitated the use of a pattern matching task strategy, and enabled subjects to correctly judge the direction of future changes and make their estimates accordingly. Such a strategy has been shown to produce good results in highly predictive environments (Hoch & Schkade, 1996).

However, the pattern matching strategy could not produce optimal performance in a non-deterministic task. Actual subjects were found to make

Copyright © 2004, Idea Group Inc. Copying or distributing in print or electronic forms without written permission of Idea Group Inc. is prohibited.

significantly greater decision errors than their nominal optimal counterparts. Greater than optimal errors suggest that the subjects tended to use substantially less potential of the available artefacts compared with their maximum potential value. Further analysis revealed that, on average, 49-37% of the total encoded knowledge was not used across the five groups; consequently a significant amount of its improvement potential remained unrealised. One possible explanation for the phenomenon may lie in the subjects' misevaluation of the worth of the repository content. Turning artefacts into tacit knowledge requires familiarity with the relevant context and the appropriate weighting models for variables. Subjects in the current research were not given any explicit analysis of the quality of their artefacts, or rules they could apply to integrate the available facts. Instead, all subjects in each group had an opportunity to learn from their own experience through task repetition and from feedback. However, the fact that the participants responded in the appropriate direction suggests that they could potentially achieve more improvement with more trials (Klayman, 1988) or with additional knowledge management support in the form of systems thinking, data mining, or knowledge sharing (Liebowitz, 2000).

As expected, our cross-group analysis indicated that the achieved decision improvement was generally consistent with each group's overall task predictability due to increased quantity and quality, but not diversity of the available artefacts. However, a more interesting finding concerns significant variations observed in the level of unused encoded knowledge when normatively irrelevant factors such as artefact quantity, quality and diversity were varied. The study found that the percentage of unused knowledge changed by 3-12%. While these demonstrated performance effects regarding quantity and diversity factors can be explained in terms of information load (Schroder et al., 1967) or task complexity (Wood, 1986), a different explanation is required to interpret the quality effect. Plausible explanations of the phenomenon may lie in Herbert Simon's notion of bounded rationality. Subjects may provide enough effort to achieve a comfortably good decision performance (Beach & Mitchell, 1978), or they may use fast and frugal heuristics and "employ limited search through objects (in satisficing) or cues and exploit environmental structure to yield adaptive decisions" (Gigerenzer, Todd & ABC Research Group, 1999). Our follow-up analysis of actual strategies employed by the subjects indeed confirmed their use of reduced search and selective weighting heuristics.

To model each subject's strategy, we applied multiple regression with the available artefacts as independent variables, and the subject's evaluation as the dependent variable. This is a common approach used to study how judges

Copyright © 2004, Idea Group Inc. Copying or distributing in print or electronic forms without written permission of Idea Group Inc. is prohibited.

weight and combine information. The model parameters were then used to indicate the importance assigned to various artefacts. It was found that subjects adapted to increased complexity of the decision problem from the cognitive load imposed on them by the need to process increased quantity of artefacts by adopting selective information utilisation. In particular, they tended to place greater reliance on some and less reliance on other available artefacts. Similarly, it was demonstrated that the increased task complexity from higher information diversity led to ignoring differences in relative importance among the individual artefacts. Such behaviour diluted the effect of the best predictor on performance, and resulted in poorer performance. The findings also indicate that subjects were aware that the additional information was less useful when the certainty of the decision outcome increased. Thus, when presented with multiple artefacts of higher quality, subjects generally tended to ignore some artefacts. Consequently, the performance was poorer than that of normative strategies.

In general, our findings indicate room for further improvement in individual decision making. The high level of unused knowledge potential from codified repositories revealed in this study suggests that individuals could potentially benefit from additional knowledge management initiatives. The prime challenge of knowledge management research is to determine innovative ways to further improve the development, transfer and use of knowledge at individual and collective levels. Currently, there are large gaps in the body of knowledge in this area, with much theory and little empirical research undertaken. The following section highlights some possible research directions for the future.

Future Research

The challenge of future research is to find ways to turn corporate memories into wellsprings of knowledge. One possible direction is to examine the potential contribution of explanatory content to knowledge utilisation. Additional analytical and procedural knowledge, as well as histories of past experiences, guiding instructions, deeper explanations and richer feedback might potentially help decision makers to better understand what works when and why (Kleiner & Roth, 1998). Such "experience factories" may also help reduce cognitive effort and minimise satisficing behaviour on the task.

"Knowledge maps" are another suggested innovative way to improve the utilisation of knowledge by providing systematic orientation in the intellectual

Copyright © 2004, Idea Group Inc. Copying or distributing in print or electronic forms without written permission of Idea Group Inc. is prohibited.

territory of a company and helping to find directions, assess situations or plan resources. With the rapid development of intranet technology it is predicted that they may soon become a standard element in companys' management repertoire. Yet, the current knowledge management literature has only a few stories to illustrate the potential of such maps (Eppler, 2003).

Another important area for research is the discovery of previously unknown patterns in vast amounts of data accumulated in organisational stores (Fayyad et al., 1996). Currently, increasingly powerful and sophisticated graphing and visualisation tools are being developed that are considered a vital aid in description and analysis. Similarly, a number of techniques that make use of the advances in the fields of artificial intelligence and statistics, such as neural networks and decision trees, have been developed to aid prediction. The challenge for research and design of knowledge discovery tools is to determine what mechanisms are most effective in eliminating/reducing human deficiencies, and enabling pattern discovery and comprehension. Our preliminary findings are encouraging in that they show improved decision makers' ability to discover trends (Handzic et al., 2002a) and associations among events (Handzic et al., 2002b) when supported by such tools.

Future research could also explore the role of social environment in knowledge enhancement. Organisations have come to realise that a large proportion of the knowledge needed is not captured on hard drives and filing cabinets, but kept in the heads of people. Sources report that 40-90% of the needed knowledge is tacit (AAOTE, 1998; Hewson, 1999). The spiral knowledge model assumes that the processes of sharing will result in the amplification and exponential growth of working knowledge (Nonaka, 1998). Yet, little is known of the ways in which tacit knowledge is actually shared, conditions under which this sharing occurs, and the impact it has on performance. Our own preliminary results suggest that the value of sharing may be contingent upon the nature of the task at hand (Handzic & Low, 2002).

Finally, research may also look at how various knowledge management initiatives when combined and integrated may interact to create a synergistic effect. According to Davenport and Prusak (1997) it is only possible to realise full power of knowledge by taking a holistic ecological approach to knowledge management. The suggested directions represent only a small selection of knowledge management issues and approaches that are currently of interest to the authors. Other research is necessary to systematically address various knowledge management issues in different tasks and contexts, and among different knowledge workers, if a better understanding of the area is to be

Copyright © 2004, Idea Group Inc. Copying or distributing in print or electronic forms without written permission of Idea Group Inc. is prohibited.

achieved. For a more comprehensive overview of research themes in the areas of knowledge processes and enablers (see also Handzic, 2003).

Conclusion

The nature of corporate memories is enhancing individual working knowledge and performance in a decision-making context. Our findings from a series of experiments indicate that people tended to use effectively up to two-thirds of the encoded knowledge, missing at least one-third of its maximum potential. Our findings also indicate that the effectiveness of knowledge repositories was highly contingent upon quantity, quality and diversity of their knowledge content. In particular, our study suggests that individuals can potentially benefit from additional knowledge management initiatives such as analytical and procedural knowledge, learning histories, guidance or interactive social environments. Future research may look at the impact of these initiatives independently, or at the possibility of a synergistic effect when combined and integrated.

References

Alavi, M., & Leidner, D.E. (2001). Knowledge management and knowledge management systems: Conceptual foundations and research issues. *MIS Quarterly, 25*(1), 107-136.

Andreassen, P.B. (1991). *Causal prediction versus extrapolation: Effects on information source on judgmental forecasting accuracy*. Working Paper, MIT.

Arthur Andersen Office of Training and Education. (1998). *BC knowledge management*. Arthur Andersen.

Ashton, R.H., & Kramer, S.S. (1980). Students as surrogates in behavioural accounting research: Some evidence. *Journal of Accounting Research, 18*(1), 1-15.

Baxter, J., & Chua, W.F. (1999). Now and the future. *Australian Accounting Review, 9*(3), 3-14.

Copyright © 2004, Idea Group Inc. Copying or distributing in print or electronic forms without written permission of Idea Group Inc. is prohibited.

Beach, L.R., & Mitchell, T.R. (1978). A contingency model for the selection of decision strategies. *Academy of Management Review, 3*(3), 439-449.

Brehmer, B. (1980). In one word: Not from experience. *Acta Psychologica, 45*(1-3), 223-241.

Brunswik, E. (1956). *Perception and the representative design of psychological experiments* (2nd ed.). Berkeley: University of California Press.

Davenport, T.H., & Prusak, L. (1997). *Information ecology.* Oxford: Oxford University Press.

Davenport, T.H., & Prusak, L. (1998). *Working knowledge.* Boston: Harvard Business School Press.

Devlin, K. (1999). *Infosense: Turning information into knowledge.* New York: W.H. Freeman and Company.

Drucker, P.F. (1993). *Post-capitalist society.* New York: Harper Business.

Earl, M. (2001). Knowledge management strategies: Toward a taxonomy. *Journal of Management Information Systems, 18*(1), 215-233.

Edmundson, R.H., Lawrence, M.J., & O'Connor, M.J. (1988). The use of non-time series information in sales forecasting: A case study. *Journal of Forecasting, 7*(3), 201.

Eppler, M.J. (2003). Making knowledge visible through knowledge maps: Concepts, elements, cases. In C.W. Holsapple, (Ed.), *Handbook on Knowledge Management 1* (pp. 189-205). Berlin: Springer.

Fayyad, U., & Uthurusamy, R. (2002). Evolving data mining into solutions for insights. *Communications of the ACM, 45*(8), 28-31.

Fayyad, U., Piatetsky-Shapiro, G., & Smyth, P. (1996). Knowledge discovery and data mining: Towards a unifying framework. *Proceedings of the Second International Conference on Knowledge Discovery and Data Mining* (KDD-96), Oregon.

Fildes, R. (1991). Efficient use of information in the formation of subjective industry forecasts. *Journal of Forecasting, 10*(6), 597-617.

Gigerenzer, G., & Goldstein, D.G. (1996). Reasoning the fast and frugal way: Models of bounded rationality. *Psychological Review, 103*(4), 650-669.

Gigerenzer, G., Todd, P.M., & ABC Research Group. (1999). *Simple heuristics that make us smart.* New York: Oxford University Press.

Copyright © 2004, Idea Group Inc. Copying or distributing in print or electronic forms without written permission of Idea Group Inc. is prohibited.

Grayson, C.J., & Dell, C.O. (1998). Mining your hidden resources. *Across the Board, 35*(4), 23-28.

Hahn, J., & Subramani, M.R. (2000, December 10-13). A framework of knowledge management systems: Issues and challenges for theory and practice. *Proceedings of* ICIS 2000, Brisbane, Australia.

Handzic, M. (2003). An integrated research framework of knowledge management. *Journal of Information and Knowledge Management, 2*(3), (pp. 245-252).

Handzic, M., & Low, G. (2002). The impact of social interaction on performance of decision tasks of varying complexity. *OR Insight, 15*(1), 15-22.

Handzic, M., Aurum, A., Oliver, G., & Logenthiran, G. (2002, September 24-25). An empirical investigation of a knowledge discovery tool. ECKM'02. *Proceedings of the 3rd European Conference on Knowledge Management* (pp. 286-291), Dublin, Ireland.

Handzic, M., Lam, B., Aurum, A., & Oliver, G. (2002, September 25-27). A comparative analysis of two knowledge discovery tools: Scatterplot versus barchart. DM'02. *Proceedings of the Third International Conference on Data Mining Methods and Databases for Engineering, Finance and other Fields,* Bologna, Italy.

Harvey, N., Bolger, F., & McClelland, A. (1994). On the nature of expectations. *British Journal of Psychology, 85*(2), 203-229.

Hewson, D. (1999, November). Start talking and get to work. *Business Life,* 72-76.

Hoch, S.J., & Schkade, D.A. (1996). A psychological approach to decision support systems. *Management Science, 42*(1), 51-65.

Jennex, M.E., & Olfman, L. (2002). Organizational memory. In C.W. Holsapple (Ed.), *Handbook on knowledge management* (pp. 207-234). Berlin: Springer-Verlag.

Klayman, J. (1988). Learning from experience. In B. Brehmer & C.R.B. Joyce (Eds.), *Human judgment: The SJT view.* Amsterdam, North-Holland: Elsevier Science Publishers.

Kleiner, A., & Roth, G. (1998). How to make experience your company's best teacher. *Harvard Business Review on knowledge management.* Boston: Harvard Business School Press.

Copyright © 2004, Idea Group Inc. Copying or distributing in print or electronic forms without written permission of Idea Group Inc. is prohibited.

Lawrence, M., O'Connor, M., & Edmundson, B. (1995, July). *A field study of sales forecasting: Its accuracy, bias and efficiency.* Working Paper, School of Information Systems, The University of New South Wales.

Liebowitz, J. (2000). *Knowledge management handbook.* CRC Press.

Lim, J.S., & O'Connor, M. (1995). Judgmental adjustment of initial forecasts: Its effectiveness and biases. *Journal of Behavioural Decision Making, 8,* 149-168.

Lim, J.S., & O'Connor, M.J. (1996a). Judgmental forecasting with time series and causal information. *International Journal of Forecasting, 12*(1), 139-153.

Lim, J.S., & O'Connor, M.J. (1996b). Judgmental forecasting with interactive forecasting support systems. *Decision Support Systems, 16*(4), 339-357.

Makridakis, S. (1993). Accuracy measures: Theoretical and practical concerns. *International Journal of Forecasting, 9*(4), 527-529.

Mathews, B.P., & Diamantopoulos, A. (1986). Managerial intervention in forecasting: An empirical investigation of forecast manipulation. *International Journal of Research in Marketing, 3*(1), 3-10.

Mathews, B.P., & Diamantopoulos, A. (1989). Judgmental revision of sales forecasts: A longitudinal extension. *Journal of Forecasting, 8*(2), 129-140.

Nonaka, I. (1998). The knowledge-creating company. *Harvard Business Review on knowledge management.* Boston: Harvard Business School Press.

O'Leary, D.E. (2002). Technologies for knowledge assimilation. In C.W. Holsapple, (Ed.), *Handbook on knowledge management* (pp. 29-46). Berlin: Springer-Verlag.

Payne, J.W. (1982). Contingent decision behaviour. *Psychological Bulletin, 92*(2), 382-402.

Sanders, N.R., & Ritzman, L.P. (1992). The need for contextual and technical knowledge in judgmental forecasting. *Journal of Behavioural Decision Making, 5*(1), 39-52.

Schroder, H.M., Driver, M.J., & Streufert, S. (1967). *Human information processing.* New York: Holt, Rinehart and Winston, Inc.

Stewart, T.A. (1997). *Intellectual capital: The new wealth of organisations.* New York: Doubleday.

Copyright © 2004, Idea Group Inc. Copying or distributing in print or electronic forms without written permission of Idea Group Inc. is prohibited.

Wolfe, C., & Flores, B. (1990). Judgmental adjustment of earnings forecasts. *Journal of Forecasting, 9*(4), 389-405.

Wood, R.E. (1986). Task complexity: Definition of the construct. *Organisational Behaviour and Human Decision Processes, 37*(1), 60-82.

Copyright © 2004, Idea Group Inc. Copying or distributing in print or electronic forms without written permission of Idea Group Inc. is prohibited.

Chapter V

Knowledge Discovery Process and Introduction of Domain Knowledge

Katsutoshi Yada
Kansai University, Japan

Abstract

This chapter describes the framework of knowledge discovery process in sales data and how the data mining system is applied to the data in the real business world by using the domain knowledge. First the framework of the knowledge discovery process in databases is reviewed. It is not clear how users construct the actual data mining process and use the domain knowledge in the existing models. We propose a two-dimensional matrix of knowledge for analysis of sales data to understand the knowledge discovery process from purchase history. Then we distinguish the data mining process from the creation of business action. We point out that efficient knowledge discovery can be achieved by intensively introducing domain knowledge of experts to the creation of business action.

Copyright © 2004, Idea Group Inc. Copying or distributing in print or electronic forms without written permission of Idea Group Inc. is prohibited.

Introduction

With the propagation of information technology typically represented by the Internet, enormous amount of data can be accumulated, and there are now strong interests in data mining in the research and business fields (Hamuro, 1998). Despite the efforts of the analysts, the useful knowledge cannot be effectively discovered very often. In Japan, many companies have also been studying the introduction of data mining systems, and effective management of business process by data mining is considered to be very important in future.

In joint research projects with many firms, we have successfully discovered useful knowledge by using data mining (Hamuro, 2001; Ip, 2000, 2002). In this paper, we try to elucidate the process of knowledge discovery from sales data and to construct a process model for efficient data mining based on these experiences. In the conventional process model, steps of typical data processing are expressed, and it gives no clear explanation as to which kind of knowledge is converted in the data mining process or how the domain knowledge should be introduced. By the use of a two-dimensional matrix for type of knowledge, we clearly identify the type of knowledge to be converted in the data mining process and the path of the conversion. We also assert that business action is created from interaction between tacit knowledge and explicit knowledge of the data analysts and the marketing staff, and that domain knowledge should be efficiently introduced to be a part of the discovery process.

Review of the Existing Studies

First, we will review the existing studies on the knowledge discovery process. The problems in the framework of the conventional knowledge discovery process are pointed out, and we will clearly define the primary aim of the present article.

Framework of Knowledge Discovery Process

Matheus et al. (1993) explained a model of the entire system and its elements along the knowledge discovery process. As major domains, they cited acqui-

Copyright © 2004, Idea Group Inc. Copying or distributing in print or electronic forms without written permission of Idea Group Inc. is prohibited.

sition of data, processing, extraction of pattern, expression of knowledge, and evaluation.

In a narrow sense, data mining is a process to extract patterns or rules in data. In this case, important elements are expression of knowledge, criteria for evaluation, and development of an algorithm. The existing study on the knowledge discovery process (Valdes-Perez, 1999) puts emphasis on the interaction between the analyst and the system. The analyzer utilizes the knowledge base currently existing inside and outside the system, such as the analysis in the past or opinions of experts, and extracts useful and beneficial rules. In knowledge discovery in the real world, it is important how human action can intervene into the knowledge discovery process (Langley, 1998), and it is asserted that we must definitely be conscious about the utilization of the introduction of domain knowledge.

Here, we will review the study of Fayyad et al. (1996) on the knowledge discovery process (Figure 1). According to their study, the starting point of knowledge discovery is to define the ultimate purpose and to understand the application area and related domain knowledge. Then the data sets necessary for the discovery are accurately defined, and various attribute groups are prepared (selection of target data). Normally, such data include plenty of noise, abnormal values, and defective values, and it is a pre-process of these data under a certain rule. Important attributes are estimated and selected from the advance analysis, and the adjusted data set is prepared. By collating these data with the purpose of analysis, the most adequate data mining algorithm is employed and a really interesting pattern is extracted.

The patterns discovered from the above steps are offered to the person in charge of evaluation. Up to the time when useful meaning will be found, the procedure is turned back to the preceding step, and the trial-and-error attempt is repeated.

Figure 1. The existing framework of knowledge discovery process.

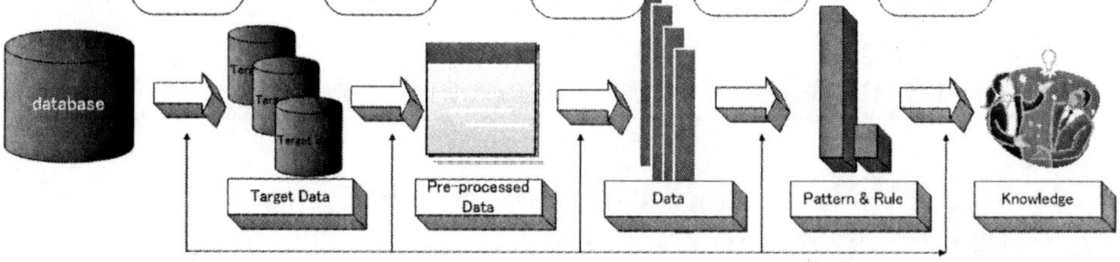

Copyright © 2004, Idea Group Inc. Copying or distributing in print or electronic forms without written permission of Idea Group Inc. is prohibited.

Problems in the Existing Studies

The framework of the conventional knowledge discovery process does not give useful suggestions almost at all for the data mining of the business field (Yada, 2002). Basically, the above model is a general model relating to knowledge discovery, and it is difficult to give sufficient suggestions to a specific problem such as purchase data analysis for the customer.

The following two points are the most important: First, what is really converted in the knowledge discovery process is the part of data with the meaning called "information" or "knowledge". In the process model as given above, it is the part where only data processing is handled. The knowledge discovery processing is a process where a wide variety of information and knowledge are integrated and are converted to new knowledge (Cowan & Foray, 1997; Tell, 1997). Nevertheless, it is not elucidated what kind of knowledge it is or how it is converted. In the course of the knowledge discovery process, we must indicate the route of concrete knowledge conversion and efficiently carry out the discovery process.

The second problem can be summarized as follows: In all of the existing models, it is suggested that the introduction of domain knowledge is indispensable for the discovery of useful knowledge, but none of these models clearly indicate how the domain knowledge should be introduced in reality. Typically, there are many models that advocate the introduction of domain knowledge to all processes. However, this is practically impossible. It is difficult to obtain suggestions as to at which stage the introduction of domain knowledge leads to more efficient knowledge discovery. For the purpose of efficiently discovering useful knowledge, we must present accurate, definite strategy on how the introduction of domain knowledge is to be utilized in the knowledge discovery process.

In the present chapter, a framework is presented by which the type of knowledge to be discovered can be classified, and the positioning of analysis to be carried out in the knowledge discovery process is defined. By the use of this framework, it is possible to understand how the discovery process is advanced and also to offer the directivity (principle) of the analysis. Then, a strategy is presented as to how domain knowledge can be effectively used in the knowledge discovery process.

Copyright © 2004, Idea Group Inc. Copying or distributing in print or electronic forms without written permission of Idea Group Inc. is prohibited.

Knowledge Discovery Process from Sales Data

The purpose of this chapter is to develop a framework for giving guidelines for the knowledge discovery process useful in the analysis of purchase history of the customers, such as POS data with customer ID. In order to increase the effectiveness of the knowledge discovery process, there will be discussion on how the domain knowledge is introduced.

Two-dimensional Matrix of Knowledge Type Extracted from Purchase History

We focused the attention not on data processing, but on the meaning of data to be processed and converted, that is, on information and knowledge in the knowledge discovery process. The data to be processed in the knowledge discovery process from purchase history and the type of knowledge to be discovered can be easily understood if these are expressed in a two-dimensional matrix as shown in Figure 2. The first is the dimension of analysis level.

Figure 2. Two-dimensional matrix of knowledge type.

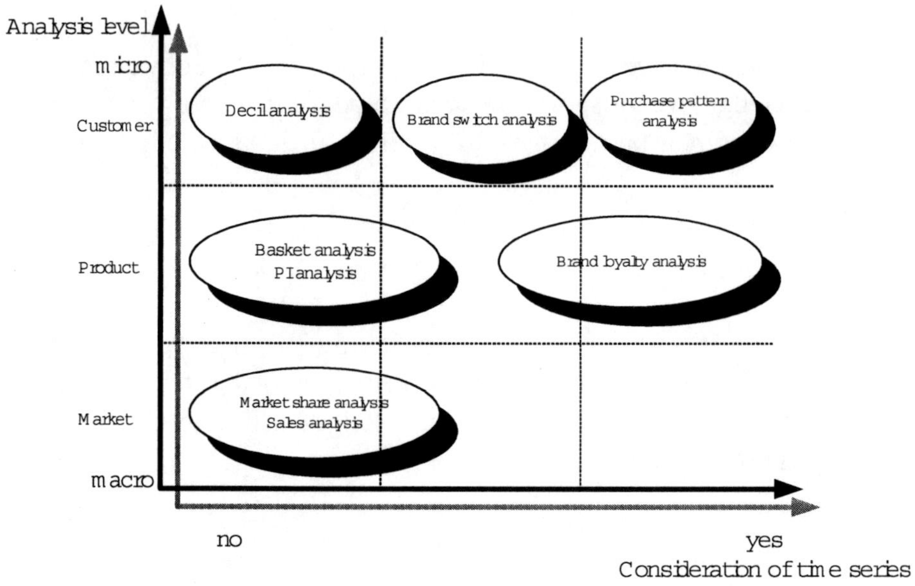

Copyright © 2004, Idea Group Inc. Copying or distributing in print or electronic forms without written permission of Idea Group Inc. is prohibited.

The analysis level ranges from macro-level such as the entire market to micro-level at each consumer behavior. In actual analysis, the data can be classified according to these levels.

The analysis of the extreme macro-level is the analysis relating to the entire market such as market share, transition of sale, and so forth. In the more detailed level, basket analysis, brand switch analysis (Berry & Linoff, 1997) and so forth are included as the analysis of commodity level. Further, in the analysis of customer level, detailed analysis is conducted such as transition analysis (decil analysis) on the amount of sales proceeds for each customer and purchase pattern analysis (Hawkins, 1999; Woolf, 1993).

The second dimension relates to how to handle the time series data in the contents of analysis. In typical POS data with ID, lines of receipts of the customer are accumulated in time series, and purchase behavior of the customer can be identified for a considerably long period. The second viewpoint is how far the changes of situation over the course of time should be considered by the use of these time series data in the analysis.

In a typical POS analysis, the accumulated time series data are aggregated and sales proceeds (e.g., sales proceeds for each commodity) are calculated. In such type of analysis, time series data are not effectively utilized almost at all. On the other hand, as the analysis for effectively utilizing the detailed time series data, there are analyses with more emphasis on the changes over time: the analysis of the changes before and after business action, that is, verification of sales promotion effects such as coupon sale, or an analysis of purchase pattern for a long period (Hamuro, 2001).

Knowledge Discovery Process and Creation of Business Action

Knowledge Discovery Process

In any of the cases, the analysis of purchase history is started from the lower left portion of the matrix. That is, to acquire basic knowledge of the entire market, it is carried out from basic analysis such as analysis of brand share, total sales amount, and so forth. In these analyses, the analyst gives no consideration on the changes over time. The time series data are aggregated and the tendency in the market is identified. Then, it is turned to the analysis with the time taken

Copyright © 2004, Idea Group Inc. Copying or distributing in print or electronic forms without written permission of Idea Group Inc. is prohibited.

into account such as expansion of the entire market, transition of sale of each individual commodity, and so forth.

Next, as the analyses of commodity level, more detailed analysis of PI (purchase index) value per number of commodities sold or basket analysis is conducted. The former is the calculation of sales proceeds per 1,000 customers who visited the store, and this is also used for the comparison of selling powers of commodities between the stores with different scale. Basket analysis is an analysis to define the characteristics of the commodities purchased at the same time. Many of these analyses are analyses for each commodity in a certain fixed period, and much consideration is not given on time base in most cases. Also, brand loyalty analysis is an analysis to elucidate loyalty and commitment of a consumer to the commodity for a long period. The change of situations due to time is taken into account in this analysis.

The analysis on the extreme micro-level and complicated analysis based on sales data are analyses with attention focused on behavior of the customers. For instance, decil analysis is an analysis for customer management. In this, the customers are divided into 10 groups depending on sales amount for each customer in a certain fixed period, and the results are utilized for identification and management of excellent customers for the store. In addition, there is brand switch analysis or purchase pattern analysis for the customers in a long period using time series data.

As described above, the typical knowledge discovery process is started from the simplest basic analysis on the lower left portion of the matrix, and it is advanced to the analysis of customer level by taking more detailed and complicated time base into consideration. Naturally, it is needless to say that the more it is advanced toward time series analysis of the customer level on the upper right portion, the higher the technical ability and analyzing ability that are required. However, it depends on the purpose of project, budget, duration of the project and strategy of the firm as to up to which step the analyses should be performed in the process.

Useful knowledge for execution of business action is acquired from a part or all of these processes. Useful knowledge is not necessarily discovered from the detailed analysis. However, in a typical analytical process, the most detailed analysis is performed, and the results of all analyses are evaluated one after another, and the usefulness of the knowledge is evaluated from the viewpoint of the execution of the business action. If the knowledge is not acquired from these processes, the viewpoint must be changed, and it should be started again from new basic analysis.

Copyright © 2004, Idea Group Inc. Copying or distributing in print or electronic forms without written permission of Idea Group Inc. is prohibited.

The Case of Analysis for New Entry

Here, we wish to introduce a case of analysis that we carried out in cooperation with an enterprise, based on the knowledge discovery process as described above.

In the autumn of 2001, a Japanese supermarket Corporation B carried out a project for analysis of POS data with customer ID, and this was officially recognized. A joint research project was initiated by a general foodstuff manufacturer (Company A) and Kansai University, and meetings were held at irregular intervals. After the arrangements were made several times, it was decided that analysis should be performed on the market of tidbits or side dishes - an imminent subject to be discussed. Company A was planning to launch sales activities newly into the market from the spring of 2002 and was already in the stage of preparation. On the foodstuff market such as supermarkets, person in charge of sales, sales counters, and so forth are clearly classified and distinguished from each other for each category of merchandise. The foodstuffs under current program were to be displayed on the sales counter for tidbits, which were to be purchased as side dishes for alcoholic drinks.

The data used this time were the membership data of a large-scale supermarket in the metropolitan area. They were the data for three months, from June to August 2001. First, to comply with the problems to be discussed, purchase history was selected for each of about 2,500 customers who had purchased the items in the category of alcohol during this period, and a data set for this purpose was prepared. Next, basic data were evaluated such as the type of customers who bought beer, number and percentage of the customers who bought sparkling wines, distribution of sale amount, and the scale of sales amount of seafood delicacies and meat delicacies among the foodstuffs of delicacies, and special features of the entire market were evaluated in detail. Seafood delicacies include side dishes prepared from seafood such as split dried cuttlefish, dried cuttlefish, and so forth. Meat delicacies include side dishes of meat line such as salami, sausage, beef jerky, and so forth. During the processes of selection, it was attempted to check for noise or abnormally priced items, and general trends of the data were accurately evaluated.

Next, the data were converted for basket analysis and trial repeating rate, and the level of each item was analyzed. When we evaluated which items were purchased concurrently at which times, it was found that the items of delicacies were mostly purchased concurrently with cakes and sweets.

Copyright © 2004, Idea Group Inc. Copying or distributing in print or electronic forms without written permission of Idea Group Inc. is prohibited.

The detailed analysis of personal attributes of the purchasers was performed to find out which group of customer likes which type of items. As a result, it was found that meat delicacies were more frequently purchased by the customers of younger generation and by unmarried persons.

Knowledge Discovery and Creation of Business Action

In this section, we will discuss the knowledge in business and the knowledge creating process. In Western epistemology, knowledge is considered as "a justified true belief," and attention is focused on explicit knowledge (Nonaka & Takeuchi, 1995). The knowledge handled in existing and our research relates only to the explicit knowledge. Is it really possible to explain knowledge discovery only from the explicit knowledge?

We believe that it is difficult to explain all of the processes to discover new knowledge using only the explicit knowledge. In the knowledge, there is also tacit knowledge (Polanyi, 1995), which cannot be expressed by words and is difficult to transfer to the other person. New knowledge is born not only from the integration of the explicit knowledge but also from interaction between tacit knowledge and explicit knowledge (Nonaka, 1994; Yada, 1998). In the organizational knowledge creating process, Nonaka (1995) defined the process of "socialization," by which two or more people have tacit knowledge in common, and the process of "externalization," by which an individual converts the tacit knowledge shared in common to explicit knowledge, and demonstrated that new innovation is developed from the interaction process between explicit knowledge and tacit knowledge in individuals and organizations. In the conventional process model, due consideration is not given to such interaction of knowledge.

We consider that the knowledge expressed by the two-dimensional matrix as given above is entirely different from the new business action. The new knowledge expressed by a two-dimensional matrix is produced by the existing analytical method or it is born through integration of knowledge. However, business action is not automatically born from new knowledge. An expert of marketing who interprets the meaning from knowledge and who has sufficient tacit knowledge on the market gives birth to the business action as a new idea. Therefore, we propose a model shown in Figure 3 as the knowledge discovery process including the new business action.

Copyright © 2004, Idea Group Inc. Copying or distributing in print or electronic forms without written permission of Idea Group Inc. is prohibited.

Figure 3. Knowledge discovery and creation of business action.

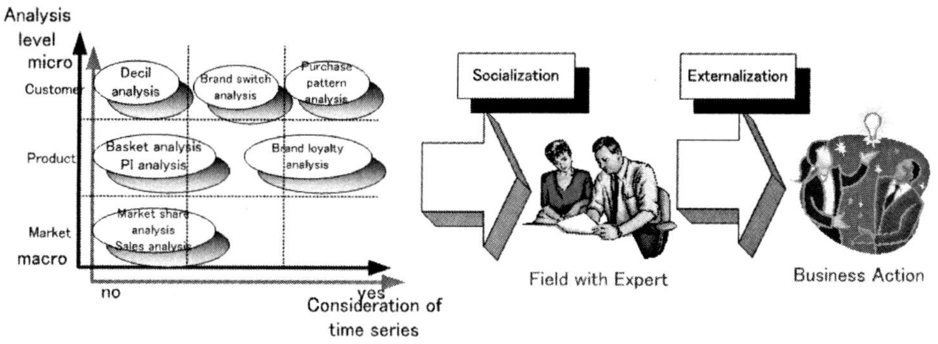

We do not believe that useful patterns and rules obtained from the data are automatically converted to business action. First, in a field where a data analyst and an expert (on marketing) commonly share the context of analysis results, tacit knowledge acquired in the data mining process is shared in common. This is what Nonaka (1995) called a process of socialization. Next, a person in charge of marketing integrates this with the accumulated experiences, and it is transferred to the process of externalization where new business action is developed. Business action is not automatically given by the data mining system. The patterns and the rules obtained are fused with the existing knowledge; that is, it is born from interaction of explicit knowledge and tacit knowledge.

Introduction of Domain Knowledge

As pointed out in many studies, the introduction of domain knowledge is indispensable for the discovery of the knowledge useful for business. Many of the existing studies recommend that the domain knowledge should be introduced in all steps of the knowledge discovery process, but this is not very efficient and not very practical. Therefore, for the purpose of efficiently introducing domain knowledge of the person in charge of marketing in the knowledge discovery process, it appears to be essential to concentrate the efforts from the scene of internalization to the step of externalization for the creation of business action. We have been making it possible to achieve efficient knowledge discovery by limiting the introduction of domain knowledge

Copyright © 2004, Idea Group Inc. Copying or distributing in print or electronic forms without written permission of Idea Group Inc. is prohibited.

to the interpretation of rules, to common sharing of the context of analysis, and to creation of business action.

In the case of analysis on the market of side dishes as given above, detailed analysis was carried out for all levels, ranging from basic market analysis, extraction of the features of purchases, and analysis on the pattern of purchase. After carrying out the analysis based on the results that there were trends to purchase these items concurrently as the purchase of beer as the result of basket analysis, it was judged by the marketing experts that for the purpose of positively launching sales activities newly into the market, these items should be displayed on sales counters in combination with the items related to beer.

In order to efficiently introduce domain knowledge, the expert must use the expression easily understandable – in other words, the rules, which can create "a clue" for the new business. In some cases, even when the accuracy of model may be low, a suggestion valuable for the marketer may be offered. Osawa (2001) expressed this phenomenon by a concept of "chance discovery" and performed a study from multilateral approaches. In order to introduce domain knowledge more efficiently, a study of chance discovery based not only on the extraction of rules but also on the development of business action has important meaning. In the future, the application of this type of study to the field of business may offer big business chances.

Conclusion

In the past, there has been only a framework as general theory for the model of knowledge discovery process, and it has been difficult to give important suggestions to the knowledge discovery in reality. In this chapter, we presented a framework with focus on the change of knowledge type in the knowledge discovery process in the data mining from purchase history data. The knowledge discovery process in reality can be understood as the conversion of knowledge on two-dimensional matrix expressed by analysis level and time base. It is important to distinguish the knowledge obtained from analysis from business action. We pointed out that it is effective to evaluate the patterns and the rules thus obtained and to introduce domain knowledge in the step to create business action.

However, we did not discuss fully the analysis of the process to create the business action to be actually constructed. In particular, the externalized

Copyright © 2004, Idea Group Inc. Copying or distributing in print or electronic forms without written permission of Idea Group Inc. is prohibited.

business action must be integrated well with the existing explicit knowledge. In the present study, we did not deal with the process of combination to full extent. This remains to be the subject of our study in future.

References

Berry, M.J.A, & Linoff, G. (1997). *Data mining techniques: For marketing, sales, and customer support.* John Wiley & Sons.

Cowan, R., & Foray, D. (1997). The economics of codification and the diffusion of knowledge. *Industrial and Corporate Change, 6*(3), 595-622.

Fayyad, U., Piatetsky-Shapiro, G., & Smyth, P. (1996). From data mining to knowledge discovery in databases. *AI Magazine, 17,* 1-34.

Hamuro, Y., Katoh, N., & Yada, K. (2001). Discovering association strength among brand loyalties from purchase history. *Proceedings of 2001 IEEE International Symposium on Industrial Electronics,* 114-117.

Hamuro, Y., Katoh, N., Matsuda, N., & Yada, K. (1998). Mining pharmacy data helps to make profits. *Data Mining and Knowledge Discovery, 2*(4), 391-398.

Hawkins, G.E. (1999). *Building the customer specific retail enterprise.* Breezy Heights Publishing.

Ip, E., Johnson, J., Yada, K., Hamuro, Y., Katoh, N., & Cheung, S. (2002). A neural network application to identify high-value customer for a large retail store in Japan. *Neural networks in business: Techniques and applications,* pp. 55-69. Hershey, PA: Idea Group Publishing.

Ip, E., Yada, K., Hamuro, Y., & Katoh, N. (2000). A data mining system for managing customer relationship. *Proceedings of the 2000 Americas Conference on Information Systems,* 101-105.

Langley, P. (1998). The computer-aided discovery of scientific knowledge. *Proceedings of 1st International Conference on Discovery Science (Lecture Notes in Artificial Intelligence* 1532), 25-39. Springer-Verlag.

Matheus, C.J., Chan, P.K., & Piatetsky-Shapiro, G. (1993). Systems for knowledge discovery in databases. *IEEE Transaction on Knowledge and Data Engineering, 5,* 903-913.

Copyright © 2004, Idea Group Inc. Copying or distributing in print or electronic forms without written permission of Idea Group Inc. is prohibited.

Nonaka, I. (1994). Dynamic theory of organizational knowledge creation. *Organization Science, 5*(1), 14-37.

Nonaka, I., & Takeuchi, H. (1995). *The knowledge-creating company.* Oxford University Press.

Osawa, Y. (2001). The scope of chance discovery. *New Frontiers in Artificial Intelligence,* LNAI 2253, 413.

Polanyi, M. (1962). *Personal knowledge – Towards a post-critical philosophy.* Routledge and Kegan Paul.

Tell, F. (1997). *Knowledge and justification – Exploring the knowledge basedfirm.* Linkoping University.

Valdes-Perez, R.E. (1999). Principles of human computer collaboration for knowledge discovery. *Artificial Intelligence 107,* 335-346.

Woolf, B.P. (1993). *Customer specific marketing.* Teal Books.

Yada, K. (2002). The future direction of active mining in the business world. *Frontiers in Artificial Intelligence and Applications, 79,* 239-245. IOS Press.

Yada, K., Katoh, N., Hamuro, Y., & Matsuda, Y. (1998). Customer profiling makes profits: How did a Japanese firm achieve competitive advantage through the knowledge creation? *Proceedings of The Practical Application of Knowledge Management, 98,* 57-66. The Practical Application Company.

Copyright © 2004, Idea Group Inc. Copying or distributing in print or electronic forms without written permission of Idea Group Inc. is prohibited.

Chapter VI

The Organizational Characteristics of Knowledge-Centricity

Jonathan Pemberton
Northumbria University, UK

George Stonehouse
Northumbria University, UK

Abstract

Knowledge focused organizations are knowledge-centric, a term that embodies the creation and management of knowledge but embedded as an integral element of an organization's strategy and performance. By devising an organizational characteristics matrix, this chapter identifies a number of essential and desirable features that comprise a knowledge-centric business. The matrix is then applied to a case study company, Black and Decker, and more specifically its European Design Center, to examine the extent to which the organization can be viewed as knowledge-centric. While the use of this first-iteration matrix is a useful mechanism for gauging knowledge-centricity, the chapter concludes with a critique of its potential limitations, with suggestions as to how it might be refined further to give a more illuminating assessment of an organization's knowledge capabilities.

Copyright © 2004, Idea Group Inc. Copying or distributing in print or electronic forms without written permission of Idea Group Inc. is prohibited.

Introduction

The issue of knowledge management is now firmly embedded within modern management thinking, as organizations re-assess their business objectives and review the operational and strategic management of their resources (Von Krogh et al., 2001; Zack, 1999). In part, a more aggressive competitive environment, coupled with a move towards creativity and innovation, has ensured that organizations are increasingly keen to exploit knowledge as a productive resource and a potential means of developing competitive advantage (Hall & Andriani, 2002). Equally, a growing awareness of the benefits that can accrue from developing collective knowledge by creating an environment that facilitates knowledge sharing has been a driver of developments in this arena for many companies in the last few years.

Interestingly, the concept of knowledge management is by no means without ambiguity and this has led to different interpretations and emphasis in the academic literature (McAdam & McCreedy, 1999). While the reasons and context for this are discussed shortly and center largely on historical evolution, knowledge "management" is insufficient to fully describe how knowledge is created and exploited. Management is essentially a "top-down" activity and relates, typically, to managing tangible resources. Knowledge, on the other hand, arises from a number of sources, with the individual, at all levels, a key ingredient throughout. Thus, knowledge creation, often tacit in nature, is a multi-faceted human activity embracing every area of an organization, with knowledge transfer occurring across organizational hierarchies, within business units, across departments, between individuals and customers, and so forth.

Knowledge is micro-managed in most everyday situations amongst individuals, but knowledge management, when used in an organizational context is, arguably, not the final stage of the knowledge journey (KPMG, 1997). *Knowledge-centricity* is a more apt term for examining the extent to which an organization is truly knowledge-focused, and while encompassing knowledge management, it encapsulates a broader view of the socio-technical and strategic issues surrounding knowledge creation, dissemination, exploitation and management.

Although this term is defined in more detail in the subsequent section, its use permits the identification of a number of characteristics that knowledge-centric organizations appear to exhibit, the latter typical of those organizations facilitating and stimulating creativity and innovation, the theme of this book. More

Copyright © 2004, Idea Group Inc. Copying or distributing in print or electronic forms without written permission of Idea Group Inc. is prohibited.

specifically, the development of an organizational characteristics matrix is the focus of this chapter, a tool for examining the degree to which an organization is viewed as knowledge-centric. Although not a definitive way of making such an assessment, its use as a means of understanding the attributes and progress of an organization in its quest to become truly knowledge focused is illustrated by reference to a large global corporation, Black and Decker. Details of ongoing refinements and testing of the matrix are then provided in the later discussion to reflect the dynamic nature of knowledge and innovation, together with the continuous learning associated with knowledge-centric organizations.

Conspicuous Beginnings: From Knowledge Management to Knowledge Centricity

The study of knowledge in a philosophical, psychological and sociological context is nothing new, but in its present incarnation, a number of business themes, including information management, organizational learning and strategic management, have informed the research and developments carried out under the banner of knowledge management (Little et al., 2002).

Historically, the information management aspect has wielded a good deal of influence on what is perceived as knowledge management, and coincides with improving and expanding information and communication systems, including the Internet, corporate intranets and extranets, and the development of so-called knowledge management systems. Indeed, there has been a widely held view that technology is synonymous with knowledge management and, unsurprisingly, this is perpetuated by many consulting organizations with a vested interest in providing technological solutions to business problems (KPMG, 2000). Ironically, while the latter groups have helped move the issue of knowledge management center-stage, such a view represents a potential barrier to developing a truly knowledge-centric organization, since technology acts largely as a knowledge enabler through which *explicit* knowledge can be captured, stored and disseminated more easily.

The true value of knowledge, however, hinges on the ability of an organization to exploit *tacit* knowledge from both internal and external sources in order to improve organizational and competitive performance (Stonehouse et al.,

Copyright © 2004, Idea Group Inc. Copying or distributing in print or electronic forms without written permission of Idea Group Inc. is prohibited.

2001). Technology has been less successful in this latter process, with human and organizational factors assuming a greater importance in this respect. Indeed, research undertaken by the UK's Cranfield School of Management reports that 83% of respondents rejected the notion that knowledge is merely an extension of the information systems function of an organization (Murray & Myers, 1998).

Investment in useful and usable technological systems is costly in terms of financial outlay, but for the benefits to be fully exploited, the management of not only the systems, but also the processes underpinning the creation and extraction of knowledge is essential. In this context, where explicit or codified knowledge is identifiable, knowledge management is an integral element of the successful implementation of any knowledge management initiative, but this term does not adequately encompass the social aspects of tacit knowledge creation through the individuals within organizations or indeed the strategic aspects of knowledge and organizational performance (Birkinshaw, 2001; Nonaka et al., 2000).

At this juncture, the notion of knowledge-centricity is helpful and acts as an all-embracing term that, broadly speaking, describes an organization in which the creation and management of knowledge are integral to its mission, strategy, operations and performance. It is, essentially, a truly knowledge-focused organization in all aspects of its internal and external business.

Such an environment does not emerge overnight and progression to knowledge-centricity is an evolutionary process, dependent on a number of factors. This is succinctly illustrated by the various stages of the *knowledge journey* outlined by consulting group KPMG (KPMG, 1997). Although originally presented from a technological standpoint, the five-stage journey refers to knowledge chaotic, knowledge aware, knowledge enabled, knowledge managed and knowledge-centric organizations, which provides a useful framework within which to examine socio-technical, cultural and managerial issues.

In order to better understand the concepts and themes involved in the development of an organizational characteristics matrix, a more detailed discussion of the various stages is desirable. It should be noted that the stages are not necessarily mutually exclusive and the boundaries between the various categories is not always precise. What follows is a broad description of the processes involved.

A knowledge-chaotic organization has, essentially, yet to recognise the importance of knowledge and its use is on an ad hoc, and often implicit, basis. Such

Copyright © 2004, Idea Group Inc. Copying or distributing in print or electronic forms without written permission of Idea Group Inc. is prohibited.

organizations typically duplicate information, brought about by incompatible systems and an unwillingness of individuals to share knowledge, assuming it is recognised in the first place (Pemberton & Stonehouse, 2002). Above all, poor leadership and a lack of vision are apparent in the knowledge-chaotic organization.

The knowledge-aware organization recognizes the need to organise knowledge and there has been a move to identify knowledge sources and processes. Typically, some systems, often technology driven, have been introduced but their implementation is uneven across the organization. Ultimately, there are no coordinated plans for dealing with knowledge as an organizational resource to improve performance.

In a knowledge-enabled company, knowledge management is beginning to benefit the business and is characterised by a reduction in the duplication of information within the organization. Standard processes and tools are visible, with knowledge resources evaluated and systems in place. There are still, however, some technological barriers centring on dissemination and a lack of structured knowledge repositories, for example. The socio-technical aspects, embodying many aspects of organizational culture, are seldom addressed at this stage and represent a significant hurdle in moving to the next phase of the knowledge journey (Pemberton & Stonehouse, 2002).

An integrated framework of procedures to create and manage information is usually prevalent in the knowledge-managed organization, with most of the technological and cultural issues of knowledge transfer and sharing largely overcome. Furthermore, a knowledge strategy exists and is reviewed and improved on a continual basis, overseen by a knowledge champion at senior management level.

Finally, within a truly knowledge-centric business, the notion of knowledge and its role in innovation figures prominently in the organization's mission and strategy. More specifically, competitive advantage typically revolves around the exploitation of its knowledge assets, supported by integrated knowledge management tools and technology. Within the general environment, leadership, structure, culture and infrastructure fully support the creation and management of knowledge, and knowledge measurement systems are generally in place. One of the distinguishing features of the knowledge centric organization, as opposed to being purely knowledge-managed, is the recognition of individual tacit knowledge in creating organizational knowledge, together with an integral "learning from learning" philosophy across the company.

Copyright © 2004, Idea Group Inc. Copying or distributing in print or electronic forms without written permission of Idea Group Inc. is prohibited.

Unravelling Critical Organizational Characteristics

Identifying the key elements that shape the knowledge-centric organization is not without its pitfalls. Conflicting views of academics and practitioners, and the differing nature of business activities undertaken by organizations, ensures that priorities and emphasis are not necessarily uniform. For example, a company producing manufactured goods may deal with its knowledge assets in a different way than that of a company selling expertise, skills and training. Yet, based on the research of academics, coupled with the practical experiences of organizations involved in capitalizing on their knowledge assets, a number of key elements that shape the knowledge-centric organization can be identified. These essentially constitute critical success factors, and can be used for developing an organizational characteristics matrix (OCM) for assessing knowledge-centricity. More specifically, as the broad subject of managing knowledge matures, commonality and convergence of themes permits the creation of an OCM, with support and evidence arising from a number of areas.

Firstly, the authors' own experience and research in the areas of knowledge management, organizational learning and performance have played a major part in identifying the key elements perceived to be important in identifying the characteristics of the knowledge-centric organization (Pemberton et al., 2002; Pemberton & Stonehouse, 2002; Stonehouse et al., 2001). In particular, research and consultancy work with large international corporations in the UK, USA, China and Russia have allowed the testing of ideas and observation of practices that appear to facilitate or inhibit the creation, management, dissemination and exploitation of knowledge within organizations.

Secondly, a study of a number of case studies from published sources, as well as annual company reports, have been used in conjunction with observations from academic and practitioner literature. Although too numerous to mention, companies such as ABB, British Petroleum, Dow Chemicals, KPMG, Microsoft, Nokia and Skandia have been used to develop the key themes and elements here (Birkinshaw, 2002; Chase, 1997; Horne, 1998; Kippenberger, 1998; McCampbell et al., 1999; Mouritsen et al., 2001; Petrash, 1996).

Thirdly, drawing upon the area of benchmarking and the notion of best practice in developing knowledge for enhanced performance has produced a number of critical success factors in the context of knowledge management and organizational learning (O'Dell et al., 1999; Pemberton et al., 2001).

Copyright © 2004, Idea Group Inc. Copying or distributing in print or electronic forms without written permission of Idea Group Inc. is prohibited.

Finally, when assessing the strengths and weaknesses of organizational capabilities in respect of its knowledge assets, the use of a knowledge audit tool covering several areas, including human and technological infrastructure, leadership and measurement, for example, provides a useful framework from which to identify key organizational characteristics. Mechanisms such as the knowledge management diagnostic (Bukowitz & Williams, 1999) and the knowledge management toolkit (Skyrme, 1999) fall within this category.

Combining these four sources, and with the earlier definition of knowledge-centricity in mind, seven themes emerge as potentially critical areas within the knowledge-centric organization, these being:

- Strategy
- Structure
- Infrastructure
- Leadership
- Culture
- Measurement
- Individual knowledge

These terms embody a number of aspects and their choice necessitates further elaboration in the ensuing section.

Developing an Organizational Characteristics Matrix

In terms of strategy, there is growing evidence that an organization's business strategy should encompass and address the issue of knowledge in strategic projects and competitive performance. O'Dell et al. (1999) discuss this in the context of benchmarking, arguing that best-practice companies explicitly incorporate knowledge management issues as part of their business strategy. Hansen et al. (2001) argue that a knowledge management strategy is critical to an organization's competitive strategy, its form dependent on the nature of the business and breaking down to a codification or personalization strategy. An ability to grasp new opportunities quickly via the development of dynamic capabilities is also a critical strategy for managing knowledge assets and sustaining competitive advantage (Teece, 2000).

Copyright © 2004, Idea Group Inc. Copying or distributing in print or electronic forms without written permission of Idea Group Inc. is prohibited.

Structure is a key factor in the sense that a traditional hierarchy, visible in earlier business models, has been shown to act as a barrier to knowledge creation and transfer (Stonehouse & Pemberton, 1999). Flatter structures, combined with local empowerment through teamwork are more conducive to developing a truly knowledge-focused organization (Bhatt, 2000; Prahalad & Hamel, 1990). The development of communities of practice can also assist in developing an environment for enhancing and sharing knowledge within an organization, although this tends to be an informal development, their success often hinging on a lack of organizational structure (Ardichvili et al., 2003; Wenger & Snyder, 2000).

Much has been written about the technological infrastructure associated with knowledge management initiatives, with communication figuring prominently in much of the discussion. The use of e-mail, together with Internet and intranet resources, is a critical element of knowledge transfer. Equally, knowledge management systems incorporating more sophisticated tools including maps, decision support facilities, intelligent systems and so forth have become an effective way of analyzing stored data and information in the generation of usable knowledge (Pemberton & Stonehouse, 2000; Vouros, 2003). Infrastructure also incorporates non-technical elements such as the human support systems that assist knowledge creation, these being closely allied with the structure of an organization.

Managerial issues come to the fore in the form of leadership. The introduction of knowledge management initiatives, and perhaps more importantly their success, is governed by the existence of so-called "knowledge champions". They act as key drivers in the knowledge journey, their expertise being used to set up projects, but they also recognise the elements that constitute such initiatives, in particular the sources of knowledge and the human input in this process (Bhatt, 2000). In particular, leaders play a critical role in developing individuals in an organization, designing an appropriate organizational context or social architecture and aligning knowledge creation with the goals of the organization (Senge, 1990).

There is a growing body of research that recognizes that cultural aspects have a major role to play in the knowledge management process. Organizational culture takes many forms and is a complex amalgam of working practices and human interaction. Elements of trust and sharing of ideas underpin the successful exploitation of knowledge aspects and parallels with the learning organization also help to understand the issues at play. A delicate balance of incentives for knowledge sharing and encouragement is also needed, if knowledge assets

Copyright © 2004, Idea Group Inc. Copying or distributing in print or electronic forms without written permission of Idea Group Inc. is prohibited.

are to be fully integrated and exploited to benefit and enhance learning within an organization (Griego et al., 2000; McDermott & O'Dell, 2001).

In recent years, the notion of measurement has surfaced in this area, broadly falling under the heading of intellectual capital. In its "hardest" form, measurement takes the form of patents and licences, but other "softer" measures also exist such as Skandia Navigator, IC Assets Monitor, and so forth, designed to assess the more intangible nature of knowledge (Liebowitz & Suen, 2000). Whether these measures, based on the indicators used, are really a true reflection of the knowledge that exists within an organization is debatable, but over time they may help to develop a picture of progression in terms of visible knowledge assets. As an absolute measure of knowledge, however, they tend to fall short of a meaningful quantitative metric. Indeed, research by O'Dell et al. suggests that even best practice organizations pay lip service to this issue and this area is driven by the philosophy that "to manage, it must be measured". (O'Dell et al., 1999)

Finally, the role of the individual in the process of knowledge creation is a major determinant of the extent to which an organization is viewed as knowledge-focused. The recognition by an individual of his or her knowledge capabilities can have either a positive or negative impact in an organization, both these latter aspects being tied into the "knowledge is power" argument. Recognition of individual knowledge by co-workers and managers is also important, the former usually facilitating better teamwork; the latter allowing managers to capitalize on individual strengths to successfully implement knowledge management strategies (Mayo, 2000; Pemberton & Stonehouse, 2002). The role of the individual is strongly linked to the cultural environment and matching individual characteristics to organizational culture and goals is recognized as a key enabler of knowledge sharing (McDermott & O'Dell, 2001).

Many of the seven issues described above implicitly incorporate a range of processes. Indeed, several authors have explicitly identified processes as a separate category in its own right, but this is typically defined in the context of a systems perspective, where knowledge is objectified, typically in the context of technological databases, and viewed from a relatively narrow angle. A wider perspective of what constitutes knowledge has been taken in this chapter and, for this reason, processes are not identified as one of the seven critical success factors, but as pervading and integral to many of them.

In devising an OCM, the issues identified above are sub-divided to create characteristics judged to be desirable features of the knowledge-centric organization. However, several of these are perceived to have greater impor-

Copyright © 2004, Idea Group Inc. Copying or distributing in print or electronic forms without written permission of Idea Group Inc. is prohibited.

Table 1. Organizational characteristics matrix.

ISSUES	CHARACTERISTIC	DESIRABLE	ESSENTIAL
Strategic	Knowledge issues are addressed explicitly in the organization's business strategy.		✓
Structural	Flatter structure with fewer layers to facilitate more effective knowledge transfer.		✓
	The use of group based teams, ideally cross-functional, as well as communities of practice, designed to encourage knowledge sharing.		✓
	Decentralization of decision making to capitalize on individual and team expertise.	✓	
Leadership	The existence of a knowledge champion at senior management level.		✓
	Management awareness of knowledge issues accompanied by an open and inclusive attitude to decision making.		✓
Infrastructure	Technical infrastructure to support knowledge transfer with tools (e.g., knowledge maps) to facilitate this.		✓
	Support systems, both human and technical, that avoid "re-inventing the wheel".	✓	
	Effective communication channels encompassing verbal, electronic and written formats.		✓
Cultural	Incentives for sharing knowledge, ideally built within appraisal regimes, emphasizing personal and organizational benefits.		✓
	High trust and supportive environment encouraging individual responsibility.		✓
	Allocation of time within the organization to actively encourage communication and knowledge transfer.	✓	
Measurement	Mechanisms exist to quantify intellectual assets.	✓	
Individual	Recognition of the individual's knowledge by:		
	▪ Individual		✓
	▪ Co-workers	✓	
	▪ Managers		✓

Copyright © 2004, Idea Group Inc. Copying or distributing in print or electronic forms without written permission of Idea Group Inc. is prohibited.

tance and are therefore essential in the sense of ensuring that the organization is truly knowledge-focused. As an interpretive benchmark, provided that all essential characteristics are apparent and the majority of the remaining desirable ones are present, an organization is judged as knowledge-centric. While an element of subjectivity is clearly evident in this process, the previous justification goes some way to explaining why certain characteristics are incorporated in the matrix, as shown in Table 1.

While it is accepted that an OCM of this nature may not be a realistic way of assessing knowledge-centricity for all organizations, particularly smaller and medium sized businesses, for larger companies, the use of such a matrix does, it is argued, help to understand whether it is truly knowledge-focused.

In this first iteration of the OCM, no weightings are given to any of the themes. Over time, however, it is envisaged that this will change as more research data become available from a number of organizations. This is particularly relevant where aspects of international culture are concerned, but this is discussed in the penultimate section of this chapter.

Mechanisms for Assessing Knowledge-Centricity

Having devised an OCM, how can it be used to assess the degree to which an organization is knowledge-centric? This is generally not an easy or quick task, and requires a combination of objectivity and subjectivity. A number of approaches can be taken:

- Many organizations now provide details of knowledge initiatives, particularly in relation to measurement of knowledge assets and intellectual capital, for example, in their published annual reports. These, however, tend to be relatively specific and only certain aspects of the OCM are covered. Consequently, such information tends to supplement other more detailed methods of inquiry.
- Knowledge audit tools exist to examine many of the areas identified in the OCM. This approach has been refined and applied over the last few years, with Skyrme's toolkit and Bukowitz and Williams' diagnostic acting as self-assessment vehicles to identify potential strengths and

Copyright © 2004, Idea Group Inc. Copying or distributing in print or electronic forms without written permission of Idea Group Inc. is prohibited.

weaknesses in their knowledge capabilities (Bukowitz & Williams, 1999; Skyrme, 1999). Such tools are based on sectionalized themes, divided by sub-themes, in which respondents indicate the strength of agreement with a number of statements using a Likert scale.

- Allied to these audit tools is benchmarking, where organizations are compared to others and best practices identified, based again on a self-completion questionnaire centring on statements and the extent to which the organization is perceived to conform. Although this is an established business tool covering a range of issues, research by O'Dell et al. (1999) for example, has helped to identify various emerging themes and aspects related to knowledge in best-practice organizations.
- The use of structured and semi-structured interviews is a valuable vehicle for assessing the various characteristics associated with an organization's knowledge capabilities. By interviewing a range of people, at all levels, an assessment can then be made. For example, interviews with senior personnel allow examination of areas such as strategy and management, issues not generally familiar to all employees. Conversely, more operational issues are better explored based on a range of personnel.
- The use of observation is also a valuable mechanism by which the findings of audits and interviews can be corroborated, allowing a full assessment of the complete picture.

Each of these approaches has strengths and weaknesses, but a combination is typically used to cross-validate the various responses and observations. Indeed, for the purposes of the Black and Decker case study presented in the next section, an audit tool, interviews and observation were used to establish the characteristics present within the organization and thus permit the application of the OCM. This pluralistic stance involves an element of objectivity and subjectivity, but this reflects the nature of the varying organizational characteristics. More detailed discussion of the approach adopted is provided in Pemberton et al. (2002).

Applying the OCM: Black and Decker

As the world's largest producer of power tools and related accessories, Black and Decker, currently valued at nearly $5 billion and a Fortune 500 global corporation (Black and Decker, 2003), has been used to examine, via the

Copyright © 2004, Idea Group Inc. Copying or distributing in print or electronic forms without written permission of Idea Group Inc. is prohibited.

OCM, the extent to which it can be viewed as knowledge-centric. As a leading international organization with approximately 23,000 employees, the development and introduction of new innovations, before their competitors, is a particular goal of the organization and a means by which it retains competitive differentiation and superior performance. More specifically, their European Design Center (EDC) based in northeast England is used as the focus of the research presented in this chapter. The EDC employs over 100 personnel with its engineers, designers and program managers, in conjunction with the marketing team, responsible for the development of many of Black and Decker's global products.

The nature of the EDC's business, highly dependent on individual expertise and creativity, necessitates the creation, sharing and dissemination of knowledge as part of its everyday operations. Initiatives to capitalize on these knowledge assets and promote good practice are in evidence within the EDC, and Black and Decker as a whole. In particular, there has been significant investment from a technological standpoint, enabling employees to access knowledge repositories, as well as utilize the technology platform for improved communication. This has been supported by structural changes with a move towards team based working, less hierarchical management structures and the development of more informal communities of practice and localized decision-making. Several of these issues are elaborated upon shortly.

In terms of applying the OCM as a means of assessing knowledge-centricity, the data used in this process arise in a number of ways. In 2001, a series of informal face-to-face interviews with senior personnel were conducted to gain a feel for the organization's approach to knowledge management issues. Semi-structured interviews were subsequently carried out with five managers to gather opinions and facts to better understand the organizational factors that influence knowledge creation, sharing and management processes. An audit questionnaire was then devised and, after a pilot survey, distributed to a random sample of 30 employees from different areas, of differing status and across different groupings within the EDC. All 30 questionnaires were returned for analysis. A detailed account of the analysis and findings of both the audit questionnaire and interviews are reported in Pemberton et al. (2002).

For reasons of brevity, a summary of the key findings is given here, these being:

- Two areas are identifiable as strong features of the organization. The role of tacit knowledge is recognized as an integral part of the EDC's business

Copyright © 2004, Idea Group Inc. Copying or distributing in print or electronic forms without written permission of Idea Group Inc. is prohibited.

and there is consensus that the technology infrastructure to support knowledge management initiatives within Black and Decker is essentially in place.
- Neutral responses are recorded for culture and structure, the role of explicit knowledge, knowledge repositories and market leverage.
- Four areas were perceived as particularly weak within the EDC, these being leadership, processes, knowledge measurement and human infrastructure.

Investment in technology appears to have been an integral element of Black and Decker's approach to knowledge management, witnessed by ongoing updating of intranet and extranet systems, with other legacy systems interacting and linking to these systems. Furthermore, there has been updating of workstations and CAD/CAM systems to ensure greater global compatibility and accessibility with other design centres. Technologies that support knowledge management such as GroupWare, data mining, document management and information repositories also exist within the organization. The use of e-mails is prevalent, with conference technologies permitting team meetings spanning differing time zones a common communication vehicle. External knowledge is also available through existing legacy systems, with access available to most employees through an integrated search engine and company intranet system that stores many types of information. Thus, for these reasons, it is no surprise that the technological infrastructure is perceived as a particular strength of the organization and is acknowledged as a mechanism that permits and encourages co-workers to share their knowledge in the form of documents and multimedia objects.

The role of tacit knowledge is also considered a strength within the EDC by the very nature of the type of work carried out at the Design Center, with its clear emphasis on product design and innovation. The expertise of groups of individuals forms the lifeblood of the Center and the use of tacit knowledge is a critical element of its core business. The research conducted found that knowledge experts are recognized within the company and their expertise is sought on a day-to-day basis by co-workers.

Conversely, the four perceived areas of weakness described above arise because:

Copyright © 2004, Idea Group Inc. Copying or distributing in print or electronic forms without written permission of Idea Group Inc. is prohibited.

- Managing the company's knowledge is not considered a core management skill with which every manager and professional has some familiarity.
- Gathering, storing information and knowledge-sharing behaviours are not recognized and rewarded by the company.
- Leadership is generally perceived as lacking a knowledge vision and failing to emphasize the role of knowledge within the organization.
- Processes and procedures to monitor external knowledge sources, particularly in relation to that of competitors, are weak.
- While tacit knowledge is generally perceived as a strength of the organization, there is limited encouragement for knowledge experts to share their expertise via formal and informal mechanisms.
- Few systems are in place to formally measure and manage its knowledge resources.

These findings arise as a direct result of the audit questionnaire, corroborated by the interviews conducted and observation of the working environment. Not all aspects can be discussed here (see Pemberton et al. (2002) for more detailed commentary), but combined, it is now possible to map the issues included in the OCM onto the research findings. The OCM for Black and Decker is shown in Table 2.

The OCM demonstrates that, on the evidence collated and analysed, Black and Decker could not be judged as knowledge-centric at the present time. Examination of the essential characteristics shows particular strengths of the company, but counter-balanced by some deficiencies too. On the positive side, knowledge is firmly on the agenda as a strategic initiative. Indeed, since this research was conducted, the organization has appointed a Vice President of Information Technology and Knowledge Management, further demonstrating its commitment to this area. The critical elements of structure and infrastructure also appear to be in place, witnessed by significant investment in information and communications technologies and a refining of the work environment to accommodate teams and communities within a generally flat structure.

The OCM does, however, highlight that critical elements of leadership and culture are absent. More specifically, it appears that managers have still to embrace the notion that managing knowledge underpins core business processes and is consequently not fully integrated into the natural flow of work. From a cultural dimension, a lack of trust and incentives for sharing knowledge

Copyright © 2004, Idea Group Inc. Copying or distributing in print or electronic forms without written permission of Idea Group Inc. is prohibited.

Table 2: Black and Decker – OCM.

ISSUES	CHARACTERISTIC	DESIRABLE	ESSENTIAL
Strategic	Knowledge issues are addressed explicitly in the organization's business strategy.		✓
Structural	Flatter structure with fewer layers to facilitate more effective knowledge transfer.		✓
	The use of group based teams, ideally cross-functional, as well as communities of practice, designed to encourage knowledge sharing.		✓
	Decentralization of decision making to capitalize on individual and team expertise.	✓	
Leadership	The existence of a knowledge champion at senior management level.		✓
	Management awareness of knowledge issues accompanied by an open and inclusive attitude to decision making.		×
Infrastructure	Technical infrastructure to support knowledge transfer with tools (e.g., knowledge maps) to facilitate this.		✓
	Support systems, both human and technical, that avoid "re-inventing the wheel".	✓	
	Effective communication channels encompassing verbal, electronic and written formats.		✓
Cultural	Incentives for sharing knowledge, ideally built within appraisal regimes, emphasizing personal and organizational benefits.		×
	High trust and supportive environment encouraging individual responsibility.		×
	Allocation of time within the organization to actively encourage communication and knowledge transfer.	✓	
Measurement	Mechanisms exist to quantify intellectual assets.	×	
Individual	Recognition of the individual's knowledge by:		
	▪ Individual		✓
	▪ Co-workers	✓	
	▪ Managers		×

Copyright © 2004, Idea Group Inc. Copying or distributing in print or electronic forms without written permission of Idea Group Inc. is prohibited.

is apparent, acting as a formidable barrier to knowledge sharing. This is strongly allied to the individual, and while within the organization there is a respect and acknowledgement of the value of knowledge between individuals and co-workers, recognition of individual knowledge by managers appears absent. This links closely with the idea that the management of knowledge is not firmly embedded within organizational culture.

It should be emphasized that the research conducted refers explicitly to Black and Decker's European Design Centre. Although designated a primary global design centre, exactly how the EDC mirrors other areas of the organization is not clear and further research is needed to corroborate these findings, if generalizations are to be made. However, given the observations based on the EDC, it is unlikely that it can be viewed as knowledge-centric.

Further Development

Although at first sight the development and use of an OCM might appear rather mechanistic, it serves two main purposes:

- The identification of organizational characteristics that describe the elements of a knowledge-focused company.
- The prioritization of these characteristics in terms of their relative importance.

In using such a matrix, the presence and importance of a characteristic requires a detailed investigation of the organization's environment, processes and activities. This is beneficial both internally and externally. In the former category, better use of knowledge assets and resources can bring substantial improvements in work practices, motivation of staff, more efficient use of technologies and greater understanding of the management of knowledge. This impacts on the external environment by providing customers with better designed and made products, together with improved service based on knowledge of the market and their target audience. A greater attention to how knowledge can be harnessed within an organization also creates greater awareness of the external environment and the ways in which competing organizations deal with their knowledge assets.

Copyright © 2004, Idea Group Inc. Copying or distributing in print or electronic forms without written permission of Idea Group Inc. is prohibited.

Of course, the OCM is not without its problems and can be criticized from a number of angles. The choice of organizational characteristics, while grounded in academic and practical research, incorporates an element of subjectivity and some have greater relevance to certain types of companies and industries than others. For example, an organization selling expertise may attach greater weight to more informal network structures than an organization selling manufactured products. This is not to say that such structures are not important, but the relative weightings are different. This highlights the limitation of using a dichotomy, desirable and essential, in the OCM. This is currently being addressed by further research in a number of companies that, it is envisaged, will assist in devising a graded scale to demonstrate the relative importance of the various organizational characteristics. This will also impact on the overall assessment of the criteria on which knowledge-centricity is based. A degree of refinement is anticipated in this respect, but this fits conveniently with the knowledge journey, since if an organization is not knowledge-centric, at which of the other evolutionary four stages, described earlier in this chapter, is an organization at? An expanded OCM will greatly assist in this assessment.

The issue of knowledge-centricity, and indeed knowledge management, is essentially the domain of large organizations, with relatively little written about small and medium-sized enterprises (SMEs). Is the OCM applicable in this context?

There are clearly certain differences between the two types of organizations. McAdam and Reid (2001) argue that the SME sector tends to be less advanced, with a mechanistic approach to knowledge and a lack of investment in knowledge management approaches and systems. Furthermore, as Sparrow (1999) and Stonehouse and Pemberton (1999) note:

- The misalignment of capability with market competitors can have a more rapid and drastic impact on SMEs in comparison with larger organizations.
- The knowledge development and competitive positioning process within SMEs is more likely to have strategic importance and affect an entire business.
- Culture is more easily managed in SMEs and represents a more realistic means of capitalizing on competitive advantage and facilitating knowledge transfer.

Copyright © 2004, Idea Group Inc. Copying or distributing in print or electronic forms without written permission of Idea Group Inc. is prohibited.

- Resources (expertise, finance, know-how, etc.) for KM initiatives in SMEs may be restricted.

Early analysis of research conducted by the authors based on the responses to a survey distributed to over 500 SMEs in 2003 has highlighted a number of pertinent issues including:

- Weak cross-team communications.
- Lack of formal information/knowledge repositories evident in most organizations surveyed.
- Lack of formal systems for environmental scanning, analysis and organizational communications in a majority of organizations surveyed.
- Weak information/knowledge retrieval processes and links with product/service offerings in over half of the organization surveyed.
- Vital knowledge is inaccessible and not integrated into the work-flow in half the organizations surveyed.
- Intellectual (intangible) assets not managed/measured or valued in majority of organizations surveyed.

There are clearly some links with the issues highlighted here and the organizational characteristics presented in the OCM. An exact mapping of the issues relevant to large companies is probably not entirely realistic, but it may be possible to devise a closely related variation of the OCM relevant to SMEs.

One final consideration is the validity of applying such a matrix across global boundaries. For example, much has been written about the differences in perspectives of knowledge management in Western and Eastern approaches over the last few years. Broadly speaking, the former tends to have historically taken a technology-oriented view, but the socio-technical aspects espoused by writers such as Nonaka et al. (2000) are now assuming greater prominence in the knowledge management area. Indeed, this is reflected in the OCM presented in this chapter. However, the relative weightings of these characteristics may not adequately explain, or account for, fundamental differences in organizational practices, structures and management. For example, in certain Eastern cultures there is a less individualistic culture compared with their Western counterparts, as well as differing attitudes towards accepting authority. Clearly, the broad characteristics of the OCM are as relevant for judging

Copyright © 2004, Idea Group Inc. Copying or distributing in print or electronic forms without written permission of Idea Group Inc. is prohibited.

knowledge-centricity in Eastern companies as those in the West, but national cultural differences, for example, are not explicitly accounted for and other nuances may also be a force at play.

Conclusion

The use of an organizational characteristics matrix is a succinct way of assessing the extent to which an organization can be viewed as knowledge-centric, a term embracing not just knowledge management, but describing all aspects of an organization's knowledge capabilities.

It should also be noted that knowledge-centricity is not necessarily retained over time and, for this reason, the application of the OCM is not a one-off activity. It is conceivable that an organization that fails to keep abreast of business and management developments, as well as the activities of those organizations competing in the same or similar marketplace, may potentially lose its knowledge-centricity status. Equally, an organization that is not judged as knowledge-centric using the OCM at a particular point in time may subsequently acquire such status when applying the OCM at a later date. A periodic application of the OCM is therefore essential to reflect the changing nature of knowledge creation and dissemination within modern organizations.

In essence, a knowledge-centric organization utilizes and exploits its knowledge assets in a variety of ways to enhance organizational and individual performance. This is, by its very nature, a dynamic process and reflects the shifting internal and external business environment in which an organization operates, and the notion of continuous learning is an integral feature of innovative organizations that are typically viewed as knowledge-centric. The characteristics comprising the OCM are vital elements of such an organization, the matrix devised by examination of a number of organizational features. In this first iteration, the OCM is a template for the assessment of knowledge-centricity, but further development is necessary to refine the matrix in line with the limitations and issues identified above. This is ongoing, and while the OCM will not be appropriate for all organizations, industries or countries, its application is useful as an internal assessment mechanism, and externally, as a means of benchmarking itself with other competing organizations.

Copyright © 2004, Idea Group Inc. Copying or distributing in print or electronic forms without written permission of Idea Group Inc. is prohibited.

Acknowledgments

The authors would like to thank Mark Francis for his collaboration in this research and his employer, Black and Decker, for allowing the work to be undertaken and reported. We would also like to thank Will Kolosz for the design and execution of the fieldwork relating to the SME survey.

References

Ardichvili, A., Page, V., & Wentling, T. (2003). Motivation and barriers to participation in virtual knowledge-sharing communities of practice. *Journal of Knowledge Management*, *7*(1), 64-77.

Bhatt, G.D. (2000). Information dynamics, learning and knowledge creation in organizations. *The Learning Organization*, *7*(2), 89-98.

Birkinshaw, J. (2001). Why is knowledge management so difficult? *Business Strategy Review*, *12*(1), 11-19.

Birkinshaw, J. (2002). Managing internal R & D networks in global firms. *Long Range Planning*, *35*(3), 245-267.

Black and Decker. (2003). *A bright future based on a solid past.* Retrieved July 5, 2003, from http://www.mmdp.co.uk/

Bukowitz, W., & Williams, R. (1999). *The knowledge management field book.* London: Financial Times - Prentice Hall.

Chase, R. (1997). Knowledge management benchmarks. *Journal of Knowledge Management*, *1*(1), 83-92.

Griego, O.V., Geroy, G.D., & Wright, P.C. (2000). Predictors of learning organizations: A human resource development practitioner's perspective. *The Learning Organization, 7*(1), 5-12.

Hall, R., & Andriani, P. (2002, February). Managing knowledge for innovation. *Long Range Planning, 35*(1), 29-48.

Hansen, M.T., Nohria, N., & Tierney, T. (2001). What's your strategy for managing knowledge. In J.W. Cortada & J.A. Woods (Eds.), *The knowledge management yearbook 2000-2001.* Boston: Butterworth Heinemann.

Copyright © 2004, Idea Group Inc. Copying or distributing in print or electronic forms without written permission of Idea Group Inc. is prohibited.

Horne, N. (1998). Putting information assets on the board agenda. *Long Range Planning*, *31*(1), 10-17.

Kippenberger, T. (1998). Sharing knowledge at BP. *The Antidote*, *3*(1), 38-40.

KPMG. (1997). *The knowledge journey: A business guide to knowledge systems.* Retrieved July 7, 2003, from *http://www.it-consultancy.com/extern/pdf/journey.pdf*

KPMG. (2000). *Knowledge management research report 2000.* Retrieved July 7, 2003, from *www.kpmg.nl/Docs/Knowledge_Advisory_Services/*

Liebowitz, J., & Suen, Y. (2000). Developing knowledge management metrics for measuring intellectual capital. *Journal of Intellectual Capital, 1*(1), 54-67.

Little, S., Quintas, P., & Ray, T. (2002). *Managing knowledge: An essential reader.* London: Sage.

Mayo, A. (2000). The role of employee development in the growth of intellectual capital. *Personnel Review*, *29*(4), 521-533.

McAdam, R., & McCreedy, S. (1999). A critical review of knowledge management models. *The Learning Organization*, *6*(3), 91-100.

McAdam, R., & Reid, R. (2001). SME and large organization perceptions of knowledge management: Comparisons and contrasts. *Journal of Knowledge Management*, *5*(3), 231-241.

McCampbell, A., Clare, L., & Gitters, S. (1999). Knowledge management: The new challenge for the 21st Century. *Journal of Knowledge Management*, *3*(3), 172-179.

McDermott, R., & O'Dell, C. (2001). Overcoming cultural barriers to sharing knowledge. *Journal of Knowledge Management*, *5*(1), 76-85.

Mouritsen, J., Larsen, H., & Bukh, P. (2001). Valuing the future: Intellectual capital supplements at Skandia. *Accounting, Auditing and Accountability Journal*, *14*(4), 399-422.

Murray, P., & Myers, A. (1998). Survey of KM practice in Europe. *Information strategy.* London: The Economist.

Nonaka, I., Toyama, R., & Konno, N. (2000). SECI, Ba and leadership: A unified model of dynamic knowledge creation. *Long Range Planning*, *33*(1), 5-34.

Copyright © 2004, Idea Group Inc. Copying or distributing in print or electronic forms without written permission of Idea Group Inc. is prohibited.

O'Dell, C., Wiig, K., & Odem, P. (1999). Benchmarking unveils emerging knowledge management strategies. *Benchmarking: An International Journal*, *6*(3), 202-211.

Pemberton, J., & Stonehouse, G. (2000). Organizational learning and knowledge assets - An essential partnership. *The Learning Organization*, *7*(4), 184-193.

Pemberton, J., & Stonehouse, G. (2002). The importance of individual knowledge in developing the knowledge-centric organization. In E. Coakes, D. Willis & S. Clarke (Eds), *Knowledge management in the socio-technical world: The graffiti continues.* London: Springer.

Pemberton, J., Stonehouse, G., & Francis, M. (2002). Black and Decker – towards a knowledge-centric organization. *Knowledge and Process Management*, *9*(3), 178-189.

Pemberton, J., Stonehouse, G., & Yarrow, D. (2001). Benchmarking and the role of organizational learning in developing competitive advantage. *Knowledge and Process Management*, *8*(2), 123-135.

Petrash, G. (1996, August). Dow's journey to a knowledge value management culture. *European Management Journal, 14*(4), 365-373.

Prahalad, C.K., & Hamel, G. (1990). The core competence of an organization. *Harvard Business Review*, *68*(3), 79-93.

Senge, P. (1990). *The fifth discipline: The art & practice of the learning organisation.* New York: Doubleday.

Skyrme, D. (1999). *Knowledge networking: Creating the collaborative enterprise.* Oxford: Butterworth Heinemann.

Sparrow, J. (1999). *Supporting knowledge management in small and medium sized enterprises.* Retrieved July 7, 2003, from University of the West of England's Knowledge Management Centre Website, http://kmc.tbs.uce.ac.uk/kmcpublications.htm

Stonehouse, G., Pemberton, J., & Barber, C. (2001). The role of knowledge facilitators and inhibitors: Lessons from airline reservations systems. *Long Range Planning, 34*(2), 115-138.

Stonehouse, G.H., & Pemberton, J.D. (1999). Learning and knowledge management in the intelligent organization. *Participation & Empowerment: An International Journal, 7*(5), 31-144.

Copyright © 2004, Idea Group Inc. Copying or distributing in print or electronic forms without written permission of Idea Group Inc. is prohibited.

Teece, D. (2000). Strategies for managing knowledge assets: The role of the firm structure and industrial context. *Long Range Planning, 33*(1), 35-54.

Von Krogh, G., Nonaka, I., & Abel, M. (2001). Making the most of your company's knowledge: A strategic framework. *Long Range Planning, 34*(4), 421-439.

Vouros, G.A. (2003). Technological issues towards knowledge-powered organizations. *Journal of Knowledge Management*, *7*(2), 114-127.

Wenger, E., & Snyder, W.M. (2000, January/February). Communities of practice: The organizational frontier. *Harvard Business Review*, 139-145.

Zack, M. (1999). *Knowledge and strategy.* Oxford: Butterworth-Heinemann.

Copyright © 2004, Idea Group Inc. Copying or distributing in print or electronic forms without written permission of Idea Group Inc. is prohibited.

Section II

Knowledge Management Tools

Chapter VII

Making Knowledge Management System an Effective Tool for Learning and Training

Albert C. K. Leung
Lingnan University, Hong Kong

Abstract

In view of the need of using knowledge management (KM) systems for learning and training, this chapter discusses six major design factors of such KM systems based on learning literatures, namely media of representation, multiple perspectives, complexity, user control, online support and navigation aids. Their implications toward learning and training effectiveness as well as various strategies and implementation methods are investigated in four categories: content, motivation, support and accessibility. It is believed that by considering the factors involved and their potential impacts on learning in the design of KM systems, the effectiveness of using these systems for learning, training and problem solving will be significantly improved.

Copyright © 2004, Idea Group Inc. Copying or distributing in print or electronic forms without written permission of Idea Group Inc. is prohibited.

Introduction

Knowledge management (KM) is becoming one of the most significant factors in determining organizational success (Bowman, 2002), because knowledge has become the key economic resource and the dominant source of comparative advantage influencing everything from a company's strategy to its products, from its processes to the very way the firm is organized (Ruggles, 1998). In fact, KM performs a range of functions for personal growth and organizational effectiveness, namely, gathering knowledge, organizing knowledge, distributing knowledge, and converting knowledge into action. Therefore, a KM system should have the capability to support knowledge acquisition, decision making, communication, reference material searching, and human resource development such as training (Plass & Salisbury, 2002).

While most businesses appreciate the strategic value of knowledge and the need to manage their knowledge assets, many of them seem unable to derive real benefits from their efforts (Murray, 2002). Fahey and Prusak (1998) summarized 11 problem areas with KM in organizations, namely working definition of knowledge, knowledge stock instead of knowledge flow, roles of individuals, creating shared context, role of tacit knowledge, knowledge of uses, thinking and reasoning, future knowledge, experimentation, technology-human interface and measures of knowledge. In another study (Hunter et al., 2002), social and cultural issues are found to be potential inhibitors for KM practices. Furthermore, lack of senior management understanding and support can also substantially reduce the gain of KM deployment (Horwitch & Armacost, 2002). As such, measures and recommendations are suggested in various literatures to make KM more effective (e.g., Bowman, 2002; Horwitch, 2002; Hunter et al., 2002; Murray, 2002). Various architectures for KM development were also proposed (e.g., Bollouju et al., 2002; Galup et al., 2002; Nemati et al., 2002; Plass & Salisbury, 2002).

Since a KM system supposedly collects all essential organizational knowledge, it has been used as a very effective tool for human resources development, such as training of new and existing staff (Carlile, 2002). Such practices are different from traditional classroom training, since they are mainly technology-based and trainee-centered. In this regard, the design of a KM system has to take consideration of other factors besides the above-mentioned factors such as knowledge presentation, system design and online support. Particularly, from the learning point of view, a KM system has to be designed to support learners' exploration, thinking and reasoning, and problem solving. Therefore, learning

Copyright © 2004, Idea Group Inc. Copying or distributing in print or electronic forms without written permission of Idea Group Inc. is prohibited.

theories are essential in the design process to ensure learning effectiveness of using such KM systems for training/learning. However, little research is found in this regard, though there is some research conducted in evaluation and design architecture of KM systems based on learning theories. For instance, in Dhaliwal and Benbasat (2001) a framework for empirical evaluation of KM systems was developed based on cognitive learning theories. Also, in Plass and Salisbury (2002), situated learning theory and cognitive flexibility theory were based on developing an information architecture for Web-based KM system development.

It is therefore the objective of this research to explore building KM systems in consideration of fundamental learning theories, which would enhance the effectiveness of learning/training by using these systems. Instead of on those technological or architectural issues about KM development, this approach is proposed based on the issues that would have potential impact on learning/training effectiveness, namely media of representation, complexity, multiple perspective, user control, online support and navigation aids. It is expected that the proposed approach would enhance the effectiveness of using KM systems for training as well as for other purposes such as decision support and knowledge searching, and provide invaluable insight toward KM development and deployment. In the following sections, learning theory development is first introduced. Thereafter, the theoretical background of the mentioned six issues as well as their implications to the design and implementation of KM systems in terms of their major training capabilities, namely contents, motivation, support and accessibility, are presented. Discussions and conclusions are given at the end of this chapter.

Learning Theory Development and Issues

Current research in learning has shifted from passive human memory to active strategies for learning: what it means to learn, the contents that learners are to acquire, and the context in which they are to acquire it (Glaser & Bassok, 1989; Greeno, 1989). There are increasing concerns about helping learners to learn to think more effectively, and to help them develop effective problem solving, reasoning and learning skills, which have brought increasing demands for more subtle methods to render overt the human thought processes (Brown, Campione

Copyright © 2004, Idea Group Inc. Copying or distributing in print or electronic forms without written permission of Idea Group Inc. is prohibited.

& Day, 1981; Resnick, 1987). This is evident from learning theory development from behaviorism to cognitivism, and then most recently to constructivism, as presented below.

Behaviorism holds that the world is completely and correctly structured in terms of entities, properties and relations (Ertmer & Newby, 1993). Hence, the goal of understanding is to know the entities, attributes and relations that exist through a process of mapping them onto learners. Learning is then operationalized as a set of stimulus-response (S-R) events such as questions and consequent responses from learners, which establish and reinforce the relevant associations in the mind of the learners (Atkins, 1993). Thus, learners become motivated to seek stimuli and make responses leading to positive consequences (Hannafin & Rieber, 1989). The lecture method of teaching embeds the pedagogical assumptions of the behaviorism theory of learning, in which the instructor is the source of objective knowledge that is related, rather than created, during class, and the instructor should be in control of the material and pace of learning (Leidner & Jarvenpaa, 1995).

The behaviorism approach has certain limitations. Firstly, no attempt is made to determine the structure of learners' knowledge nor to assess which mental processes are necessary for them to use (Winn, 1990). Also, learners are characterized as being reactive to conditions in a learning environment (Ertmer & Newby, 1993). Furthermore, it is difficult to define a series of behaviors, starting with the entering behavior and leading to the desired terminal behavior of a learning process (Case & Bereiter, 1984). Therefore, the resulting instruction teaches components but not integrated knowledge and skills, and the resulting learning is poorly retained, which does not relate well to previously learned materials. More importantly, learners often have trouble generalizing their learned knowledge from one situation to another, remaining poor in divergent reasoning, problem solving, and troubleshooting (Hannafin & Rieber, 1989). Due to these shortcomings, it is generally agreed that behavioral principles cannot adequately explain the acquisition of higher level skills or those that require a greater depth of processing, and are effective for low-level learning, such as rote recall or simple concept acquisition (Hannafin & Rieber, 1989).

In view of the shortcomings of behaviorism, learning research has shifted from behavioral psychology to cognitive psychology since the mid-1980s. Explication of the process of learning, by contrast, the least developed component of behaviorism, became the major concern (Glaser & Bassok, 1989). Cognitive approaches advocate leaning in the context of working on specific problems,

Copyright © 2004, Idea Group Inc. Copying or distributing in print or electronic forms without written permission of Idea Group Inc. is prohibited.

and learners are required initially to have a certain amount of declarative knowledge of a particular domain before proceeding to the problem solving. Moreover, they all recommend explication and modeling of the appropriate problem-solving structure and of the procedures or strategies entailed. However, the cognitive approaches do seem to have different stances toward instruction in terms of learner control, feedback, knowledge transition path and shared or individualized learning. In addition, the actual goal of instruction is often to communicate or transfer knowledge to the learners in the most efficient and effective manner through simplification and standardization (Bednar, Cunningham, Duffy & Perry, 1991). The process of reducing the complexity of learning tasks may well be misrepresenting the thinking or mental processing required by the task (Jenkins, 1979). Due to these limitations, it is argued that cognitivism has not provided enough of a paradigm shift in terms of learning and problem solving, and to a certain extent, it is still primarily objectivistic (Jonassen, 1991b).

Recently, it is the constructivism that attracts lots of attention. Constructivism can be considered to be an extension of cognitivism characterized by discovery and experiential learning (Rieber, 1992), which provides learners with the conceptual power needed to deal with complex and ill-structured problems or domains (Ertmer & Newby, 1993). It is reminiscent of the discovery approaches to learning, whereby learners learn best when they discover or can be led to discover for themselves (Brush, Armstrong, Barbrow & Ulintz, 1999). It claims that everyday learning always takes place within a social context, instead of as largely independent situational variables (Jonassen & Rhrer-Murphy, 1999). Constructivism focuses on creating authentic problems within authentic environments for learning, environments that correspond to the real world, so that learners build personal interpretations of the world based on individual experiences and interactions with those environments (Ertmer & Newby, 1993). In fact, many learning approaches such as cognitive apprenticeship, anchored instruction, problem-based learning and case approach, generally support the theme of constructivism. In particular, these approaches provide various kinds of generative learning environments in laboratory-based (e.g., apprenticeship), videodisc-based (e.g., anchored instruction), text-based (e.g., case approach) and action-based contexts (problem-based learning).

The evolution of the learning theories indicates that learning focus has been shifting from direct instruction of objectivism to a more opened and learner centred learning process of constructivism, which requires high-order reason-

Copyright © 2004, Idea Group Inc. Copying or distributing in print or electronic forms without written permission of Idea Group Inc. is prohibited.

ing and knowledge construction. As the main objective of constructivism is to provide shared environments that permit sustained exploration by learners and enable them to understand the kind of problems, opportunities and knowledge that experts in various areas would encounter and apply (CTGV, 1993a), it is feasible to provide such meaningful and problem-solving contexts in a KM system. Users can then explore, interrogate, discover, and learn within a KM system, that is, a knowledge construction process. Based on these learning theories, six issues were found influential on learning effectiveness of KM systems, namely media of representation, complexity, multiple perspectives, user control, online support and navigation aids as outlined in the following.

- Media of representation: It addresses the ways that various types of media should be used to build a KM system.
- Multiple perspectives: It concerns problem solving across analogous or even different domains or the possibility of multiple solutions to a single problem.
- Complexity: It concerns the complexity of a knowledge management system, that is, how it should be designed to reflect the real-world complexity.
- User control: It concerns the amount of control given to the users for free exploration as well as the amount of coaching and guidance regulated in a KM system.
- Online support: It deals with various kinds of supports that should be provided in a KM system in terms of type and amount of support, also including the linkage between goals and required prior knowledge/experience.
- Navigation aids: It concerns not only the physical mapping of resources contained in a KM system, but also the concept mapping in structuring users' prior experience and current knowledge, which is especially useful for novices in ill-structured domains.

These issues by no means are exhaustive, but they potentially address the major concerns of learning effectiveness of KM. Most of these issues have been reviewed, validated and applied in learning related applications, and it is expected that by introducing these issues into the development of KM systems, they should have positive impact on effectiveness when such systems are used for staff training as well as for performing other functions such as decision

Copyright © 2004, Idea Group Inc. Copying or distributing in print or electronic forms without written permission of Idea Group Inc. is prohibited.

support. As noted in Carlile (2002), without a focus on learning, KM is really only information management or management of potential knowledge. Thus, in the following sections, the implications of these issues toward the development of KM systems are discussed in view of their major capabilities for personal growth as well as organizational effectiveness.

Knowledge Management Systems

Knowledge management (KM) is generally developed within businesses as a part of the strategic planning and management sector with the promise that it can help solve business problems. It is an integrated, systematic approach to identifying, managing, and sharing all of an enterprise's information assets, including databases, documents, policies and procedures, as well as previously unarticulated expertise and experience held by individual workers. A KM system is an IT-based system developed to support the organizational knowledge management behavior, which would help users find short, focused and just-in-time knowledge on a variety of related topics (Plass & Salisbury, 2002). The primary goal of a KM system is to promote the use of the built-in knowledge throughout an organization, and the secondary goals are (a) the capturing of knowledge from experienced members of the organization and (b) training new employees who are inexperienced. Therefore, the main abilities of a KM system are to gather knowledge, organize knowledge, distribute knowledge, convert knowledge into action, train ourselves continuously, and repeat the cycle (Zahner, 2002).

While this research mainly focuses on the training/learning aspects of using KM systems, knowledge capturing/gathering is not the major concern of this study. Rather, the study is based on the following four aspects to enhance effectiveness of training and other applications, namely content, motivation, support and accessibility. According to Carlile (2002), in order to truly be knowledge management, the learning segment of the process must take place, and these four areas can enhance effectiveness of learning/training of using a KM system. Content provides resources and data to support programs and their development; motivation is essential to encourage people to seek out KM resources when they need knowledge and skills; support is needed for users to find/access specific information/knowledge/solutions in an effective and efficient manner; rapid accessibility allows users to access KM system faster and more

Copyright © 2004, Idea Group Inc. Copying or distributing in print or electronic forms without written permission of Idea Group Inc. is prohibited.

conveniently. In the following sections, discussion is conducted investigating how the six issues can contribute to the development of KM systems in the above four aspects.

Contents of KM System

Media of Representation

There is evidence that use of multisensory and multimedia materials increases educational effectiveness (Gerlic & Jauxs, 1999; Mayer, 1997; Mayer & Moreno, 1998), because there are separate spaces for storing and rehearsing verbal information and visual or spatial information in human memory (Silber, 1998). In addition, it seems that we encode verbal and visual information differently in memory (Paivio & Wallace, 1981), and we remember visual information very well, even more so if we can place a meaningful interpretation on the visuals. Therefore, in a multimedia environment, users can more easily form rich mental models of even complex problem situations (Schank, 1993).

While multimedia can potentially make learning more effective and efficient, the multitude of media and display options, and the requirements of a KM system can magnify the difficulty in determining the appropriate combination of presentation features and events (see Hannafin & Rieber, 1989). There are also varied research efforts on presentation variables regarding learning, such as visualization, text design, graphics applications, text display variables and user interface design (e.g., Gillingham, 1988; Lee & Boling, 1999). However, it is practically impossible to isolate which features or attributes of media affect learning; thus media should be synergistic combinations of technology, task and context to facilitate knowledge construction and meaning making on the part of the learner instead of mere knowledge conveyors (Cobb, 1997; Jonnassen et al., 1994).

Although multimedia can provide rich, robust, and motivated representation of a problem domain, they are not typically thought of as artifacts for problem solving and inquiry. Particularly, videos and photographs are more likely to be treated as visual aids to accompany text or audio information (Smith & Blank, 2000). For instance, the narratives that accompany documentary films focus attention on salient issues, but the narrator's voice often becomes the principal source of information (Wetzel et al., 1994). Users may rely on the narratives to explain the "right" interpretations of the video content instead of framing their

Copyright © 2004, Idea Group Inc. Copying or distributing in print or electronic forms without written permission of Idea Group Inc. is prohibited.

own questions and generate hypotheses. Thus, the use of video as primary data rather than as supplements to textual or audio explanation is crucial, particularly for discovery-based or open-ended learning environments (Smith & Blank, 2000).

According to Zack (1999), there are generally three types of knowledge in an organization: declarative knowledge, procedural knowledge and causal knowledge. Thus, in a KM system, different knowledge should be represented in diversified types of media, such as video, animations, diagrams, text, maps and photos. The knowledge is then divided into knowledge units, which are labeled, indexed, and stored in the system for user retrieval and manipulation. A knowledge platform may then consist of several repositories, each with a structure appropriate to a particular type of knowledge or content. This includes schemes for linking and cross-referencing knowledge units in terms of association, order sequence and causality, and is discussed in the following sections.

Multiple Perspectives

Complex domains usually require multiple perspectives of representations due to their ill-structured and highly conditional nature (Gagne, 1990). No single perspective is adequate to the task of representing ill-structured problems (Lewis, Stern & Linn, 1993). Therefore, in a relatively complex domain, users should be given the opportunity to experience an event from multiple perspectives in terms of multiple solutions or views of a phenomenon under study (Cobb, 1997; Park & Hannafin, 1993), as well as to solve comparative problems under different settings or even in different domains (Choi & Hannafin, 1995). Indeed, unlike solutions to well-structured problems that can simply be right or wrong, in complex domains such as business, law and medicine, it is often unrealistic to have one single answer to a problem. Rather, solutions to ill-structured problems should be divided into different categories such as better, good, bad and worse. For instance, in Dick (1991), the integration of multiple objectives is proposed in terms of the more comprehensive range of activities in which a learner is engaged, and therefore integrative learning goals are achieved.

Thus, to help learners react in response to varying situational demands, they must understand problems in their full complexity and must "criss-cross" the problem space in multiple passes in order to observe how shifts in variables and

Copyright © 2004, Idea Group Inc. Copying or distributing in print or electronic forms without written permission of Idea Group Inc. is prohibited.

goals alter the space (Lewis et al., 1993). Sometimes, wrong solutions may also be incorporated in a learning system to let users learn from failures. It helps users understand the circumstance under which one solution is the best and may not be the best under other circumstances (Minstrell, 1989); thus the objective of multiple perspectives is achieved. On the other hand, by observing the reasoning processes and strategies that experts usually employ when applying knowledge and performing complex tasks, learners can also acquire the ability to discriminate among subtle features by virtue of experience across a range of situations that provide relevant contrasts (Honebein, Duffy & Fishman, 1993).

Such multiple perspective requirements in a KM system were also pointed out in Fahey and Prusak (1998) as "creating shared context" and "importance of experimentation," which represent a shared understanding by differing individuals of an organization's external and internal worlds and how these worlds are connected, and the need for exploitation over exploration. Accordingly, a KM system should contain an integrated knowledge base built on differing perspectives, beliefs, assumptions, and even views across different domains, which are categorized according to their respective levels of appropriateness toward a solution confronting similar problems.

Complexity

The complex content is characterized by high cognitive demands due to contextually induced variability, multiple knowledge representation and multiple interconnectedness of knowledge components (Spiro, Feltovich, Jacobson & Coulson, 1991). Effective learning is an individual and personal implication in the process of schematization and abstraction of the complexity of reality (Mendelsohn, 1996). However, if a problem is too complex, a novice may easily be overwhelmed by the complexity, become distracted by surface features of a problem, and fail to see the important underlying principles (Chi, Feltovich & Glaser, 1981). This is because knowledge is stored as chunks in memory, with each chunk containing the amount of information based on a learner's existing knowledge (Miller, 1956). There is also evidence that learners pass through a series of stages or phases during which the learning process and the variables influencing it change systematically (Shuell, 1990).

Hence, in a KM system, knowledge can be layered to accommodate multiple levels of complexity and accommodate differences in related prior knowledge (e.g., Park & Hannafin, 1993). A novice may start out with a simplified

Copyright © 2004, Idea Group Inc. Copying or distributing in print or electronic forms without written permission of Idea Group Inc. is prohibited.

representation of a task domain, and gradually move on to more and more complex representations, until the user is able to deal with the full complexity of the content domain (e.g., Levin & Waugh, 1988). To do so, the developers must understand how fluently those required skills are arrived at and how this process might be enhanced within a learning environment (CTGV, 1992). Such design is essential to ensure the learning effectiveness of various levels of users. It is also important to encourage the use of a KM system if users find it satisfactory, easy to use and useful: the three major determinants of user acceptance of a KM system (see Dhaliwal & Benbasat, 1996). Furthermore, complexity of a KM system can also be coped with by more user control, online support and navigation aids as presented in the following sections respectively.

Motivation with More User Control

Same as learner control, user control refers to the freedom with which a user can take command of the selection and sequencing of content, display and conscious cognition; whereas by contrast, program control gives less control to users (see Nicaise & Crane, 1999). It has been long discussed that individuals should be more involved in choice-making on control of learning (e.g., Beasley & Waugh, 1995), and the research also shows that under greater learner control, learners can learn better (Brown et al., 1981) and become more concentrated and motivated (MacLachlan, 1986; Perfetto, Bransford & Franks, 1983). However, there are also mixed results regarding learner control due to many influential factors, such as learners' learning attitudes (Cunningham, 1991), learners' ability (Cunningham, 1991; Gillingham, 1988), prior knowledge of tasks (McKeachie, 1990), type of tasks, that is, procedural or declarative in nature (Gick & Holyoak, 1980) and time-on-task (Nicaise & Crane, 1999). Yet still, according to Honebein et al. (1993), learners should have more control over their knowledge exploration in terms of content, sequence, pace, iteration and review, particularly in ill-structured domains.

Accordingly, in a KM system, it is necessary to provide functions to speed up, slow down, and freeze or repeat physical occurrences, which would give users the options to see and experience events in the ways not normally possible in real situations (e.g., Greeno, 1989). Since in complex domains, the availability of information at any given moment often exceeds the individual's ability to process it (Greeno, 1989), thus users may need to visit the same material at different times, in rearranged contexts, for different purposes, and from

Copyright © 2004, Idea Group Inc. Copying or distributing in print or electronic forms without written permission of Idea Group Inc. is prohibited.

different conceptual perspectives, with each iteration providing new insight (Park, 1984). Furthermore, a wide range of increasingly complex environments can be provided that allow a novice to start with a fairly constrained environment, and gradually assume more control of his/her solution process until that the last world is as similar as possible to the real domain (Honebein et al., 1993). Additionally, variation in level of expertise and audio-visual cues can also be made available to suit different users' needs (Greeno, 1989).

However, some program control may be necessary for effective learning in a KM system. As pointed out by Fahey and Prusak (1998), getting to different states of knowledge development requires some form of reasoning, which has been downplayed in many KM systems. Thus, users should be challenged, or even prompted to generate questions, hypotheses or theories themselves at various stages during their exploration of a KM system to facilitate metacognitve thinking, and also to focus on important aspects of tasks (e.g., Hooper & Hannafin, 1991). Environments designed to invoke conceptual, strategic and evaluative processes are more likely to prove successful when facilitation is provided for the use of available tools, activities and resources (Hicken, Sullivan & Klein, 1992). These embedded questions/tasks should be distributed systematically within a KM system for users to accomplish (Honebein et al., 1993), because it is not uncommon for users to fail to recognize the need of it and then ignore suggested strategies or questions, believing that the challenges are unnecessary or a hindrance to progress (Hay & Barab, 2001). Such control structures can potentially integrate concepts and skills between adjacent levels of knowledge (Jonassen & Reeves, 1996).

Online Support

In ill-structured domains, it usually requires more information than is available to initially understand a situation or problem (Land & Greene, 2000); thus if one's goal is to help users become independent learners and problem solvers in specific areas, more guidelines and domain related information should become available within a learning/training program (Minstrell, 1989). Generally, three basic types of support are available: just-in-time support, scaffolding and coaching. Just-in-time support provides hints, clues, concepts to reflect upon, or contextualized support to help users as they progress through to their problem solution when needed. On the other hand, scaffolding is to provide hints as to facilitate the transfer of what users already know to the task at hand,

Copyright © 2004, Idea Group Inc. Copying or distributing in print or electronic forms without written permission of Idea Group Inc. is prohibited.

allowing them to accomplish otherwise impossible tasks (Harley, 1993). Coaching is to make additional resources available to users as they search for a solution to a particular problem (Hoffman & Rtchie, 1997). It includes directing user attention, reminding of overlooked steps, providing hints and feedback, challenging and structuring ways to do things, and providing additional tasks, problems, or problematic situations (Choi & Hannafin, 1995). Furthermore, guidance and advice are implicit rather than explicit, and non-directive rather than directive, being provided when needed by users (Choi & Hannafin, 1995).

In a learning/KM system, technology can be used to build these user supports competently. For instance, in Tobin and Dawson (1992), learners are provided menu access to possible questions to be answered, descriptions of available resources and their functions, and advice on ways to proceed. More specifically, for each task to be accomplished, especially for novice learners, the program outlines the goals, what it means, why it is important, the amount of work they should expect to carry out, advice on how they might start the investigation, good practice hints, prior knowledge needed, and possible approaches, under the condition that the freedom of exploration is not undermined (Scardamalia, 1989). In addition, heuristics can be used to characterize the relative significance of links among various ideas (e.g., Scardamalia, 1989). A more comprehensive approach, however, is described in Laurillard (1998), where a multiply-linked audio-visual database containing linked commentaries, videos and pictures of archaeological artifacts is built to support learners' exploration. Furthermore, the databases of insights, problems and goals are compiled and accessible to cross-domain searches, so that a keyword search could bring together entries not only from the current context but also from other related domains to facilitate cross-domain knowledge transfer (e.g., Plass & Salisbury, 2002; Schank & Jona, 1991).

Systems response/feedback can also serve as a form of user support by providing feedback on users' actions and inquiries including tool manipulations, resource utilization, and requests for guidance, and the opportunity to receive feedback related to learner actions is critical to understanding (Dhaliwal & Benbasat, 1998; Land & Hannafin, 1996). Unlike conventional approaches, feedback involves more than confirmation of the accuracy of a response. For instance, a program may respond using visual (e.g., video or graphical display of an action), verbal (e.g., textual or aural information), sensory-tactile (simulator movement), or combined representations, related to the problem itself, the strategies used by the learner, or the learning context (Hannafin et al., 1993).

Copyright © 2004, Idea Group Inc. Copying or distributing in print or electronic forms without written permission of Idea Group Inc. is prohibited.

Through feedback, users re-evaluate their beliefs, explore alternative explanations, and revise understanding (Edwards, 1995). It further facilitates the connections among learner actions, intentions, and underlying theories (Land & Hannafin, 1996; Schwartz et al., 1999). However, the mere provision of tools, resources, and feedback does not inherently induce thought-based action and theory development. Users must think and act with intention to generate and solve problems, test ideas, and seek objective feedback related to their exploration (Land & Hannafin, 1996).

Rapid Accessibility with Navigation Aids

In a KM system, navigation is very important to keep users moving toward a goal in an information space encompassing thousands of pages of information, which is not only showing directions, but also building a mental model of the knowledge structure, that is, a cognitive control structure that guides users for effective learning and problem solving (Burk et al., 1998; Choi & Hannafin, 1995). Users who are impulsive, display spatial difficulties, do not possess a prerequisite amount of information, and have less practice with broad goal-oriented learning tasks, may get lost in a complex environment, unable to comprehend the information presented and to identify what information is needed or where to locate it (Chiu & Wang, 2000; Lawless & Brown, 1997). Successful navigation occurs when there is a correspondence between the physical representation of the world and the learners' mental representation of the world. When this correspondence is broken, disorientation occurs, and then learning suffers (Tripp & Roby, 1990). As Shasta (1986) pointed out, movement through multimedia systems is under-constrained without cognitive control structures. Hence, when using a multimedia or Web-based system, behavior tends to become entropic, goal-less, impulsive, and distracted by the many opportunities to browse offered by the system. Therefore, it is essential to provide some navigational aids to promote more explanatory behavior or interaction for users under learner control conditions (Burke et al., 1998).

There is no generic approach to provide navigation aids. In fact, it appears that various types of aids can be valuable cognitive management tools for piloting and navigating vast multimedia information spaces, such as timelines, graphs, navigation map (or browse), narrative sequences, index of the information in a program, hot words embedded in text, guide tool (e.g., suggestions for where to go next in a program), and concept map indicating structure, units, or domain

Copyright © 2004, Idea Group Inc. Copying or distributing in print or electronic forms without written permission of Idea Group Inc. is prohibited.

knowledge (Chiu & Wang, 2000; Scardamalia et al., 1989; Trumbull et al., 1992; Vargas & Alavaz, 1992). The effects of hot words, spider maps and hierarchical maps in a hierarchically organized hypertext have been studied, and the results revealed that learners using the hierarchical map felt significantly less disoriented than the learners using the hot words (Beasley & Waugh, 1995). It is also found that a global map showing the entire hierarchical knowledge structure reduces searching steps of a learner; that is, the larger the map, the better the help (Chiu & Wang, 2000). However, other research found that maps do not necessarily help navigation and reduce disorientation due to increased cognitive load in using the map (Stanton et al., 1992).

On the other hand, concept maps provide a rich view of knowledge and the ability to differentiate among concepts, and they provide a useful way to assess different levels of understanding and cognitive growth (Cliburn, 1990). Concept maps are diagrams that indicate the organization of lesson, unit, or domain knowledge (Vargas & Alartz, 1992). They should represent both primary aspects of a concept as well as their conceptual associations, that is, prior knowledge, which in turn designate both nodes and their corresponding links, and therefore support the learner's efforts to navigate (Park & Hannafin, 1993). Such a visual guide can effectively function as a prior knowledge retrieval plan, where stored knowledge is effectively associated with relationships governing the retrieval context (Hooper & Hannafin, 1991). It may also be used to form relevant associations among current knowledge and prior experience (Hooper & Hannafin, 1991), and cognitive control structure (CTGV, 1993), which are often lacking in users with learning problems.

Discussions

The six factors discussed above, namely media of representation, multiple perspectives, complexity, user control, online support and navigation aids, shed light on their influences on knowledge management from a learning standpoint. The various implementation methods of each factor also provide a base for future development of respective constructs representing these factors. These factors are by no means exhaustive, but they are drawn from a wide range of learning theories, approaches, and practices. In the following sections, the interrelationships, especially the intervening effects among these factors are discussed, which will provide further insight to actual implementa-

Copyright © 2004, Idea Group Inc. Copying or distributing in print or electronic forms without written permission of Idea Group Inc. is prohibited.

tion of KM systems. However, these relationships are projected based on the qualitative analysis, and need to be further verified, preferably through empirical studies in the future.

First of all, media of representation can have major impact on complexity and multiple perspectives, because powerful media such as multimedia can present very complex situations in an effective and efficient manner, which in turn will influence multiple perspectives required in knowledge representation. Since complexity is represented by induced variability, multiple knowledge representation, and multiple interconnections of knowledge components (Spiro et al., 1991), thus the various levels of complexity can be positively determined by the degree of multiple perspectives. Therefore, the selected combination of media will affect the design and implementation of KM programs in terms of complexity and multiple perspectives.

Secondly, in a KM system, complexity also influences navigation aids and online support. A complex learning/training environment will need more learning support to support users' learning and exploration. Also, multiple perspectives would only be achieved when users are given more control of their own learning paths, paces, internal process control, or even goals. Obviously, multiple levels of controls can accommodate users with different abilities, experience and pre-knowledge of a subject/problem/topic concerned. Additionally, measures may also be taken to challenge users to generate or answer questions and hypotheses. Furthermore, it is also a good idea to evaluate a user's learning processes in terms of learning paths, choices made, any repetitions, rehearsals, challenges tackled or even time spent at each step in a program. These data can be valuable to evaluate the performance and achievement of a user, to further examine a user at a cognitive level in terms of learning method, that is, how to study or learn, and to make further improvement of the program.

Thirdly, navigation aids are closely associated with user control. In a complex situation, sufficient aids can reduce the cognitive load of a user when s/he uses the KM system for learning/training purposes; thus it can potentially allow users more control while not creating disorientations. In general, navigation aids can be measured by types of aids such as timelines, hierarchical map, spider map and concept map, extent of these aids in terms of the comprehensiveness, and their accessibility.

Similarly, online support also positively related to user control. When given more user control, users are more likely to encounter difficulties during their exploration and tend to look more frequently for support. Thus, sufficient and

Copyright © 2004, Idea Group Inc. Copying or distributing in print or electronic forms without written permission of Idea Group Inc. is prohibited.

well-placed online support is essential for effective and efficient learning/training. By the same token, online support can be measured by the type of support offered, the comprehensiveness of support provided, and the way that this support is accessed.

From a research point of view, a model can be built that shows the intervening effects among these six factors contributing to learning effectiveness. This chapter certainly has paved the way for constructing such a model, and subsequently conducting in-depth empirical analysis to determine the strength of these relationships as well as integrative influences on learning/training effectiveness. Toward this direction, the measurement variables and their corresponding constructs will have to be developed, refined and validated.

Conclusion

To make knowledge management (KM) systems more effective and successful, they should support users' thinking, reasoning and learning to facilitate decision support, problem solving and knowledge transfer. Particularly, when KM systems are used in training for personal growth and organizational effectiveness, they should be designed paying more attention to modern learning theories.

The review of the learning theory developments indicates that the focus of learning has been shifting from direct instruction of the objectivism to a more opened and learner centered learning process of constructivism. Its implication to KM system development is that KM systems should provide users shared environments for sustained exploration, problem solving and learning. Toward this endeavor, six issues were considered and discussed in the chapter, namely media of representation, complexity, multiple perspective, user control, online support and navigation aids. Under each issue, various strategies and implementation methods were proposed, most of which were based on validated learning research as well as successful applications. It is believed that when a KM system is built inline with the six issues, its training effectiveness as well as for other purposes of use will be significantly improved.

Overall, this chapter provides invaluable insight into the development of KM systems in view of the lack of support of learning theories in many KM applications. It shows how the learning principles can be implemented in a KM

Copyright © 2004, Idea Group Inc. Copying or distributing in print or electronic forms without written permission of Idea Group Inc. is prohibited.

system for effective learning, problem solving and knowledge transfer. For further research, empirical study may be conducted to show actual evidence of improvement in learning effectiveness. Also, additional issues or strategies may be continuously identified and explored.

References

Atkins, M.J. (1993). Theories of learning and multimedia applications: An overview. *Research Papers in Education, 8*(2), 251-271.

Beasley, R.E., & Waugh, ML. (1995). Cognitive mapping architectures and hypermedia disorientation: An empirical study. *Journal of Educational Multimedia and Hypermedia, 4*(2/3), 239-255.

Bednar, A.K., Cunningham, D., Duffy, T.M., & Perry, J.D. (1991). Theory into practice: How do we link? In G.L. Anglin (Ed.), *Instructional technology: Past, present, and future* (pp. 88-101). Englewood, CO: Libraries Unlimited.

Bolloju, N., Khalifa, M., & Turban, E. (2002). Integrating knowledge management into enterprise environments for the next generation decision support. *Decision Support Systems, 33*(2), 163-176.

Bowman, B.J. (2002). Building knowledge management systems. *Information Systems Management, 19*(3), 32-40.

Brown, A.L., Campione, J.C., & Day, J.D. (1981). Learning to learn: On training students to learn from texts. *Educational Researcher, 10*(2), 14-21.

Brush, T.A., Armstrong, J., Barbrow, D., & Ulintz, L. (1999). Design and delivery of integrated learning systems: Their impact on student achievement and attitudes. *Journal of Educational Computing Research, 21*(4), 475-486.

Burke, P.A., Etnier, J.L., & Sullivan, H.L. (1998). Navigational aids and learner control in hypermedia instructional programs. *Journal of Educational Computing Research, 18*(2), 183-196.

Carlile, L.W. (2002). Knowledge management and training: The value of collaboration. *Performance Improvement, 41*(4), 37-43.

Copyright © 2004, Idea Group Inc. Copying or distributing in print or electronic forms without written permission of Idea Group Inc. is prohibited.

Case, R., & Bereiter, C. (1984). From behaviorism to cognitive behaviorism to cognitive development: Steps in the evolution of instructional design. *Instructional Science, 13*(2), 141-158.

Chi, M.T.H., Feltovich, P.J., & Glaser, R. (1981). Categorization and representation of physics problems by experts and novices. *Cognitive Science, 5*(2), 121-152.

Chiu, C., & Wang, F. (2000). The influence of navigation map scope on disorientation of elementary students in learning a Web-based hypermedia course. *Journal of Educational Computing Research, 22*(2), 135-144.

Choi, J., & Hannafin, M. (1995). Situated cognition and learning environments: Roles, structures, and implications for design. *Educational Technology Research and Development, 43*(2), 53-69.

Cliburn, J.W. (1990). Concept maps to promote meaningful learning. *Journal of College Science Teaching, 19*(4), 212-217.

Cobb, T. (1997). Cognitive efficiency: Toward a revised theory of media. *Educational Technology Research and Development, 45*(4), 21-35.

Cognition and Technology Group at Vanderbilt. (1992). The Jasper Experiment: An exploration of issues in learning and instructional design. *Educational Technology Research and Development, 40*(1), 65-80.

Cognition and Technology Group at Vanderbilt. (1993). Examining the cognitive challenges and pedagogical opportunities of integrated media systems: Toward a research agenda. *Journal of Special Education Technology, 8*(2), 119-124.

Cunningham, D.J. (1991). Assessing construction and constructing assessments: A dialogue. *Journal of Educational Technology, 5,* 13-17.

Dhaliwal, J.S., & Benbasat, I. (2001). The use and effects of knowledge-based system explanations: Theoretical foundations and a framework for empirical evaluation. *Information Systems Research, 7*(3), 342-362.

Dick, W. (1991). An instructional designer's view of constructivism. *Educational Technology, 31*(5), 41-44.

Edwards, L.D. (1995). The design and analysis of a mathematical microworld. *Journal of Educational Computing Research, 12*(1), 77-94.

Ertmer, P.A., & Newby, T.J. (1993). Behaviorism, cognitivism, constructivism: Comparing critical features from an instructional design perspective. *Performance Improvement Quarterly, 6*(4), 50-72.

Copyright © 2004, Idea Group Inc. Copying or distributing in print or electronic forms without written permission of Idea Group Inc. is prohibited.

Fahey, L., & Prusak, L. (1998). The eleven deadliest sins of knowledge management. *California Management Review, 40*(3), 265-276.

Gagne, R.M. (1990). Integrative goals for instructional design. *Educational Technology Research and Development, 38*(1), 23-30.

Galup, S.D., Dattero, R., & Hicks, R.C. (2002). Knowledge management systems: An architecture for active and passive knowledge. *Information Resources Management Journal, 15*(1), 22-27.

Gerli, I., & Jaušovec, N. (1999). Multimedia: Differences in cognitive processes observed with EEG. *Educational Technology Research and Development, 47*(3), 5-14.

Gick, M.L., & Holyoak, KJ. (1980). Analogical problem solving. *Cognitive Psychology, 12*(3), 306-365.

Gillingham, M.G. (1988). Text in computer-based instruction: What the research says. *Journal of Computer-Based Instruction, 15*(1), 1-6.

Glaser, R., & Bassok, M. (1989). Learning theory and the study of instruction. *Annual Review of Psychology, 40,* 631-666.

Greeno, J.G. (1989). A perspective on thinking. *American Psychologist, 44*(2), 134-141.

Hannafin, M.J., & Rieber, L.P. (1989). Psychological foundations of instructional design for emerging computer-based instructional technology: Part II. *Educational Technology Research and Development, 37*(2), 102-114.

Hannafin, M.J., Hannafin, KM., & Dalton, DW. (1993). Feedback and emerging instructional technologies. In J. Dempsey & G. Sales (Eds.), *Feedback and interactive instruction* (pp. 263-286). Englewood Cliffs, NJ: Educational Technology Publications.

Harley, S. (1993). Situated learning and classroom instruction. *Educational Technology, 33*(3), 46-51.

Hay, K.E., & Barab, S.A. (2001). Constructivism in practice: A comparison and contrast of apprenticeship and constructionist learning environments. *The Journal of the Learning Sciences, 10*(3), 281-322.

Hicken, S., Sullivan, H., & Klein, J.D. (1992). Learner control modes and incentive variations in computer-delivered instruction. *Educational Technology Research and Development, 40*(4), 15-26.

Hoffman, B., & Rtchie, D. (1997). Using multimedia to overcome the problems with problem based learning. *Instructional Science, 25*(2), 97-115.

Copyright © 2004, Idea Group Inc. Copying or distributing in print or electronic forms without written permission of Idea Group Inc. is prohibited.

Honebein, P.C., Duffy, T.M., & Fishman, B.J. (1993). Constructivism and the design of learning environments: Context and authentic activities for learning. In T.M. Duffy, J. Lowyck & D.H. Jonassen (Eds.), *Designing environments for constructive learning* (pp. 87-108). Heidelberg: Springer-Verlag.

Hooper, S., & Hannafin, M.J. (1991). Psychological perspectives on emerging instructional technologies: A critical analysis. *Educational Psychologist, 26*(1), 69-95.

Horwitch, M., & Armacost, R. (2002). Helping knowledge management be all it can be. *Journal of Business Strategy, 23*(3), 26-31.

Hunter, L., Beaumont, P., & Lee, M. (2002). Knowledge management practice in Scottish law firms. *Human Resource Management Journal, 12*(2), 4-21.

Jenkins, J.J. (1979). Four points to remember: A tetrahedral model and memory experiments. In L.S. Cermak & F.I.M. Craik (Eds.), *Levels and processing in human memory* (pp. 429-446). Hillsdale, NJ: Lawrence Erlbaum.

Jonassen, D.H. (1991). Objectivism versus constructivism: Do we need a new philosophical paradigm? *Educational Technology Research and Development, 39*(3), 5-15.

Jonassen, D.H., & Reeves, T.C. (1996). Learning with technology: Using computers as cognitive tools. In D.H. Jonassen (Ed.), *Handbook of research for educational communications and technology* (pp. 693-719). New York: Macmillan Library Reference.

Jonassen, D.H., & Rohrer-Murphy, L. (1999). Activity theory as a framework for designing constructivist learning environments. *Educational Technology Research and Development, 47*(1), 61-79.

Jonassen, D.H., Campbell, J.P., & Davidson, M.E. (1994). Learning with media: Restructuring the debate. *Educational Technology Research and Development, 42*(2), 31-39.

Land, S.M., & Greene, B.A. (2000). Project-based learning with the World Wide Web: A qualitative study of resource integration. *Educational Technology Research and Development, 48*(1), 45-68.

Land, S.M., & Hannafin, M. (1996). A conceptual framework for the development of theories-in-action with open-ended learning environments. *Educational Technology: Research and Development, 44*(3), 37-53.

Copyright © 2004, Idea Group Inc. Copying or distributing in print or electronic forms without written permission of Idea Group Inc. is prohibited.

Laurillard, D. (1998). Multimedia and the learner's experience of narrative. *Computers & Education, 31*(2), 229-242.

Lawless, K.A., & Brown, S.W. (1997). Multimedia learning environments: Issues of learner control and navigation. *Instructional Science, 25*(2), 117-131.

Lee, S.H., & Boling, E. (1999). Screen design guidelines for motivation in interactive multimedia instruction: A survey and framework for designers. *Educational Technology, 39*(3), 19-26.

Leidner, D.E., & Jarvenpaa, S.L. (1995). The use of information technology to enhance management school education: A theoretical view. *MIS Quarterly, 19*(3), 265-291.

Levin, J.A., & Waugh, M. (1988). Educational simulations, tools, games, and microworlds: Computer-based environments for learning. *Journal of Educational Research. 12*(1), 71-79.

Lewis, E., Stern, J., & Linn, M. (1993). The effect of computer simulations on introductory thermodynamics understanding. *Educational Technology, 33*(1), 45-58.

MacLachlan, J. (1986). Psychologically based techniques for improving learning within computerized tutorials. *Journal of Computer-Based Instruction, 13*(3), 65-70.

Mayer, R.E. (1997). Multimedia learning: Are we asking the right questions? *Educational Psychologist, 32*(1), 1-19.

Mayer, R.E., & Moreno, R. (1998). A split-attention effect in multimedia learning: Evidence for dual processing systems in memory. *Journal of Educational Psychology, 90*(2), 312-320.

McKeachie, W.J. (1990). Research on college teaching: The historical background. *Journal of Educational Psychology, 82*(2), 189-200.

Mendelsohn, P. (1996). Mapping models of cognitive development to design principles of learning environments. In S. Vosniadou, E.D. Corte, R. Glaser & H. Mandl (Eds.), *International perspectives on the design of technology-supported learning environments* (pp. 323-345). Mahwah, NJ: Lawrence Erlbaum Associates.

Miller, G. (1956). The magical number seven, plus or minus two: Some limits on our capacity for processing information. *Psychological Review, 63*(1), 81-97.

Copyright © 2004, Idea Group Inc. Copying or distributing in print or electronic forms without written permission of Idea Group Inc. is prohibited.

Minstrell, J.A. (1989). Teaching science for understanding. In L.B. Resnick & L.E. Klopfer (Eds.), *Toward the thinking curriculum: Current cognitive research* (pp. 129-149). Alexandria, VA: American Society for Curriculum Development.

Murray, P. (2002). Knowledge management as a sustained competitive advantage. *Ivey Business Journal, 66*(4), 71-76.

Nemati, H.R., Steiger, D.M., Iyer, L.S., & Herschel, R.T. (2002). Knowledge warehouse: An architectural integration of knowledge management, decision support, artificial intelligence and data warehousing. *Decision Support Systems, 33*(2), 143-161.

Nicaise, M., & Crane, M. (1999). Knowledge constructing through hypermedia authoring. *Educational Technology Research and Development, 47*(1), 29-50.

Paivio, A., & Wallace, L. (1981). Dual coding and bilingual memory. *Journal of Verbal Learning and Verbal Behavior, 20*(5), 532-539.

Park, I., & Hannafin, M.J. (1993). Empirically-based guidelines for the design of interactive multimedia. *Educational Technology Research and Development, 41*(3), 63-85.

Park, O. (1984). Empirically based procedures for designing a response-sensitive sequence in computer-based instruction: An example from concept-teaching strategies. *Journal of Computer-Based Instruction, 11*(1), 14-18.

Perfetto, G.A., Bransford, J.D., & Franks, J.J. (1983). Constrains on access in problem solving context. *Memory & Cognition, 11*(1), 24-31.

Plass, J.L., & Salisbury, M.W. (2002). A living-systems design model for Web-based knowledge management systems. *Educational Technology Research & Development, 50*(1), 35-57.

Resnick, L.B. (1987). Learning in school and out. *Educational Researcher, 16*(9), 13-20.

Rieber, L.P. (1992). Computer-based microworlds: A bridge between constructivism and direct instruction. *Educational Technology Research and Development, 40*(1), 93-106.

Ruggles, R. (1998). The state of the notion: Knowledge management in practice. *California Management Review, 40*(3), 80-89.

Copyright © 2004, Idea Group Inc. Copying or distributing in print or electronic forms without written permission of Idea Group Inc. is prohibited.

Scardamalia, M., Bereiter, C., Mclean, R.S., Swallow, J., & Woodruff, E. (1989). Computer-supported intentional learning environments. *Journal of Educational Computing Research, 5*(1), 51-68.

Schank, R.C. (1993). Learning via multimedia computers. *Communications of the ACM, 36*(5), 54-56.

Schank, R.C., & Jona, M.Y. (1991). Empowering the student: New perspectives on the design of teaching systems. *Journal of the Learning Sciences, 1*(1), 7-35.

Schwartz, D., Brophy, S., Lin, X., & Bransford, J. (1999). Software for managing complex learning: Examples from an educational psychology course. *Educational Technology Research and Development, 47*(2), 39-59.

Shasta, D. (1986). *Netbook: A data model to support knowledge exploration.* Courant Institute, New York University.

Shuell, T.J. (1990). Phases of meaningful learning. *Review of Educational Research, 60*(4), 531-547.

Silber, K.H. (1998). The cognitive approach to training development: A practitioner's assessment. *Educational Technology Research and Technology, 46*(4), 58-72.

Smith, B.K., & Blankinship, E. (2000). Justifying imagery: Multimedia support for learning through explanation. *IBM Systems Journal, 39*(3/4), 749-767.

Spiro, R.J., Feltovich, P.L., Jacobson, M.L., & Coulson, R.L. (1991). Cognitive flexibility, constructivism, and hypertext: Random access instruction for advanced knowledge acquisition in ill-structured domains. *Educational Technology, 31*(5), 24-33.

Stanton, N.A., Taylor, R.G., & Tweedie, L.A. (1992). Maps as navigational aids in hypertext environments: An empirical evaluation. *Journal of Educational Multimedia and Hypermedia, 1*(4), 431-444.

Tobin, K., & Dawson, G. (1992). Constraints to curriculum reform: Teachers and the myths of schooling. *Educational Technology Research and Development, 40*(1), 81-92.

Tripp, S.D., & Roby, W. (1990). Orientation and disorientation in a hypertext lexicon. *Journal of Computer-Based Instruction, 17*(4), 120-124.

Copyright © 2004, Idea Group Inc. Copying or distributing in print or electronic forms without written permission of Idea Group Inc. is prohibited.

Trumbull, D., Gay, G., & Mazur, J. (1992). Students' actual and perceived use of navigational and guidance tools in a hypermedia program. *Journal of Research on Computing in Education, 24*(3), 315-328.

Vargas, E.M., & Alvarez, H.J. (1992). Mapping out students' abilities. *Science Scope, 15*(6), 41-43.

Wetzel, C.D., Radtke, P.H., & Stern, H.W. (1994). *Instructional effectiveness of video media.* Hillsdale, NJ: Lawrence Erlbaum Associates.

Winn, W. (1990). Some implications of cognitive theory for instructional design. *Instructional Science, 19*(1), 53-69.

Zack, M.H. (1999). Managing codified knowledge. *Sloan Management Review, 40*(4), 45-58.

Zahner, J. (2002). Teachers explore knowledge management and e-learning as models for professional development. *TechTends, 46*(3), 11-16.

Copyright © 2004, Idea Group Inc. Copying or distributing in print or electronic forms without written permission of Idea Group Inc. is prohibited.

Chapter VIII

Web Service Modeling Framework for the Enhanced Data Warehouse

Krzysztof Wecel
The Poznan University of Economics, Poland

Pawel Jan Kalczynski
University of Toledo, USA

Witold Abramowicz
The Poznan University of Economics, Poland

Abstract

This chapter presents how Web services architecture can be leveraged to extend an existing system to an open and flexible platform. It reviews crucial issues related to modularization, properties of the Web services, integration of heterogeneous services and incorporating new services. We describe the modeling framework used, which is the Web Service Modeling Framework (WSMF). As a case we show how the enhanced data warehouse system was remodeled in order to transform it from a closed solution to an open Web services-based system called the enhanced Knowledge

Copyright © 2004, Idea Group Inc. Copying or distributing in print or electronic forms without written permission of Idea Group Inc. is prohibited.

Warehouse (eKW). We analyze eKW as a Web service and show how eKW conforms to the eight layers of functionality in Web services. We also speculate about the future of eKW in the semantic web and innovations it can contribute to knowledge management. In the semantic Web eDW should be used as a source of knowledge, hence the name "knowledge warehouse".

Introduction

Until now the Web has focused on publishing information that is readable primarily by humans. However, recently more and more attention has been paid to processing information automatically by computers. To achieve this goal, sophisticated systems are designed. They use various techniques of artificial intelligence, for example, shallow text processing (Neumann & Piskorski, 2002).

Tim Berners-Lee suggested another solution – to create the Web so that it can be easily processable by machines. Such a Web is called the *semantic Web* (Berners-Lee, Hendler & Lasilla, 2001).

Another issue is making a computer application accessible through the Web. The ultimate vision is that of the Web as a distributed computation device.

According to the IBM Web Services Tutorial, "web services are a new breed of web applications. They are self-contained, self-describing, modular applications that can be published, located, and invoked across the Web" (Leymann, 2001).

The idea we extend in this chapter was originally called the *enhanced Data Warehouse* (eDW) (Abramowicz, Kalczynski & Wecel, 2002). As a response to numerous proposals to improve the original concept of data warehousing, (e.g., Gray & Watson, 1998; Nemati et al., 2002), eDW extends the existing enterprise data warehouse with unstructured information filtered from selected sources on the Web. eDW was primarily designed as a closed system; that is, only users of a particular data warehouse could take advantage of this solution. Moreover, eDW was entirely based on internal modules without taking advantage of other systems. According to recently observed trends, we decided to re-engineer the architecture of the eDW system.

Copyright © 2004, Idea Group Inc. Copying or distributing in print or electronic forms without written permission of Idea Group Inc. is prohibited.

Background

eDW is an agent-based system that allows the automatic filtering of information from the Web to the data warehouse and automatic retrieval of this information through the data warehouse (Abramowicz, Kalczynski & Wecel, 2002). The overview of the system is presented in Figure 1.

Components of the eDW system were divided into two main types: agents and servers. Software agents are software entities that carry out some set of operations on behalf of a user or another program with some degree of independence or autonomy, and in so doing, employ some knowledge or representation of the user's goals or desires (Grosof & Kephart, n.d.). In turn, servers are components that are responsible for creating agents, serving as a contact point for agents, and storing the complete knowledge of the eDW agents.

The eDW system comprises four main servers:

- Profiling Server – personalizes the data warehouse and discovers the long-term information needs of data warehouse users.

Figure 1. Overview of the enhanced data warehouse (Abramowicz, Kalczynski & Wecel, 2002).

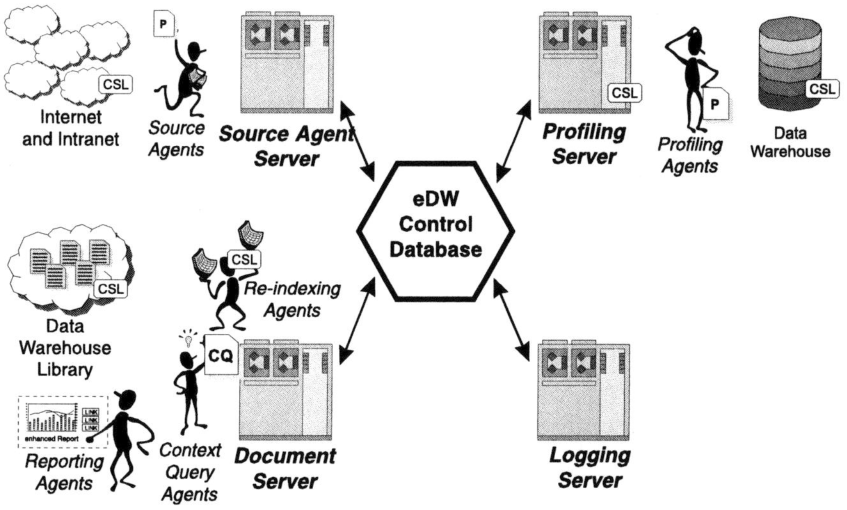

Copyright © 2004, Idea Group Inc. Copying or distributing in print or electronic forms without written permission of Idea Group Inc. is prohibited.

- Source Agent Server – explores pre-defined sources of information and searches for potentially interesting documents that would satisfy information needs discovered earlier.
- Document Server – handles documents once they are acquired to the system; presents users with documents relevant to data warehouse reports in response to their short-term information needs.
- Logging Server – tracks all the activity of servers, agents, and users.

Each server is accompanied by its agents that act in the environment for which they were designed, that is, the Web, data warehouse, and digital library, to complete their tasks.

In the original concept of eDW, the profiling server was used to discover long-term information needs of data warehouses and to store these needs as profiles (Abramowicz, Kalczynski & Wecel, 2001). The profiles were then used by the source agent server to filter relevant documents from the Web, and store them in the data warehouse library (Abramowicz, Kalczynski & Wecel, 2001). Documents were accessed by users through the document server that responded to context queries, which represent temporary, short-term information needs of users.

The originally proposed eDW system has many features that distinguish it from other information systems. These advantages point us in the direction in which the eDW should be further developed and improved. The new version of the system should be:

- *flexible:* the presented four server components of the system can be developed separately, but they should be able to communicate in a formalized manner
- *extensible:* the new components can be easily added to the system, especially specialized agents for different Internet sources or data warehouses
- *distributed:* the agents and the servers can be run on different machines; therefore we are not limited by local computational resources and load-balancing is made possible
- *learning:* the agents can extend and share knowledge acquired while interacting with users and also build up the knowledge base by inferencing

Copyright © 2004, Idea Group Inc. Copying or distributing in print or electronic forms without written permission of Idea Group Inc. is prohibited.

- *adaptive:* the addition of new information sources requires learning just a few new parameters or at most creating a new source agent that will specialize in this source, while the rest of the systems remain unchanged

The original eDW has some drawbacks that should be addressed in the new implementation. One is related to retrieving new information from external sources to the data warehouse library. These sources are usually heterogeneous and they require creating specialized agents. Therefore, it is justified to join the forces of different communities that try to automate the process of information acquisition.

Another weak part of eDW is the component responsible for matching documents with information needs. This important issue is addressed later in this chapter. We need a better integration with external information providers in order to serve user needs better.

All these considerations are related to the new trend in application development and architectures – Web services. An open interface that we need can be implemented as Web services. If this can be accomplished we will be able to easily integrate with content providers, use other services that we do not have (e.g., extract information from CNN financial news), and also offer and sell our services to other external entities. Therefore, the remaining part of this chapter is devoted to new concepts that can help in overcoming the existing problems with eDW and in transforming it into a Web service-based solution – the enhanced knowledge warehouse.

Web Service Modeling Framework

In order to model eDW in terms of the new architecture, we need an appropriate framework. We decided to use a full-fledged Web service modeling framework, and we will briefly describe it below. The Web service modeling framework (WSMF) is based on two principles (Fensel & Bussler, 2002):

- strong *de-coupling* of the various components that realize a business application, and

Copyright © 2004, Idea Group Inc. Copying or distributing in print or electronic forms without written permission of Idea Group Inc. is prohibited.

- strong *mediation* service enabling anyone to exchange information with anyone else.

The first principle requires that any complex service should be decomposed into a number of smaller modules. Therefore, as the first change in the architecture, eDW was decomposed into five services that can act independently. These are:

a) *Profiling Service,* evolved from the profiling server
b) *Filtering Service,* previously the source agent server
c) *Indexing Service,* derived from the back-office part of the document server
d) *Library Service,* the former data warehouse library (DWL), derived from the document server
e) *Reporting Service,* derived from the front-office part of the document server

The second principle states how to connect the de-coupled services together. This is achieved by mediation of different vocabularies as well as by different interaction styles. The principle behind the approach presented in WSMF is to provide a scalable interoperability among services.

Web service modeling framework consists of four main elements: ontologies, goal repositories, Web services, and mediators, which are described in detail below.

Ontologies

Ontologies are considered a key enabling technology for the semantic Web. Thanks to them, it is possible to represent knowledge that is understandable for humans and readable for computers (Fensel, 2001). According to the formal and the most often cited definition (Gruber, 1995), an ontology is a "formal explicit specification of a shared conceptualization".

When it comes to the application areas, we can point out the following (Gruninger & Lee, 2002):

Copyright © 2004, Idea Group Inc. Copying or distributing in print or electronic forms without written permission of Idea Group Inc. is prohibited.

a) communication:
- between computer systems
- between people
- human-computer interaction

b) inferencing:
- for internal representation and manipulation of information
- for the analysis of internal structures, algorithms, inputs, outputs of the implemented system in the conceptual modeling

c) knowledge reuse and organization:
- for structuralization and organization of libraries.

In WSMF, the ontology provides the terminology that is used by all other WSMF elements.

Ontologies define the following:

- *formal semantics*, allowing information to be processed by a computer
- *real-world semantics*, linking the machine-processable content with certain meaning for a human user.

Goal Repositories

A *goal* is an objective that a client may achieve while in contact with a Web service. A goal specification consists of two elements (Fensel & Bussler, 2002):

- pre-conditions, that is, what a service expects as an input
- post-conditions, that is, what a service returns as an output.

It is advised that goal specifications are kept separately from actual Web service descriptions, because one service can help in achieving different goals and one goal can be achieved by employing different services.

What is stressed in WSMF is that the goal should be precisely described. This is achieved by utilizing ontologies in the goal specification.

Copyright © 2004, Idea Group Inc. Copying or distributing in print or electronic forms without written permission of Idea Group Inc. is prohibited.

Table 1. Goal repositories in eKW.

Service	pre-conditions	post-conditions
Profiling	- information system (e.g., data warehouse)	- profiles
Library	- context query	- relevant documents
Filtering	- profiles	- relevant documents
Reporting	- data warehouse report	- *enhanced report*
Indexing	- Web document	- document indices

In eKW the ontology is utilized to build profiles and context queries. In a natural way they are well-defined pre-condition goal specifications. In particular, profiles specify what documents should be returned by the filtering service, and context queries specify what documents should be returned by the library service, for example, documents for a given period, for a given subject, by a selected author, of a specified length, and so forth.

The eKW goal repositories are presented in Table 1.

Web Service

In a general sense, a Web service is complex when it is composed of other services. However, in the WSMF there is a specific distinction between elementary and complex services. The criterion that matters is a complexity of service description (its interface).

According to WSMF, eKW is considered a simple Web service, although it consists of a number of sub-services (see Figure 2). Private processes are hidden from external users, and only external aspects (interfaces) of the service are taken into account when determining the complexity of the system.

There are some issues that should be discussed in more detail. Web service descriptions, like these of the goals, contain pre-conditions and post-conditions. These conditions can be linked directly or indirectly (via a mediator) to goal conditions. In the second case a Web service can strengthen a pre-condition, that is, more parameters are required, or weaken a post-condition of a goal, because not all results of the Web service fulfill the goal descriptions. When applied to the library service of eKW, these considerations resemble the precision-recall tradeoff known from the information retrieval systems area. The stronger the goal conditions, the more accurate the results are, and the smaller number of documents is returned.

Copyright © 2004, Idea Group Inc. Copying or distributing in print or electronic forms without written permission of Idea Group Inc. is prohibited.

Going down to the technical architecture level, we notice that a concurrent service binding method should be introduced in eKW. In this case, it would be possible to choose different Web services for the same task; for example, in eKW we can use different specialized indexing services. For example, if our service does not know how to parse and index Adobe PDF files, we can use another service to perform this task.

For each service in eKW we can declare an *invoked Web service proxy.* This is useful when one Web service may invoke other Web services to provide its service. For example, the reporting service has to invoke the profiling service in order to obtain the profile of the user report. The proxy allows referring to the Web service, without defining which Web service will be invoked. The binding takes place during runtime, which is similar to late binding in programming. Moreover, different profiling services may be called for different types of reports.

Special attention should be paid to errors. Complex services may use specialized *error ports.* If a Web service performs long transactions, it should inform the service requester about it. For example, the filtering service requires time to find appropriate documents on the Web. Sometimes Web services include concurrent data input and output streams. For example, the reporting service may negotiate input parameters, such as specifying more accurate time constraints, and requesting more or fewer documents in the list with the library service. If the library service does not return any documents that meet the criteria specified in the context query, the reporting service may negotiate different input parameters (weaker conditions) with the user.

Mediator

The concept of a mediator was developed in heterogeneous and distributed information systems. A mediator translates user queries into sub-queries on different information sources and integrates the sub-answers (Wiederhold, 1992).

WSMF distinguishes different types of mediation: mediation of data structures, business logics, message exchange protocols, and dynamic service invocation (Fensel & Bussler, 2002). Actually, the entire eKW is a data structure mediator. It allows mediation between a data warehouse and the Web. Therefore, other types of mediations will not be analyzed in this chapter.

Copyright © 2004, Idea Group Inc. Copying or distributing in print or electronic forms without written permission of Idea Group Inc. is prohibited.

Data could be mediated by direct mapping, for example, using XSL-T rules for XML documents. However, this technique is rather inefficient, especially when the number of services increases. Omelayenko and Fensel (2001) suggest a layered integration architecture, in which the mediation of data structures can be solved in two steps:

1. intermediate data model and three sub-steps: extract, map, rewrite; to cope with different syntactical standards
2. intermediate conceptualization (i.e., ontology); to cope with the number of mappings.

Mediation could be a Web service itself; hence the idea of eKW as a Web service. There is one interface for the Web, but many interfaces for different data warehouse implementations. Also, other decision support systems may be taken into account.

eKW as a Web Service

To consider eKW a Web service, we need to analyze Web services in more detail. Fensela and Bussler (2002) and Bussler (2001) identified eight layers necessary to achieve automatic Web service decomposition into complex services. They are discussed in this section. First, we need to distinguish and define different document types that will be exchanged within the eKW system.

Document Types

Document types describe the content of business documents, and are defined in terms of elements. They are instantiated when the service requester and provider exchange data.

In eKW we have to distinguish at least the following document types:

- *profile:* representation of relatively constant user information needs, that can be automatically built based on the content of the information system (e.g., the data warehouse in eDW)

Copyright © 2004, Idea Group Inc. Copying or distributing in print or electronic forms without written permission of Idea Group Inc. is prohibited.

- *context query:* unlike the profile, it defines temporary user information needs that result from the user activity and interactions with this information system in everyday work (e.g., looking for the information about companies-clients that made the highest-value purchases in our outlets)
- *Web documents:* documents retrieved from the Web (e.g., HTML, XML, PDF)
- *indices:* representations of Web documents that can be matched with profiles or context queries (e.g., weighted vectors of keywords)
- *ranked list of Web documents:* the system's response to a profile or a context query.

Semantics

Documents should be semantically correct. This ensures that they are properly interpreted. One of the most popular ways to conform to the semantics is to use *ontologies,* which provide a means for defining the concepts of the exchanged data. Documents may refer to the ontology concepts; therefore the system knows proper element values. This ensures consistency and allows the same interpretation by all participants of the data exchange process.

Originally, the semantic layer in eDW was provided by the *common semantic layer* (CSL) (Abramowicz, Kalczynski & Wecel, 2001). It was defined as a set of concepts used to index documents. The main drawback of this solution was the lack of explicitly-defined relations between terms. Moreover, CSL was only used to index documents and not to represent any knowledge in the system.

In eKW, we introduce ontologies to express semantics, and also supply the system with learning capabilities. The ontology occupies a central place in the model. Because eKW is primarily designed to satisfy user information needs, these needs should be specifically well described. Both profiles and context queries are expressed in terms of ontologies. The on-going D-Leap project at the PoznaD University of Economics (Poland) aims at developing ontologies for representing user skills, so-called skill maps (Abramowicz, Kowalkiewicz & Zawadzki, 2002). From these maps we can derive organizational capabilities, which create a broader context for information retrieval and filtering tasks. User information needs are the function of capabilities of the organization, the user's skills, and projects that the user is working on.

Copyright © 2004, Idea Group Inc. Copying or distributing in print or electronic forms without written permission of Idea Group Inc. is prohibited.

Table 2. Intentions in eKW in relation to document types.

Document	Intentions
Profile	- create a new profile - store the profile in a database - search for documents (request for filtering)
Context query	- create a new query - search for documents (request for retrieval)
Indices	- create new indices (for a given document) - store indices in a database as semantic descriptions of documents
Web document	- filter from the Web - store in a library - retrieve from a library - deliver to the user
list of Web documents	- compose the list - present the list to a user

While talking about exchanging documents, we also have to define the intents of the message exchange, which are summarized in Table 2.

Process Definition

When implementing Web services, it is important to define the business message exchange sequence. The business logic of eKW is presented in Figure 2.

The central module of eKW is the library service (former data warehouse library). The first block of the processes refers to so called *transparent filtering*. The initial step is to find out what kind of information should be collected. Therefore the library service consults the profiling service to get some representation of information needs (profiles). Then it can formulate new filtering criteria and pass them to the filtering service. When the new documents that meet the criteria are found on the Internet, they are sent to the library service. In order to organize them, the library service sends documents to the indexing service, and receives their indices: subject and temporal (Kalczynski et al., 2003). Thus the documents are ready for retrieval.

The second block of processes, referred to as *transparent retrieval,* starts with a request for the report, submitted by a user. The user expects to get a data warehouse report accompanied by a list of documents relevant to this report,

Copyright © 2004, Idea Group Inc. Copying or distributing in print or electronic forms without written permission of Idea Group Inc. is prohibited.

Figure 2. Message exchange sequence in eKW.

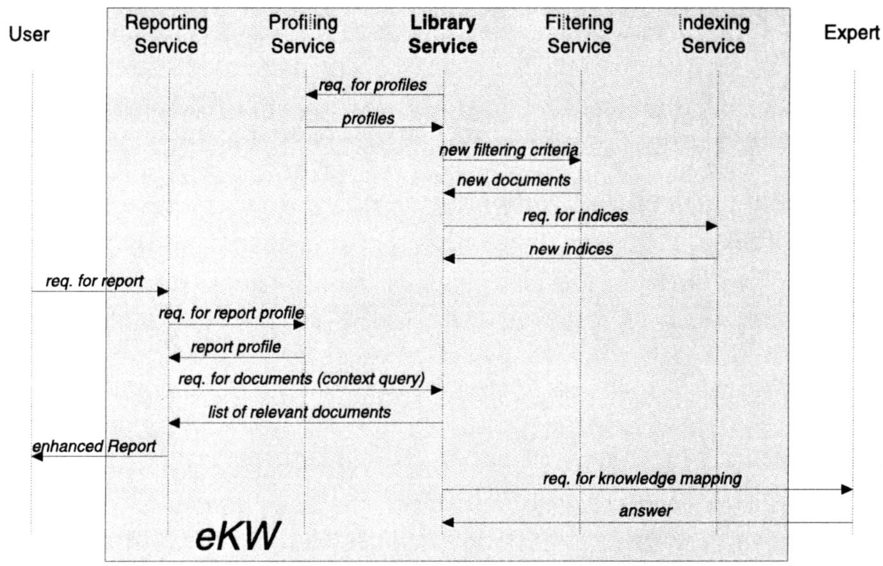

automatically retrieved by the system. The request is handled by the reporting service. In order to retrieve relevant documents, the profile of the report is required. This profile can be obtained from the profiling service and it describes a report in terms of the ontology that allows matching documents with the report. Based on the profile, the time constraints of the report, and some sophisticated algorithms (Abramowicz, Kalczynski & Wecel, 2002, pp. 231-258), the reporting service builds an appropriate context query and submits it to the library service. In response, the library service returns a set of documents. Finally, the reporting service prepares the *enhanced report.*

The final block of processes allows improving the knowledge of library service by consulting external experts. When some documents cannot be found automatically, an expert can suggest the matching and changes in ontologies.

Other Layers of a Web Service

Transport Binding

There are plenty of data transport mechanisms available at the moment. The most popular are HTTP and HTTPS. It is also possible to use FTP or even SMTP when exchange is asynchronous. Prior to the exchange of data, the

Copyright © 2004, Idea Group Inc. Copying or distributing in print or electronic forms without written permission of Idea Group Inc. is prohibited.

service requester and provider have to agree on the protocol. eKW will not use any sophisticated mechanism beyond SOAP, and so HTTP was considered the most appropriate.

Exchange Sequence Definition

Due to the unreliability of networks, service providers have to define a sequence of acknowledgement messages. Each message should be transmitted only once. This is a technical issue and it will not be addressed separately in eKW.

Security

Security is also a technical issue, and eKW will utilize standardized solutions. These solutions should provide encryption to ensure privacy and also signing to ensure non-repudiation.

Syntax

The most popular syntax is XML, and it was selected for eKW. For storing ontologies, we can consider a language that allows higher abstraction levels and controls better what actually is stored in files. One of them is the resource description framework (RDF) (Beckett, 2003), but there are also some languages for storing ontologies, the DARPA agent markup Language (DAML) (Hendler & McGuinness, 2001), the ontology inference language (OIL), and recently the Web ontology language (OWL) (McGuinness & Van Harmelon, 2003).

Trading Partner Specific Configuration

Each service requester or provider has different business logic. When partners want to cooperate, they have to start with some adjustments of these logics. Interaction should be formalized when using the Web services.

Copyright © 2004, Idea Group Inc. Copying or distributing in print or electronic forms without written permission of Idea Group Inc. is prohibited.

Future Trends

Consistency of Web Documents and Data: A Knowledge Management Case

Although we describe the consistency of documents and data in the enhanced knowledge warehouse, the principles behind the idea may be applied to other business information systems. By definition, the data warehouse is an integrated, subject oriented, non-volatile and time-variant collection of organizational data (Gray & Watson, 1998). In order to introduce consistency among Web documents and data, the library service must enjoy similar features. Hence, documents are never removed from the library; all documents are properly described with metadata and dynamically linked to data warehouse objects when a system request for document is being processed. There are four levels of consistency (contexts) between the Web documents and DW that enable the eKW system to build context queries: subject context, temporal context, semantic context and personal context. These four contexts together provide constraints for sub-setting documents accessible through the library service and producing relatively small ranked lists of relevant documents associated with data warehouse reports.

Three of the four contexts are encoded in the context query produced by the library service each time a user requests a new state of any data warehouse report. Personalization is applied by the reporting service right before the results of the context query are returned to the user.

To illustrate how the context query is created in eKW let us define the SUBSET operation on the set of Web documents, such that SUBSET(*document_set, constraints*)=*document_subset*.

Subject Consistency

In eKW all documents accessible through the library service should match at least one version of any profile. Profiles are built for metadata objects; thus each document is linked to one or more nodes in business metadata. Because warehouse elements are organized hierarchically in metadata, a structure of document clusters based on the metadata hierarchy emerges. These clusters may overlap, but they provide the first level of sub-setting Web documents for the purpose of extending the data warehouse report. The desired detail level of

Copyright © 2004, Idea Group Inc. Copying or distributing in print or electronic forms without written permission of Idea Group Inc. is prohibited.

sub-setting may be preset and changed. The subset of documents linked to the present node (object) and to all children of this node (recursively) can serve as an example.

Subject consistency among Web documents and the data warehouse is based on the assumption that only documents that belong to the warehouse subject of the report are considered relevant to this report.

Once a report is launched, the collection of Web documents (D) is mechanically subset to a smaller collection of documents, which are linked to the warehouse context of a given report. In other words:

$$S1 = \text{SUBSET}(D, \text{Subject}).$$

Because at the filtering stage all documents that have at least one term similar with at least one profile were accepted, subject consistency produces relatively large subsets of documents. Hence, more rigid constraints must be introduced to produce more precise results.

Temporal Consistency

The principal assumption of temporal consistency in the eKW system is that documents that are irrelevant to time constraints specified are completely irrelevant to information consumers' needs. Hence, measuring temporal consistency should precede measuring semantic consistency among the Web documents and DW reports.

Time constraints may be easily extracted from the current view of any data warehouse report. The constraints are usually organized into granules of predefined granularities, for example, years, quarters, months or weeks, and this may facilitate optimization of measuring temporal consistency.

In our model, we assumed that the time constraints of a data warehouse report might be represented as a single weighted range in time (weight=1). However, one may think of more complex constraints like "every first week of March, April and May between 1999 and 2002".

Having temporal references extracted from Web documents, it is possible to measure temporal consistency among the aforementioned range and the temporal representation of every document. This could be done by various methods (Berlanga et al., 2001; Kalczynski, 2002; Kalczynski et al., 2003).

Copyright © 2004, Idea Group Inc. Copying or distributing in print or electronic forms without written permission of Idea Group Inc. is prohibited.

As a result of applying time constraints of the report, the following subset of the library Service collection emerges:

$$S2 = SUBSET(S1, time) = SUBSET(SUBSET(D, subject), time).$$

Due to its sub-setting power, temporal context plays a key role in eKW.

Semantic Consistency

Semantic consistency among Web documents and data warehouse reports is based on the extension of profiles. Since the current profiles for a given report exist in the eKW system, they may be adjusted to the current view of the data warehouse report. For instance, if a user drills down to the certain product name, only this name – not the whole inventory – will provide input for further sub-setting of the collection. Unlike subject and temporal contexts, semantic context cannot be applied with SQL statements. Instead, it is based on measuring angular distances among document representation (indices) and semantic context representations (queries). After computing this distance, all documents that match the query with the value greater than an arbitrary threshold are included in the resulting subset.

$$S3 = SUBSET(S2, semantic)$$
$$= SUBSET(SUBSET(SUBSET(D, subject), time), semantic)$$

However, the same data warehouse reports may be viewed by many different users. This means that S3 for a given state of the report may not look the same for all eKW users. In order to intersect individuals' long-term information interests with documents, one more level of sub-setting is introduced in eKW - personalization.

Personalization

Personalization is the final level of assuring consistency among Web documents and data warehouse reports in the eKW system. It is based on the implicit

Copyright © 2004, Idea Group Inc. Copying or distributing in print or electronic forms without written permission of Idea Group Inc. is prohibited.

feedback technique that enables the system to learn about an individual's information interests by analyzing his or her actions (e.g., view, print, hide). As it is distinct from the subject, temporal and semantic contexts, personalization is maintained by the reporting service. The reporting service records user actions and converts them into a personalized profile. This profile is then used to filter and reorder S3. Techniques for reordering and filtering query results with a profile are known as document scoring. Those documents, for which the value of the score measure is above an arbitrary threshold, are included in the final subset.

S4 = SUBSET(S3, personal)

= SUBSET(SUBSET(SUBSET(SUBSET(D, subject), time), semantic), personal)

When the library service executes an appropriate query for a given state of the report, the reporting service scores the results according to individual user profiles, creates a ranked list and presents it with the data warehouse report to the user. Thus, the enhanced report emerges as the final product of the system.

One may think of other contexts (e.g., localization, status) that may be useful for further subsetting of document collections. We believe that the four contexts used to subset a document collection in eKW are sufficient for automated (transparent) document retrieval. Future research may include studying the potential application of context queries in various information systems.

eKW in the Semantic Web

The semantic Web will provide access to heterogeneous and distributed information, thus enabling software products to mediate between user needs and the information sources available. On the other hand, the Web is a huge collection of information, and there are no means to process this information. SWWS (semantic Web-enabled Web services) is a combination of Web services together with the semantic Web.

For the proper functioning of the semantic Web the following elements are required (Berners-lee, Hendler & Lasilla, 2001):

Copyright © 2004, Idea Group Inc. Copying or distributing in print or electronic forms without written permission of Idea Group Inc. is prohibited.

- information sources with a specific structure
- sets of the inference rules that allows automatic drawing of conclusions
- sets of information called ontologies.

If we want to take advantages of the semantic Web to further develop eKW, we have to make it accessible through the Web. eDW is modularized, so we were able to easily transform each module into a self-contained service. The main role of eKW in the semantic Web is mediation. eKW is a kind of data mediator that employs ontologies as a conceptualization layer. This implies that one of the most important things that should be developed within eKW is ontologies. The first phase in the evolution of the semantic Web will most likely be to develop decentralized and adaptive ontologies (Kim, 2002). Business related ontologies should be developed first. The necessary mediation between different information systems could be then carried out based on the ontologies. The use of ontologies would also allow better representation of user information needs.

Introduction of ontologies is a straightforward consequence of the architecture of the semantic Web, which, similarly to the Internet, will be decentralized. Traditional systems of knowledge representation were usually centralized; they required identical definitions of shared concepts. Those systems were hardly flexible, and it was hard to add new vocabulary or inference rules. In the semantic Web various communities can create their own concepts, which, thanks to the ontology, can be mapped onto other concepts, whether their own or belonging to another community.

The creators of the semantic Web assume that it will be primarily used by software agents. Thus, the language for those agents is required. Information is properly structuralized in XML, and the semantic is stored with resource description framework (RDF). RDF demonstrates how ontologies can be stored and is widely utilized by other standards. New directions of research show that information agents together with ontologies can provide breakthrough technologies for Web applications.

The semantic Web should not only provide better access to data and information (content) but also to services. One of the most important languages for eKW is DAML-S, the DARPA agent markup language with ontology for services (Ankolenkar et al., 2001). It is the ontology for services, and should make it possible to discover, invoke, compose, and monitor Web resources,

Copyright © 2004, Idea Group Inc. Copying or distributing in print or electronic forms without written permission of Idea Group Inc. is prohibited.

which offer particular services and have particular properties. DAML-S could be then used as the service profile for advertising services.

The most important elements of DAML-S are structure of the ontology, service profile to be advertised, and the process model for the detailed description of the service functioning. So far, the DAML-S working group has developed the so-called *upper ontology,* which consists of ontologies for profiles, processes and time. Further work is carried out on ontologies designed for controlling the processes.

The ancestor of all classes representing services is Service class. The interdependences between classes are illustrated in Figure 3.

For description of the service we need the following information:

- what the service requires from the user: the answer for this question is contained in a profile, so the service has to *present* `ServiceProfile`
- how the service works: the answer is contained in a model, so the service has to be *described by* `ServiceModel`
- how we can use the service: the answer is contained in a `Service Grounding`.

Figure 3. Specification of the services in DAML-S (Ankolenkar et al., 2001).

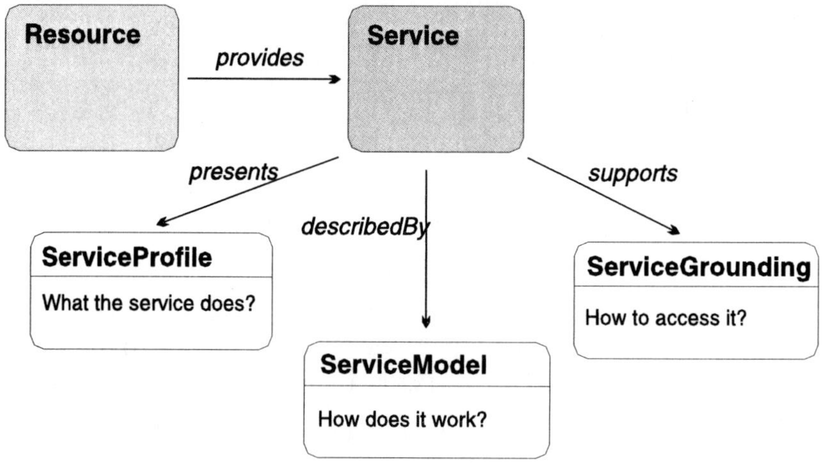

Copyright © 2004, Idea Group Inc. Copying or distributing in print or electronic forms without written permission of Idea Group Inc. is prohibited.

The service profile provides three types of information:

- human-readable description of the service and its provider
- specification of the functionality offered by a service
- additional attributes for distinguishing the service, for example, quality of service, expected response time, geographical restrictions.

The service model describes how processes are executed. The basic class here is `Process`. It is characterized by many features, but the most important are input parameters. Three types of processes are distinguished:

- `AtomicProcess`, containing no sub-processes, can be directly invoked
- `SimpleProcess`, executed in one step, but cannot be directly invoked; realized by an atomic process or developed into composite process
- `CompositeProcess`, a process composed of sub-processes.

Grounding specifies details of the service interface. Usually, it contains communication protocols, with additional parameters, for example, port numbers. Also, it should specify an unambiguous way of exchanging data with the service.

Knowledge Supply Chain Management

Knowledge supply chain management (KSCM) is a particular case of the adaptive knowledge chain management (Wecel, Zalech & Jakubowski, 2003). Forrester defines adaptive supply networks as business networks of supply chain partners that use technology to sense changes in their environment and to respond to them. Adaptive knowledge chain arises when providers of knowledge are not official members of the chain, that is, they are not known in advance, when the chain is defined.

KSCM is used originally to introduce new technologies. We assume that mainly external (to the company) sources of knowledge are utilized. Every member can retrieve knowledge from many sources, enhance it, and sell it to many external entities. Members can also request knowledge from their predeces-

Copyright © 2004, Idea Group Inc. Copying or distributing in print or electronic forms without written permission of Idea Group Inc. is prohibited.

Figure 4. Knowledge supply chain.

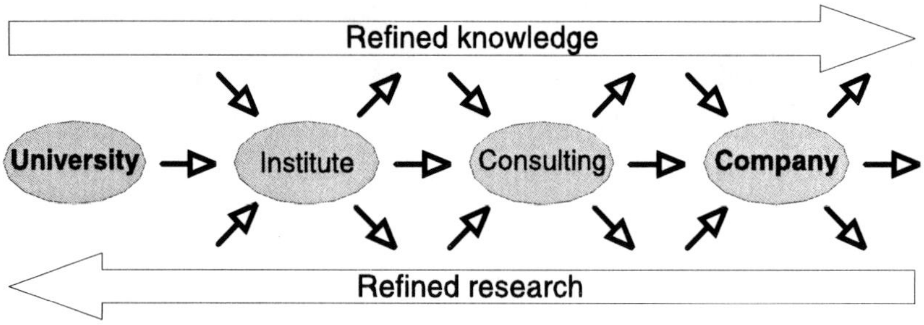

sors. Complex solutions are created by cumulating knowledge of many members. The hypothetical configuration of a chain is depicted in Figure 4.

In order to make the collaboration between partners possible, they have to integrate their internal knowledge management systems. In the KSCM solution we proposed to use the eKW system. eKW is responsible for transferring knowledge between partners. eKW is capable of filtering new information from preceding members based on the information needs of the chain member. In fact, eKW joins the D-Leaps that serve as electronic marketplaces for knowledge and as knowledge repositories, and are used by every member in a chain. The information needs can be defined based on D-Leap content, which reflects organizational knowledge, company activity area, and is represented using ontologies: topic maps (ontologies representing the areas of expertise) and skill maps (ontologies representing the skills of workers, their education, trainings, certificates, etc.).

When we look at the relation between the two partners, the situation can resemble this depicted in Figure 5.

Figure 5. KSCM overview.

Copyright © 2004, Idea Group Inc. Copying or distributing in print or electronic forms without written permission of Idea Group Inc. is prohibited.

Between the university and the company there is a marketplace, the meeting point of supply and demand. An organization running the marketplace, that is, a broker, should also be equipped with the D-Leap. In this case, the D-Leap is understood as market of knowledge. All D-Leaps can communicate through eKWs by utilizing topic maps and skill maps.

The Web becomes a natural environment for KSCM. eKW will be further developed to be settled in the context of the semantic Web. The semantic Web offers the new foundations for organizing knowledge; therefore, it could also be used in KSCM.

Conclusion

This chapter presented how a Web services paradigm can be used to extend the existing closed systems. Thus, the enhanced knowledge warehouse was modeled to conform to a new way of building applications, namely to the approach based on Web services.

This chapter showed how the terminology of WSMF is utilized to model a system as a Web service. According to WSMF, we de-coupled our original eDW system into separate modules, thus creating basic Web services. These services were then analyzed in terms of the eight layers of the Web services' functionality. We showed that only a few layers require special treatment in eKW.

We did not propose any formal notations. In future work, the following languages will be useful to formally describe eKW in the semantic Web-enabled Web services:

- WSFL (Web Services Flow Language) (Leymann, 2001), a foundation for WSMF
- DAML-S (DARPA agent markup language with ontology for services) as Web-based syntax (Ankolenkar et al., 2001)
- PSL (Process Specification Language) as formal semantics (Schlenoff et al., n.d.)

Copyright © 2004, Idea Group Inc. Copying or distributing in print or electronic forms without written permission of Idea Group Inc. is prohibited.

The Web becomes a global platform where organizations communicate with each other to exchange value-added services. The main service offered by eKW on this platform is to deliver information relevant to the user activities in a given context.

References

Abramowicz, W., Kalczynski, P.J., & Wecel, K.A. (2001). Common semantic layer to support integration of the data warehouse and the Web. *Human computer interaction* (HCI 2001). Gdansk, Poland: Akwila, Gdynia.

Abramowicz, W., Kalczynski, P.J., & Wecel, K.A. (2001). Information ants to explore Internet sources of business information. *ISCA 14th International Conference on Computer Applications in Industry and Engineering CAINE-2001*, Las Vegas, NV.

Abramowicz, W., Kalczynski, P.J., & Wecel, K.A. (2001). Profiling the data warehouse for information filtering. *Proceedings of 2001 Information Resource Management Association International Conference.* Hershey, PA: Idea Group Publishing.

Abramowicz, W., Kalczynski, P.J., & Wecel, K.A. (2002). *Filtering the Web to feed data warehouses.* London: Springer-Verlag.

Abramowicz, W., Kowalkiewicz, M., & Zawadzki, P. (2002). Enhancing searching and navigation of knowledge repositories using skill maps technology. *5th UICEE Conference*, Chennai, India.

Ankolenkar, A. et al. (2001). DAML-S: Semantic markup for Web services. Available: http://www.daml.org/services/daml-s/2001/10/daml-s.html

Beckett, D. (2003). *RDF/XML Syntax Specification, W3C.* Available: http://www.w3.org/TR/rdf-syntax-grammar/

Berlanga, R. et al. (2001). Techniques and tools for temporal analysis of the retrieved information. *Database and Expert Systems Applications, 12th International Conference* (DEXA-2001). Berlin: Springer-Verlag.

Berners-Lee, T., Hendler, J., & Lasilla, O. (2001). The semantic Web. *Scientific American.*

Copyright © 2004, Idea Group Inc. Copying or distributing in print or electronic forms without written permission of Idea Group Inc. is prohibited.

Bussler, C. (2001). B2B protocol standards and their role in semantic B2B integration engines. *IEEE Data Engineering, 24*(1).

Fensel, D. (2001). *Ontologies: Silver bullet for knowledge management and electronic commerce.* Berlin: Springer-Verlag.

Fensel, D., & Bussler, C. (2002). The Web service modeling framework WSMF. *Electronic Commerce Research and Applications, 1*(2), 113-137.

Fensel, D. et al. (2000). OIL in a nutshell. *European Knowledge Acquisition Conference (EKAW-2000).* Springer-Verlag.

Gray, P., & Watson, H.J. (1998). Present and future directions in data warehousing. *ACM SIGMIS Database, 29*(3), 83-90.

Grosof, B., & Kephart, J. (n.d.). *Intelligent agents project at IBM.* Available: http://www.research.ibm.com/iagents/home.html

Gruber, T.R. (1995). Toward principles for the design of ontologies used for knowledge sharing. *Int. J. Hum. Comp. Stud., 43*(5/6), 907-928.

Gruninger, M., & Lee, J. (2003). Ontology applications and design. *Communications of the ACM, 45*(2), 39-41.

Hendler, J., & McGuinness, D.L. (2001). Darpa agent markup language. *IEEE Intelligent Systems, 15*(6), 72-73.

Kalczynski, P.J. (2002). Software agents to filter business information from the Web to the data warehouse. *Management information systems.* The Poznan University of Economics.

Kalczynski, P.J. et al. (2003). Time indexer: A tool for extracting temporal references from business news. *2003 Information Resource Management Association International Conference.* Hershey, PA: Idea Group Inc.

Kim, H. (2002). Predicting how ontologies for the semantic Web will evolve. *Communications of the ACM, 45*(2), 48-54.

Kreger, H. (2001). *IBM Web services tutorial.* Available: http://www-3.ibm.com/software/solutions/webservices/pdf/WSCA.pdf

Leymann, F. (2001). *Web Services Flow Language* (WSFL 1.0). Available: http://www-3.ibm.com/software/solutions/webservices/pdf/WSFL.pdf

McGuinness, D.L., & Van Harmelen, F. (2003). *OWL Web Ontology Language Overview, W3C.* Available: http://www.w3.org/TR/owl-features/

Copyright © 2004, Idea Group Inc. Copying or distributing in print or electronic forms without written permission of Idea Group Inc. is prohibited.

Nemati, H.R. et al. (2002). Knowledge warehouse: An architectural integration of knowledge management, decision support, artificial intelligence and data warehousing. *Decision Support Systems, 33*(2), 143-161.

Neumann, G., & Piskorski, J. (2002). A shallow text processing core engine. *Journal of Computational Intelligence, 18*(3), 451-476.

Omelayenko, B., & Fensel, D. (2001). A two-layered integration approach for product information in B2B e-commerce. *Second International Conference on Electronic Commerce and Web Technologies* (EC-WEB 2001), Munich, Germany.

Schlenoff, C. et al. (2000). *The Process Specification Language (PSL): Overview and Version 1.0 specification,* NISTIR 6459, NIST. Gaithersburg, MD. Available: http://www.mel.nist.gov/psl/pubs/PSL1.0/paper.doc

Wecel, K., Zalech, W., & Jakubowski, T. (2003). Knowledge supply chain management to support technology transfer. *Business Information Systems* (BIS2003). University of Colorado in Colorado Springs.

Wiederhold, G. (1992). Mediators in the architecture of future information systems. *IEEE Computer, 25*(3), 38-49.

Copyright © 2004, Idea Group Inc. Copying or distributing in print or electronic forms without written permission of Idea Group Inc. is prohibited.

Chapter IX

Enterprise Portals and Knowledge Management Processes

Abdus Sattar Chaudhry
Nanyang Technological University, Singapore

Abstract

Many portal products have been marketed as knowledge management tools, implying that benefits of knowledge management can be achieved by implementing a portal. Our research suggests that portal products are not able to fully support the requirements of knowledge management functions. Products reviewed were strong in providing personalization, content management, folder-sharing and search or retrieval services. However, they lacked in services such as categorization, workflow, document management, collaboration, and business intelligence. In order to improve on the support for knowledge management, portals should be able to handle multimedia, incorporate metadata or taxonomy into their content and provide tools for workflow and mining. Enterprise portals might not fully support the processes within the knowledge management life cycle, but they remain as the only technology with the most potential to serve as the main infrastructure for knowledge management.

Copyright © 2004, Idea Group Inc. Copying or distributing in print or electronic forms without written permission of Idea Group Inc. is prohibited.

Introduction

Enterprise portals have been considered by software vendors and researchers as the main technological infrastructure that provides a complete solution in supporting enterprise knowledge management. Davydov (2001) stated that an enterprise portal fulfilled the need for a knowledge management application to synthesize data by filtering and refining. The technology was able to support advanced information dissemination and knowledge management features such as specialized directories, bulletin boards, comprehensive searching and identification of experts. Kotorov and Hsu (2001) confidently referred to portals as enterprise knowledge management systems. Szuprowicz (2000) also believed that the portals could be used to facilitate, capture and share knowledge. However, few studies have been done to verify these claims. In this chapter, we have attempted to review salient features of portal products and examined to what extent they support the knowledge management processes. The scope of our research is restricted to enterprise portal as a type of tool for knowledge management with the following objectives in view:

- Review the availability and comprehensiveness of portal features in supporting knowledge management processes. These features include personalization, collaboration, search and retrieval, categorization, business intelligence, content management and publishing, document management, workflow process and folder sharing.
- Review the capabilities of enterprise portals in supporting knowledge management processes such as capturing, sharing, storing, classifying, retrieving, maintaining, presenting and generating.

In the chapter, the processes in the knowledge management life cycle refer to acquiring knowledge, organizing, maintenance, retrieval and distribution. Acquiring knowledge refers to the capturing of explicit and tacit knowledge. These are then categorized in some form of taxonomy and indexed in a repository. Content editors will update the knowledge stored, insert metadata and delete obsolete knowledge. Lastly, a powerful search engine and intelligent agents are used to assist in the retrieval of relevant knowledge for targeted dissemination to the knowledge workers. The discussion in this chapter is focused around these processes.

Copyright © 2004, Idea Group Inc. Copying or distributing in print or electronic forms without written permission of Idea Group Inc. is prohibited.

Literature Review

The knowledge management tools market has over 200 tools that range widely in terms of technology, functionality and price (Natarajan & Shekhar, 2000). Software vendors such as Baan, Cognos, Documentum, IBM, Intraspect, Open Text, PeopleSoft and Verity were considered as vendors providing knowledge management tools (Jackson, 1998). It became extremely difficult to distinguish between knowledge management tools and mere IT solutions. Researchers have been listing tools they considered as knowledge management tools and classifying them according to the type of tools, the stream of technology, the knowledge services, functions of tools, type of knowledge, two dimensions and by the knowledge management processes.

A poll in July 2002 conducted by Meta Knowledge Management portal (*www.metakm.com*) showed that 67.2% of 342 surfers perceived the Internet, enterprise information portals and collaborative tools as the technology to implement for knowledge management systems. Another survey by the Delphi Group (1997) indicated that the primary technologies of knowledge management were databases and knowledge bases, followed by document management, intranets and groupware, and search and retrieval technology.

Merlyn (1998) proposed three main process categories for knowledge management tools, and they were knowledge retrieval, knowledge capture and knowledge navigation and discovery. Similarly, Hills (1998) mentioned that knowledge management tools should support the following tasks: knowledge creation, organisation, retrieval and delivery. Tiwana (2000) argued that knowledge management was neither about building a "smarter" intranet nor was it document management. He classified elements of knowledge utilization and basic technology support under these processes. Another interesting classification was also developed by Tiwana (2000) based on the knowledge spiral model proposed by Nonaka and Takeuchi. When evaluating knowledge management tools, one should also study the characteristics of the tool. These include context sensitivity, user sensitivity, flexibility, heuristic and suggestiveness (Frappaolo & Toms, 1997). Similarly, Nesbitt (2001) advised the consideration of organisation, flexibility, security, maintenance and accessibility when assessing knowledge management tools.

There were no absolute tools that could satisfy all requirements of a knowledge management tool. A survey conducted by Bain and Co. found that only 2% of respondents were highly satisfied with their knowledge management tools

Copyright © 2004, Idea Group Inc. Copying or distributing in print or electronic forms without written permission of Idea Group Inc. is prohibited.

(Bartlett, 2000), while 64% were not satisfied with their tools and felt that IT tools were not a quick fix for achieving knowledge management.

The enterprise portal was referred to as the *logical culmination of technological advances* in the areas of knowledge archival and dissemination, the Internet, intranets and extranets, and managerial innovations in the area of shared learning and corporate experience building (Natarajan & Shekhar, 2000). It enabled the conversion, storage and on-tap availability of tacit knowledge in explicit and accessible formats. Enterprise portal could also be thought of as a one-stop concept. Kounadis (2000) defined an enterprise portal as a personalised, *single point of access* through a Web browser to critical business information located inside and outside of an organisation. An extension of the enterprise portal included personal digital assistants, handheld devices, mobile phones, and other Internet appliances. The Delphi group also defined a portal as a single point of access window that opens not into just information but the connections between the information that transforms it into knowledge (CA, 2000).

It was anticipated that an enterprise portal would become a key component of *unified applications access,* information management and knowledge management within enterprises, and between enterprises and their trading partners, channel partners and customers. The enterprise portal relied on vast databases of information and presented them in a Web browser using intelligent retrieval and personalisation mechanisms (Michaluk, 2000). Data sources included intranets, e-mail, enterprise resource planning systems and data warehouse systems.

White (2000) equated enterprise information portal as *corporate portal* and referred to it as a customisable *Web browser interface* that provides users with access to internal and external information resources. The characteristics of a portal should include management of heterogeneous databases and document types, structured access, customised interfaces, collaborative working, multi-level security, high levels of currency and future proof. An enterprise portal was a convenient centralised *doorway* to an organisation's internal data, which included its information, systems and processes. It was also known as intranet portal, business portal, corporate portal or enterprise information portal (Barnick et al., 1999; Phifer, 1999). Today, enterprise portals serve as the digital *gateway* (Kozlowski, 1999) connecting knowledge workers to a wide spectrum of information, from corporate data to human resources information, policies, procedures, client details, product preferences and project specifications. By providing this centralised repository of information,

Copyright © 2004, Idea Group Inc. Copying or distributing in print or electronic forms without written permission of Idea Group Inc. is prohibited.

enterprise portals literally pulled the organisation together, leading to an increased internal awareness. At present, enterprise portal is the second most-mentioned item in the IT market, right after e-business. However, the term *portal* has been used loosely and abused by IT vendors with aggressive sales tactics.

An Enterprise portal solution should enable organisations to integrate internal and external sources information regardless of platform, applications and data type (structured or unstructured). Specific adaptors, portlets, gadgets, plug-ins or database drivers developed for the Enterprise portal could used to perform such integration. If certain data sources were authenticated, a separated or built-in single sign-on module has to be incorporated into the portal architecture to achieve seamless access. Open standards such as Extensible Markup Language (XML) were gradually used in enterprise portals to facilitate the future integration to back-end applications. Phifer (2000) indicated that an enterprise portal solution that provided robust interoperability across different vendors' products would emerge in 2001 but would not mature until 2003.

Most enterprise portals included a personalisation feature with which the user could specify his or her preferences over the layout and content. Presentation of specific information helped to increase productivity, and save time, effort and money in a business sense. This customisation produced a portal that was content rich yet highly focused (Michaluk, 2000). Users no longer needed to search through vast amount of data. For example, a customer would be presented with information on products related to his or her buying habits. Personalisation could be performed on group as well as personal levels. The delivery of the right information at the right time to the right people could be achieved by monitoring and notification (Phifer, 2000).

Ruber (2000) also classified the types of portals into *corporate* portal, *customer* portal, *vertical* portal, *commerce* portal and *Internet* portal. These portals served the employees, customers, business professionals in a single discipline, business professional in any discipline and consumers, respectively. In this research, we will concentrate on the internally facing enterprise portal or corporate portal, and its relationship with knowledge management and the business objectives of the enterprise. There were also horizontal and vertical enterprise portals. Phifer (2000) defined a *horizontal* enterprise portal as one that provided broad access to many types of repositories and generic application-integration features. This type of enterprise portal serviced the needs of users with no business functionality, and provided the foundation for a true enterprise-wide portal, but lacked integration with popular application pack-

Copyright © 2004, Idea Group Inc. Copying or distributing in print or electronic forms without written permission of Idea Group Inc. is prohibited.

ages. On the other hand, a *vertical* enterprise portal focused on a specific application or business functionality, and was usually associated with packaged applications, for example, enterprise resource planning, customer relationship management, sales force automation or supply chain management. These enterprise portals also provided enhancements to the applications they support but they were so focused that they could not provide the foundation for a true enterprise-wide portal.

Only recently, enterprise portals were considered as one of the knowledge management tools. While disparate applications existed in many organisations, there was no co-ordinated effort by IT department to bring these applications together in the past, probably due to insufficient funds, messy corporate structure or the technology was not available yet. Tiwana (2000) was one of the researchers who termed enterprise portal as a knowledge server. It was an integrating technology that provided an extensible architecture for unifying and organising access to disparate corporate repositories and Internet data sources.

There were overlapping areas between enterprise portals and knowledge management as the technologies behind them shared the same parentage – the Internet and its indexing, search and retrieval of data from disparate sources. Both enterprise portals and knowledge management focused on productivity and sophisticated access, organisation and control of the organisation's information sources. Both aimed to maintain productivity and close information gaps through profiling and personalisation. However, the rationale behind knowledge management was more business oriented: to optimise inter- and extra-enterprise collaboration and to leverage knowledge and collaboration to improve business responsiveness, reuse and innovation (Harris et al., 1999). Knowledge management was more concerned with people and culture. Any technology related to knowledge management must be able to stimulate and augment knowledge sharing, collaboration and innovation without instilling technology-phobia behaviour among the staff.

Some researchers preferred using the new term of *enterprise knowledge portal* over the term *enterprise information portal.* Widmayer (2000) put forward an argument that an enterprise information portal was a system of integrated applications usually implemented through a Web browser that offered a single gateway into a universe of information about a specific area. However, as an enterprise information portal dealt only with explicit knowledge and not tacit knowledge, it was not a complete knowledge. Widmayer further explained that an enterprise knowledge portal was a clearer knowledge management application and it was a type of enterprise information portal with

Copyright © 2004, Idea Group Inc. Copying or distributing in print or electronic forms without written permission of Idea Group Inc. is prohibited.

the extra functions to search and retrieve documents, proprietary methods, and other documents related to competitive abilities. The knowledge portal was also able to distinguish knowledge from information. A detailed evaluation has been done by SPEX on 10 portal products (SPEX, 2001). Criteria for the evaluation process include personalisation, integration, query and navigation, development capabilities and security. For example, Figure 5 was the results of the evaluation done on HummingBird enterprise information portal.

Our review of literature has indicated that information technology does play an important role in all knowledge management projects. While there existed a wide range of tools for knowledge management, enterprise portals were perceived as the most comprehensive knowledge management tools ever developed. Portal products have been evaluated based on a checklist of features, structure of knowledge, benefits and technology but not with relation to the knowledge management processes. We hope that our study will make a modest contribution in this regard.

Methodology

Two studies have provided the basis for the methodology used in this study. The first study was the Knowledge Structure and Services (KSS) matrix developed by Valente and Housel (2001) to evaluate all knowledge management tools. In the KSS matrix, the horizontal axis represented the core knowledge services while the vertical axis displayed the knowledge structure. The second study was by Chaudhry (1997), who proposed a quantitative evaluation method for library automation systems. On this model, users assigned different weights to all features of the system depending on the importance and computed the capability score and functionality score using the vendor scores and user scores respectively. The capability score and functionality score were then used to compute the composite score for each feature. Lastly, a numerical value was calculated for each feature and compared across products during the selection process. A modified method of evaluation will be used for this research as it was not possible to obtain vendors' scores for so many portal products and the scoring scheme was different.

We used a checklist to review features of portal products based on two parameters: portal infrastructure services and knowledge management processes. A sample of portal products available in the market at the time of study

Copyright © 2004, Idea Group Inc. Copying or distributing in print or electronic forms without written permission of Idea Group Inc. is prohibited.

was assessed using the checklist. Depending on the number of components described in the portal product, scores on a scale of 0 to 5 were inserted into the checklist. These scores were collated and analyzed to come up with mean scores on indicated support for knowledge management functions and processes.

The portal infrastructure services were used as the first parameter in the checklist. These services or features were selected based on surveys conducted by the Delphi Group, the Gartner Group, the Butler Group, information in journal articles written by authorities in portals as well as personal experience with portal products. Nine functional requirements related to information and knowledge used as a basis included the following: personalization, collaboration, search and retrieval, categorization, business intelligence, content management and publishing, and document management.

Knowledge management processes were the second parameter assessed through the checklist. The processes used in this research were those built around core processes of creating, organising and using knowledge repositories (Valente & Housel, 2001). Eight processes were used, as these played a crucial role in the knowledge management lifecycle, handled some form of knowledge, were supported by some form of enablers and were dependent on other processes. These include capture, share, storage, classify, retrieve, maintain, presentation, and generate.

A sample of portal products in the market was selected for this research considering various factors. Firstly, vendors selling portal products were found by searching the Internet using "portal vendor" or "enterprise portal" as the keywords in the Google search engine. From Web sites that displayed the whole list of vendors, each link was visited and scrutinized for portal products. Faulty links were not chosen, but in the process of searching, many appeared to have changed their Web site or merged with other vendors. Apart from listings from the Internet, lists of portal participants at exhibitions such as "Portals World Asia 2000," "Knowledge Management Asia 2001" and "Made-in-Singapore & proud of I.T. 2001," listings in surveys, journal articles, and books were used to locate the sample. Only portal products with product information or white papers available from the product Web site were considered for this study. The samples were selected based on the portal product descriptions and only products that claimed to promote knowledge management and contained two or more features listed in the checklist were examined.

The latest version of the portal product was studied together with all out-of-the-box features. Add-on software components that were not offered in the

Copyright © 2004, Idea Group Inc. Copying or distributing in print or electronic forms without written permission of Idea Group Inc. is prohibited.

product suite would not be considered. For example, if the portal product required a separate search engine product to take care of search and retrieval features, the original portal product did not satisfy the search function. The criteria was important, as portal products are usually extensible and other products could be added on to beef-up a particular feature that was lacking in the original portal product suite. A list of portal vendors included in the study is given in Appendix C.

Information on the portal product was important for a complete understanding of the product so that a fair score could be allocated for each service. The information sources included:

a) Survey reports
b) Interviews with the product vendors
c) Detailed product information, brochures and white papers available over the Internet
d) Multimedia demonstration of the portal
e) Participation in a free-online demonstration of the portal
f) Extended literature review on the portal product
g) Installation of an evaluation copy of the portal product

A study on survey reports from consulting companies allowed quick access to authoritative evaluation results of different portal products. However, these reports were costly and in some cases were conducted on earlier versions of the portal products. Moreover, only a few such reports existed and the set of features used in these reports was different from those used in this research. Thus, a study on survey reports was not selected. Interviews with vendors provided in-depth information on selected features of portal products and allowed vendors to defend a feature if it scored less than what the vendors expected. However, as this research did not provide any business opportunities for these vendors, they were not forthcoming to accept such interviews. Product specialists also tended to overstate the ability of their products. Therefore, interviews were not used as a main source of information. Mainly these were used for verification and validation of information.

Detailed product brochures and information on the overall portal architecture were available from the product Web sites. Sometimes case studies on that particular portal product and informative white papers were also available. This

Copyright © 2004, Idea Group Inc. Copying or distributing in print or electronic forms without written permission of Idea Group Inc. is prohibited.

option was a feasible source of information. Some portal vendors were willing to provide a free online trial of the portal product after registration. This free trial offered a hands-on approach to better understand the features of the portal product and was a more accurate information source than product brochures. However, not all vendors provided such free demonstrations. Nevertheless, this option was most suitable for a complete understanding of the product.

Portal products Web sites might provide multimedia downloads that illustrate the functions in the portal. These multimedia files were mostly created using Macromedia Flash and were interactive in nature. Though only certain features were shown in the clip and only some sites offered such multimedia, they offered a better visual understanding over that achieved by reading a printout on the product. This information source was selected for this research.

In certain cases, published journals and books contained discussion on the portal products. We used these discussions on selected portal products for examples to illustrate certain features. An installation of an evaluation copy of the portal was the best way to understand the functions of all the features of the product. Such a setup required hardware, network connections and back-end applications that were not available for this research. Besides, not all vendors were willing to provide copies of their products for evaluation. In summary, the information sources used were *detailed product information, brochures, white papers* from the product Web site, *multimedia demonstrations* and participation in *free-online demonstrations* of the portal. In order for portal products to be assessed accurately, effort focused on finding and understanding all available portal information.

For each portal product, all the information sources were studied carefully and used to assign scores in the checklist depending on the number of components per service or process, using a scale of 0 to 5. Below were the components for every portal infrastructure service and knowledge management process. For example, if there was no component for workflow process in the portal product, a score of 0 was inserted into the row for workflow process on the checklist. If the product had status tracking and customizable action for the workflow process, a score of 2 would be assigned. When the product had all five components for that feature, the maximum score of 5 would be allocated to that feature. The scoring of portal products aimed to quantify the degree in which these products can substantiate infrastructure services and processes. Every portal product had a different set of scores. The score of all portal products for each service or process was summed up and divided by the total number of portal products to calculate the mean score. Using Microsoft Excel,

Copyright © 2004, Idea Group Inc. Copying or distributing in print or electronic forms without written permission of Idea Group Inc. is prohibited.

the standard deviation was also calculated. The mean scores were later sorted in descending order and represented in a bar chart. From the bar chart, services or processes above or equal to the mean score of 2.5 can be differentiated from those below the mean score of 2.5.

Findings and Discussion

The facts and figures were presented in an aggregated manner and the results explained the overall trends of enterprise portals from the 58 product samples. The mention of individual product name was avoided, unless necessary. In instances where the name of products was mentioned, they only served as examples to illustrate a certain point. It was not the intention of this study to describe portal products in comparative terms or to provide a complete evaluation of all portal products. A sample size of 58 portal products was evaluated using a checklist of services and processes (Appendix A, B, and C). The results of the review of features are presented in the next section.

Portal Infrastructure Services

Each service or feature of portal products was graded based on five essential components. A score on a scale of 1 to 5 was assigned depending on the number of components provided by the product. To calculate the mean score for each service, the scores of 58 products for that service was summed up and divided by the total number of products. Figure 1 presents a summary of the mean scores of all the services ranked from the highest mean score to the lowest. Standard deviation for each service is illustrated as a black line over the top of the bar. It estimates how widely values were dispersed from the average value (the mean).

It was found that none of the portal services was able to achieve the maximum mean score of 5. This could be due to the strict criteria used to measure each service, or perhaps portal products in general could never satisfy the requirements of a complete knowledge management system. There was always a gap between portal products and their expected functions. Five of the portal services (categorization, workflow, document management, collaboration and business intelligence) have a mean score below 2.5, while four of the services

Copyright © 2004, Idea Group Inc. Copying or distributing in print or electronic forms without written permission of Idea Group Inc. is prohibited.

Figure 1. Ranking of portal infrastructure services.

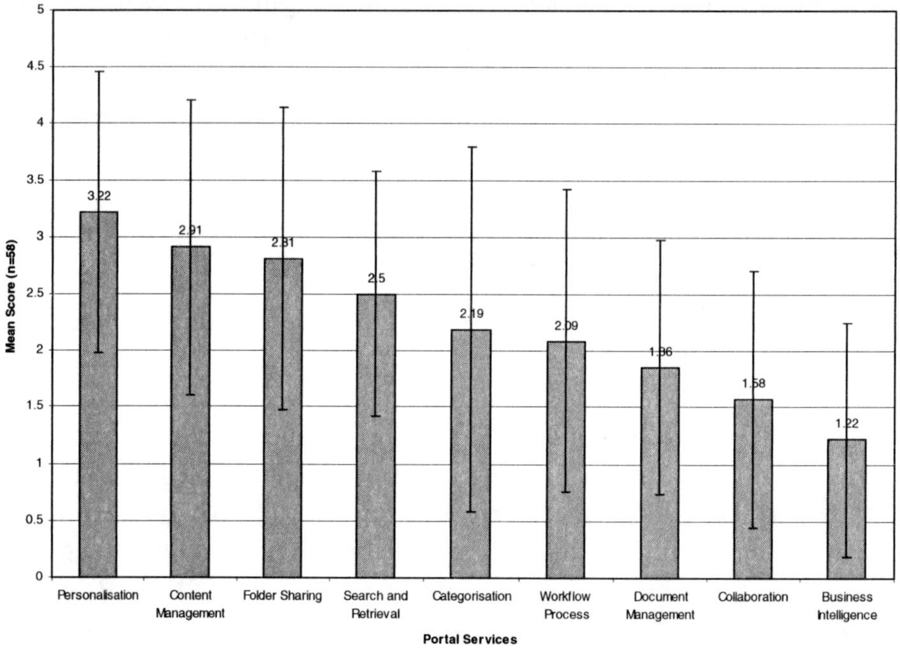

(personalization, content management, folder sharing and search) showed a mean score equal to or above 2.5.

The most supported services were personalization, with a mean score of 3.22, followed by content management with 2.91, folder sharing with 2.81, and lastly search & retrieval with 2.5. Contradictory to the findings from Delphi (2001), the survey by Delphi Group in 2000 found that portals actually provide services in the order of categorization, publishing, search and retrieval, personalization and collaboration. As the sample size and methodology of the Delphi survey was not described, it was not possible to single out the reasons for the different findings.

Knowledge Management Processes

Eight processes were selected for assessing portal products in this study. They were crucial to the knowledge management life cycle and are expected to contribute to the success of knowledge creation, sharing and retention. The 58

Copyright © 2004, Idea Group Inc. Copying or distributing in print or electronic forms without written permission of Idea Group Inc. is prohibited.

Figure 2. Ranking of knowledge management processes.

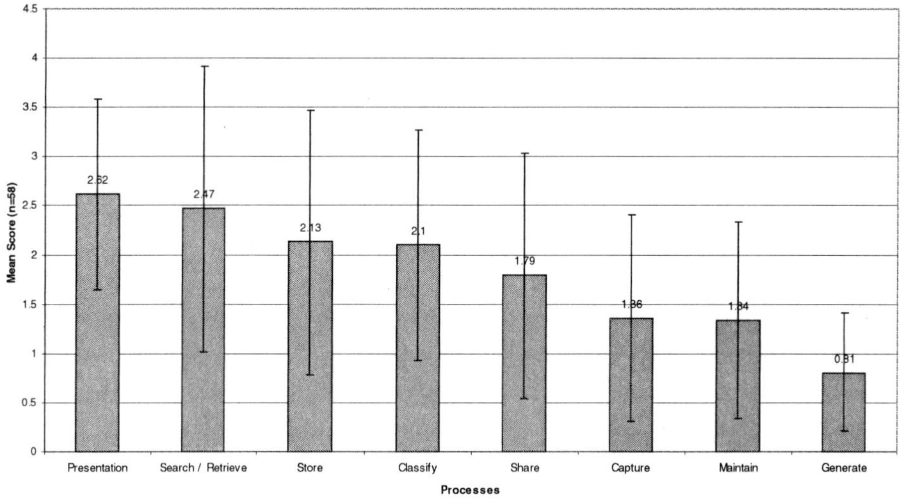

portal products were assessed again on their support for these processes and their mean scores and standard deviations have been presented in Figure 2. Only the presentation process has a mean score above 2.5, while the rest were below 2.5. Thus, presentation was the most supported process in portal products.

It was found that the top five portal products that achieved the best individual scores in portal infrastructure services were HummingBird EIP, FileNet, Citrix Nfuse, Brio Portal and DataChannel Server. As for knowledge management processes, the top five products were HummingBird EIP, Brio Portal, Comintell Knowledge XChanger, Sybase EP and Autonomy-in-a-box. Different portal products were strong in different services or processes.

Our study focused on the overall trends of support of all portal products with respect to their support for knowledge management. Over the years, many companies have implemented knowledge management using highly-hyped technology such as portals, but the results have been lacking and the price tag higher than originally anticipated. Deveau (2002) attributed this to the wrong perception of knowledge management. Likewise, Widmayer (2000) insisted that portals are ill equipped to do the total knowledge management job. What was missing between the implementation of enterprise portals and the realization of a knowledge management organisation?

Copyright © 2004, Idea Group Inc. Copying or distributing in print or electronic forms without written permission of Idea Group Inc. is prohibited.

Interpretation on Portal Infrastructure Services

From the findings of this study, portal products in the market should examine ways to improve on categorization, workflow, document management, collaboration and business intelligence in order to realize a better portal infrastructure for knowledge management. This was close to what Choksy et al. (2001) had stated, in which categorization, collaboration and expert identification were found to be still lacking in many portal offerings today. Both collaboration and collaboration services achieved a low mean score in this study.

Results from the survey of 58 portal products have shown that the portal service with the highest mean score was personalization service, at 3.22. Although this was not a very high mean score out of the maximum of 5, we inferred that most of the portal products satisfied the personalization function that allowed the customization of content for dissemination to the individual. This finding reinforced Collins' (2001) argument that portals were able to create a central "window" that presented information to users and a "door" that allowed users to pass through to reach other destinations. The ability of a portal to provide information tailored to the preferences or needs of the user must be one of the key value propositions of a portal (Choksy et al., 2001). Although the overall mean score was 3.22 for personalization service, some portal products were able to achieve the maximum score of 5, and they were Broadvision Infoexchange Portal, Brio Portal, HummingBird EIP, PeopleSoft Portal, Mediapps Net.Portal, Sybase EP and BEA Weblogic Portal. Please refer to Appendix A for the complete list of components for each portal service.

The second and third highest mean scores were 2.91 for content management service and 2.81 for folder sharing service respectively. It could be deduced that most portal products have the infrastructure services to support information sharing and publication. In the sample, Citrix NFuse, DataChannel Server, Documentum Portal CM edition, Elipva Portal, HummingBird EIP, FileNet and Webridge PX were able to achieve the maximum score of 5 in content management service. Whereas, in folder sharing service, portal products with the maximum score of 5 were Citrix, DataChannel Server, Documentum Portal CM edition, HummingBird EIP, Hyperwave Information Portal and FileNet.

Search and retrieval service had a mean score of 2.5 out of 5, which indicated that an average of only 50% of the components were present for this service. Objectively, portal products in the market were neither developed with the retrieval of information as the most important function nor had powerful search

Copyright © 2004, Idea Group Inc. Copying or distributing in print or electronic forms without written permission of Idea Group Inc. is prohibited.

engines bundled with the product. Of the 58 products, only Hyper wave Information Portal product achieved the maximum score of 5.

In the fifth position was the categorization service, with a mean score of 2.19. This was a relatively low score and it may be due to the lack of focus in facilitating the navigation through loads of information using thesaurus, taxonomy and metadata. Automatic categorization was also not well developed. Of the 58 portal products, Brio Portal, Comintell Knowledge XChanger, HummingBird EIP, Knowledge Insight and Verity PortalOne were found to be strong in categorization service, each achieving the maximum score of 5.

Workflow process service obtained a mean score of 2.09. This indicated the low priority placed by vendors on the routing of electronic documents with the approval cycle and actions from the different roles. In the survey, workflow process was mostly restricted to the approval of documents within content and document management. However, a flexible system that can accommodate different business processes would be more practical. Portal products with the maximum score of 5 were Convera RetrievalWare, EnterWorks Suite, and Enformia Enterprise Portal.

An interesting observation was the low mean score of 1.86 for document management services. Of the 58 portal products, the maximum score was 4 and only Livelink, Intraspect and Cyknit were able to receive this score. Overall, all portal products sampled were deficient in the incorporation of metadata into information sources, the indexing of scanned images, and did not integrate well with desktop programs. Since CIO (1999) mentioned that the ability to digitize documents was the first step in any knowledge management hierarchy, portal products would not be useful if they were unable to process digitized images or document.

Collaboration and business intelligence services obtained the lowest mean score of 1.58 and 1.22, respectively. Results showed that portal products were lacking in providing a platform for effective communication with multimedia content, filtering mechanisms and asynchronous technology. Likewise they were poor in the ability to analyze data and to integrate with existing enterprise resource planning systems. These findings challenged Szuprowicz's (2000) claim that a significant portion of the portal market has already developed powerful reporting and data analysis abilities. Of the 58 products, the maximum score for collaboration services was 4, and only Covia InfoPortal, Elipva Portal, HummingBird EIP and Livelink could achieve this. As for business intelligence services, only Brio Portal and HummingBird EIP were able to obtain the maximum score of 5.

Copyright © 2004, Idea Group Inc. Copying or distributing in print or electronic forms without written permission of Idea Group Inc. is prohibited.

Interpretation on Knowledge Management Processes

Many portal products claimed that they could support processes within the knowledge management life cycle. However, it was found that 7 out of 8 processes have a mean score of below 2.5 out of the possible maximum of 5. These seven processes were: search/retrieve, store, classify, share, capture, maintain and generate. This finding quantified and magnified the gap between enterprise portals and knowledge management processes. Please refer to Appendix B for the complete list of components for each portal process.

Presentation process has the highest mean score of 2.62, and this could be due to the popular presence of simple personalization and text support in the portal products. On the other hand, presentation process was lacking in advanced personalization, intuitive search results and multimedia content. Out of the 58 portal products reviewed, only Datachannel server, HummingBird EIP and Intraspect were able to achieve a maximum score of 5.

The study showed a mean score of 2.47 for the search process. Although search or retrieval could be done across different knowledge domains, portal products were weak in an intelligent push technology, fuzzy search, and knowledge mining and did not allow the storage of search results for reuse or sharing. Nevertheless, many products were able to incorporate all the five components, and they were Brio Portal, Comintell Knowledge XChanger, Convera Retrievalware, Eoexchange UniversalSearch, HummingBird EIP, Verity PortalOne and Autonomy-in-a-box. The store process obtained the third highest mean score of 2.13. The most common component was the ability to link information sources. Components that were less common were multi-dimensional cataloguing/indexing, subject experts' directory, knowledge bases and filtering. iPlanet Portal Server, Orbital Organik and Plumtree Corporate Portal were the only products out of the 58 products included in the sample that could achieve the maximum score of 5 for this process.

Overall, the classify process could only obtain a low mean score of 2.1. Except for push technology, components such as customized publishing tools, information refinery tools, discussion groups and metadata were consistently lacking in the portal product samples. Individual products such as Brio Portal, Comintell Knowledge XChanger and Autonomy-in-a-box have managed to achieve the maximum score of 5. Four of the processes, namely share, capture, maintain and generate processes, had an unexpected low mean score of less than 2. This means that each of them has less than 2 out of the 5 possible components.

Copyright © 2004, Idea Group Inc. Copying or distributing in print or electronic forms without written permission of Idea Group Inc. is prohibited.

The mean score for share process was 1.79 and the push-publishing-notification component was more common than online collaboration, group decisions, multimedia support, groupware and video-conferencing. Thus, knowledge sharing was not as easily implemented by using a portal product as previously claimed by vendors. Of the sample, HummingBird EIP and Intraspect Portals were the only products that scored 5 (the maximum score).

It was found that the capture process achieved a low mean score of 1.36. This process was particularly weak in tracking personal navigational trail, user audit trail and employee skills yellow pages. Out of 58 portal products, none of them was able to achieve a score of 4 or 5. This finding indicated the failure of portals to capture knowledge and to enable them for reuse by other knowledge workers.

Equally neglected was the maintain process, with a mean score of 1.34. Most of the portal products allowed the knowledge source to be manually validated but did not provide project databases, customer support databases, automatic validation and communities of practice. Lotus Kstation and Intraspect were the only products with the maximum individual score of 5.

The generate process obtained the lowest mean score of 0.81. This inferred the inability of portals to externalize knowledge, mine data and to incorporate conceptual mapping and pattern recognition. However, out of 58 portal products, only Brio Portal was able to achieve the maximum score of 5.

In summary, only four out of nine portal infrastructure services and one out of eight processes were well supported by enterprise portals. Therefore, there exist large gaps between what the vendors claimed that their portal products could do and what these products can actually contribute in any knowledge management initiative. If enterprise portals were seen as a form of technology, then portals alone were not able to meet all the criteria of a knowledge management system. On the other hand, for a portal product to improve its support for knowledge management, it must also improve in the services and processes that it is weak in.

There were many reasons why certain services or processes were deficient in portal products. One possible reason was that vendors might not have a full understanding of knowledge management. With insufficient knowledge or a wrong perception, vendors who were not ready continued to penetrate the portal market and positioned themselves as the pioneer of enterprise portals. As each vendor has his or her own interpretation of knowledge management, naturally the vendors' products were aligned towards those features consid-

Copyright © 2004, Idea Group Inc. Copying or distributing in print or electronic forms without written permission of Idea Group Inc. is prohibited.

ered as essential for knowledge management. As a consequence, services or processes that portal products were found lacking might actually be considered as non-essential items by the vendors.

Yet another possible reason was that portal vendors might have originated from a specialized area before they started producing portal products. For example, Cognos, Convera and Documentum were originally vendors specializing in business intelligence, search engine and content management, respectively. Thus, apart from the original area of specialization, other features were not as well developed in their portal product. Moreover, the R&D department of portal vendors might not have all the necessary expertise and resources to conduct research in all aspects of enterprise portals. For example, many R&D staff knew the details of personalization service, as it was common in Internet portals such as My Yahoo, but they did not understand the details of business intelligence service, as this was a very specialized field. Besides, developers might be constrained by the time and budget allocated for the development of the product. Their scope in the development of portal features could also be attributed to the product's selling price that was pegged at a lower level than competing products. As a result, not all portal features were developed up to a standard necessary to support knowledge management.

Summary and Conclusion

This study found that enterprise portals were well equipped with personalization service, content management service, folder sharing service and search or retrieval services. Technically, enterprise portals must improve on other services such as categorization, workflow, document management, collaboration and business intelligence in order to better support knowledge management. They should handle contextual media such as images, audio and video files, incorporate an accurate metadata or taxonomy system, allow business processes to be mapped to a workflow and offer informative mining of structured and unstructured information.

Where the knowledge management cycle was concerned, using enterprise portal technology was not sufficient to support all processes. From the results, it was inferred that enterprise portals were excellent in supporting the presentation process but weak in supporting the retrieval, storage, classification, sharing, capture, maintenance and generation processes. In order for enter-

Copyright © 2004, Idea Group Inc. Copying or distributing in print or electronic forms without written permission of Idea Group Inc. is prohibited.

prise portals to strengthen their support for knowledge management, the portal products could improve in the deficient area by being extensible or combine with other products.

One inference from this study was that most enterprise portals offered personalization service and this will most likely be the single service that can help bridge the gaps and improve on support for knowledge management. Extensible Web parts already existed for a number of products such as Broadvision's Portlets, Brio's SmartObjects, Citrix's Content Delivery Agent, Cognos's Gadgets, DataChannel's Portlets, Plumtree's Gadgets, PeopleSoft's Pagelets and HummingBird's eClips. As there were many third-party companies who could develop Web parts for a small fee or make them available as free downloads, these portal products can incorporate almost any objects in their portals' interface. For example, if the portal product was weak in business intelligence service and generate process, one can develop and insert a specific Web part to provide data mining, data extraction and transformation so that knowledge can be discovered from meaningless information. Thus, it would be important for enterprise portals to include extensible Web parts in their mission to be a knowledge management tool.

Another deduction was that other technologies should be combined with portal products to support knowledge management processes. For example, if a portal product needs improvement in categorization service and classify process, it should be integrated with Inxight's Categorizer or Semio's Taxonomy, which are specialized products in such areas. By identifying the weakness of an enterprise portal, one can mix-and-match with the right technology to improve the infrastructure for knowledge management.

Although enterprise portals were lacking in certain areas and cannot be guaranteed to be a complete knowledge management solution, they remain the most promising technology to serve as the infrastructure to accommodate the broad and extensive processes within the knowledge management life cycle.

References

Barnick, D., Smith, D., & Phifer, G. (1999, September 27). *Q&A: Trends in Internet and enterprise portals.* GartnerGroup RAS Services No. QA-09-0602.

Copyright © 2004, Idea Group Inc. Copying or distributing in print or electronic forms without written permission of Idea Group Inc. is prohibited.

Bartlett, J. (2000, September). KM Tools are in the pit. *Knowledge management* (p. 12).

Buckman, B. (1997). *Lions and tigers and bears: Following the road from command and control to knowledge sharing.* Buckman Laboratories International, Inc.

Butler Group. (2001). *Corporate portals: Survey analysis.* USA: The Butler Group.

Chaudury, A.S. (1997). How to evaluate a library automation system. *Singapore Libraries, 26*(2), 3 - 16.

CIO. (1999, September 15). *Knowledge management: Big challenges, big rewards.* CIO special advertising supplement. Available: http://www.cio.com/sponsors/091599_km_1.html

Computer Associates. (2000). *Knowledge portals: Integrating Web sites without going insane. Paper presented at CA-World 2000.* Available: http://www.caworld.cpm/proceedings/2000/general/gp102pn/ [2001, Oct 1].

Davydov, M.M. (2001). *Corporate portals and e-business integration.* USA: McGraw-Hill.

Delphi Group. (1997). *Delphi on knowledge management: Research and perspectives on today's knowledge landscape.* Boston: The Delphi Group.

Delphi Group. (2001, April). *Application portals: Maximising existing computing resources in a changing business and technology environment.* Boston: The Delphi Group.

Deveau, D. (2002). No brain, no gain. *Computing Canada, 28*(10), 14-15.

Frappaolo, C., & Toms, W. (1997). Knowledge management: From terra incognita to terra firma. In J.W. Cortada & J.A. Woods (Eds.), *The knowledge management yearbook 1999-2000* (pp. 381-388). Boston: Butterworth-Heinemann.

Harris, K., Phifer, G., & Hayward, S. (1999, August 2). *The enterprise portal: Is it knowledge management?* GartnerGroup RAS Services No. SPA-08-8978.

Hills, M. (1998). New tools for knowledge management. *Knowledgies.* Available: http://www.cnilive.com/docs_pub/html/p0798mh.html

Copyright © 2004, Idea Group Inc. Copying or distributing in print or electronic forms without written permission of Idea Group Inc. is prohibited.

Jackson, C. (1998). Process to product: Creating tools for knowledge management. *The BizTech Network.* Available: http://www.brint.com/members/online/120205/jackson/secn1.htm

Kotorov, R., & Hsu, E. (2001). A model for enterprise portal management. *Journal of Knowledge Management, 5*(1), 86 - 93.

Kounadis, T. (2000, August). How to pick the best portal? *E-business Advisor.* Available: http://www.advisor.com/Articles.nsf/aid/KOUNT01

Kozlowski, M.A. (1999). New Delphi methodology facilitates organizational success with corporate portals. *The Delphi Group.* Available: http://www.delphigroup.com/pressreleases/1999-PR/19990618-PortalDesignMethod.htm

Merlyn, P.R. (1998, December). From information technology to knowledge technology. *Journal of Knowledge Management, 2*(2), 28-35.

Michaluk, D. (2000). *Enterprise information portals comparison & selection guide.* Faulkner Information Services Docid. 00017648.

Natarajan, G., & Shekhar, S. (2000). *Knowledge management: Enabling business growth.* New Delhi: Tata McGraw-Hill Publishing Company.

Nesbitt, K. (2001). *The evolution of knowledge management.* Faulkner Information Services Docid. 00017607.

Phifer, G. (1999, April 20). *Enterprise portal trends emerge among confusion.* GartnerGroup RAS Services No. SPA-07-6037.

Phifer, G. (2000, April 19). *CIO Alert: Be prepared to support multiple portals in your enterprise.* GartnerGroup RAS Services No. IGG-04192000-02.

Phifer, G. (2000, August 2). *CIO Alert: Best practises in deploying enterprise portals.* GartnerGroup RAS Services No. IGG-08022000-01.

Ruber, P. (2000, April). Portals on a mission. *Knowledge Management,* 35-44.

SPEX. (2001). *Enterprise Portals 2000/2001 research module.* Available: http://www.checkspex.com/catalog/index.htm

Szuprowicz, B. (2000). *Implementing enterprise portals: Integration strategies for intranet, extranet and Internet resources.* USA: Computer Technology Research Corp.

Tiwana, A. (2000). *The knowledge management toolkit: Practical techniques for building a knowledge management system.* Upper Saddle River, NJ: Prentice Hall.

Copyright © 2004, Idea Group Inc. Copying or distributing in print or electronic forms without written permission of Idea Group Inc. is prohibited.

Valente, A., & Housel, T. (2001). Electronic tools for knowledge management. In H. Bell (Ed.), *Measuring and managing knowledge* (pp. 109 - 125). Boston: McGraw Hill.

White, M. (2000). Enterprise information portals. *The Electronic Library, 18*(5), 354-362.

Widmayer, K. (2000, December 5). *Enterprise information portals and knowledge management.* Paper presented at the International Knowledge Management meeting.

Copyright © 2004, Idea Group Inc. Copying or distributing in print or electronic forms without written permission of Idea Group Inc. is prohibited.

Appendix A

Checklist for Assessing Portal Products
Portal Infrastructure Services

Personalization	❑ Content personalization ❑ Color and layout ❑ Notification using push and pull technology ❑ Dynamic based on user activity ❑ Extensible Web parts
Collaboration	❑ Synchronous (e.g., online chat) ❑ Asynchronous Linked (e.g., forums) ❑ Asynchronous separate (eg., e-mail) ❑ Moderation or filtering mechanism ❑ Multimedia content
Search and retrieval	❑ Simple search, e.g., keywords ❑ Advanced options pattern matching or concept-based ❑ Ability to search across all data sources ❑ Automatic searching while performing other task ❑ Storing search results for sharing and reference
Categorization	❑ Manual categorization by content owner ❑ Automatic ❑ Thesaurus or taxonomy available ❑ Hierarchical navigation available ❑ Uses XML or some sort of metadata
Business Intelligence	❑ Mining of structured data ❑ Mining of unstructured data ❑ Intelligent agent ❑ ETL (data extraction, transformation, load) ❑ Integration to ERP
Content Management and Publishing	❑ Simple uploading of documents available ❑ Version control and author support ❑ Complex composition mechanism available, e.g., the use of customizable XML template ❑ Multimedia, e.g., video files ❑ Push or pull technology and subscription services
Document Management	❑ Version control ❑ Document history, file tracking or audit and control access ❑ Indexing of scanned images ❑ Metadata tag to contents ❑ Integrated with desktop programs, eg.,Word
Workflow Process	❑ Approval cycle ❑ Status tracking ❑ Files uploading and comments allow ❑ Action customizable ❑ Control access
Folder Sharing or Document Directory	❑ Control access ❑ Folder in physical drive ❑ Folder in central database ❑ Structured data ❑ Unstructured data

Copyright © 2004, Idea Group Inc. Copying or distributing in print or electronic forms without written permission of Idea Group Inc. is prohibited.

Appendix B

Knowledge Management Processes

Presentation	❑ Simple personalization, e.g., limited layout ❑ Advanced personalization, e.g., library for Web components ❑ Intuitive search result presentation ❑ Text support ❑ Multimedia support
Share	❑ Online collaboration and learning ❑ Multimedia support ❑ Group decisions ❑ Push, publishing, notification ❑ Groupware, video-conferencing, Web camera
Search / Retrieve	❑ Fuzzy ❑ Intelligent push based on a profile/event ❑ Knowledge mining ❑ Multiple knowledge domains ❑ Summary of results
Classify	❑ Customized publishing tools ❑ Information refinery tools ❑ Push technology ❑ Customized discussion groups ❑ Concepts of metadata
Capture	❑ Personal navigational trail ❑ User audit trail ❑ Employee skills yellow pages ❑ Pull technology ❑ Intelligent agent
Store	❑ Multi-dimensional cataloging/indexing ❑ Resource directories (subject experts) ❑ Knowledge bases ❑ Linking ❑ Filtering
Maintain	❑ Past project databases ❑ Customer support knowledge bases ❑ Communities of practice ❑ Manual validation ❑ Automatic validation
Generate	❑ Data mining ❑ Collaborative decision-making processes ❑ Externalization tools ❑ Conceptual mapping ❑ Pattern recognition

Copyright © 2004, Idea Group Inc. Copying or distributing in print or electronic forms without written permission of Idea Group Inc. is prohibited.

Appendix C

List of Portal Vendors Included in the Study

1. 2Bridge
2. Activenavigation
3. Adenin
4. Aptech
5. Autonomy
6. BCN3net
7. BEA Systems
8. Brio
9. Broadvision
10. Business Objects
11. Chrystal
12. Citrix
13. Cognos
14. Comintell
15. Computer Associates
16. Convera
17. Corechange
18. Covia
19. Data Channel
20. CyKnit
21. Divine
22. Documentum
23. Elipva
24. Enformia
25. Enterworks
26. EoExchange
27. eRoom Tech
28. Factiva
29. Intraspect
30. FileNet
31. Hummingbird
32. Hyperwave
33. IBM
34. iManage
35. InfoImage
36. Insight Technologies
37. Intervate
38. Interwoven
39. iPlanet
40. Knowledge-Track
41. Lotus
42. Mediapps
43. Microsoft
44. Net Objects
45. Onyx
46. Open Text Livelink
47. Oracle
48. Orbital
49. PeopleSoft
50. Plumtree
51. Sagent Technology
52. SAP
53. Sybase
54. Tibco
55. Verity
56. Viador
57. Webridge
58. Zap Ucone

Copyright © 2004, Idea Group Inc. Copying or distributing in print or electronic forms without written permission of Idea Group Inc. is prohibited.

Chapter X

Amalgamating Ontological Modeling with Bluetooth Service Discovery

Maria Ruey-Yuan Lee
Shih Chien University, Taiwan

Ching Lee
Hyper Taiwan Technology Inc., Taiwan

Abstract

This chapter introduces ontology conceptual modeling for discovering Bluetooth Services in m-commerce. Discovery services in a dynamic environment, such as Bluetooth, can be a challenge because Bluetooth is unlike any wired network, as there is no need to physically attach cables to the devices you are communicating with. Regular Bluetooth service discovery protocol may be inadequate to match different service naming attributes. To support the matching mechanism and allow more organized service discovery, service relation ontology is proposed to extend and

Copyright © 2004, Idea Group Inc. Copying or distributing in print or electronic forms without written permission of Idea Group Inc. is prohibited.

enhance the hierarchical structure introduced in the Bluetooth specification. Frame-based and XML-based approaches are used to codify the service relation ontology, which represents the relations of service concepts. A semantic matching process is introduced to facilitate inexact matching, which leads to a situation in which a simple positive or negative response can be meaningful. The Bluetooth ontology modeling represents a broad range of service descriptions and information. The semantic matching process improves the quality of service discovery. We believe that Bluetooth wireless networks' amalgamation with the ontology conceptual modeling paradigm is a necessary component of creating a new path in the field of m-commerce infrastructures.

Introduction

Bluetooth™ is set to be the fastest growing technology since the Internet or the cellular phone (Bray & Stuman, 2002). Bluetooth has created the notion of a Personal Area Network (PAN), a close range wireless network set to revolutionize the way people interact with the information and technology around them. Bluetooth is unlike any wired network, as there is no need to physically attach a cable to the devices you are communicating with. In other words, you may not know exactly what devices you are talking to and what their capabilities are. To cope with this, Bluetooth provides inquiry and paging mechanisms and a Service Discovery Protocol (SDP). Service discovery, normally, involves a client, service provider, and seek out or directory server. Bluetooth does not define a human-machine interface for service discovery; it only defines the protocol to exchange data between a server offering services and a client wishing to use them. The SDP in Bluetooth provides a means for applications to discover which services are available and to determine the characteristics of those available services (Bluetooth Specification, 2001). However, service discovery in the Bluetooth environment is different from service discovery protocol in traditional network environments. In the Bluetooth environment, the set of services that are available changes dynamically based on the RF proximity of the device in motion.

The Bluetooth SDP uses 128-bit university unique identifiers (UUIDs) that are associated with every service and attributes of that service. However, UUID-based description and matching of services are often inadequate (Avancha,

Copyright © 2004, Idea Group Inc. Copying or distributing in print or electronic forms without written permission of Idea Group Inc. is prohibited.

Joshi & Finin, 2002). For example, consider a wireless hotspot such as airport terminal or shopping mall where clients use handheld devices to discover information about available services such as the "railway service". Using regular Bluetooth SDP, the request may fail if a series of UUIDs stores its service as "metro" or "train" or "bart," and so forth. In addition, the current version of Bluetooth SDP does not support service registration. Thus, the airport information would likely not be able to register its services to facilitate users' needs.

To tackle this problem and enhance the quality of service discovery, we provide the Bluetooth SDP matching and browsing mechanism to use ontology modeling concepts associated with UUIDs to service in hotspot environments. After introduction, the body of this chapter is organized into five sections. The first section describes state-of-the-art approaches to the service discovery. The second section provides a brief explanation of Bluetooth service discovery application profile and shows its objectives and supports. The third section focuses on service browsing. A Service Relation Ontology (SRO) is introduced to model the service ontology. A frame-based representation is used to present the service concepts. The fourth section examines service searching, which describes semantic searching processes. It provides a service records example and also introduces the concepts of service search patterns. The final section discusses the different ontological approaches and shows their advantages and disadvantages.

Background

Most common service discovery protocols have been designed mainly for use on the Internet (Chakraborty & Chen, 2002; Davis, Fensel & Harmelen, 2002; Ludwig, 2002; Ludwig & Santen, 2002). These protocols mostly use string matching, the simplest matching mechanism. Service Location Protocol (Veizades et al., 1997), Jini (Amold et al., 1999) and Salutation (Salutation, 1999) are well-known service discovery protocols that use string matching. However, one of the limitations of string matching is when clients and service providers do not share a common understanding of something, which could result in false matching.

In order to make the service discovery more powerful and flexible, one of the requirements of the design of Bluetooth service discovery protocols is

Copyright © 2004, Idea Group Inc. Copying or distributing in print or electronic forms without written permission of Idea Group Inc. is prohibited.

interoperability with existing service discovery protocols. Miller and Pascoe (1999) describe such an effort to map the Bluetooth service discovery protocol to the Salutation protocol. It has also been suggested to add the IP layer on top of the Bluetooth stack and support TCP and/or UDP connections. This is a feasible solution, which could replace Jini, SLP, Salutation and so on. However, these IP-based protocols suffer from deficiencies similar to Bluetooth SDP because Bluetooth does not allow broadcasting of data (Chakraborty et al., 2001). The IP-based service discovery protocol therefore cannot use multicasting either for service discovery by clients or service advertisements by providers.

We believe that ontological support can enhance the interaction with clients and other services across enterprises. Service descriptions and information need to be understood and agreed upon among various parties. Common ontology infrastructures must be present in the existing service discovery architectures. However, they are often either missing from or not well represented in the existing service discovery architectures. We believe that the amalgamating ontological modeling with service discovery provides a more flexible and feasible solution as far as Bluetooth networks are concerned. The emergence of ontology and Bluetooth wireless networks creates a new path in the field of m-commerce infrastructure.

Bluetooth Service Discovery Application Profile

Service discovery is a process by which devices and services in networks can locate, gather information and interact with other services in the network. Service discovery is fundamental to all Bluetooth profiles and is expected to be a key component of most Bluetooth applications (Miller & Bisdikian, 2001).

The identified objectives for Bluetooth SDP are:

- Simplicity: Because service discovery is a part of nearly every Bluetooth usage case, it is desirable that the service discovery process be as simple as possible to execute.

Copyright © 2004, Idea Group Inc. Copying or distributing in print or electronic forms without written permission of Idea Group Inc. is prohibited.

- Compactness: Since service discovery is a typical operation to perform soon after links are established, the SDP air-interface traffic should be as minimal as feasible so that service discovery does not unnecessarily prolong the communication initialization process.
- Versatility: It is important for SDP to be easily extensible and versatile enough to accommodate the many new services that will be deployed in Bluetooth environments over time.

SDP supports the following service inquires:

- Search by service class
- Search by service attributes
- Service browsing

Service Browsing

Service browsing in Bluetooth is used for a general service search and provides the user with answers to such questions as: "What services are available?" or "What services of type X are available?" In the Bluetooth specification, a service browsing hierarchy is suggested. The hierarchy includes browse group descriptor services records (G) and other service records with (S) (Bluetooth Specification, 2001).

Service Relation Ontology

We propose service relation ontology to extend and enhance the hierarchical structure introduced in the Bluetooth specification. The ontological relation model has been applied to e-commerce (Lee, Sim & Kwok, 2002). Ontology represents an explicit specification of a domain conceptualization (Gruber, 1993). The classes and relations of the service relation ontology are shown in Figure 1, which support *gradation, dependence* and *association* classes among concepts. The hierarchical graph illustrates inheritance, where each class on the lower level inherits properties from the preceding level.

Copyright © 2004, Idea Group Inc. Copying or distributing in print or electronic forms without written permission of Idea Group Inc. is prohibited.

Figure 1. Service relation ontology.

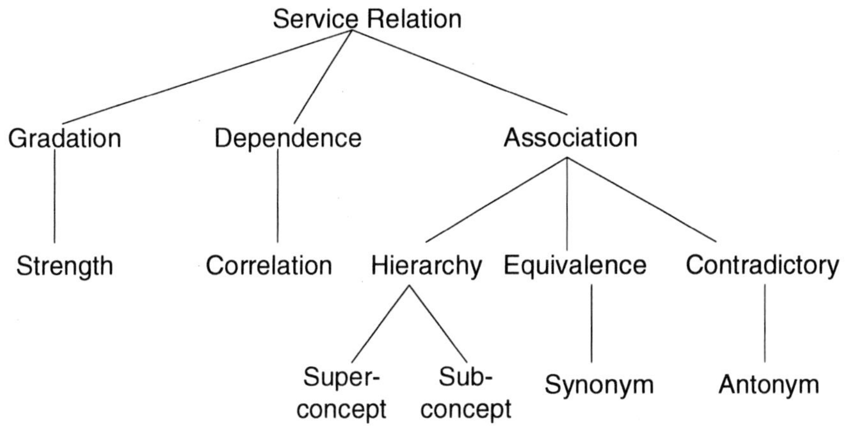

The three classes identified in Figure 1 are:

- Class gradation – to order strength of a concept, which represents a semantic relation for organizing lexical memory of adjectives (Fellbaum, 1998).
- Class dependence – to model the semantic dependence relations between concepts, also known as correlation.
- Class association – consists of three sub-classes:
    - Equivalence – represents the same concept meaning between or among concepts.
    - Hierarchy – represents the broader or narrower concept relations.
    - Contradictory – represents opposing values of an attribute.

The six ontological relations identified in Figure 1 facilitate the effective application of electronic lexicons for Bluetooth service discovery. The operations of the relations are given as follows:

Copyright © 2004, Idea Group Inc. Copying or distributing in print or electronic forms without written permission of Idea Group Inc. is prohibited.

- Super-concept: If a concept has a broader meaning than another concept, then the concept is called super-concept. For example, "audio" is a super-concept of "cellular" and "intercom".
- Sub-concept: If a concept has a narrower meaning than another, then the concept is called sub-concept. For example, "cordless phone" and "mobile phone" are sub-concepts of "phone," whereas "phone" is a super-concept.
- Synonym: If two concepts share similar properties, then they are synonyms. For example, "cell phone" and "cellular phone" are synonyms.
- Antonym: If two concepts have opposite properties, then they are antonyms. For example, "wire" and "wireless" are antonyms or "symmetric" and "asymmetric" are antonyms.
- Strength: If a concept is associated with a scale (such as short, square and long) representing degree and grades, then the concept has strength. For example, "decline," "plummet" and "nosedive" are concepts that are similar in meaning but differ in their strengths.
- Correlation: If a concept is dependent on another concept, then they have correlation. For example, the relationship between bandwidth of a transmission system and the maximum number of bits per second that can be transferred over that system.

Concept Representation

Two approaches can be used to codify the service relation ontology; for example a frame-based approach represents the gradation, dependence and association of service concepts (Lee, Sim & Kwok, 2002). Figure 2 shows an example of a frame and various slots to represent a concept.

The above service name slot is self-explanatory; both sub-concept and super-concept facilitate categorization, sub-assumption and inheritance. The property slot captures the features, attributes, and characteristics of service concepts. The frame-based representation has the same interpretation as the notion of property of objects in an object-oriented paradigm, which is a class of objects that inherit prosperities from an ancestor class. In the above formalism, a concept inherits the features (attributes and properties) from concepts that subsume it. The synonym and antonym slots define the (inter-)

Copyright © 2004, Idea Group Inc. Copying or distributing in print or electronic forms without written permission of Idea Group Inc. is prohibited.

Figure 2. An example of the service concept representation.

```
<concept>
  Service Name: Mobile phone
  Property:{ }
  Super-concept: {Phone }
  Sub-concept: { }
  Synonym: { Cellular phone}
  Antonym: { Wire phone}
  Correlation: { }
  Strength: { }
<end_concept>
```

relations between (and among) concepts with similar or opposite meanings, respectively. The correlation slot models depend on concepts.

A thesaural markup language (TML), specified as an XML, can also be used to define the permitted markup element types and embedding structure (Lee, Baillie & Dell'Oro, 1999). For example, the representation of the above service concept can be marked up in TML. The ontology markup element is used to define service concepts.

```
<ontology>
        <setHierarchy          type=”HI”        name=”Hierarchy”/>
        <setHierarchy          type="SC"        name="Super-concept"/>
        <setHierarchy          type="SU"        name= "Sub-concept"/>
        <setEquivalence type="EQ"      name= "Equivalence"/>
        <setEquivalence type="SY"      name= "Synonym"/>
        <setContradictory      type="CO"        name= "Contradictory"/>
        <setContradictory      type="AN"        name= "Antonym"/>
<ontology/>
```

The instance markup element is used to populate the ontology structure with instances:

Copyright © 2004, Idea Group Inc. Copying or distributing in print or electronic forms without written permission of Idea Group Inc. is prohibited.

```
<instances>
        <Hierarchy        type="HI"        value="Mobile Phone">
                          <superConcept  type="SC"        value="Phone">
                          <subConcept          type="SU"        value="">
        </Hierarchy>
        <Equivalence              type="EQ"        value="Mobile Phone">
                                  <Synonym        type="SY"  value=" Cellular Phone">
        </Equivalence>
        <Contradictory  type="CO"        value="Mobile Phone">
                                  <Antonym        type="AN"        value="">
        </Contradictory>
</instances>
```

Service Searching

Service searching in Bluetooth is used to search services by service class and attributes. In particular, it is used when searching for a specific service and provides the user with the answers to such questions as: "Is service X available, or is service X with characteristics 1 and 2 available?" (Muller, 2001). However, the class of the service defines the meanings of the attributes, so an attribute might mean something different in different service records.

Semantic Searching Process

Based on the proposed service ontology, we provide a semantic matching process to allow matching different naming attributes. Figure 3 shows the semantic matching process. The key of the searching engine process is a knowledge base, the service ontology, with information about service instances. The searching process first listens to the query and extracts the service name. It then matches to the service records to determine whether it can answer the query. Upon failure, it responds with a "no matching" message. Otherwise, the engine extracts the relationships that the service ontology describes and uses them to arrive at a service searching pattern solution to a given service discovery query.

Copyright © 2004, Idea Group Inc. Copying or distributing in print or electronic forms without written permission of Idea Group Inc. is prohibited.

Figure 3. Semantic matching process.

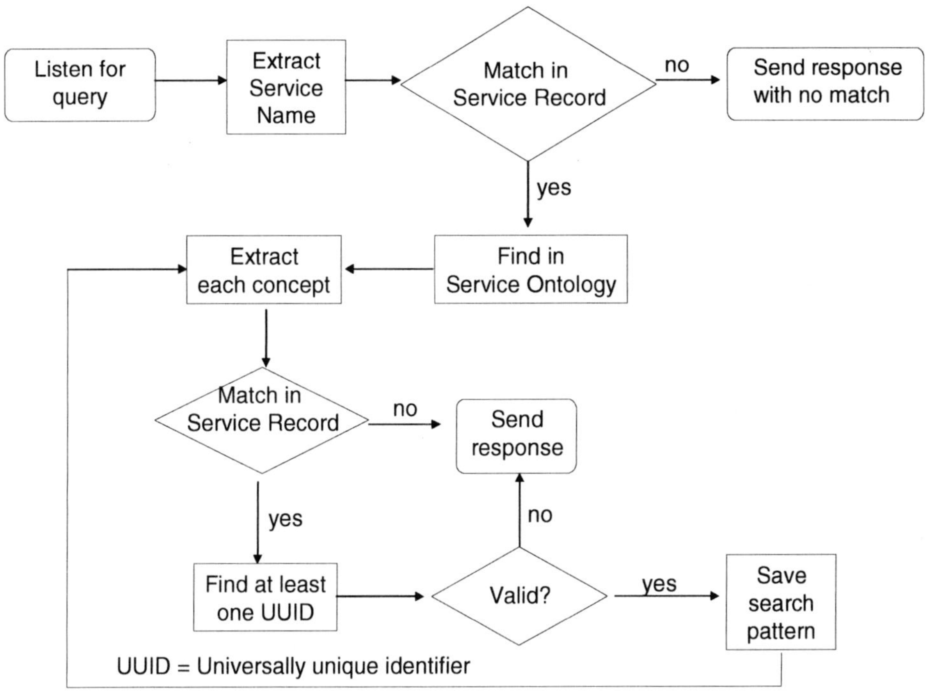

Service Records

A service record holds all the information a server provides to describe a service. Table 1 shows an example of the Bluetooth headset service record (Bray & Sturman, 2001).

The example table illustrates how a service record is made up. For example, when a client acquires a "headset" service, the semantic searching engine reaches the service name in the service record. It then goes to the service ontology to get its related concepts, such as its "synonym" concept, earphone. The process continues until the ontology concept frame ends.

Copyright © 2004, Idea Group Inc. Copying or distributing in print or electronic forms without written permission of Idea Group Inc. is prohibited.

Table 1. Bluetooth headset service record example (Source from: Bray & Sturman, 2001).

Item	Type	Value	Attribute
ServiceRecordHandle	Unit 32	Assigned by Server	0x000
ServiceClassDList			0x001
ServiceClass0	UUID	Headset	0x1108
ServiceClass1	UUID	Generic Audio	0x1203
ProtocolDescriptorList			0x0004
Protocol0	UUID	L2CAP	0x0100
Protocol1	UUID	RFCOMM	0x0003
ProtocolSpecificParamater()	Unit8	Server Channel #	
BluetoothProfileDescriptorList			0x0009
Profile()	UUID	Headset	0x1108
Parameter()	Unit 16	Version 1.0	0x0100
ServiceName	String	"Headset"	0x0000+language offset
Remote Audio Volume Control	Boolean	False	0x0302

Service Search Patterns

A service search pattern is used to support a list of UUIDs to locate matching service records. A service search pattern matches a service record if each and every UUID in the service search pattern is contained within any of the service records' attribute values. A valid service search pattern must contain at least one UUID. The UUIDs need not be contained within any specific attributes or in any particular order within the service record.

Discussion

Avancha, Joshi and Finin (2002) have discussed that using ontology to describe services can facilitate inexact matching because it provides a structure for reasoning about how knowledge is derived from the given descriptions. They have commented that describing service ontologically is superior to UUID-based descriptions. They use the DAML+OIL (Darpa Agent Markup Language and Ontology Inference Layer) to describe their ontology and a Prolog-

Copyright © 2004, Idea Group Inc. Copying or distributing in print or electronic forms without written permission of Idea Group Inc. is prohibited.

based reasoning engine to use the ontology. Although DAML+OIL is becoming a standard for use in the semantic Web, the ontology developers may have difficulty understanding implemented ontologies or even building new ontologies because they focus too much on implementation issues. Moreover, direct coding of the resulting concepts is too abrupt a step, especially for complex ontologies.

In this chapter, we provide a language-independent concept model for representing the "context-dependent" classification knowledge. The classification knowledge is to organize words into groups that share many properties. The context is dependent on Bluetooth service discovery concepts. One of the advantages of using ontology is to validate conceptual models (Shanks, Tansley & Weber, 2003). The proposed ontology model represents specific domain phenomena and clarifies ambiguous semantics in the model; for example, in Figure 4, which outlines an example of an ontology conceptual model used in practice, all phenomena in the domain are represented as either concepts or relationships.

The conceptual model (Figure 4) enables ontologists to distinguish different types of phenomena in their theories. This is important because people can view the various distinctions as real. The ontology model can identify misclassified phenomena, which assists the validation of the conceptual model. The repre-

Figure 4. An example of ontology conceptual model.

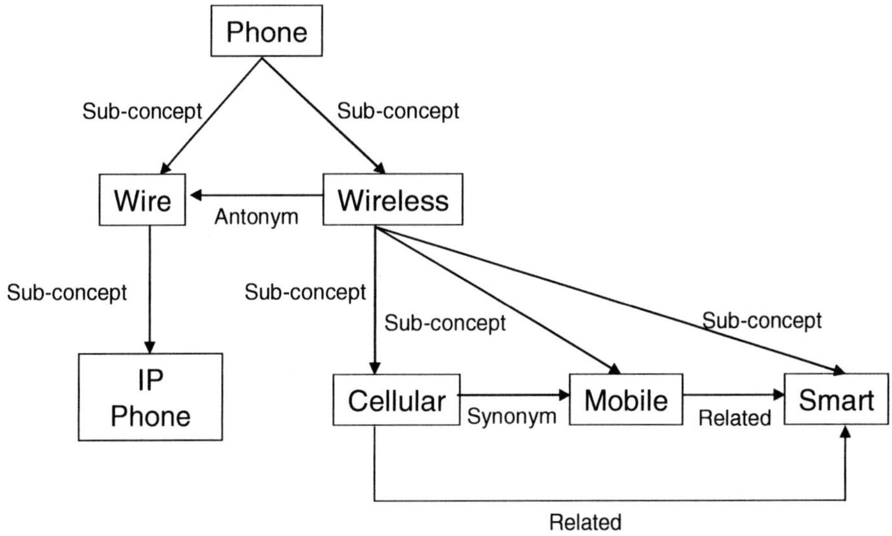

Copyright © 2004, Idea Group Inc. Copying or distributing in print or electronic forms without written permission of Idea Group Inc. is prohibited.

sentation with the figure can motivate ontologists to ask validation questions about the focal domain as though all phenomena in it were either entities or relationships. In addition, the proposed model can help generate clear, complete description of the domain and help make sense of ambiguous semantics in conceptual models that need to be validated.

Conclusion

We have introduced a service ontology concept modeling to enhance the Bluetooth service discovery. We have shown a frame-based presentation to support gradation, dependence and association classes among concepts. The semantic searching process allows matching different naming attributes to increase the quality of service discovery.

We envision the semantic service discovery solution can also be applied to wireless LAN, IEEE 802.11b and wide-area wireless networks. By looking at the rapid deployment of wireless technologies in hot spots such as cafes, shopping malls and restaurants around the world, semantic service discovery will play an important role in future mobile-commerce applications.

Our future work includes evaluating semantic matching performance both in response time and processing time. We will need to compare the response and processing times for service discovery queries in the enhanced Bluetooth SDP with those in the regular system. We will also investigate the possibilities of developing m-commerce applications using semantic service discovery.

Acknowledgments

This work reported in this paper has been funded in part by the Department of Information Management, Shih Chien University and Hyper Taiwan Technology Inc. The authors would like to thank Scott Lai of Hyper Taiwan Technology for his helpful discussions and useful suggestions.

Copyright © 2004, Idea Group Inc. Copying or distributing in print or electronic forms without written permission of Idea Group Inc. is prohibited.

References

Amold, K., Wollrath, A., O'Sullivan, B., Scheiffer, R., & Waldo, J. (1999). *The Jini specification.* Addison-Wesley.

Avancha, S., Joshi, A., & Finin, T. (2002, June). Enhanced service discovery in Bluetooth. *Communications of the ACM,* 96-99.

Bluetooth Specification Version 1.1. (2001, February).

Bray, J., & Sturman, C. (2001). *Bluetooth connect without cables.* Prentice-Hall.

Chakraborty, D., & Chen, H. (2002). Service discovery in the future for mobile commerce. *ACM Crossroads,* winter. ACM Press.

Chakraborty, D., Perich, F., Avancha, S., & Joshi, A. (2001). DReggie: A smart service discovery technique for e-commerce applications. Workshop on Reliable and Secure Applications in Mobile Environment, in conjunction with *20th Symposium on Reliable Distributed Systems (SRDS).*

Davies, J., Fensel, D., & Harmelen, F. (Eds.). (2002). *Towards the semantic Web: Ontology-driven knowledge management.* John Wiley & Sons.

Fellbaum, C. (1998). *WordNet: An electronic lexical database.* The MIT Press.

Gruber, T.(1993). Translation approach to portable ontology specifications. *Knowledge Acquisition, 5*(9), 199-220.

Lee, M., Baillie, S., & Dell'Oro, J. (1999). TML: A Thesaural Markup Language. *Proceedings of the 4th Australasian Document Computing Symposium,* Australia.

Lee, M., Sim, K., & Kwok, P. (2002). Concept acquisition modeling for e-commerce ontology. In K. Sollten (Ed.), *Optimal information modeling techniques* (pp. 30-40). IRM Press.

Ludwig, S. (2002). *Review of service discovery systems.* Technical Report, TR-DGRG695. Department of Electrical and Computer Engineering, Brunel University.

Ludwig, S., & Santen, P. (2002). A grid service discovery matchmaker based on ontology description. *Proceedings of the EuroWeb 2002 Conference,* UK.

Miller, B., & Bisdikian, C. (2001). *Bluetooth revealed.* Prentice Hall.

Copyright © 2004, Idea Group Inc. Copying or distributing in print or electronic forms without written permission of Idea Group Inc. is prohibited.

Miller, B., & Pascoe, R. (1999). *Mapping salutation architecture APIs to Bluetooth service discovery layer.* Available: http://www.bluetooth.com

Salutation Architecture Specification (Part-I). (1999). *The Salutation Consortium,* 2.1 edition.

Shanks, G., Tansley, E., & Weber, R. (2003, October). Using ontology to validate conceptual models. *Communication of the ACM, 46*(10), 85-89.

Veizades, J., Cuttman, E., Perkins, C., & Kaplan, S. (1997). *Service location protocol.* Available: http://www.rfc-editor.org/rfc/rfc2165txt

Copyright © 2004, Idea Group Inc. Copying or distributing in print or electronic forms without written permission of Idea Group Inc. is prohibited.

Chapter XI

Effective Integration of Computer-Supported Collaborative Learning into Knowledge Management Structures: A Model and an Evaluation Framework

Francisco Milton Mendes Neto
Federal University of Campina Grande, Brazil and
Serpro – Federal Service of Data Processing, Brazil

Francisco Vilar Brasileiro
Federal University of Campina Grande, Brazil

Abstract

Support for knowledge management (KM) requires mechanisms for creation, mapping and transference of knowledge. Many organizations use computer tools, like knowledge mapping tools, knowledge repositories, tools to support communities of practice and computer-supported collaborative learning (CSCL), to achieve these goals. In particular,

Copyright © 2004, Idea Group Inc. Copying or distributing in print or electronic forms without written permission of Idea Group Inc. is prohibited.

CSCL can support knowledge transfer at the same time that it improves the process of creating new knowledge. However, whole CSCL potential to transfer knowledge and foment learning is not being used adequately, mainly because of the lack of appropriate integration with other KM tools. In fact, there is a lack of guidance on how to effectively integrate CSCL into KM and how to evaluate the benefits of this integration. This chapter fills in this gap by proposing a model to improve KM through the consistent and effective integration of CSCL into the KM structure of organizations. It also describes a framework to evaluate the results of this integration.

Introduction

The main functionalities of an organizational knowledge management (KM) structure are: creation, mapping and transference of knowledge. *Knowledge creation* occurs in people's minds through the interaction between tacit and explicit knowledge (Joshi et al., 2002; Nonaka & Takeuchi, 1995). *Knowledge mapping* consists of the identification and classification of the existent organizational knowledge. This, in turn, is embedded in documents, repositories, routines, processes, practices, norms and, mainly, in people's minds. Finally, *knowledge transfer* consists of moving knowledge to where it can generate value. That is, to where it can be used to support the execution of some organizational activity (Davenport & Prusak, 1998).

Many organizations use computer tools to support the functionalities of KM structures. As for instance, we can cite: knowledge mapping tools, knowledge repositories, tools to support communities of practice, and computer-supported collaborative learning (CSCL) tools (Baloian et al., 2000; Guzdial & Turns, 1998; Hsiao, 1996; Joshi et al., 2002; Whitelock, 1993), among others.

These tools together support the three main functionalities of a KM structure. Some organizations use, among other tools, CSCL to transfer knowledge. Because of its focus on both communication techniques used and what is being communicated (knowledge content), CSCL can support knowledge transfer at the same time that it improves the creation process of new knowledge (Hsiao, 1996). We advocate that the judicious integration of CSCL into a KM structure

Copyright © 2004, Idea Group Inc. Copying or distributing in print or electronic forms without written permission of Idea Group Inc. is prohibited.

allows the provision of more reach (knowledge for more workers), speed (knowledge is generated as soon as its lack is detected), objectivity (right knowledge to the right person on the right time) and effectiveness (more knowledge application) in the knowledge transfer.

Although many KM structures use CSCL tools nowadays, their use is, normally, implemented in an independent way; that is, without a great integration with other KM tools. To the best of our knowledge, there is no literature that gives guidance on how to effectively and consistently integrate CSCL into KM, which may also be perceived as an indication that this integration is not being carried out at all. Consequently, the whole CSCL potential to transfer knowledge and foment organizational learning is not being used adequately.

In this chapter we describe a model to integrate CSCL into a KM structure in a consistent and effective way. We also analyze the benefits that this integration brings to organizational KM by discussing the main requirements that should be satisfied by KM and how CSCL contributes to the fulfillment of these requirements. Then, we propose a process for defining capable measures to evaluate the results obtained with this integration.

The remaining of this chapter is structured in the following way. Firstly, we discuss the requirements that should be satisfied by a KM structure. In the following, we present an analysis on how CSCL tools can help in satisfying these requirements. Then, an integration model is detailed and its benefits are discussed. After that, we describe a process to define measures to evaluate this integration. Finally, the chapter is concluded with our final remarks on how to effectively integrate CSCL into KM structure of organizations and evaluate the results.

Requirements for the Success of KM

KM is a relatively new research area; thus, neither the correct directions to be followed nor the difficulties to be faced when implementing it are yet very clear. However, a number of requirements that need to be satisfied in order to achieve success in KM have already been identified. Some of them are:

Copyright © 2004, Idea Group Inc. Copying or distributing in print or electronic forms without written permission of Idea Group Inc. is prohibited.

Requirement 1: To promote the workers' creativity and the innovation of products and services

The incentive to workers' creativity and innovation of products and services inside the organization is an important issue to be considered when implementing KM. Organizations must pursue a balance between rigidity and flexibility excess of their KM structures. Rigidity inhibits creativity, while flexibility improves it. However, too much flexibility precludes the control of creativity so that it can be successfully addressed to the needs of a product or a service. Consequently, a tension is created between process and practice, that is, between the way that the organizational activities are formally organized and the way that these activities are actually accomplished. Practice contributes to the appearance of new ideas, while process allows their control and implementation to take place (Brown & Duguid, 2000).

Requirement 2: To share essential knowledge to the business

One of the main KM requirements is to increase the intellectual capital of the organization; however, it is not sufficient to share knowledge for this to happen. It is necessary to share knowledge that can be useful to create value to the business (Mouritsen et al., 2001).

Requirement 3: To increase the access to the knowledge

One of the difficulties faced by KM is how to share the knowledge necessary for the business improvement among all the workers. Some organizations only stimulate creativity among elite professionals, as an attempt at solving the tension between process and practice. Other workers' jobs remain predictable and very close to process structures. Nowadays, due to constant changes on the business strategies caused by the market, all organizational sectors need to be creative (Brown & Duguid, 2000).

Requirement 4: To facilitate the knowledge transfer

Qualified workers' lack of structure and plans on how to share their knowledge is a problem faced by most of the organizations during KM implementation.

Copyright © 2004, Idea Group Inc. Copying or distributing in print or electronic forms without written permission of Idea Group Inc. is prohibited.

Usually, the few workers that possess these abilities do not have time to place their knowledge into a system (Davenport & Prusak, 1998).

Requirement 5: To increase the amount of explicit knowledge

KM structures require definition and storage of the best practices of the organization for posterior searches. There are, however, some reasons that make this a difficult task. Firstly, because of the difference between what workers are expected to do and what they really do, normally there are great differences between tasks' specifications presented in process handbooks (explicit knowledge) and their practical execution. Secondly, due to the difference between what workers think they do and what they really do, tasks' effective execution is full of tacit improvisations, which are difficult to be articulated by their executioners. A KM structure has to surpass these barriers when defining the organization's best practices and storing them in the form of explicit knowledge (Brown & Duguid, 2000).

Requirement 6: To increase the exchange of tacit knowledge

How to foment the exchange of tacit knowledge is another problem that should be considered when implementing KM. Tacit (or implicit) knowledge cannot be easily articulated, formalized, communicated or codified, because it contains personal aspects. It is deeply rooted in the action, in the engagement and in the involvement in a specific context (Nonaka & Takeuchi, 1995).

Requirement 7: To increase the workers' motivation and engagement to the learning process

A challenge faced by KM relates to how to motivate the workers to search for knowledge. It is not sufficient to offer an effective tool to promote the organizational learning. It is necessary that workers are motivated to use it (Mouritsen et al., 2001).

Copyright © 2004, Idea Group Inc. Copying or distributing in print or electronic forms without written permission of Idea Group Inc. is prohibited.

Requirement 8: To make the execution of the activities more efficient

Although great progress has been observed in KM, most organizations continue not using adequately the knowledge distributed inside them. This knowledge could be used to optimize the execution of the business processes and the use of the organizational resources. These organizations cannot capitalize on their intellectual resources nor use the existent knowledge in the improvement of their activities. They also cannot combine this knowledge with existent processes to create something new. This would help them in answering a number of new challenges, enabling them to be more efficient than their competitors (Hansen & Von Oetinger, 2001).

Requirement 9: To improve the quality of products and services

KM should contribute to increase the intellectual capital of the organization, that is, to increase the amount of knowledge (business competencies) that has been applied to products and services of the organization. An increase in the amount of intellectual capital of the organization can bring improvement in the quality of its products and services.

Requirement 10: To increase the profitability of the organization

The focus of most business strategies is on the increase of the profitability. If financial outcomes have not been improved, the business strategy's basic statements should be reviewed (Kaplan & Norton, 1992). One of the main KM goals is also to fulfill this requirement. According to Davenport and Prusak (1998), business initiatives involving intellectual capital tend to have strong focus on the conversion of knowledge in revenues or profits.

Copyright © 2004, Idea Group Inc. Copying or distributing in print or electronic forms without written permission of Idea Group Inc. is prohibited.

CSCL Tools and Their Contributions to the Fulfillment of KM Requirements

A Brief Description of CSCL Tools

CSCL is a research area of specialized domain inside CSCW (Computer-Supported Cooperative Work) (Greenberg, 1991). CSCW studies the use of groupware in any business area and it has as its main focus to facilitate the communication among a group to increase productivity. CSCL is limited to study of the use of groupware in the educational area. It has as its main focus to support knowledge recipients (e.g., trainees, students, etc.) in the process of effectively learning in groups, using computer tools.

The learning process is related to the acquisition and the constant renewal of competenceies (knowledge and skills), in which the collaboration among a group plays a fundamental role. The main difference between CSCL and other computer-mediated learning modalities is that it focuses on collaboration. It allows interaction with both learning environment and other training participants (e.g., workers, experts, facilitators, students, teachers, etc.).

The knowledge required for workers changes daily. CSCL tools allow adapting the training materials to the current organizational needs in an easier way than face-to-face learning. In the latter, training materials are normally prepared with greater antecedence; thus they quickly become outdated (Allinson & Hammond, 1989; Levy, 2001a).

CSCL was idealized initially as a potential substitute to the face-to-face learning, but it did not reach the expected results. Now, after a better understanding of the technology, methodologies and potential of this learning modality, the focus has changed. It was verified that CSCL would be better used if it was addressed to more specific learning objectives; that is, if it was addressed to business goals (Levy, 2001b; Rossett, 2001, 2002a).

An environment to support collaborative learning must offer mechanisms for knowledge recipients to interact with both colleagues and knowledge providers (e.g., experts, teachers, instructors, etc.). Knowledge recipients should interact in the same way that they would interact in the face-to-face learning. They should acquire in this learning modality, at least, the same knowledge that they would obtain if accomplishing training in a face-to-face way. This interaction is supported by the integration of tools for both communication and cooperation,

Copyright © 2004, Idea Group Inc. Copying or distributing in print or electronic forms without written permission of Idea Group Inc. is prohibited.

which can be synchronous or asynchronous. These tools are important in a number of group activities for solving problems. Some examples of these tools are detailed below.

Synchronous Communication Tools

Chat Tool: chat tools allow online communication in text format with the other training participants. These tools can also offer for participants an interface to search for past conversations, facilitating the retrieval of the training memory.

Audio Conference Tool: the audio conference tool allows carrying out a conference among the training participants using audio resources.

Videoconference Tool: This tool allows carrying out a conference among the training participants using audio and video resources.

Asynchronous Communication Tools

Electronic Mail: the electronic mail allows sending messages over the Internet to all training participants.

Discussion List: this tool allows participants to engage themselves in the discussion of any subject and recover past discussions.

Interest Groups: interest groups allow participants to discuss the main subjects of the training, which were identified by the knowledge providers of the training. These tools can also offer for participants an interface to search for past discussions.

Synchronous Cooperation Tools

Whiteboard: the whiteboard consists of a drawing area that can be visualized by all training participants. It is useful to discuss models, diagrams, graphs, flow charts and other things that facilitate the development of a task. Whiteboards are usually used together with a chat tool.

Tool to Share Applications: a training participant using this tool can share with other participants any application that is executing at his or her computer.

Copyright © 2004, Idea Group Inc. Copying or distributing in print or electronic forms without written permission of Idea Group Inc. is prohibited.

This is useful, for example, to share applications required for the development of the training with geographically distant participants.

File Transfer Tool: this tool facilitates files interchange among the training participants. It allows, for example, sending or receiving documents complementing the training subjects or programs to support the training activities.

Asynchronous Cooperation Tools

Materials Repository: the materials repository allows recovering the training materials, which can be files or references to files (URLs[1]). Materials shared in this repository are normally materials to complement the knowledge recipients' learning, such as homework, complementary readings, and so forth.

Frequently Asked Questions (FAQ): this tool allows accessing the most frequent questions about the training subject, which were previously sent to knowledge providers of the learning process.

News Mural: the news mural allows consulting the training events (event description, day, hour, etc.) and news that are related to the training.

Fulfilling KM Requirements with the Support of CSCL

CSCL contributes to *promote the workers' creativity and the innovation of products and services* because it allows greater flexibility in the acquisition and transference of knowledge. It also offers the necessary framework to support, control and address what has been learned to a product or service of the organization.

Greater flexibility is possible due to a number of media formats (image, audio, video, hypertext, etc.) that can be used for knowledge acquisition via CSCL tools. The appropriate format can be chosen depending on the aptitudes and individual preferences (Allinson & Hammond, 1989). Further, CSCL tools normally offer a number of interaction mechanisms (synchronous and asynchronous), which can be used for knowledge transfer. This learning modality offers a much greater degree of flexibility for workers participating in the learning process: flexibility in both time (access to knowledge at any time) and space (access to knowledge from anywhere possessing network connection or

Copyright © 2004, Idea Group Inc. Copying or distributing in print or electronic forms without written permission of Idea Group Inc. is prohibited.

Internet connection) dimensions, mainly, if the CSCL interface is the World Wide Web (Berners-Lee et al., 1994).

On the other hand, structure can be supported by the coordination tools existent in some CSCL environments that allow registering most decisions that users (e.g., workers, experts, facilitators, students, teachers, etc.) take within the environment. Further, these environments allow knowledge providers to closely follow, motivate and interact with knowledge recipients in learning activities that can bring significant outcomes to the organization.

The use of CSCL tools integrated to other KM tools can help in *sharing essential knowledge to the business,* because CSCL tools allow offering training as soon as the lack of this knowledge has been detected by other KM tools. The integration of CSCL tools into KM structures allows *increasing the access to the knowledge;* that is, it supplies more reach in the knowledge transfer. This integration yields sharing knowledge in a uniform way in the whole organization, independently of geographical location, physical limitations, organizational position, and so forth. This learning modality allows easy access to knowledge, which can be shared with more people. In this way, it also helps in fomenting creativity into all organizational sectors.

CSCL tools can facilitate the knowledge transfer, and consequently increase the speed with which the knowledge arrives where it can generate value. Workers using them can easily share their knowledge with colleagues, mainly through the several tools of communication and cooperation. CSCL can also be used to qualify workers in technologies, methodologies and required abilities to implement KM by releasing training to workers. This is another way of attenuating the problem of qualified workers' shortcomings in this area.

Some CSCL modalities promote problem resolution activities, in which knowledge recipients participate in discussions to identify more effective ways of accomplishing their tasks. These can be added to the database of best practices contributing to *increasing the amount of explicit knowledge.* CSCL can also help in *increasing the exchange of tacit knowledge* into organizations. It can stimulate workers with common interests to use its tools to interact with each other. Moreover, knowledge providers can foment the formation of groups with common interests around projects that can bring interesting outcomes to the organization.

CSCL can be useful to *increase the workers' motivation and engagement to the learning process,* since knowledge providers can supply support to workers in the planning and structuring of their learning. This support allows

Copyright © 2004, Idea Group Inc. Copying or distributing in print or electronic forms without written permission of Idea Group Inc. is prohibited.

knowledge acquisition in a simple, fast and efficient way. The several tools for communication and cooperation existent in most CSCL environments can facilitate this support. The effective integration of CSCL into KM can also provide more objectivity to the knowledge transfer. It makes it possible to provide a learning process that is both continuous and personalized. Further, it allows aiming this learning at the business goals, because CSCL allows mediation. Knowledge providers can guide the knowledge transfer process to business goals. Once identified which knowledge is more important for the organization, CSCL tools allow giving priority to them during the learning process. In this way, CSCL contributes directly to *improving the quality of products and services* of the organization. Consequently, it contributes to *increasing the profitability of the organization* by the improvement of the business competitive advantages.

Finally, CSCL can provide more effectiveness in the knowledge transfer, since it can increase the percentage of knowledge that is really assimilated and applied. This will bring benefits to the workers, because they will learn what they really need to know in order to accomplish their daily tasks. Consequently, CSCL will *make the execution of the activities more efficient* (Levy, 2001a).

A Model for the Effective Integration of CSCL into KM Structures

We now present a model to improve organizational KM through the effective integration of CSCL. It is represented in UML (Unified Modeling Language) (Quatrani, 1998), which allows object oriented modeling. Figure 1 illustrates the model, which consists of a diagram showing the collaboration between CSCL and other KM tools. This model gives a general view of how CSCL can bring benefits to a KM structure.

T(in a1, a2..., out b1, b2...) represents messages exchanged among objects, where: *T* is the message type, *in a1, a2...* represents the list of request arguments and *out b1, b2...* represents the list of reply arguments. The message types can be:

Copyright © 2004, Idea Group Inc. Copying or distributing in print or electronic forms without written permission of Idea Group Inc. is prohibited.

Figure 1. The model for integration of CSCL into KM structures.

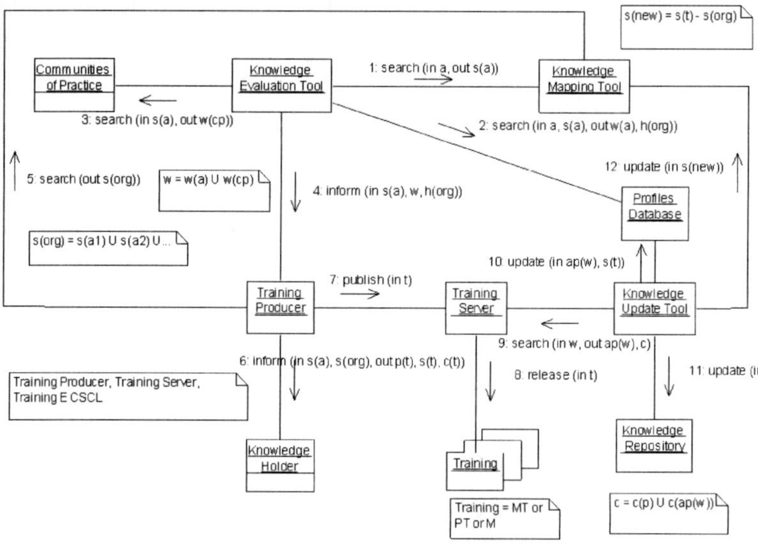

- Informative: message updating an object with necessary information (e.g., inform() and update());
- Interrogative: message requesting information from an object (e.g., search());
- Imperative: message requesting an object to execute some task (e.g., publish() and release()).

Components of the Model

Knowledge Mapping Tool

Knowledge mapping tools are used to build the knowledge map of the organization; that is, to detect existent organizational knowledge and its location. They generally point to people (tacit knowledge sources), but they can also address explicit knowledge sources, such as documents and databases (Davenport & Prusak, 1998). They also identify the knowledge required for the

Copyright © 2004, Idea Group Inc. Copying or distributing in print or electronic forms without written permission of Idea Group Inc. is prohibited.

effective execution of the business (Hansen et al., 1999). Knowledge tree (Levy, 1997a) is an example of a tool for knowledge mapping.

Profiles Database

Profiles databases are tools that store information on the workers' competencies (knowledge and skills) as well as how to locate them. The location of knowledge holders is useful because they can provide support to colleagues during the processes of solving a problem, developing solutions, and so forth. Profiles databases can also facilitate the workers' selection for both teaching activities and representation of the organization in external events.

Knowledge Repository

Knowledge repositories are tools that provide a uniform access to the knowledge embedded in documents and databases. In this way, the knowledge can be easily stored and recovered (Davenport & Prusak, 1998). Knowledge repositories can store documents or URLs that were submitted by workers. These documents can be in several formats (texts, images, videos, etc.). Reviewers or content managers can appraise the submitted contents before they can be published in the repository.

Communities of Practice

Communities of practice (Wenger & Snyder, 2000) are groups of people that informally share knowledge and impressions in specific areas. They arise within organizations that stimulate knowledge transfer. However, it is not easy to build, sustain and, mainly, integrate them into organizations. Due to their informal and spontaneous nature, as well as their natural isolation, communities of practice are normally resistant to supervision and interference (Wenger & Snyder, 2000). They can exist with or without mediation of information technology. For example, they can operate via either the regular meetings among their members or the use of electronic mail or other technology. However, the use of a computer tool in order to support communities of practice can increase the reach and the effectiveness of the transference, storage and recovery of the knowledge by the communities' members as well.

Copyright © 2004, Idea Group Inc. Copying or distributing in print or electronic forms without written permission of Idea Group Inc. is prohibited.

Knowledge Evaluation Tool

Knowledge evaluation tools identify the knowledge required for the fulfillment of some particular function within the organization. They use both knowledge mapping tools, which identify the knowledge necessary for an organizational area, and profiles databases, which identify the workers' knowledge. Knowledge evaluation tools should allow searching both the knowledge required for an area (using knowledge mapping tools) and the workers' competencies (using profiles databases). Then they point out both the competencies required for the workers and the knowledge subjects that they should know to execute their work in an efficient way.

Knowledge Update Tool

A knowledge update tool detects, automatically, the existence of new knowledge that has been generated in training. After carrying out the training, this tool updates the profiles database (tacit knowledge) and the knowledge repository (explicit knowledge) with the new acquired knowledge. This tool can also update, if necessary, the knowledge map of the organization with new subjects acquired during the accomplishment of trainings.

CSCL Tools

Most CSCL environments are composed of three basic components: *training producer,* which can be used to create trainings; *training server,* which releases trainings to workers; and *training,* which includes both contents and tools for navigation, coordination and interaction. The latter can consist of tools for both communication and cooperation.

Behavior of the Model

The *knowledge evaluation tool* facilitates the identification of the knowledge necessary for some particular organizational area by searching in the *knowledge mapping tool.* This operation is represented in the model of Figure 1 by message *search (in a, out s(a)),* which provides as input the identifier of an area

Copyright © 2004, Idea Group Inc. Copying or distributing in print or electronic forms without written permission of Idea Group Inc. is prohibited.

of the organization (a) and receives as result the list of subjects required for the effective execution of its activities (s(a)).

This information can be used, for example, to search in the *profiles database* for any worker within that area that does not hold the necessary knowledge to execute his or her tasks with efficacy; further, the search can also discover whether there are workers holding such knowledge within the organization. This operation is represented in the model by message *search (in a, s(a), out w(a), h(org))*, which provides as input the organizational area that is being evaluated (a) and the required subjects for the execution of its activities (s(a)). This message receives as results the list of workers of the organizational area that do not hold the necessary knowledge (w(a)) and the list of holders of such knowledge in the organization (h(org)).

The *knowledge evaluation tool* can also search for *communities of practice* related to the identified subjects. It can discover the workers belonging to these communities (w(cp)) that may have interest in these subjects (s(a)). This is represented by message *search (in s(a), out w(cp))*. The *knowledge evaluation tool* allows associating new training with *communities of practice* as well as offering them automatically for the communities' members.

The information collected by the *knowledge evaluation tool* can be used to inform the *training producer* about: subjects (knowledge) that should be covered in the training (s(a)), list of workers that should be trained - $w = w(a) \cup w(cp)$ - and specific knowledge holders (h(org)), that is, workers that hold specific knowledge about a subject (specialists). This can help define training scope, and target public and possible knowledge providers, respectively. This operation is represented in the model by message *inform (in s(a), w, h(org))*.

Then, the *training producer* can recover the organizational knowledge map from the *knowledge mapping tool*. This map is the union of the required subjects for each organizational area - $s(org) = s(a_1) \cup s(a_2) \cup ...$, where $s(a_i)$ are the subjects that such areas need to execute their activities. This is represented in the model by message *search (out s(org))*. After obtaining this map, the *training producer* can inform the *knowledge holders* that they were listed as possible knowledge providers. It also informs the subjects that the knowledge providers should teach in the training.

The *training producer* can also offer the organizational knowledge map for the *knowledge holders*, which facilitates the selection of other subjects related to the business to be included in the training. Finally, the *training producer* waits for a confirmation of some knowledge holders, which will be the knowledge

Copyright © 2004, Idea Group Inc. Copying or distributing in print or electronic forms without written permission of Idea Group Inc. is prohibited.

providers of the training. After that, the knowledge providers must supply the training scope and its respective contents, as it is represented in the model by message *inform (in s(a), s(org), out p(t), s(t), c(t))*. This message provides as input the list of subjects that the training should cover (s(a)) and the organizational knowledge map (s(org)). It receives as results the list of knowledge providers (p(t)), the list of subjects that will be instructed in this training (s(t)) and the training content (c(t)).

The training to provide the required knowledge can be published in the *training server*. This is represented by message *publish (in t)*, where *t* is the training material (e.g., a course). Later on, this training can be released to its target public, which can be: the whole organization (Mass Training - MT), an individual group (Personalized Training - PT) or a particular worker (Mentoring - M). This operation is represented by message *release (in t)*.

After the accomplishment of the training, the *knowledge update tool* searches for both the approved workers (ap(w)) and the generated contents (c) in the *training server*. The training content include the contents produced by both the knowledge providers (c(p)) and the approved workers (c(ap(w))) - c = c(p) $\cup$ c(ap(w)). This operation is represented in the model by message *search (in w, out ap(w), c)*, which provides as input the list of workers that participated in the training (w) and receives as results the list of approved workers (ap(w)) and the generated contents (c).

After getting this information, the individual knowledge map of the *profiles database* of all workers that were trained (ap(w)) should be updated with the new knowledge (s(t)). This is represented by message *update (in ap(w), s(t))*. The *knowledge update tool* also updates the *knowledge repository* with: (i) the contents that were generated during the training (c); (ii) the list of subjects that are related to these contents (s(t)); and (iii) the list of knowledge providers that selected them (p(t)). This is represented by the message *update (in c, s(t), p(t))*. Finally, the *knowledge update tool* updates the knowledge map of the organization with the new subjects acquired during the accomplishment of the training still not included in the *knowledge mapping tool* (s(new)). This is represented in the model by message *update (in s(new))* - s(new) = s(t) - s(org), closing, in this way, the model cycle.

Application of the Model

We accomplished empirical research on the application of the model in a real context to verify its suitability for the business world and provide practical

Copyright © 2004, Idea Group Inc. Copying or distributing in print or electronic forms without written permission of Idea Group Inc. is prohibited.

guidelines on how to use the model. This research was carried out in a large Brazilian company whose business is mainly the provision of information technology services. In the following, the steps to apply the integration model in this organization are listed:

1. Identify the tools that support the model's functionalities in the organization;
2. Verify whether the tools identified in the previous step supply the information required for the model's messages exchange;
3. Plan how to adapt the existent similar tools and implement the new required tools;
4. Implement the plan generated in step 3.

As our objective in this empirical research is only to show that it is possible to apply the model in a real case, we have limited it to the implementation of steps 1 to 3. We believe that they are enough to demonstrate the practical significance of the model. The last step is currently being implemented and its results will be shown in future works.

Identifying the Organizational Tools that Support the Model's Functionalities

Among the tools supporting the KM functionalities of this organization, we identify four tools that are similar to the integration model's tools. The similarities among these tools and the model's tools are described next.

- *Profile System:* This tool supports the mapping of organizational knowledge and the storage of information on workers' competencies and their localization. The former is supported in the integration model by the knowledge mapping tool and the latter is supported by the profiles database.
- *Knowledge Database:* This tool is similar to the model's knowledge repository, storing contents that were shared by workers.
- *Knowledge Communities:* This tool is similar to the communities of practice shown in the model of Figure 1.

Copyright © 2004, Idea Group Inc. Copying or distributing in print or electronic forms without written permission of Idea Group Inc. is prohibited.

Figure 2. An instance of the model for a particular organization.

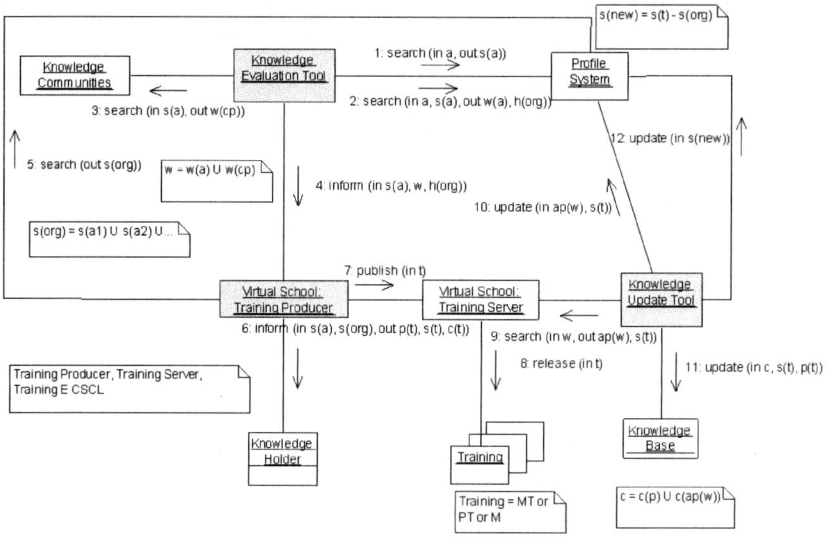

- *Virtual School:* This tool is a CSCL environment, being composed of both a tool to create training materials (training producer) and a training server, besides the training.

Then, replacing the integration model's tools viewed in Figure 1 by the tools listed before, we have the model's instance shown in Figure 2. The gray rectangles represent the tools that need to be adapted or implemented.

Verifying whether the Organizational Tools Supply the Required Information

The profile system (see Figure 2) provides all information supplied by both the knowledge mapping tool and the profiles database, shown in the model of Figure 1. In the same way, the knowledge database and the knowledge communities (Figure 2) are similar to the knowledge repository and the communities of practice, respectively (Figure 1). However, in this organization, there are no tools that supply all information or execute all functionalities provided by both the knowledge evaluation tool and the knowledge update tool. Moreover, the training producer of the Virtual School is limited to create

Copyright © 2004, Idea Group Inc. Copying or distributing in print or electronic forms without written permission of Idea Group Inc. is prohibited.

the training materials and does not execute the additional functionalities of the model's training producer (see Figure 1). Consequently, these functionalities need to be implemented.

Planning How to Adapt the Existent Similar Tools and Implement the new required tools:

We verify that this organization uses a relational database management system for storing the data of its knowledge management tools. Thus, we will use the database language SQL to create queries for recuperating and storing data in these tools. Next, we will outline how these tools can be implemented.

a) Knowledge Evaluation Tool

According to the model's instance of Figure 2, the knowledge evaluation tool can be implemented in this organization as a software component composed of four methods, which implement the messages 1, 2, 3 and 4 of the model. These methods are presented in the following.

- Implementing the Method 1:

  Considering *db-PS* as the relational database that stores the Profile System's data and *t-knowledge_tree* as the table storing the knowledge mapping's data, the first method's sketch can be:

```
search(in a, out s(a)){
    ...
        a ⟵ organizational area for evaluating;
        s(a) ⟵ select knowledge subjects from db-PS.t-knowledge_tree
                where t-knowledge_tree.organizational area=a;
    ...
}
```

- Implementing the Method 2:

  In the same database, considering *t-profiles* as the table storing the workers profiles' data, the method implementing the message 2 can be sketched as we show next.

Copyright © 2004, Idea Group Inc. Copying or distributing in print or electronic forms without written permission of Idea Group Inc. is prohibited.

```
search(in a, s(a), out w(a), h(org)){
    ...
        w(a) ⟵ select workers from db-PS.t-profiles
                where t-profiles.organizational area=a and t-profiles.knows-s(a)=false;
        h(org) ⟵ select workers from db-PS.t-profiles
                where t-profiles.organizational area=* and t-profiles.knows-s(a)=true;
    ...
}
```

- Implementing the Method 3:

  Considering *db-KC* as the relational database that stores the knowledge communities' data and *t-members* as the table storing the members' data of the communities, the method's sketch for implementing the message 3 can be:

```
search(in s(a), out w(cp)){
    ...
        w(cp) ⟵ select workers from db-KC.t-members
                where t-members.subject discuted=s(a);
    ...
}
```

- Implementing the Method 4:

  Consider *db-TP* as the relational database that stores the training producer's data and *t-trainings* as the table storing the future training data, whether $s(a) = \{s_1, s_2,\ldots, s_i\}, i>=1$; $w = \{w_1, w_2,\ldots, w_j\}, j>=1$; and $h(org) = \{h_1, h_2,\ldots,h_n\}, n>=1$. Then, the method implementing the message 4 is outlined next:

```
inform(in s(a), w, h(org)){
    ...
    For s ⟵ s_1 to s_i and k ⟵ w_1 to w_j and h ⟵ h_1 to h_n {
        ...
        insert into db-TP.t-trainings (new training subjects, target public, instructors)
        values (s, k, h);
        ...
    }
    ...
}
```

Copyright © 2004, Idea Group Inc. Copying or distributing in print or electronic forms without written permission of Idea Group Inc. is prohibited.

b) Virtual School: Training Producer

The training producer used by the virtual school of this organization contemplates essentially two functionalities: training materials creation and their publication in the training server. However, the training producer of the integration model contemplates two additional functionalities, which are represented in the model of Figure 2 by messages 5 and 6. These functionalities can be implemented by the methods outlined next:

- Implementing the Method 1:

  The sketch of the method that implements the message 5 of the model, recovering the organizational knowledge map, that is, the organization's areas and the knowledge subjects required for accomplishing their activities, can be viewed next.

```
search(out s(org)){
  ...
   s(org)) ⟵ select knowledge subjects, organizational area from db-PS.t-knowledge_tree ;
  ...
}
```

- Implementing the Method 2:

  Considering $h(org) = \{h_1, h_2,...,h_n\}$, $n>=1$, part of the method implementing the message 6 of the model, which informs the organization's knowledge holders about useful information for creating future trainings, is sketched next.

```
inform(in s(a), s(org), out p(t), s(t), c(t)){
   ...
         For h ⟵ h1 to hn{
           ...
                 Send message()
                   To: h.email
                   Subject: training program
                   Content:
                   "The subjects that should be contemplated are:" s(a)
                   "and the organizational knowledge map is:" s(org)
                   "Please use this information for creating the training materials
                    in the training producer."
                   ...
         }
   ...
}
```

Copyright © 2004, Idea Group Inc. Copying or distributing in print or electronic forms without written permission of Idea Group Inc. is prohibited.

c) Knowledge Update Tool

The knowledge update tool can be implemented in this organization as a software component composed of four methods, which implement the messages 9, 10, 11 and 12 of the model (see Figures 1 and 2).

- Implementing the Method 1:

  Considering *db-TS* as the database that stores the training server's data about the accomplished trainings, *t-students* as the table storing the data about students' activities and *t-contents* as the table storing information about the generated contents, the sketch of the method implementing the message 9 can be:

```
search(in w, out ap(w), s(t)){
    ...
            ap(w) ←  select worker's register from db-TS.t-students
                     where t-students.status=approved;
             s(t) ←  select subject from db-TS.t-contents
                     where t-contents.author-type=instructor or student;
    ...
}
```

- Implementing the Method 2:

  Considering $ap(w) = \{ap_1, ap_2,...,ap_i\}$, $i>=1$ and $s(t) = \{s_1, s_2,...,s_j\}$, $j>=1$, the method implementing the message 10 of the model of Figure 2 is outlined next.

```
update(in ap(w), s(t)){
    ...
        For ap ← ap_1 to ap_i{
          ...
            For s ← s_1 to s_j{
              ...
                Insert into db-PS.t-profiles (worker' knowledge)
                values (s);
              ...
            }
          ...
        }
    ...
}
```

Copyright © 2004, Idea Group Inc. Copying or distributing in print or electronic forms without written permission of Idea Group Inc. is prohibited.

- Implementing the Method 3:

  Consider *d-KDB* as a directory for storing the contents released by workers in the knowledge database of this organization, *db-KDB* as the database that stores the knowledge database's data and *t-contents* as a table storing the data about these contents, whether $c = \{c_1, c_2, \ldots, c_i\}$, $i>=1$; $s(t) = \{s_1, s_2, \ldots, s_j\}, j>=1$; and $p(t) = \{p_1, p_2, \ldots, p_n\}, n>=1$. Then, the method's sketch implementing the message 11 can be:

```
update(in c, s(t), p(t)){
  ...
    For k ← c1 to ci {
      ...
      upload (k, d-KDB);
      For s ← s1 to sj and p ← p1 to pn {
        ...
        insert into db-KDB.t-contents (content's subject, content's provider)
        values (s, p);
        ...
      }
      ...
    }
  ...
}
```

- Implementing the Method 4:

  Finally, considering $s(new) = \{s_1, s_2, \ldots, s_i\}$, $i>=1$, the method that implements the message 12 of the model, that is, the method responsible for updating the organizational knowledge map with the new subjects acquired during the accomplishment of the training, can be outlined as shown next.

```
update(in s(new)){
  ...
    For s ← s1 to si {
      ...
      insert into db-PS. t-knowledge_tree (knowledge subjects)
      values (s);
      ...
    }
  ...
}
```

Copyright © 2004, Idea Group Inc. Copying or distributing in print or electronic forms without written permission of Idea Group Inc. is prohibited.

Conclusions of the Empirical Research

We showed with this empirical research in a real context that it is perfectly possible and is not complex to apply the model for integrating CSCL into KM structures in the business world. Although we have shown the use of all tools of the model, it can also be partially used by an organization. The actual use will depend on a cost-benefit analysis. For example, if an organization wishes to select the training subjects, due to its business strategy or the lack of a computer tool to indicate the required knowledge, it can ignore steps 1 and 12 of the model. Consequently, the necessary subjects for an organizational area (s(a)) should be supplied to the *knowledge evaluation tool* by somebody of the organization.

The cost-benefit analysis can point out, for example, that it is more suitable for an organization to indicate both the knowledge providers of trainings (p(t)) and the target public (w). An organization can manage the information about the knowledge of its workers in a non-automated way and may not have interest in implementing (or acquiring) a *profiles database*. In this case, it can ignore steps 2 and 10 of the model. Consequently, this information should be manually supplied to the *training producer* by somebody of the organization, and so on.

The model allows setting up the training content with a basis on the organizational knowledge map using the *training producer*. That guarantees that the released trainings will be in total conformity with the knowledge map structure. Further, it will allow evaluating the training effectiveness directly by the growth of the organizational knowledge map.

Benefits of the Effective Integration of CSCL into KM Structures

Among the direct benefits of the effective integration of CSCL into organizational KM, we can list: reach, objectivity, speed and effectiveness. How these benefits are attained is discussed next.

Reach

Generally, knowledge transfer is local and fragmented. The larger the organization, the greater the probability of the existence of some required knowledge,

Copyright © 2004, Idea Group Inc. Copying or distributing in print or electronic forms without written permission of Idea Group Inc. is prohibited.

but the lesser the probability of a worker (who needs it) to know how and where to find it (Davenport & Prusak, 1998; Kock, 2000). A solution to this problem is to offer knowledge automatically to workers when they need it, that is, without the need of explicit requisition of knowledge. This is important because most workers do not know which knowledge is available and, consequently, they never search for it (Maurer & Tochtermann, 2002).

The effective integration of CSCL into KM allows releasing knowledge to workers without need of explicit requisition. Our model allows the identification of the knowledge necessary for workers and the automatic release of appropriate training to them. Automatic identification of workers needing particular knowledge and implementation of personalized training targeted for this public allow greater reach in knowledge transfer. Mass training in strategic knowledge areas can also be released to all workers as another way of obtaining reach. In this case, workers should decide on participating or not in the training offered.

Objectivity

It is possible to release personalized training to train a specific public after the identification of the knowledge necessary for some particular organizational function or worker, as it was discussed before. Personalized training allows more objectivity in knowledge transfer, because it avoids waste of time and resources with knowledge transfer to workers that do not need it. Knowledge will be transferred objectively to workers that can really use it for the execution of their activities (right knowledge to the right person on the right time). This increases the possibility of knowledge use and adds more value to the organizational intellectual capital, which increases when knowledge is used.

Speed

The speed with which knowledge arrives where it can generate value is an important evaluation factor on how effectively the organizational intellectual capital is being used. Usually, knowledge transfer happens on demand in the organizations. When a worker needs specific knowledge, either he or she searches in the knowledge database or interacts with specialists in this subject. In both cases, this might take precious time. The integration of CSCL into KM allows releasing focused training as soon as the lack of a particular knowledge is detected, thus increasing the knowledge transfer speed.

Copyright © 2004, Idea Group Inc. Copying or distributing in print or electronic forms without written permission of Idea Group Inc. is prohibited.

Effectiveness

Knowledge transfer effectiveness, that is, the knowledge percentage that has been really assimilated and applied, is influenced mainly by the method used in the transfer process (Kock, 2000). Further, the richer and more tacit is the knowledge, the more effort should be placed to enable workers to share it directly (Davenport & Prusak, 1998).

It is possible to reach greater effectiveness in knowledge transfer through the use of mentoring. Direct interaction with a specialist (knowledge provider) during certain periods of time allows acquiring more consistent and deeper knowledge about a particular area, as well as obtaining a greater amount of knowledge. This is true because the knowledge recipient obtains more detailed and implicit knowledge. The long process of trying to extract and understand specialists' knowledge, by conversation, observation, interrogation, and so on provides workers with a better comprehension of the subject being learned than that acquired through learning processes based on non-interactive means (e.g., searching in knowledge repositories, reading papers, etc.).

Our model creates the means to efficiently identify knowledge requirements to improve organizational activities, workers requiring this knowledge, as well as specialists to act as mentors in a mentoring training program.

Evaluation Process

The process of defining measures (indicators) to measure the CSCL effectiveness as a KM tool is not a trivial task, mainly because what will be measured is the knowledge that has been aggregated and shared into the organization by virtue of the use of CSCL. Since knowledge is an intangible resource, it is not captured easily by the traditional measurement systems (Bontis et al., 1999; Lopez et al., 2001).

Several measurement systems have been proposed to measure intangible assets value. Next we briefly describe the most important measurement systems available.

Copyright © 2004, Idea Group Inc. Copying or distributing in print or electronic forms without written permission of Idea Group Inc. is prohibited.

APQC Recommendations (Lopez et al., 2001)

The recommendations of the American Productivity & Quality Center (APQC) on how to evaluate KM are classified in five stages. According to this measurement system, the initial stages (1 and 2) of the process of KM implementation do not require a formal evaluation and it rarely happens. The need for evaluation and measurement grows as KM becomes more structured and more diffused in the organization (stage 3). On the other hand, the importance of specific measures for KM is decreased as KM becomes more institutionalized in the organization. These measures are gradually replaced by measures to evaluate the effectiveness of knowledge-intensive business process (stages 4 and 5).

Intellectual Capital Statements (Mouritsen et al., 2001)

The intellectual capital statements are a new form of reporting KM activities. They facilitate the calculation and management of the organizational knowledge, including the implicit (tacit) knowledge of workers. Mouritsen (2001) accomplished a case study of 17 organizations, trying to evaluate their intangible assets. This research originated a model to state intellectual capital. This model can be used to closely follow KM activities, besides facilitating the management and the evaluation of the organizational knowledge assets. Intellectual capital statements define both the KM strategy and what the organization is prepared to do.

KCO Model (Smith et al., 2001)

The knowledge centric organization model (KCO model) was proposed by the Department of the Navy (DoN) of the United States of America. This model uses three types of measures to monitor KM initiatives of different perspectives: outcome, output and system. *Outcome measures* are related to the whole organization and they measure characteristics in organizational level, such as productivity increase and business profits. *Output measures* measure characteristics at project level, such as the effectiveness of the learned lessons and the amount of new business markets discovered during a project. *System measures* monitor the usefulness and the responsibility of tools to support the technology.

Copyright © 2004, Idea Group Inc. Copying or distributing in print or electronic forms without written permission of Idea Group Inc. is prohibited.

The KCO model also classifies measures in quantitative or qualitative terms. *Quantitative measures* can be expressed by numbers. Typically, they provide objective data (hard data) to evaluate the performance between two points or see tendencies. *Qualitative measures* use the situation context to provide a value sense. They are related to subjective data (soft data). These measures include stories, anecdotes and projections.

Balanced Scorecard (Kaplan & Norton, 1992)

The balanced scorecard (BSC) uses a balanced group of tangible and intangible assets for performance evaluation. It supplies a general vision of the business performance by a multidimensional system. BSC combines financial measures with operational measures. The former shows the result of already executed actions. The latter is related to the customers' satisfaction, the internal processes, the organizational innovation and the learning activities (future performance indicators). The four interrelated BSC perspectives are described below (Kaplan & Norton, 1992).

- Innovation and Learning Perspective

  This perspective evaluates the capacity to innovate, improve and learn of the organization (Kaplan & Norton, 1992). It includes all the measures related to both the workers and the organizational systems that facilitate the learning and the knowledge diffusion.
- Internal Perspective

  This perspective focuses on critical internal operations. Organizations need to decide which processes and competencies should be improved continually (essential competencies), besides specifying measures to evaluate them (Kaplan & Norton, 1992).
- Customer Perspective

  This perspective tries to evaluate the business performance in the customers' vision. It identifies the customers and establishes measures specifically related to these customers. These measures normally belong to one of the following categories: time, quality, performance/service and cost (Kaplan & Norton, 1992).

Copyright © 2004, Idea Group Inc. Copying or distributing in print or electronic forms without written permission of Idea Group Inc. is prohibited.

- Financial Perspective

  This perspective evaluates whether the implementation and the execution of the business strategy are contributing to the financial goals. Usually, these goals are related to the profitability improvement, organizational growth and market value increase (Kaplan & Norton, 1992; Smith et al., 2001).

An Evaluation Framework for the Integration of CSCL into KM Structures

The proposed framework is based on BSC. We have chosen the BSC to support the evaluation of the integration of CSCL into KM, among other reasons, because it avoids that the measures are excessively focused on any particular aspect. As previously discussed, BSC allows evaluating the business performance under four interrelated perspectives. It tries to reach a balance between short and long-term goals, financial and non-financial measures and internal and external perspectives (Arveson, 1999; Bontis et al., 1999; Kaplan & Norton, 1992; Smith et al., 2001).

Figure 3. Framework for evaluating the integration of CSCL into KM.

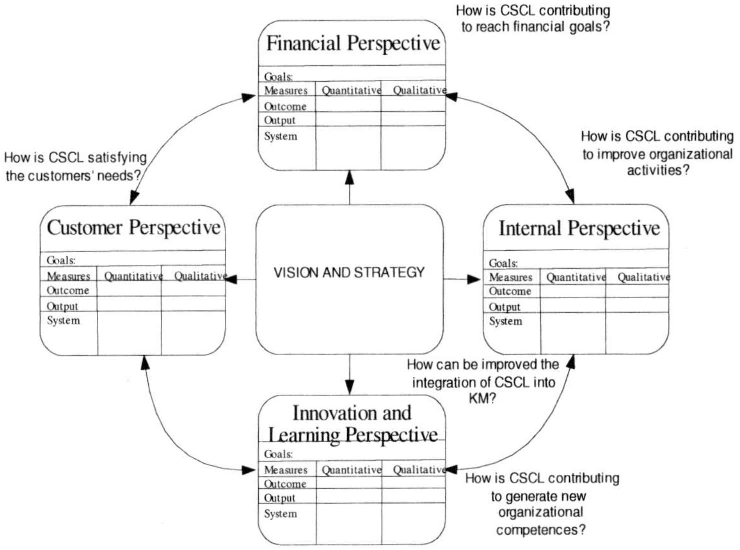

Copyright © 2004, Idea Group Inc. Copying or distributing in print or electronic forms without written permission of Idea Group Inc. is prohibited.

BSC's traditional perspectives can be shaped for a particular KM initiative. We have adapted the BSC perspectives to reflect the specific goals of the integration of CSCL into KM (see Figure 3). We also complemented the BSC with a classification matrix, which was proposed in the KCO model. This matrix classifies measures into two distinct dimensions (Smith et al., 2001). The first dimension allows monitoring KM initiatives of three different perspectives: outcome, output and system. The second dimension of the matrix classifies measures for KM initiatives' evaluation in either quantitative or qualitative terms.

Evaluation Framework Use for Defining Measures

According to the proposed evaluation framework, we should define the goals of each BSC perspective before the definition of the measures. We have defined a number of measures to evaluate the effective integration of CSCL into KM. These measures are distributed in 10 strategic goals, which were classified inside of the four BSC perspectives. We also classify the necessary measures to evaluate these goals in outcome, output or systems measures and in quantitative or qualitative measures.

However, it is important to point out that the process of defining measures for evaluation of the integration of CSCL into KM, like KM in itself, is not an exact science. It is necessary to apply a careful judgment to determine what is suitable for a particular KM structure and organization. The goals of the integration define what the organization is trying to reach and they should guide the measurement process. These goals should also clarify how measures should be used to generate value and improve the business performance.

We do not intend to exhaust all possibilities of measures or goals for this type of evaluation. Our intention is to facilitate the process to obtain these measures. We propose a set of goals and measures that we believe to be effective for this type of evaluation. However, each organization may select the subset of goals and measures more suitable for its context and available resources.

The goals of the integration of CSCL into KM are, in fact, the fulfillment of the requirements that should be satisfied by KM, which were discussed before. One way of evaluating the CSCL effectiveness as a KM tool is measuring its contribution in the achievement of these requirements. The defined goals, besides some examples of measures that can be used to evaluate them, are shown here.

Copyright © 2004, Idea Group Inc. Copying or distributing in print or electronic forms without written permission of Idea Group Inc. is prohibited.

Innovation and Learning Perspective

The innovation and learning perspective is the most important perspective for evaluation of KM initiatives (Arveson, 1999). For that reason, 7 of the 10 defined goals belong to this category.

- Goal 1: To promote the workers' creativity and the innovation of products and services.

  Measure Examples: percentage of new services (or products) that can be related to CSCL training subjects (quantitative/outcome); percentage of new competencies in the organizational knowledge map related to CSCL training subjects (quantitative/output); and so on.
- Goal 2: To share essential knowledge to the business.

  Measure Examples: percentage of competencies in the organizational knowledge map that were covered in CSCL training (quantitative/output); workers' perception rate in relation to the content importance to the business (qualitative/output); and so forth.
- Goal 3: To increase the access to the knowledge.

  Measure Examples: workers' satisfaction rate in relation to accessibility of CSCL trainings (qualitative/system); percentage of workers that were trained in this learning modality in relation to the total number of workers (quantitative/system); and so forth.
- Goal 4: To facilitate the knowledge transfer.

  Measure Examples: workers' satisfaction rate in relation to the usability of the CSCL tools (qualitative/system); average of distinct contributions shared by each worker during CSCL trainings (quantitative/system); and so forth.
- Goal 5: To increase the amount of explicit knowledge.

  Measure Examples: percentage of contents that were added to the knowledge repository that can be related to CSCL training subjects (quantitative/output); average of contributions shared by workers during CSCL trainings (quantitative/system); and so forth.
- Goal 6: To increase the exchange of tacit knowledge.

  Measure Examples: percentage of new competencies that were added to the profiles database that can be related to CSCL training subjects

Copyright © 2004, Idea Group Inc. Copying or distributing in print or electronic forms without written permission of Idea Group Inc. is prohibited.

(quantitative/output); average of personal interactions accomplished by each worker during CSCL trainings (quantitative/system); and so forth.

- Goal 7: To increase the workers' motivation and engagement to the learning process.

  Measure Examples: percentage of workers that did enroll in CSCL training (quantitative/system); percentage of evasion or waiver of CSCL training (quantitative/system); and so forth.

Internal Perspective

- Goal 8: To make the execution of the activities more efficient.

  Measure Examples: percentage of projects that were concluded before the deadline (cycle time decrease) that can be related to CSCL training subjects (quantitative/outcome); workers' perception rate in relation to the CSCL training's usefulness for execution of their activities (qualitative/output); and so forth.

Customer Perspective

- Goal 9: To improve the quality of products and services.

  Measure Examples: percentage of growth in products (or services) sales related to CSCL training subjects (quantitative/outcome); customers' satisfaction rate in relation to products (time, quality, performance and cost) that can be related to CSCL training subjects (qualitative/outcome); and so forth.

Financial Perspective

- Goal 10: To increase the profitability of the organization.

  Measure Examples: percentage of business processes that increased the profitability that can be related to CSCL training subjects (quantitative/outcome); percentage of economy with training - registration, fees and passages (quantitative/outcome); and so forth.

Copyright © 2004, Idea Group Inc. Copying or distributing in print or electronic forms without written permission of Idea Group Inc. is prohibited.

Conclusion

We discussed before that many organizations use CSCL tools to support a number of functionalities of their KM structures, but these tools are seldom efficiently integrated with other KM tools. In an attempt at solving this problem, we have provided an evaluation of the interrelation between KM and CSCL, that is, evaluation of the requirements that should be satisfied by the KM implementation and how CSCL tools can be useful to satisfy them. In the following, we presented a model for integration of CSCL into KM structures of organizations and an analysis of its benefits for organizational KM.

The model that was proposed is generic enough to cover the main aspects involved in different structures of KM and CSCL. It can be used in an organization that already implements KM and CSCL but does not obtain benefits of the effective integration of these structures. It can also be used in an organization where some integration already exists but it is not complete. In both cases, the model should allow verifying whether the tools that are being used in these structures satisfy all KM requirements. This model also covers the utilization of the main tools that can be used in these structures and it allows the accomplishment of a cost-benefit analysis, which will facilitate the decision on both which tools should be used and how they should be used to achieve particular goals.

After the model description, we described a process for defining measures to evaluate this integration. Firstly, we discussed the main measurement systems that have been proposed to evaluate intangible assets. After that, we presented a framework to evaluate the integration of CSCL tools into KM structures of organizations. Then we used this framework to define goals that should be achieved by the integration as well as some measures capable of evaluating their results.

From now on, it is necessary to experiment with the judicious integration of KM tools into the business world; that is, we really need to implement this integration in organizations to know its results. But how can we verify whether this integration truly improves the business performance? The evaluation framework that we proposed together with its set of goals and measures can answer this question. However, it needs to be used in a practical context to verify its effectiveness.

Copyright © 2004, Idea Group Inc. Copying or distributing in print or electronic forms without written permission of Idea Group Inc. is prohibited.

Endnote

[1] URL (Uniform Resource Locator) is the address pattern of any resource in the Web.

References

Allinson, L., & Hammond, N. (1989). A learning support environment - the hitchhiker's guide. In R. McAleese (Ed.), *Hypertext: Theory into practice* (pp. 62-74). Norwood, NJ: Ablex Publishing.

Arms, W. (2001). *Digital libraries.* MIT: CEFET-CE.

Arveson, P. (1999). *The balanced scorecard and knowledge management.* Retrieved March 1, 2003, from Balanced Scorecard Institute Web site: http://www.balancedscorecard.org/bscand/bsckm.html

Baloian, N.A., Pino, J.A., & Hoppe, H.U. (2000). A teaching/learning approach to CSCL. *Proceedings of Hawaii International Conference on System Sciences, 33* (p. 10). IEEE.

Berners-Lee, T., Cailiau, R., Luotonen, A., Nielsen, H.F., & Secret, A. (1994). The World-Wide Web. *Communications of the ACM, 37*(8), 76-82.

Bontis, N., Dragonetti, N.C., Jacobsen, K., & Roos, G. (1999). The knowledge toolbox: A review of the tools available to measure and manage intangible resources. *European Management Journal, 17*(4), 391-402.

Brown, P.S., & Duguid, P. (2000). Balancing act: How to capture knowledge without killing it. *Harvard Business Review, 78*(3), 73-80.

Davenport, T., & Prusak, L. (1998). *Working knowledge: How organizations manage what they know.* Boston: Harvard Business School Press.

Greenberg, S. (1991). *Computer-supported cooperative work and groupware.* New York: Academic Press.

Guzdial, M., & Turns, J. (1998). Supporting sustained discussion in computer-supported collaborative learning: The role of anchored collaboration. *Journal of the Learning Sciences.*

Copyright © 2004, Idea Group Inc. Copying or distributing in print or electronic forms without written permission of Idea Group Inc. is prohibited.

Hansen, M.T., & Von Oetinger, B. (2001). Introducing t-shaped managers: Knowledge management's next generation. *Harvard Business Review, 79*(3), 106-116.

Hansen, M.T., Nohria, N., & Tierney, T. (1999). What's your strategy for managing knowledge? *Harvard Business Review, 77*(2), 106-116.

Hsiao, W.D.L. (1996). *CSCL theories*. Retrieved April 30, 2003, from University of Texas, College of Education Web site: http://www.edb.utexas.edu/csclstudent/Dhsiao/theories.html

Joshi, S.M., Pushpanadham, K., & Khirwadkar, A. (2002). Knowledge management through e-learning: An emerging trend in the Indian higher education system. *International Journal on E-Learning, 1*(3), 47-54.

Kaplan, R.S., & Norton, D.P. (1992). The balanced scorecard - measures that drive performance. *Harvard Business Review, 70*(1), 71-79.

Kock, N. (2000). Sharing interdepartmental knowledge using collaboration technologies: An action research study. *Journal of Information Technology Impact, 2*(1), 5-10.

Levy, J.D. (2001a). Measuring and maximizing results through elearning. Retrieved March 1, 2003, from Cornell University, Jonathon D. Levy Web site: http://www.people.cornell.edu/pages/jl63/Measuring and Maximizing Results102401.doc

Levy, J.D. (2001b). The ecosystem of elearning 2005. Retrieved March 1, 2003, from Cornell University, Jonathon D. Levy Web site: http://www.people.cornell.edu/pages/jl63/Ecosystem_of_eLearning_2005102401.doc

Levy, P. (1997). *Odile jacob/du conseil de l'enveloppe* (pp. 214-222). Paris.

Levy, P., & Authier, M. (1992). *Les arbres de connaissances*. Paris: La D'couverte.

Lopez, K., Hartz, C., Sammis, S., Hofer-Alfeis, J.C.R., & Wilson, J.N. (2001). *Measurement for knowledge management*. Retrieved April 30, 2003, from American Productivity & Quality Center Web site: http://www.kmadvantage.com/docs/km articles/Measurement for KM.pdf

Maurer, H., & Tochtermann, K. (2002). On a new powerful model for knowledge management and its applications. *Journal of Universal Computer Science, 8*(1), 85-96.

Copyright © 2004, Idea Group Inc. Copying or distributing in print or electronic forms without written permission of Idea Group Inc. is prohibited.

Mouritsen, J., Larsen, H.T., & Bukh, P.N.D. (2001). Intellectual capital and the 'capable firm': Narrating, visualizing and numbering for managing knowledge. *Accounting, Organizations and Society, 26,* 735-762.

Nonaka, I., & Takeuchi, H. (1995). *The knowledge-creating company: How Japanese companies create the dynamics of innovation.* New York: Oxford University Press.

Quatrani, T. (1998). *Visual modeling with rational rose and UML.* Massachusetts: Longman.

Rossett, A. (2001, June). E-trainer evolution. *ASTD's Online Magazine*, Retrieved March 1, 2003, from http://www.learningcircuits.org/2001/jun2001/rossett.html

Rossett, A. (2002a). *The ASTD e-learning handbook: Best practices, strategies and case studies for an emerging field.* New York: McGraw-Hill.

Rossett, A. (2002b, March). Overcoming insomnia in the big tent of e-learning. *International Society for Performance Improvement Newsletter*, Article 0203. Retrieved April 30, 2003, from http://www.performanc express.org/0203/

Smith, S., Carberry, J., Dean, C., Hall, I., Hawhurst, J., Jones, B., Kanter, J., Kim, M., Mills, C., Pawley, M., Pierce, L., Poage, J., Pollock, N.,

Schmitz, E., Smith, P., White, T., & Hiser, M. (2001). *Metrics guide for knowledge management initiatives.* Retrieved March 1, 2003, from U.S. Government, Department of the Navy Web site: http:// www.km.gov/documents/

Wenger, E.C., & Snyder, W.M. (2000). Communities of practice: The organizational frontier. *Harvard Business Review, 78*(139-145).

Whitelock, D., Taylor, J., O'Mhea, T., Scanlon, E., Clark, P., & O'Malley, C. (1993). What do you say after you have said hello? Dialogue analysis of con and cooperation in a computer supported collaborative learning environment. *International Peg Conference, 11,* 2-4. Edinburgh.

Copyright © 2004, Idea Group Inc. Copying or distributing in print or electronic forms without written permission of Idea Group Inc. is prohibited.

Section III

Knowledge Management for Attaining Strategic Advantage

Chapter XII

The European Challenge of KM and Innovation: A Skills and Competence Portfolio for the Knowledge Worker in SME's

Ana Maria R. Correia
Universidade Nova de Lisboa, Portugal

Anabela Sarmento
Instituto Politécnico Porto, Portugal and
University of Minho, Portugal

Abstract

Globalization, bringing about universal and dynamic transformations in every sector of the economy, is placing organizations everywhere in new and different competitive situations. In this context, the improvement of enterprise performance and economic growth makes increased demands for timely knowledge in the workplace to deliver competitive, knowledge-intensive work, enabling institutions and nations to maintain their vitality

Copyright © 2004, Idea Group Inc. Copying or distributing in print or electronic forms without written permission of Idea Group Inc. is prohibited.

through economic growth and increased productivity. This chapter highlights the European strategy towards a knowledge-based society where innovation and competitiveness are the goals to be achieved. The Portuguese scenario concerning small and medium enterprises and the creation of a Portuguese knowledge and information economy are also described. Some approaches to knowledge management (KM), contributing to understanding the scope of this emergent domain, are introduced. The skills and competencies that a knowledge manager should develop in order to perform his/her job are discussed. The chapter concludes by mapping the main areas of study and practice that the authors consider as relevant to performing an effective knowledge management function.

Introduction

In a contemporary world, where markets, products, technology, competitors, regulation, and even societies are undergoing universal and dynamic transformation, demands have increased for customised and more sophisticated products and services. Innovation, together with the knowledge that enables it, has become a vital source of sustainable and competitive advantage, that is, the basis of economic growth and productivity increase.

Information and knowledge are creating new industries around them and, at the same time, are pervading all sectors of economy (Skyrme, 1999, p. 12), assuming a vital role in the economic change taking place over recent years, together with "technology, information, business processes, quality control, human capital and corporate capabilities and competences – all knowledge related factors" (Burton-Jones, 2001, p. vi).

Globalization has created a business environment where components/inputs are available to all firms at similar prices. Through the Internet, firms can reach distant markets at competitive prices, enabling innovative firms to respond to regional specialization and to the expansion of long distance relationships and markets.

Increased virtualisation in business activities, facilitating new ways of working, such as self-managed teams, virtual teams, flexible offices and teleworking, is prevailing as a consequence of information and communication technologies development (Skyrme, 1999, pp. 20, 34).

Copyright © 2004, Idea Group Inc. Copying or distributing in print or electronic forms without written permission of Idea Group Inc. is prohibited.

Such pressures are transforming "the nature of production and thus work, jobs, firms, markets and every aspect of economic activity" (Burton-Jones, 2001, p. 4) worldwide, impacting knowledge, skills, talents and the know-how required by individuals in the workplace (Quinn, Baruch & Zein, 2002). As Wiig (1999, p. 156) points out, "knowledge workers, everywhere, can access the latest information on advanced concepts and methodologies, business issues and technologies".

Companies that are better able to utilise information and knowledge can make decisions faster and closer to the point of action, overcome internal and external barriers, provide more opportunities to innovate, reduce product development time and enhance customer relationships (Hackett, 2002, p. 727).

Although the recognition of the importance of knowledge as a source of economic wealth and political power is not a new idea, it is only recently that the concepts, principles and practices related with the management of knowledge – aiming to increase an organization's ability to exploit knowledge – left the periphery of management thought and practice (Little, Quintas & Ray, 2002, p. 1).

Moreover, in the context of continuous technological advance in computational power and communication technologies, in which the volume of data and information being produced is constantly expanding (Lyman & Varian, 2000), knowledge itself, understood as "the capacity for effective action" (Senge, 2000, p. 56), remains the crucial resource to good performance of any organization and the key to wealth creation. This explains why it is important to move from information management – understood as the management of anything that is or can be digitised – to a broader concept of knowledge management, "which deals with all aspects of how people in organizations are enabled in performing knowledge-based functions" (Dawson, 2000, p. 321).

The main challenge is to stimulate knowledge production (learning) and its management. The development of intellect, innovation, technology and services – not the management of physical resources – is the key for most companies, as well as of industries and countries (Quinn, Baruch & Zein, 2002, pp. 7-8).

The transformations taking place at the enterprise level as well as at the workplace call for a new kind of worker/employee, with competencies, attitudes and intellectual agility "conductive to systemic and critical thinking within a technologically oriented environment" (Bontis, 2003, p. 7) and who is able to recognise that his/her "behaviour contributes much more to the enterprise success than conventional assets" (Wiig, 1999, p. 164).

Copyright © 2004, Idea Group Inc. Copying or distributing in print or electronic forms without written permission of Idea Group Inc. is prohibited.

This chapter begins by briefly referring to the European strategy, set in 2000 at the Lisbon Summit of the European Council, to build a knowledge-based economy in the European Union and some policies aiming at promoting such a goal. We also describe the Portuguese scenario concerning SMEs and the creation of a Portuguese knowledge and information economy. In this context, the importance to undertake comprehensive and systematic knowledge management within European organizations in order to compete with world markets is essential. Knowledge and knowledge management (KM) are broadly defined and discussed by introducing several approaches emerging in the literature, each one contributing with a fragmented perspective, helping to understand the scope of KM as a new management approach. Grounded in a literature review, it offers a map to the core areas that, at present, are considered as contributing towards an effective knowledge management function.

Innovation and Competitiveness in a Knowledge-Based Society

European Policies

The development of a knowledge-based society in Europe and the preparation of workers and citizens to deal with the new challenges and opportunities were discussed at the Lisbon European Council Summit in March 2000 (Lisbon European Council, 2000). The Summit's conclusions outline a strategy to transform the European Union into the "the most competitive and dynamic knowledge based economy in the world" by 2010, through being knowledge-based and able to guarantee a sustainable growth, with more jobs and greater social cohesion.

The progress towards this strategic goal was reviewed in the European Council meeting in Barcelona (March 2002). Several concerns were expressed and the strategies to attain such a goal were revised. Furthermore, the Barcelona Summit called on the Commission to draw up an *eEurope Action Plan* focusing on widespread availability of broadband networks throughout the Union by 2005 and actions on *eGovernment*, *eLearning*, *eHealth* and *eBusiness* to foster the development of new services. This led to the *e-Europe*

Copyright © 2004, Idea Group Inc. Copying or distributing in print or electronic forms without written permission of Idea Group Inc. is prohibited.

2005 Action Plan, which puts "users at the centre". It aims to improve participation, open up opportunities for everyone and enhance skills (*e-Europe2005*, 2002). To achieve such an objective, it is crucial to provide "opportunities for people to participate in society and help the workforce to acquire the skills needed in a knowledge-driven economy" (*op.cit,* para 1).

Later, in the Brussels European Council Summit (2003), the following were defined as priority actions: (1) raising employment and social cohesion (e.g., life-long learning should be promoted, and closer cooperation in enhancing transparency about skills standards across Europe encouraged; also investing in human capital is a prerequisite for the promotion of European competitiveness), (2) giving priority to innovation and entrepreneurship, (3) connecting Europe and (4) developing environmental protection for growth and jobs.

The same concerns and recommendations were already reflected in the *UNICE Benchmarking Report 2000.* This report recommends to European governments and companies, as a priority action, to increase the level of innovation in Europe (a) to improve attitudes towards creativity and innovation, (b) to release the full potential of new products and markets, (c) to facilitate the creation and exploitation of knowledge and new ideas, (d) to improve the knowledge and competence of people, and (e) to improve the financing of innovation (UNICE, 2000, p. 7). Furthermore, the same document emphasises that, in order to improve the employability of people within the European innovation system, governments must help develop a workforce capable of meeting the challenges of the future, must ensure that individuals have sufficient incentive to work, obtain additional skills, change work practices, accept new responsibilities, must encourage the expansion of the use of high performance work systems that support innovation, and companies must improve the skills and abilities of their employees, particularly in the area of innovation (UNICE, 2000, p. 38). The *UNICE Benchmarking Report 2001* explores the impact of the new economy on Europe's competitiveness, stating that entrepreneurship is the key to growth. It stresses the fact that the business environment in Europe is not as supportive for the development of new companies as it is in the US. The report concludes by saying that "if Europe is to be a dynamic and competitive knowledge-based economy, it needs to have a stronger spirit of enterprise, a more competitive environment, a world class knowledge infrastructure and a society more supportive of change" (UNICE, 2001a, p. 1). The same concerns are expressed in the document *Lisbon Strategy: Status 2003,* from UNICE. The idea that entrepreneurship should be fostered in Europe together with the insurance of the human resources strength and efficiency is

Copyright © 2004, Idea Group Inc. Copying or distributing in print or electronic forms without written permission of Idea Group Inc. is prohibited.

again stressed. As a matter of fact, one can read (UNICE, 2002b, p. 6) that "entrepreneurs create new sources of wealth, replace old inefficient firms with new innovative ones, and create new jobs" and thus "an entrepreneurial culture and skills should be supported in schools and universities and among the working population to encourage individuals to become entrepreneurs".

To meet the target agreed on by the European Council in Lisbon (2000), it is widely recognized that innovation is the "cornerstone" of the strategy (COM, 2003a). And this recognition is evident in the efforts of the EU in its promotion. The creation of a (1) *Trend Chart on Innovation in Europe* that provides collection, analysis and dissemination of information on innovation policies at national and EU level[1], (2) *European Innovation Scoreboard,* that presents, annually, quantitative data on framework conditions, the science and engineering operational environment, and innovation behaviour within firms[2], and (3) an *Innobarometer* that is a survey of the framework conditions[3], are some examples.

As seen in previous paragraphs, in order to attain the goals set in the Lisbon summit, that is, to transform the European Union into a knowledge-based society, innovation is needed. Innovation is a core characteristic of a knowledge-based economy; it is a source of competitiveness for firms and industries (whether small, medium or big enterprises). Innovation can: 1) take the form of invention arising out of the research laboratory, 2) happen by taking an idea from another business sector and adapting it for use in other production processes or markets, 3) be the search for new, untapped, market space, 4) be the development of a new approach to a business (COM, 2003a). Moreover, innovation is not only the province of research and development centres. It can be technological but also organizational (new ways of organizing work in areas such as workforce management, distribution, finance, manufacturing, etc., which can have a positive influence on competitiveness). The driving force for innovation can be external or internal. Externally, one identifies the enterprise's operating environment, the networks established with other enterprises, the market demands and conditions, the customer attitudes, the external inputs (technology, cooperation networks, advice) and the framework conditions (market capital, support regulatory environment and flexible, mobile and skilled human resources). As for the internal motivation, there is the ability of the enterprise to recognise market opportunities, its capabilities to respond innovatively, the education and training of the staff and the enterprise's knowledge base (COM, 2003a).

Copyright © 2004, Idea Group Inc. Copying or distributing in print or electronic forms without written permission of Idea Group Inc. is prohibited.

Fostering innovation requires more than R&D centres. It needs people with the right skills, initiative and creativity. And in this context, the Higher Education Institutions (HEI) play an important role in the innovation process. They are described as "sources of human capital and creativity, as well as themselves being the source of many innovations and of the knowledge that underpins many more" (European Commission, 2002a, p. 13). HEI should be encouraged to provide high-quality training in innovation-related matters (*op. cit.*). Furthermore, and as far as SMEs are concerned, they will remain an important focus on innovative effort and of policy making. To help innovation to emerge in SMEs, "links with HEI and business services that can assist SME's choice and implementation of innovations and the further development and commercialisation of their own ideas, should be fostered" (*op. cit.,* p. 14). SMEs need assistance in the adoption of innovations, especially for those that will "allow them to participate on a more equal footing in the knowledge-based economy, and in some cases achieve entry to new markets and more independence from large-firm-oriented networks" (*op.cit.,* p. 14).

To sum up, one can see that the political thrust in Europe is towards the development of a knowledge-based economy, in order to generate the required innovation to promote its competitiveness on a global scale. This economy can only be attained through innovation (e.g., entering in new markets, commercialising different products, improving business processes). SMEs play an important role in this activity as they represent an important part of the entrepreneurship capacity in Europe. But all the objectives established in the Lisbon summit in 2000 can only be achieved with the development of an adequate workforce with the necessary skills and knowledge. As Pfeffer (2002) notes, one crucial source and differentiating factor for competitive success is employees and how they work. This author states that some companies' successes are due, not to economies of scale, but rather to their skilled workforce and the way they are managed; if competitiveness is achieved through people, "then the skills of those people are critical" (*op. cit.,* p. 67). And this knowledge could be obtained by training/education and through the networks that could be established among HEI and SMEs – the knowledge obtained would help to foster the necessary innovation and help SMEs to become more competitive.

SMEs play an important role as a "major source of job creation and entrepreneurial experimentation" (European Commission, 2002a, p. 118). As a matter of fact, one can read in the Communication of the European Communities (2003b, p. 1) that "Europe's competitiveness depends strongly on its small

Copyright © 2004, Idea Group Inc. Copying or distributing in print or electronic forms without written permission of Idea Group Inc. is prohibited.

businesses, which are a key source of jobs, a breeding ground for business ideas and a main driver for entrepreneurship". And this role is even more relevant, as most of the EU employment is accounted for by firms with less than 250 employees (SMEs) mostly in the services. Also, "new business models are emerging, from 'virtual organisations' to integrated supply chains" (European Commission, 2002a, p. 119). Thus, "enterprises should be encouraged to explore new business models, both in terms of their internal organisation, and in relation to participation in networks and value chains of various kinds" (*op. cit.*, p. 119). Also, "one issue related to organisational innovation is e-business, the use of the Internet for marketing, financial transactions and networking more generally. Broadband penetration and mobile networking can only accelerate the increasing use of such potentials" (*op. cit.*, p. 120). Additionally, more sophisticated and specialised ways of exploiting knowledge are emerging and thus "new management skills will be needed to run these companies, where innovation will be the normal way of doing business rather than a perturbation" (*op. cit.*, p. 120).

The Creation of a Knowledge and Information Economy: The Portuguese Scenario Concerning SMEs

As one can draw from what is stated above, the role of the SMEs in the development of a knowledge driven society and in the competitiveness of the EU is crucial.

In this context, and taking into account the central role knowledge plays in European policies for the construction of a knowledge economy, we have undertaken our research, trying to characterize the Portuguese situation and then to identify the goals and strategies drawn up by the Portuguese government, in order to help Portugal move towards a knowledge driven society. In the following paragraphs, the results of this research are outlined.

According to data available in the *Innovation Scoreboard* 2002[4], "Portugal's current innovation performance is below the EU mean for all indicators, but trends show signs of catching up". As a matter of fact, "Portugal scores very high for trends in two indicators related to the information society: ICT expenditures and home Internet access". However, this report also states that Portugal has "levels about half those of the EU mean for the supply of new S&E[5] graduates, tertiary education and life-long learning". Finally, one can also read that, "the business sector is among the weaker areas of innovation performance

Copyright © 2004, Idea Group Inc. Copying or distributing in print or electronic forms without written permission of Idea Group Inc. is prohibited.

in Portugal". Summing up, the major relative strengths of Portugal concern ICT expenditures and home Internet access, while the major weaknesses are related to education, the development of a highly skilled workforce and adult participation in further education.

Lately, policies have been introduced to close the existing gap between the EU mean and Portuguese performance in this sector. On June 26, 2003, the Council of Ministers of Portugal approved the *Plano de Acção para a Sociedade da Informação* (Action Plan towards the Information Society), stating that it would be the "most important strategic and operational coordination tool of the policies of the XVth Government towards the Information Society"[6]. This action plan establishes goals considering the impact of the development of the information society on the country, the competitiveness of its enterprises, on modernization of public administration and on the citizens' quality of life, while also recognising that Portugal occupies a less favourable position, in the European context.

Thus, according to the *Plano de Acção para a Sociedade da Informação*[7], to the *Programa do XV Governo* - The Programme of the XVth Government of Portugal[8] and to the *Unidade de Missão Inovação e Conhecimento - Unit of Innovation and Knowledge Mission*[9], the main Portuguese concerns regarding the development of the information society and the knowledge economy will address four objectives:

a) To increase the effectiveness of the economic system and the competitiveness and productivity of Portuguese enterprises;
b) To increase the qualifications, competencies and knowledge of the Portuguese population;
c) To contribute to the modernization, rationalization, responsibility and revitalization of the public administration and official departments;
d) To increase the dynamics of the civil society through the promotion of the citizens' quality of life.

These objectives are then developed in several lines of action. It is not our task to detail all the actions established by the Portuguese government to promote the full participation of Portugal in the global knowledge economy; this paper highlights only those concerning SMEs.

Copyright © 2004, Idea Group Inc. Copying or distributing in print or electronic forms without written permission of Idea Group Inc. is prohibited.

Among the concerns of the present government, as far as the development of the Portuguese Information Society is concerned, it is relevant to note that the increase in the level of qualification of citizens assumes a high priority. As a matter of fact, one of the action lines within the Plan towards the Information Society aims to promote the development of "new skills". However, the projects expected to be developed within this plan only tackle: 1) the promotion of the education of Portuguese people concerning information and communication technologies (ICT); 2) the integration of ICTs in the education system and 3) the promotion of digital products and services. They include wider access to the Internet and increased numbers of computers in schools.

Despite the effort being made by the government to close the existing gap between the Portuguese level and the average of the other European countries, as far as the Information Society is concerned, after analysing these goals and lines of action we fear that the Portuguese vision of such goals is too technologically oriented. Concerns are still biased towards the development of infrastructures, bandwidth, access cost to the Internet, equipment in schools and numbers of home computers. There is no concern regarding the development of the needed competencies to live and succeed in a knowledge society. We understand that the technologies are necessary, but they become useless if the user does not understand why s/he should use and benefit from them (e.g., connecting with other people, establishing networks, gathering information). One way to develop this kind of knowledge is through training and qualification (European Commission, 2002b). As a matter of fact, "qualifications of their staff and their professionalism" is the factor most often mentioned when explaining the company's strength in innovation, according to the replies of managers in 11 of the 15 Member States. Portugal is one of the 11. But there is, apparently, a gap between the needs in this field and the efforts deployed. Indeed, although the importance of training is recognised, Portugal is still below average regarding enterprises and business training budgets. "A considerable high proportion of enterprises in Portugal (15%) (...) did not devote any working time to training efforts during the last year [2001]" (European Commission, 2002b, p. 49). This survey also shows some features that characterise the profile of enterprises that do not allocate a training budget to their employees. These features are: enterprises established for more than 30 years, mostly in the construction sector, small and medium enterprises and non-exporting companies. Results also show that, as far as Portugal is concerned, in order to be more innovative efforts must be made "to motivate staff at all levels to acquire new competencies and to adapt to change" (European

Copyright © 2004, Idea Group Inc. Copying or distributing in print or electronic forms without written permission of Idea Group Inc. is prohibited.

Commission, 2002b, pp. 52-53). It suggests a need for "change management" in the policies within companies, towards a more pro-active participation concerning future changes and a motivation to embrace innovation (*op. cit*).

Knowledge and Knowledge Work Management

Knowledge – Some Approaches

To define knowledge is not an easy task. This is a complex and ambiguous term, which has generated wide debate in the literature.

There are two philosophical perspectives that may be used to approach knowledge (Newell, Robertson, Scarborough & Swan, 2002; Yates-Mercer & Bawden, 2002). Newell et al. (2002) refer to these perspectives as *structural* and *processual,* while Yates-Mercer and Bawden name them as *scalar* and *cognitive* models.

According to the *structural* perspective (or scalar model), knowledge is perceived as a "discrete, objective, largely cognitive entity" (Newell et al., 2002, p. 3), susceptible of being classified as tacit (which includes judgement, "feel" and deep understanding, i.e., unarticulated expertise and experience) and explicit (knowledge that is formalised and expressed – e.g., technical drawings, policies, manuals of procedures, information existing in computer memories) (Nonaka & Takeuchi, 1995). Information and knowledge are seen as "closely related entities which can be transformed into one another, outside human mind" (Yates-Mercer & Bawden, 2002, p. 20). An organization that embraces this perspective will develop knowledge stores (repositories) and will try to capture the organization's knowledge by software.

Under this perspective, there are a number of frameworks developed recently in order to help us to understand the types of knowledge involved in the knowledge creation processes and the conditions under which they are applied and created. These frameworks are known by their authors' names: Nonaka, Spender and Blackler.

i) Nonaka's framework (1994) – suggests that "knowledge creation can only occur at the level of the individual". Furthermore, Newell reinforces

Copyright © 2004, Idea Group Inc. Copying or distributing in print or electronic forms without written permission of Idea Group Inc. is prohibited.

this view, saying that "Nonaka stresses that creative individuals need to be supported in their endeavours and management needs to provide the necessary context for such individuals to share and create knowledge" (Newell et al., 2002, p. 5).

ii) Spender's framework (1996, 1998) – "where collective knowledge has a prominent role, as it is the most useful because this is a type of knowledge that other firms would find difficult to understand and imitate" (Spender quoted in Newell et al., 2002, p. 5). The concept of collective knowledge can be mirrored in communities of practice, well explored by Wenger, McDermott and Snyder (2002).

iii) Blackler's framework (1995) – according to this author there are five types of knowledge in an organization – embrained, embodied, encultured, embedded and encoded knowledge, explained as:

> *"Embrained knowledge is knowledge that is dependent on conceptual skills and cognitive abilities. Embodied knowledge is action oriented and is only partly explicit. Encultured knowledge refers to the process of achieving shared understanding through the development of an organizational culture. Embedded knowledge is knowledge that resides in systemic routines. It can be analysed by considering the relationships between technologies, roles, procedures and emergent routines. Finally, encoded knowledge is information conveyed by signs and symbols either in manual or electronically transmitted form"* (Blackler, 1995, pp. 1025-5 quoted in Newell et al., 2002, p. 6).

According to this latter perspective, knowledge exists at the individual and collective level. Yet, "different types of knowledge dominate in different types of organisations" (*op. cit.,* p. 6).

The *processual* perspective (or cognitive model) suggests that we should focus our attention on the processes or practices of knowing, emphasizing that knowledge is socially constructed and embedded in practice. This means that more importance is given to the process of knowing and knowledge creation and the context that made possible this creation, rather than the knowledge per se, seen as something static or objective. Nonaka, Toyama and Konno (2002, p. 49) designate this context as *ba,* which means, "a shared context in which knowledge is shared, created and utilized. (...) *Ba* is the place where information is interpreted to become knowledge". In this perspective, the author argues that a "substantial part of an individual's tacit knowledge will

Copyright © 2004, Idea Group Inc. Copying or distributing in print or electronic forms without written permission of Idea Group Inc. is prohibited.

always remain tacit, resistant to articulation or codification". And, "this tacit knowledge only exists as conscious experience and behaviour which are rooted and manifest in processes of knowing an action" (Newell et al., 2002, p. 7). Furthermore, the cognitive model:

> " *regards knowledge as something intrinsic to, and only existing within, the human mind and cognition. Knowledge, being subjective cannot be directly transferred or communicated from one person to another, but must be converted into information first. Information is then regarded as the objective – and then a communicable and recordable form of knowledge*" (Yates-Mercer & Bawden, 2002, p. 21).

An organization that adopts the *cognitive model* will consider that knowledge resides in the minds of its employees and cannot be captured. Instead, such an organization will:

> "*implement knowledge management largely by cultural means, by organizing their physical space appropriately and by using appropriate communication tools – thus encouraging and enabling staff to share knowledge. Examples are: financial and other rewards for knowledge sharing; provision of well appointed informal meeting areas; encouraging face-to-face discussion rather than email communication*" (*op.cit*., 2002, p. 21).

Thus, managing knowledge becomes managing people and the interactions among them.

Swan and Scarbrough (2002), based on an analysis of the number of articles on KM published between 1990-2000 available at the *ABI/Inform Proquest* database, concluded that it is possible to identify two waves concerning the interest for this emerging management approach. The first one corresponds to a dominance of the IT/IS community in the diffusion of KM, and generated "an emphasis on knowledge capture and codification" (Swan & Scarbrough, 2002, p. 11) in parallel with the development and promotion of "knowledge technologies" (e.g., data warehouses, intranets, data mining). As for the second wave, the emphasis is on social and behavioural concerns (e.g., the development of "communities of practice"). Despite this evidence, these authors also state that KM cannot be polarised between "KM as systems" and "KM as people". It means that KM should be concerned not only with the capture and codification of tacit knowledge, but also with the creation of learning organizations – that is,

Copyright © 2004, Idea Group Inc. Copying or distributing in print or electronic forms without written permission of Idea Group Inc. is prohibited.

the process that enables an organization to adapt to change and move forward by acquiring new knowledge, skills or behaviour and thereby transforming itself (Hackett, 2002, p. 727) and organizational culture – that is, building, creating and developing cultures and communities. The main idea is that these two perspectives, taken separately, represent a partial view of KM and that:

> *"Personnel professionals, organizational analysts, IT professionals and accountants each have something to contribute to developing coherent and workable KM practices"* (Swan & Scarbrough, 2002, p. 12).

In turn, Davenport and Cronin (2000) consider that KM is being used differently across domains, with each claiming that its partial understanding represents a definitive articulation of the concept. These domains are Library and Information Systems (LIS), Process Engineering (PE) and Organizational Theory (OT).

To the LIS, KM is seen as management of know-how, which corresponds to the "coding and classification of recorded material (content) embedded in artefacts, structures, systems and repositories," without trying to understand how business value is perceived and created. In the Process Engineering (PE) approach, KM is perceived as the discovery and extraction of value through existing processes that are disintegrated and re-compiled. This:

> *"... process approach does not do justice to the application of people's competencies, skills, talents, thoughts, ideas, intuitions, commitments, motivations and imaginations, in short, the realm of tacit knowledge"* (*op. cit.*, p. 2).

In both perspectives – LIS and PE – knowledge is seen as something that can be codified. Thus, both are incomplete, as other perspectives take into consideration the knowledge that cannot be codified, or tacit knowledge.

However, there is a growing recognition that the:

> *"knowledge of experts is an accumulation of experience – a kind of residue of their actions, thinking, and conversations – that remains a dynamic part of their ongoing experience"* (Wenger, McDermott & Snyder, 2002, p. 9).

Copyright © 2004, Idea Group Inc. Copying or distributing in print or electronic forms without written permission of Idea Group Inc. is prohibited.

As noted, knowledge is simultaneously tacit and explicit; each one depends on the other[10] (*op. cit.*). From a business standpoint, the tacit aspects of knowledge are often the most valuable as they consist of embodied expertise – a deep understanding of complex, interdependent systems that enable dynamic responses to context specific problems.

The importance of interaction and informal learning processes such as storytelling, conversation, coaching and apprenticeship of the kind that communities of practice provide for sharing of tacit knowledge, justifies their importance. (Wenger, McDermott & Snyder, 2002, p. 9).

It is in this context that the third domain (OT) emerges, where KM is perceived as a capacity for allowing the organizations to develop, to innovate and to strengthen their competitiveness. Thus, in the OT perspective, KM is not the management of the knowledge resource but of the context in which the knowledge is used.

To sum up what has been discussed so far, KM cannot be regarded from a single point of view – either seeing knowledge as susceptible of capture, codification and transfer, or recognising it as a human process in which only tacit knowledge would make the difference – but should be understood as the confluence of several disciplines and sciences, each contributing towards the definition and comprehension of this concept.

In line with this, Little, Quintas and Ray (2002) have defended that the interest for knowledge as an area of research and practice within the field of management has its origins in the convergence of different perspectives, including information management, organizational learning, strategic management, management of innovation, and the measurement and management of intangible assets. Thus, KM emerges as a pluri- and interdisciplinary area (*op. cit.,* p. 2) that has a vital role for organizations.

Moreover, Bontis (2002a, p. 20) defines KM as "how an organization makes use of its intellectual capital," which embraces human[11], structural[12] and relationship[13] capital. Petty and Guthrie (2000, p. 4) strengthen this perspective, stating that:

> *"Knowledge management is about the management of the intellectual capital controlled by a company. Knowledge management, as a function, describes the act of managing the object, intellectual capital."*

Copyright © 2004, Idea Group Inc. Copying or distributing in print or electronic forms without written permission of Idea Group Inc. is prohibited.

Carlisle (2002) reinforces that KM is more than information management, by specifying that:

> *"It requires the pursuit of different types of objectives and the development of different types of resources, strengths, process capabilities and organizational structures"* (*op. cit.*, p. 123).

To summarise what has been said till now, knowledge is very complex and its understanding and management cannot be done from just a single point of view. One should consider the multiple perspectives brought up by its history, development and the contributions of the different disciplines.

Importance Of KM: Some Evidence

Since 1997, one can witness an increase in the interest for KM, manifested through the growth in the number of conferences and publications addressing KM or related aspects (Little, Quintas & Ray, 2002). The first international conference to have KM as the main topic was held in September 1995 and the first periodicals in the field, including *Knowledge Management, Knowledge Inc., Knowledge Management Review* and the *Journal of Knowledge Management* have been published from 1997 onwards. The publication of journal articles regarding KM rose from about 25 (1995) up to about 625 in 1999 (number of knowledge management articles on *ABI/Inform* database) (*op.cit.,* p. 3).

At present, it is possible to find a diversity of good examples of events related to knowledge management. The "KM Europe 2003" (http://www.kmeurope.com), the "CIKM2003 – 12th Conference on Information and Knowledge Management" (http://bit.csc.lsu.edu/~cikm2003/), "The Fifth European Conference on Organizational Knowledge and Learning Capabilities" (http://www.uibk.ac.at/congress/oklc2004/), and "The 4th European Conference On Knowledge Management" (*http://www.mcil.co.uk/2o-eckm2003-home.htm*) are only some of the them to take place during the current year (2003).

Furthermore, other projects and activities are being carried out in order to develop the management of knowledge in Europe and foster innovation and competitiveness. The Knowledge Board (http://www.knowledgeboard.com) is one of those projects. This is the European KM Community, created with the

Copyright © 2004, Idea Group Inc. Copying or distributing in print or electronic forms without written permission of Idea Group Inc. is prohibited.

support of European Commission's Information Society Technologies (IST) Programme, which provided the framework for implementing a thematic network on the area of KM, and was launched in 2000, with representatives from 13 European research projects; at present this number exceeds 40. At present (July 2003) there are more than 4,000 individuals and 170 enterprises contributing to this network.

Within this community, some projects are being carried out. The development of the "European Guide to Good Practice in Knowledge Management" (http://www.knowledgeboard.com/cgi-bin/item.cgi?id=109306) is one of those deserving mention.

The Knowledge Manager Profile

Competitiveness depends not on knowledge per se, but in the addition of value where it is created and applied for specific tasks and purposes and in the way it is applied to strategic organizational objectives and to promote innovation (Newell et al., 2002). Frequently, innovation is the primary purpose for knowledge management; it can only be accomplished through the involvement of people with different expertise and experience, working together.

It is easy to find in the literature examples of large corporations implementing KM initiatives. Among these are the Ford Motor Company, Chevron, Texas Instruments, Canadian Centre for Management Development, Health Canada (Bontis, 2002b), Microsoft, Coca-Cola, Merck, Intel, and Skandia (Snyder & Pierce, 2002).

Taking into account that the large majority of firms worldwide are small and medium ones (SMEs) (EUROSTAT, 2002), why is it that the literature does not offer as many references to applications of KM in this sector? Is KM of any relevance to SMEs? If so, are their KM needs analogous to those of large corporations?

One could argue that the solution to KM lies in education and in the training and preparation of a particular kind of worker – the knowledge worker. As referred to in the document "Innovation Tomorrow," from the European Commission (2002a), education is central to the development of the knowledge-based society.

Copyright © 2004, Idea Group Inc. Copying or distributing in print or electronic forms without written permission of Idea Group Inc. is prohibited.

Furthermore, in the *Innobarometer 2002*[14], one of the main conclusions expressed is that managers attribute their strength in innovation mostly to the qualification and professionalism of the staff. Moreover, it should be recognised that the biggest contributors to GNP in Europe are the SMEs, who cannot afford the resources to formally "compartmentalize the information gathering and use functions, nor do they have the resources to develop the infrastructure necessary to access and use the information" (Rosenberg, 2002, p. 2). It is argued that these competencies should be developed by all employees, regardless of the dimension of the enterprise in which they are working. These would be called *KM professionals,* who, apart from having the general knowledge worker skills, should also be equipped with the skills, capabilities and competencies required to manage organizational knowledge assets to increase an organization's ability to exploit knowledge as a resource to "increase productivity, quality and innovation" (Hackett, 2002, p. 727). As a matter of fact, innovation is "stimulated by, and creates requirements for, a skilled workforce. (...) Skills are required to generate, implement, effectively use, and generate new uses for innovations (organizations as well as technological)" (European Commission, 2002a, p. 144).

Furthermore, firms should provide training opportunities to their employees to enhance their KM skills and foster an environment where knowledge is created and disseminated through the organization (Zack, 2002).

As outlined in the previous sections, the recognition of the importance of knowledge for wealth creation in organizations and in society (Newell et al., 2002, pp. 16-18), the rise of knowledge work in parallel with the corresponding decline of traditional forms of work and the restructuring of work and organizations as a consequence of the use and limitations of information and communication technologies have all brought to the fore the importance of KM practices, both at the institutional and at country level.

This section describes the competencies, skills, abilities and attitudes required by a workforce able to take advantage of the opportunities brought about by the implementation of knowledge management to create and leverage intellectual capital for business performance and in public management (Wiig, 2002, p. 225). We will concentrate on those who have the responsibility to perform knowledge management functions in institutions, that is, the KM professionals. Nevertheless, one should bear in mind that the development of such competencies, at every level, is vital to work in a knowledge-based society and should be a goal to be pursued by every knowledge worker.

Copyright © 2004, Idea Group Inc. Copying or distributing in print or electronic forms without written permission of Idea Group Inc. is prohibited.

Competencies and Skills For KM

Abell and Oxbrow (2001, pp. 105-126), in a research study completed in 1999 covering professionals that perform KM related jobs in a variety of organizations – private (financial services, consultancy, lawyers, industry, engineering and services) and public (Central Administration, health services, education, police, etc.) in Europe and USA, concluded that the required skills and competencies fall within one of a set of three categories, namely: 1) Professional and technical core competencies; 2) Organizational skills, and 3) KM enabling skills.

The first two relate to individuals and the third relates to KM teams, communities and networks skills. Together, these three sets represent the competency building blocks that an individual, group or organization requires in order to possess KM capability. Each of those sets are briefly explained:

i) Professional and technical core competencies

   They are acquired through educational, professional or technical qualifications, training and experience and reflect personal attributes, preferences and background; usually they are continually developed. Generally considered, they are not the primary focus of KM approaches, although it is essential that any knowledge worker is able to maintain and develop these occupational competencies. Quinn, Anderson and Finkelstein (2002, p. 86) name these as "cognitive knowledge" or "know-what".

ii) Organizational competencies

   These are the most frequently cited as key skills for KM teams. They are also those required to apply professional or technical competencies effectively and include communication[15], negotiation and persuasion[16]. To these may be added facilitation, mentoring and coaching. The ability to contribute to work teams, where individuals have to play different roles according to circumstances falls also under this set of competencies. The understanding of business processes and its interpretation are at the core of this set, as the individuals need to understand the value adding impact of their contribution. Such capacity requires the ability to learn and absorb, effectively, all aspects of the organization's business. Quinn, Anderson and Finkelstein (2002, p. 86) name these competencies as "advanced skills" (know-how) and "systems understanding" (know-why).

Copyright © 2004, Idea Group Inc. Copying or distributing in print or electronic forms without written permission of Idea Group Inc. is prohibited.

iii) KM enabling competencies

The third KM skills set relates to the capacity to plan and implement KM approaches. The emphasis on these skills may change as KM becomes embedded in the organization. For instance, in the initial phase of a knowledge strategy implementation, emphasis should be on the development of corporate KM behaviours and processes, requiring a stronger input regarding human resources management, the establishment of business processes and the development of management skills.

Those authors have also identified within this set of competencies two key areas enabling KM:

- Understanding the knowledge process, and
- Change management, which includes the ability to: 1) identify the benefits of change for the organization and for individuals; 2) involve people in the development of ideas and thinking about direction; 3) identify barriers and obstacles; d) understand the art of achieving the possible before tackling the impossible; e) influence the organizational and infrastructure developments and, f) retain a missionary zeal for the process (Abell & Oxbrow, 2001, p. 118).

Furthermore, the creation of value from knowledge and the implementation of strategies to attain these objectives imply that all organizations from all sectors express a need to increase their capability to define information requirements, find, analyse, use, share, store and create information. This capability requires an information-literate workforce (ALA, 1989, 1998; Bawden, 2001; Webber & Johnstone, 2001). Rosenberg (2002, p. 2) defines information literacy as the "ability to know when information is needed and then having the skill to identify, locate, evaluate, organize and effectively use that information". This means that due to the characteristics of an uncertain and global environment and work settings, a new kind of worker is needed for contemporary organizations to compete and innovate:

> *"who have to access, manage and use the vast amount of information delivered to them through multiple channels (e.g., phone, Internet, e-mail, printed documents, Web-cast) in a wide variety of formats (e.g., video, printed, electronic text)"* (Cheuk, 2002, p. 2).

Copyright © 2004, Idea Group Inc. Copying or distributing in print or electronic forms without written permission of Idea Group Inc. is prohibited.

In these circumstances, information literacy must be part of the "skill set of almost every employee who works with information" in a business or an institution (Rosenberg, 2002, p. 3).

Mapping the New Professional Profile

KM is a multi- and pluri-disciplinary area. This has strong implications concerning the education and training of those with competencies to perform the KM function in organizations. As referred to above, KM has its roots either in the perspective of "KM as systems," where knowledge is susceptible to creation, codification and transfer, or in the perspective of "KM as people" (Swan & Scarbrough, 2002, p. 11), where knowledge cannot be easily extracted and recorded. The first perspective has evolved with the work and research of the libraries and information sciences, together with those coming from process engineering. The second perspective developed with those coming from organizational theory, psychology and sociology. Bringing those perspectives together allows us to map KM. Furthermore, each perspective stresses a particular aspect of KM, contributing to a deeper understanding of knowledge and its management. The proliferation of perspectives and the diversity of areas contributing to KM suggest that the professional profile emerging should not be seen only from one, but should be at the confluence of the contributing disciplines.

Figure 1. Knowledge Management map in order to prepare the new professional profile.

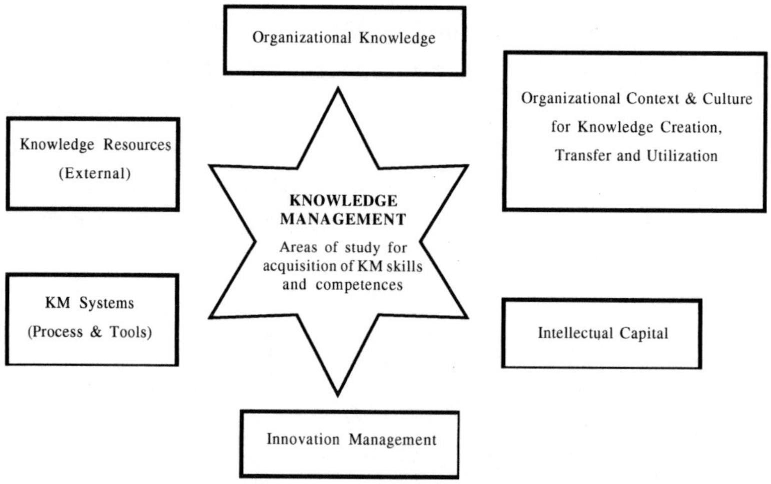

Copyright © 2004, Idea Group Inc. Copying or distributing in print or electronic forms without written permission of Idea Group Inc. is prohibited.

Figure 1 aims to broadly sketch the landscape of domains that, in our opinion, should be addressed in any plan of study to convey KM competencies to those who will be performing knowledge management functions.

In the six areas of study every contribution to KM described above is built avoiding any of the partial perspectives referred to in 3. The topics covered in each area are briefly explained in the following paragraphs. These are only illustrative and by no means an extensive list of what has to be addressed:

i) Knowledge resources – the knowledge manager should be able to understand how information and knowledge resources – for example, databases, Web-based and other information and knowledge resources, usually available through library and information services, are created, organized, accessed and retrieved to enable him/her to fully exploit all the information that is being made available, both internally and externally to the organization, which is crucial to the decision making process by everyone in the organization;

ii) KM systems (KMS) – these are seen as the enabling technologies for an effective and efficient KM. As Maier (2002, p. 20) states, these tools and systems must have

   1) basic functionalities - for example, intranets (for communication; as well as storage, exchange, search and retrieval of data and documents); CSCW - Computer Supported Collaborative Work - (enables real-time collaboration among geographically-distributed work group members); groupware (supports time management, discussions, meetings or creative workshops of creative work groups), workflow management systems (support well-structured organizational processes and handle the execution of workflows);

   2) Integrative KMS - support codification (to create cognitive categories, through which the person makes sense), search and retrieval - for example, data mining for KM, CRM;

   3) Interactive KMS - support KM processes - for example, locating experts and building communities, e-business, ERP (op. cit., p. 20); and

   4) Bridging KMS - provide contextualized knowledge repositories - for example, portals, decision support systems, CRM, ERP (*op. cit.,* 20).

Copyright © 2004, Idea Group Inc. Copying or distributing in print or electronic forms without written permission of Idea Group Inc. is prohibited.

Generally speaking, KMS are intended to organize, interpret and make widely accessible the expertise of an organization's human capital; they help to maintain a well-informed, productive workforce (Leidner, 1998).

iii) Organizational knowledge – the notion that while individuals learn, so also do groups and organizations, has gained wide acceptance in the last decade (Bood, 1998, p. 210). *Organizational learning* occurs as knowledge, acquired and developed by individual members, is embedded in *organizational memory* or pasted into the *organizational knowledge base* (*op.cit.,* p. 216). This draws on the idea that organizational knowledge can be stored, retrieved and recollected. Karreman (2002) points out that:

> *"organizational (collective) memory is socially constructed, culturally maintained and dispersed, and as indeed is indicated by the concept of knowledge management – a possible target for managerial efforts".*

Within organizational knowledge, *competitive intelligence* (CI) is also referred to as *competitor intelligence, business intelligence* or *environment scanning* (Bergeron & Hiller, 2002, p. 355). It covers numerous sectors of intelligence – competitor, technology, product/service, environment (ecology), economy, legislation/regulation, acquisition/merger, customer/supplier, market, partner/collaborator, social/historical/political environment and the organization's internal environment (Fahey, 1999); CI's goal is to stimulate the organization's creativeness, innovativeness and willingness to change. *Social intelligence,* which is the process by which a society, organization or individual scans the environment, interprets what is there and constructs versions of events that may afford competitive advantage (Cronin & Davenport, 1993, p. 8), falls also within organizational knowledge. As Davenport (2000) points out, "social intelligence has reached maturity in the age of networks" and suggests that in a world of virtual workplaces it may be defined as "insight which is based on collective understanding of work practices " (*op. cit.,* p. 145) and can be used; project management and learning how to work professionally with others are vital skills for everyone who performs knowledge management functions.

Copyright © 2004, Idea Group Inc. Copying or distributing in print or electronic forms without written permission of Idea Group Inc. is prohibited.

iv) Organizational context and culture - as already stated, traditional sources of success - product and process technology, protected or regulated markets, access to financial resources and economies of scale - have been in the past the sources of competitive advantage. These have become less important and what remains as a crucial, differentiating factor, difficult to be imitated/duplicated by competitors is the organizational culture and its capabilities. How people are managed, effectively motivated and the effects of this on their behaviour and skills are becoming vital (Pfeffer, 2002, pp. 62–66). Furthermore, as referred to above, knowledge creation implies more than information codification. It includes the development of a "knowledge culture" that can be translated into the nurturing of communities of practice (Davenport & Hall, 2002; Wenger, 1998; Wenger, McDermott & Snyder, 2002), trust among people, rewards, incentives, motivation (Hall, 2001) as well as the establishment of communication channels and organizational structure (Maier, 2002).

v) Intellectual capital – although knowledge creation by business organizations has been almost neglected in management studies, it is now recognized as the most important source of organizational competitiveness at the international level. The importance of intangible resources instead of tangible ones for company value, gave rise to a growing interest in developing methods and tools that enable companies "to analyse their intellectual capital stocks" and "organizational learning flows" (Bontis, 2002b, p. 623); intellectual capital includes the human, structure and relations, as mentioned above. This area, within a KM plan of study, will contribute to the understanding of the role of intangible assets in an organization and will address the measures and metrics to assess and evaluate the IC.

vi) Innovation management – knowledge management for S&T innovation is the goal of any organization in order to remain competitive in a rapidly changing environment; for that effect, those who are going to perform the knowledge management function should be able to identify KM resources to support a knowledge strategy for technical/scientific innovation, contribute to the writing of a development plan for an innovative product or service in a scientific or technical organization, search for development funds, contribute to the strategic understanding of the regulatory and standards environment of scientific and technical organizations and identify and evaluate knowledge markets opportunities.

Copyright © 2004, Idea Group Inc. Copying or distributing in print or electronic forms without written permission of Idea Group Inc. is prohibited.

These areas of study should not be seen as independent of each other, nor as mutually exclusive. For instance, the development of communities would benefit from the use of groupware; organizational learning will need a culture that encourages and stimulates people to share their knowledge. All these processes will need knowledge and information resources repositories.

The education and training of a KM professional should cover all these fields. Furthermore, it should also take into consideration the development of competencies and skills identified by Abel and Oxbrow (2001) jointly with those concerning infoliteracy.

Conclusion

Change is at the core of business life as organizations try to keep up with continuously evolving clients' tastes, competition on a global scale and shorter product life cycles. Stimulated by the policies defined by the European Councils, Europe is trying to develop towards "the most competitive and dynamic knowledge-based society in the world, by the year 2010". Portugal is not an exception and in the last three years some projects came to fruition, namely the creation of the *Unidade de Missão Inovação e Conhecimento*, together with the setting up of the *Plano de Acção Sociedade da Informação*. The effort that is being made is recognized but some shortcomings are identified – for example, the adoption of a technological perspective of a knowledge-driven society and the under-development of the required competencies to live and succeed in such an environment.

To attain the goals concerning innovation and competitiveness, it is necessary to recognize the importance of intangible resources, such as people and their expertise, and to develop new capabilities and competencies by the general worker as well as by the knowledge manager specialist.

The broad areas of study required to train the KM professionals include knowledge resources, KM systems, organizational knowledge, organizational context and culture, intellectual capital and innovation management. The development of adequate competencies of such professionals could be the basis for a strategy to help Portuguese SMEs to catch up with other European countries.

Copyright © 2004, Idea Group Inc. Copying or distributing in print or electronic forms without written permission of Idea Group Inc. is prohibited.

Endnotes

[1] http://trendchart.cordis.lu

[2] http://trendchart.cordis.lu/Scoreboard2002/index.html

[3] http://www.cordis.lu/innovation-smes/src/innobarometer.htm

[4] http://trendchart.cordis.lu/Scoreboard2002/html/eu_member_states/country_performances/country_pages/portugal_page.html

[5] Science & Engineering

[6] http://www.portugal.gov.pt/pt/Conselho+de+Ministros/Comunicados/20030626.htm

[7] http://www.portugal.gov.pt/pt/Conselho+de+Ministros/Documentos/20030627_PM_SInformacao.htm

[8] http://www.portugal.gov.pt

[9] http://www.umic.pcm.gov.pt/UMIC/. This Unit has been created by the XVth Government of Portugal with the objective to set a transversal and integrated perspective of all the activity of the Government as well as the operational and politic articulation among Governmental members in order to attain the goals established in the Lisbon Summit, in 2000.

[10] "Even explicit knowledge is dependent on tacit knowledge to be applied" (Wenger, McDermott & Snyder, 2002, p. 9).

[11] "Human capital is the stock of knowledge that exists at the individual level in an organization" (Bontis, 2002a, p. 24). It includes the knowledge that resides in the minds of employees (tacit knowledge and difficult to codify and transfer) as well as the firm's processes, strategies and tactics (*op. cit.*). According to Sveiby, "Human capital is the accumulated value of competence, training, skills and knowledge residing within organizational members" (Snyder & Pierce, 2002, p. 477).

[12] Bontis (2002a, p. 24) describes structural capital, as the "… Knowledge embedded in the non-human storehouses and routines of organisations. (…) Consists of the mechanisms and structures of the organization that can help support employees in their quest for optimum performance". Structural capital, also named "organizational capital", includes all forms of intellectual property as well as the knowledge embedded in the routines of the company, such as organizational or operating systems (Snyder & Pierce, 2002, p. 478).

Copyright © 2004, Idea Group Inc. Copying or distributing in print or electronic forms without written permission of Idea Group Inc. is prohibited.

[13] Relationship capital "... Comprises customer and supplier relationships, knowledge of market channels and an understanding of the impact of governmental or industry association" (Bontis, 2002a, p. 24). Customer (relational) capital is the value derived from connections outside the organization; it includes reliable suppliers and loyal customers (Snyder & Pierce, 2002, p. 478).

[14] http://www.cordis.lu/innovation-smes/src/innobarometer.htm

[15] Represent the ability to express oneself clearly to explain complex situations or thoughts, to get one's point across, listening, understanding and being aware of the needs of one's audience (Abel & Oxbrow, 2001, p. 116).

[16] Consists of the ability to influence and will determine the ability to act effectively (Abel & Oxbrow, 2001, p. 116).

References

Abell, A., & Oxbrow, N. (2001). *Competing with knowledge.* London: TFPL and Library Association Publishing.

American Library Association. (1989). *Presidential committee on information literacy.* Final eeport. Chicago: American Library Association. Retrieved March 12, 2004, from http://www.ala.org/Content/NavigationMenu/ACRL/Publications/White_Papers_and_Reports/Presidential_Committee_on_Information_Literacy.htm

American Library Association. (1998). *A progress report on information literacy. An update on American Libraries Association.* Presidential Committee on Information Literacy. Retrieved March 12, 2004, from the National Forum on Information Literacy Web site: http://www.ala.org/Content/NavigationMenu/ACRL/Publications/White_Papers_and_Reports/A_Progress_Report_on_Information_Literacy.htm, and from http://www.infolit.org/documents/progress.html

Barcelona European Council. (2002, March 15-16). *Presidency conclusions.* Retrieved March 12, 2004, from http://ue.eu.int/pressData/en/ec/71025.pdf

Copyright © 2004, Idea Group Inc. Copying or distributing in print or electronic forms without written permission of Idea Group Inc. is prohibited.

Bawden, D. (2001). Information and digital literacies: A review of concepts. *Journal of Documentation, 57*(2), 218-259. Retrieved March 12, 2004, from http://gti1.edu.um.es:8080/jgomez/hei/intranet/bawden.pdf

Bergeron, P., & Hiller, C. (2002). Competitive intelligence. In B. Cronin (Ed.), *Annual review of information science and technology* (pp. 353-390). Medford, NJ: Information Today.

Bontis, N. (2002a, March/April). The rising star of the Chief Knowledge Officer. *IVEY Business Journal,* 20-25. Retrieved March 12, 2004, from http://www.business.mcmaster.ca/mktg/nbontis/ic/publications/BontisIBJ.pdf

Bontis, N. (2002b). Managing organizational knowledge by diagnosing intellectual capital: Framing and advancing the state of the field. In N. Bontis & C.W. Choo (Eds.), *The strategic management of intellectual capital and organizational knowledge* (pp. 621-642). New York: Oxford University Press.

Bontis, N. (2003). *National intellectual capital index: The benchmarking of Arab countries.* UNDP/RBAS working paper, Hamilton, Ontario. Retrieved March 12, 2004, from http://www.business.mcmaster.ca/mktg/nbontis/ic/publications/BontisUNJIC.pdf

Bood, R. (1998). Charting organizational learning: A comparison of multiple mapping techniques. In C. Eden & J. Spender (Eds.), *Managerial and organizational cognition* (pp. 210-230). London: Sage.

Brussels European Council. (2003). *Presidency conclusions – Brussels European council 20 and 21 March 2003.* Retrieved March 12, 2004, from http://ue.eu.int/newsroom/makeFrame.asp?MAX=&BID=76&DID=75136&LANG=1&File=/pressData/en/ec/75136.pdf&Picture=0

Burton-Jones, A. (2001). *Knowledge capitalism – Business, work and learning in the new economy.* New York: Oxford University Press.

Carlisle, Y. (2002). Strategic thinking and knowledge management. In S. Little, P. Quintas & T. Ray (Eds.), *Managing knowledge – an essential reader* (pp. 122-138). London: Sage.

Cheuk, B. (2002). *Information literacy in the workplace context: Issues, best practices and challenges.* White Paper prepared for UNESCO, the U.S. National Commission on Libraries and Information Science, and the National Forum on Information Literacy, for use at the Information

Copyright © 2004, Idea Group Inc. Copying or distributing in print or electronic forms without written permission of Idea Group Inc. is prohibited.

Literacy Meeting of Experts, Prague. Retrieved March 12, 2004, from http://www.nclis.gov/libinter/infolitconf&meet/papers/cheuk-fullpaper.pdf

Commission of European Communities. (2003a). *Innovation policy: Updating the Union's approach in the context of the Lisbon strategy* (COM(2003)112 final). Communication from the Commission. Brussels: Commission of the European Communities.

Commission of European Communities. (2003b). *Thinking small in an enlarging Europe* (COM(2003)26 final). Communication from the Commission. Brussels: Commission of the European Communities. Retrieved March 12, 2004, from http://europa.eu.int/comm/enterprise/enterprise_policy/sme-package/doc/com26_en.pdf

Conselho de Ministros. (2003). *Plano de _Acção para a Sociedade da Informação.* Retrieved March 12, 2004, from http://www.portugal.gov.pt/pt/Conselho+de+Ministros/Documentos/20030627_PM_SInformacao.htm

Cronin, B., & Davenport, E. (1993). Social intelligence. In M. Williams (Ed.), *Annual review of information science and technology* (ARIST), *28,* 3-43.

Davenport, E. (2000). Social intelligence in the age of networks. *Journal of Information Science, 26*(3), 145-152.

Davenport, E., & Cronin, B. (2000). *Knowledge management: Semantic drift or conceptual shift?* Retrieved March 12, 2004, from http://www.alise.org/conferences/conf00_Davenport-Cronin_paper.htm

Davenport, E., & Hall, H. (2002). Organizational knowledge and communities of practice. In B. Cronin (Ed.), *Annual review of information science and technology* (pp.171-228). Medford, NJ: Information Today.

Dawson, R. (2000). Knowledge capabilities as the focus of organizational development and strategy. *Journal of Knowledge Management, 4*(4), 320-327.

eEurope2005. (2002). *Executive summary.* Retrieved March 12, 2004, from http://europa.eu.int/information_society/eeurope/news_library/documents/eeurope2005/execsum_en.pdf

European Commission. (2002a). *Innovation tomorrow – Innovation policy and the regulatory framework: Making innovation an integral part of the broader structural agenda.* Luxembourg: Office for Official Publications of the European Communities.

Copyright © 2004, Idea Group Inc. Copying or distributing in print or electronic forms without written permission of Idea Group Inc. is prohibited.

European Commission. (2002b). *Inobarometer 2002.* Retrieved March 12, 2004, from http://www.cordis.lu/innovation-smes/src/innobarometer.htm

EUROSTAT. (2002). *SMEs in Europe: Competitiveness, innovation and the knowledge-driven society* (CAT No KS-CJ.02-001-EN-N). Luxembourg: Office for Official Publications of the European Communities.

Fahey, L. (1999). *Competitors: Outwitting, outmanoeuvring, outperforming.* New York: Wiley.

Hackett, J. (2002). Beyond knowledge management – New ways to work. In N. Bontis & W.C. Choo (Eds.), *The strategic management of intellectual capital and organizational knowledge* (pp. 715-738). New York: Oxford University Press.

Hall, H. (2001, April 10-11). *Social exchange for knowledge exchange.* Paper presented at the International Conference on Managing Knowledge, University of Leicester. Retrieved March 12, 2004, from http://www.bim.napier.ac.uk/~hazel/esis/hazel1.pdf

IRG3. (2002, May 13). *Technologies for major work and businesses challenges.* Information Society, Information Society Internal Reflection Group 3.

Karreman, D. (2002, April). *Knowledge management and "organizational memory" - remembrance and recollection in a knowledge intensive firm.* Paper presented at the conference Organizational Knowledge and Learning Capabilities (ALBA).Retrieved March 12, 2004, from http://www.alba.edu.gr/OKLC2002/Proceedings/pdf_files/ID312.pdf

Leidner, D. (1998). *Understanding information culture: Integrating knowledge management systems into organizations.* INSEAD working paper. Paris: INSEAD.

Lisbon European Council. (2000). *Presidency Conclusions - 23-24 March 2000.* Retrieved March 12, 2004, from http://ue.eu.int/Newsroom/LoadDoc.asp?BID=76&DID=60917&LANG=1

Little, S., Quintas, P., & Ray, T (2002). *Managing knowledge: An essential reader.* London: Sage.

Lyman, P., & Varian, H. (2000). *How much information.* Retrieved July 18, 2003, from http://www.sims.berkeley.edu/how-much-info/index.html

Maier, R. (2002). State-of-practice of knowledge management systems: Results of an empirical study. *Informatik/ Informatique – Knowledge Management, 1,* 14-22.

Copyright © 2004, Idea Group Inc. Copying or distributing in print or electronic forms without written permission of Idea Group Inc. is prohibited.

Newell, S., Robertson, M., Scarbrough, H., & Swan, J. (2002). *Managing knowledge work.* Houndmills: Palgrave.

Nonaka, I. (1994). A dynamic theory of organisational knowledge creation. *Organization Science*, *5*(1), 14-37.

Nonaka, I., & Takeuchi, H. (1995). *The knowledge creating company: How Japanese companies create the dynamic innovation.* New York: Oxford University Press.

Nonaka, I., Toyama, R., & Konno, N. (2002). SECI, ba and leadership: A unified model of dynamic knowledge creation. In S. Little, P. Quintas & T. Ray (Eds.), *Managing knowledge – an essential reader* (pp. 41-67). London: Sage (reprint).

Petty, R., & Guthrie, J. (2000). Intellectual capital literature review: Measurement, reporting and management. *Journal of Intellectual Capital, 1*(2), 155-176.

Pfeffer, J. (2002). Competitive advantage through people. In J. Henry & D. Mayle (Eds.), *Managing innovation and change* (pp. 61-73). London: Sage.

Quinn, J., Anderson, P., & Finkelstein, S. (2002). Managing professional intellect: Making the most of the best. In J. Henry & D. Mayle (Eds.), *Managing innovation and change* (pp. 87-98). London: Sage.

Quinn, J., Baruch, J., & Zein, K. (2002). Intellect, innovation and growth. In J. Henry & D. Mayle (Eds.), *Managing innovation and change* (pp. 5-22). London: Sage.

Rosenberg, V. (2002). *Information literacy and small business.* White Paper prepared for UNESCO, the U.S. National Commission on Libraries and Information Science, and the National Forum on Information Literacy, for use at the Information Literacy Meeting of Experts, Prague. Retrieved March 12, 2004, from http://www.nclis.gov/libinter/infolitconf& meet/papers/rosenberg-fullpaper.pdf

Sawn, J., & Scarbrough, H. (2002). The paradox of knowledge management. *Informatik/Informatique – Knowledge Management, 1*(Fev), 10-13.

Senge, P. (2000). Reflection on a leader's New York: Building learning organizations. In D. Morey, M. Maybury & B. Thuraisingham (Eds.), *Knowledge management – Classic and contemporary works* (pp. 53-60). Cambridge, MA: MIT Press.

Copyright © 2004, Idea Group Inc. Copying or distributing in print or electronic forms without written permission of Idea Group Inc. is prohibited.

Skyrme, D. (1999). *Knowledge networking – Creating the collaborative enterprise.* Oxford: Butterworth Heinemann.

Snyder, H., & Pierce, J. (2002). Intellectual capital. In B. Cronin (Ed.), *Annual Review of Information Science and Technology, 36* (pp. 467-500). Medford, NJ: Information Today.

UNICE. (2000). *Stimulating creativity and innovation in Europe: The UNICE benchmarking report 2000.* Retrieved March 12, 2004, from http://212.3.246.118/1/LJDBFBPDFEGFKIGHIBBNFPLOPDBY9DA1BG9LTE4Q/UNICE/docs/DLS/2002-03509-E.pdf

UNICE. (2001a). *Unice benchmarking report 2001: EU must make a reality of reform* (press release). Retrieved March 12, 2004, from http://212.3.246.118/2/LJDBFBPDFEGFKIGHIBBNFPLOPDBY9DANT19LTE4Q/UNICE/docs/DLS/2002-03675-E.pdf

UNICE. (2001b). *The ReNEWed economy – Business for a dynamic Europe - Unice benchmarking report 2001.* Retrieved March 12, 2004, from http://212.3.246.118/3/LJDBFBPDFEGFKIGHIBBNFPLOPDBY9DANCD9LTE4Q/UNICE/docs/DLS/2002-03680-E.pdf

UNICE. (2002a). *The Lisbon strategy/status 2003 - Time is running out, action needed now* (press release). Retrieved March 12, 2004, from http://212.3.246.118/4/LJDBFBPDFEGFKIGHIBBNFPLOPDB69DBDB39LI71KM/UNICE/docs/DLS/2003-00007-EN.pdf

UNICE. (2002b). *Lisbon strategy: Status 2003 – Time is running out, action needed now.* Retrieved March 12, 2004, from http://212.3.246.118/5/LJDBFBPDFEGFKIGHIBBNFPLOPDB69DB1CG9LI71KM/UNICE/docs/DLS/2003-00589-EN.pdf

Webber, S., & Johnston, B. (2001). *Information literacy: Standards and statements.* Retrieved March 12, 2004, from http://dis.shef.ac.uk/literacy/standards.htm

Wenger, E. (1998). *Communities of practice – Learning, meaning and identity.* New York: Cambridge University Press.

Wenger, E., McDermott, R., & Snyder, W. (2002). *Cultivating communities of practice.* Boston: Harvard Business School Press.

Wiig, K. (1999). What future knowledge management users may expect. *Journal of Knowledge Management, 3*(2), 155-156.

Wiig, K.M. (2002). Knowledge management in public administration. *Journal of Knowledge Management, 6*(3), 224-239.

Copyright © 2004, Idea Group Inc. Copying or distributing in print or electronic forms without written permission of Idea Group Inc. is prohibited.

Yartes-Mercer, P., & Bawden, D. (2002). Managing the paradox: The valuation of knowledge and knowledge management. *Journal of Information Science, 28*(1), 19-29.

Zack, M. (2002). Developing a knowledge strategy. In C.W. Choo & N. Bontis (Eds.), *The strategic management of intellectual capital and organizational knowledge*. New York: Oxford University Press.

Copyright © 2004, Idea Group Inc. Copying or distributing in print or electronic forms without written permission of Idea Group Inc. is prohibited.

Chapter XIII

The Role of Knowledge Creation in Competitive Advantage

Patricia C. Miller
University at Albany, USA

Abstract

The ability of an organization to better utilize its current stock of knowledge or position itself to identify opportunities to create knowledge faster than its competitors is key to increasing organizational wealth. Knowledge can be defined as that core asset that adds wealth to an organization and when properly implemented, results in new or improved products or services. Opining on the core competency model (Hamel & Prahalad, 1994) and on the concept of intellectual bandwidth (Nunamaker et al., 2001), the author suggests that an organization can enhance its performance and increase its competitive standing by making a careful assessment of its intellectual bandwidth for knowledge creation. In this chapter, the key enablers that influence the level of knowledge creation that occurs within an organization are identified. The chapter lists the organizational characteristics that will help ensure the high level of intellectual bandwidth needed for knowledge creation.

Copyright © 2004, Idea Group Inc. Copying or distributing in print or electronic forms without written permission of Idea Group Inc. is prohibited.

Introduction

> *"Knowledge [is] the new resource for economic performance..."* (Drucker, 1994, p. 11)

In a world where knowledge is power, the ability of an organization to better utilize its current stock of knowledge or position itself to identify opportunities to create knowledge faster than its competitors will result in increased organizational wealth. Davenport and Prusak (1998) contend that organizations that are first to acquire and use new knowledge will gain a competitive advantage. To maintain this competitive advantage, however, the organization must be able to continually absorb new knowledge and employ this knowledge in new or innovative ways.

The organization must be able to recognize changes in the environment that require new knowledge; therefore it must engage in scanning activities, both internal and external. The organization must also be flexible in order to respond and exploit these new opportunities (Cohen & Levinthal, 1990). It must be capable of applying this knowledge, thereby helping to ensure that it will gain a competitive edge or maintain its competitive standing (Cohen & Levinthal, 1990; Kogut & Zander, 1988; Zack, 2003). This requires that the organization be in a state of continual learning.

This chapter explores an organization's ability to create knowledge and increase its competitive standing. The intellectual bandwidth for knowledge creation model is presented and the key enablers that make up this model and influence the level of knowledge creation are examined. The author suggests that an organization can enhance its performance and increase its competitive standing by making a careful assessment of its intellectual bandwidth for knowledge creation.

Background

Knowledge is often thought of as the end state along a continuum from data to information to knowledge (Grover & Davenport, 2001). It is often hard to give a concise definition of knowledge, as noted by the following characterizations.

Copyright © 2004, Idea Group Inc. Copying or distributing in print or electronic forms without written permission of Idea Group Inc. is prohibited.

- Knowledge is information that has meaning and is always in a state of becoming. It results from taking information that is inert and static, and transforms it, giving it new meaning (Bhatt, 2000).
- Knowledge is a justified belief system that leads to action (Nonaka & Takeuchi, 1995).
- Knowledge is personalized information residing in the minds of individuals (Alavi & Leidner, 2001).

It is often easier to say what knowledge is not; for example, knowledge is not neat and simple (Davenport & Prusak, 1998). This last statement best sums up the fluid character of knowledge. Knowledge can be intuitive, such as knowing how much and what type of persuasion will be effective with one's partner, or it can be formally structured, as in DaimlerChrysler's "Engineering Books of Knowledge."

Tacit and Explicit Knowledge

Knowledge resides in the minds of individuals and in organizations. It is frequently categorized as either explicit or tacit (Nonaka & Takeuchi, 1995; Polyani, 1998). Explicit knowledge can be codified, communicated without difficulty, recorded, written, and transferred into other formats or embedded in technology (Davenport & Prusak, 1998). Organizations make use of explicit knowledge in best practices, manuals, specifications and routine, programmed activities. Tacit knowledge, on the other hand, is content specific, abstract, and difficult to articulate because of its cognitive, intuitive and technical components (Alavi & Leidner, 2001; Bhatt, 2000; Nonaka & Takeuchi, 1995). Tacit knowledge is flexible, fluid and self-fortifying. It builds on an individual's experiences and mental models, combining them and giving new meaning as the context changes (Davenport & Prusak, 1998). This is why it is so difficult to teach someone how to ride a bicycle or even recognize the meaning of the sounds a favorite pet makes.

Organizations need to be able to draw on the tacit knowledge found in individuals and transform it into tacit knowledge held by a group and, when possible, converted into an explicit form. This is a difficult task since tacit knowledge results from life experiences which include the social, cultural,

Copyright © 2004, Idea Group Inc. Copying or distributing in print or electronic forms without written permission of Idea Group Inc. is prohibited.

emotional and cognitive backgrounds of individuals. Therefore, the ability to externalize this knowledge so that others might learn from it may not be possible (Nestor-Baker & Hoy, 2001; Polyani, 1998). Hence, organizations must provide the environment that will enable individuals to utilize their tacit knowledge and expertise to increase organizational performance and productivity. "Managers need to provide the following conditions: the right amount of autonomy for participants; a certain level of creative chaos, redundancy, and variety to make the environment stimulating…" (Von Krogh et al., 2000, p. 179).

Knowledge, Competitive Advantage and Innovation

"To remain competitive-maybe even to survive-businesses will have to convert themselves into organizations of knowledgeable specialists." (Drucker, 1998, p. 11)

Knowledge can be defined as that core asset that when properly employed results in new or improved products or services. These products and services help create organizational wealth, enabling the organization to gain or maintain a competitive advantage, that is, by employing strategies of differentiation, cost or niche (Porter, 1998). Competitive advantage can be defined as profit above the industry average for a sustained period. It usually has as its foundation a core competency, that "thing" that the organization does better than its competitors do. In order to be considered core, a competency must meet the following criteria. It must provide customer benefits, it must be extendable and it must be difficult to imitate (Hamel & Prahalad, 1994). According to Forbes Magazine, the average age of organizations worldwide is less than 20 years, so their survival depends on their ability to engage in activities that can help ensure a competitive advantage.

In today's rapidly changing global economy, innovation is the number one creator of organizational wealth (Baum et al., 2000). Innovation is defined as the creation or discovery of novel products or services. Knowledge, while a necessary adjunct to innovation, is not sufficient to ensure competitive advantage. An organization might be able to innovate but not properly implement the result or it might not choose the right product for the market. Polaroid

Copyright © 2004, Idea Group Inc. Copying or distributing in print or electronic forms without written permission of Idea Group Inc. is prohibited.

Corporation, which filed for Chapter 11 bankruptcy in 2001, is an example an industry leader that failed to recognize the impact that computer technology such as the digital camera, would have upon its industry.

Innovation increases the chances that an organization will survive and it is essential to competitive advantage.

> *"Innovation is essential to competitive advantage and the chances of survival will be enhanced when the organization attends and responds to more and different stimuli."* (Belardo & Belardo, 2002, p. 71)

Innovation requires that the organization engage in continuous learning. To do so, it must acquire the knowledge needed to close what Zack (2003) describes as the strategic gap. Determining the knowledge needed to close this gap requires a process not unlike the knowledge management process described by Huber (1991), Nevis et al. (1995), and Belardo (2001). This process includes the following stages: identification, elicitation, dissemination and utilization. While discussion of these stages is beyond the scope of this chapter, it is necessary to draw attention to the identification stage because it is here that the knowledge needed to enhance competitive advantage is identified. It is in the identification stage that organizations determine and answer questions such as the following. What are our knowledge needs? Who possesses this knowledge? Where can it be found? "From a macro perspective, identification is important because knowledge is essential for competitive intelligence which can help the firm determine strategy. From a micro perspective, identification is essential to successful knowledge management because, in order to get the right knowledge to the right person at the right time, it is essential that the organization know who possesses this knowledge" (Belardo & Belardo, 2002, p. 28)

Intellectual Bandwidth for Knowledge Creation

The term *bandwidth* is normally associated with circuit or transmission capacity, such as 56 K or Fast Ethernet, while the transmission speed is dependent on the type of transmission media used, such as copper or glass. It

Copyright © 2004, Idea Group Inc. Copying or distributing in print or electronic forms without written permission of Idea Group Inc. is prohibited.

Figure 1.

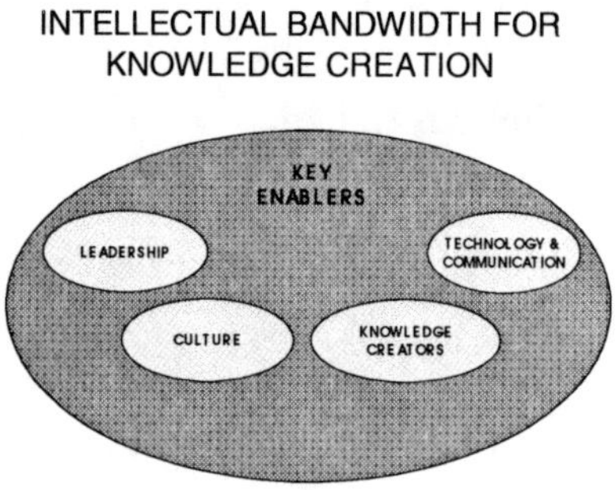

is advantageous for organizations to be able to have the largest transmission capacity and the fastest transmission speed that they can afford to transmit large amounts of data, and bandwidth-hungry video, graphics and sound. Additionally, the extensive use of the Web for e-commerce requires the ability to produce images quickly and relies on secure, stable and swift communications. The concept of an intellectual bandwidth has been discussed in conjunction with an organization's ability to create value. "The effectiveness with which an organization can create value is bounded by its potential intellectual bandwidth, which is its collective potential to acquire information, make sense of it, and take action with respect to a goal." (Nunamaker et al., 2001, p. 5). Opining on this concept and building on previous literature on knowledge creation, absorptive capacity, and innovation, the author suggests that any organization can gauge its potential to create knowledge by considering "media" or enablers influencing the rate of knowledge creation. These key enablers, listed in Figure 1, are leadership, culture, knowledge-creators and technology and communication (Belardo & Belardo, 2002; Cohen & Levinthal, 1990; Von Krogh, et al., 2000).

Leadership

> *"Knowledge creation is often chaotic and disorderly but if managed correctly can result in the creation of new skills and competencies"* (Bhatt, 2000).

Copyright © 2004, Idea Group Inc. Copying or distributing in print or electronic forms without written permission of Idea Group Inc. is prohibited.

Leadership plays a critical role in identifying the knowledge that an organization will acquire and use and should define the organization's mission in terms of knowledge (Zack, 2003). Leaders determine whom the organization listens to externally and to what degree this knowledge is disseminated within the organization. Leaders must understand the difference between the overt demonstrations of organizational behavior and the inherent thinking that leads to such demonstrations and develop the strategic architecture to reengineer the organizational genetic code, as it were (Hamel & Prahalad, 1994). They must also examine the basis for rewarding employee performance and a fine balance must be struck between rewarding units or teams for the sharing of knowledge and rewarding individuals in cases where their tacit knowledge leads to innovations. Jack Welch of General Electric Corporation and Leif Edvinsson of Skandia Insurance Company, Ltd are examples of leaders that helped make these organizations innovation forerunners.

Culture

> *"Culture shapes the processes by which new organizational knowledge—with its accompanying uncertainties—is created, legitimated, and distributed."* (DeLong & Fahey, 2000, p. 126)

Culture is a reflection of the values and practices of the organization; it can serve to facilitate or restrict the flow of knowledge. While organizations may have difficulty distinguishing the true culture from the espoused culture, people learn quickly by observation what values and practices are acceptable, despite what is formally advertised by management (Schein, 1999). Strategies for change need to be grounded in a clear understanding of the true organizational culture and the mental models that shape beliefs. It is important that the models that shape individuals beliefs about the organization include a firm conviction that it encourages experimentation and risk-taking and does not punish failures, because it realizes that all are essential parts of new competency development (Belardo & Belardo, 2002; Zack, 2003). Chaparral Steel is an example of an organization that recognizes that not all experimentation leads to successful outcomes. Individuals are not penalized when their efforts fail; the information is used as a learning tool.

Copyright © 2004, Idea Group Inc. Copying or distributing in print or electronic forms without written permission of Idea Group Inc. is prohibited.

While culture has a significant influence in the management of knowledge, the ability of an organization to put together teams of individuals with diverse but complementary experiences can serve to ignite sparks of creativity where they might otherwise lie dormant. Socialization and activities where individuals can informally share knowledge with teammates and other colleagues is vital (Brown & Duguid, 2001; Davenport & Prusak, 1998; Von Krogh et al., 2000). The development of micro-communities and virtual communities, which allow individuals to meet across geographic regions and functional titles, is essential to the development of knowledge.

Knowledge Creators

> *"Knowledge workers cannot be bullied into creativity or information sharing; and the traditional forms of compensation and organizational hierarchy do not motivate people sufficiently for them to develop the strong relationships required for knowledge creation on a continuing basis."* (Von Krogh et al., 2000, p. 4)

The capability of an organization to build on existing knowledge is affected by an organization's intellectual capacity, which is largely a function of the level of prior related knowledge (Cohen & Levinthal, 1990; Kogut & Zander, 1992). It is important that the organization employ individuals whose experience will enable them to recognize and assimilate new sources of information, produce something unique and innovative or contribute to team productivity.

Knowledge creators are knowledge workers; they are individuals who have a role in seeking out knowledge sources. Knowledge creators recognize the potential of information to be reused in novel ways and are able to create new or improved products and services by working individually or in groups with other knowledge creators. Gatekeepers are knowledge workers who play an important role in the organization, for they constantly span the external environment for sources of new information. Organizations that realize the importance of having individuals who function as gatekeepers and individuals who can absorb this information and see new possibilities will actively seek these characteristics in those they employ. They will provide intellectual sustenance needed to allow this potential to develop more fully among their employees (Davenport & Prusak, 1998). They will foster an environment that

Copyright © 2004, Idea Group Inc. Copying or distributing in print or electronic forms without written permission of Idea Group Inc. is prohibited.

facilitates relationship formation and collaboration. Siemens's "Xenia," *City of Knowledge,* is an example of a vehicle for people to meet and exchange ideas and solutions.

Technology & Communication

> *"The mere presence of technology won't create a learning organization, a meritocracy, or a knowledge creating company."* (Davenport & Prusak, 1998, p. 142)

One of the biggest misconceptions about managing knowledge is the belief that technology plays a salient role in the success of any knowledge management initiative. Getting the right information to the right people at the right time is important, and technology is a key enabler in disseminating information throughout the organization. However, technology is limited in its ability to facilitate teammaking, elicit tacit knowledge or build trust (Belardo & Belardo, 2002; Davenport & Prusak, 1998). As knowledge creation has more to do with "relationships and community-building than databases...." "Investments in information technology alone cannot make the knowledge-creating company happen" (Von Krogh et al., 2000). Technology should be used to design systems to support collaboration and communication, and to facilitate the flow of information throughout the organization. There are knowledge management tools and technologies that support the identification of new knowledge opportunities, such as sophisticated GroupWare, Web retrieval software and recommender systems (Resnick & Varian, 1997; Stenmark, 2001). However, unless the information system is user-friendly and is perceived as beneficial, there will be little incentive to use it (Davis, 1989). The *right* technology can increase business performance by bringing about reduced work-coordination costs, streamlined work processes, and increased interorganizational relationships (Sambamurthy et al., 2003).

Communication should be multi-dimensional, that is, formal, informal, social, oral and written, and it must initiate at all levels within the organization. The ability to express and share ideas must be encouraged and fostered. When people trust that what they say will not result in negative criticism or retribution, they will feel free to communicate their ideas (DeLong & Fahey, 2000). When communication is encouraged and varied opportunities to foster dialogue are

Copyright © 2004, Idea Group Inc. Copying or distributing in print or electronic forms without written permission of Idea Group Inc. is prohibited.

facilitated by the organization, people learn to understand each other and develop the relationships that are so important to the sharing of tacit knowledge (Belardo & Belardo, 2002; Davenport & Prusak, 1998; Von Krogh et al., 2000).

Characteristics of Organizations with High Intellectual Bandwidth

Organizations with high intellectual bandwidth for knowledge creation are regularly in the forefront of innovation and share certain characteristics in the areas of leadership, culture, and technology and communication. Organizations seeking to innovate need to identify opportunities for improvement and they should determine how many of the following characteristics, which are found in innovative organizations, are present in their organization.

Leadership

- Creates a clear, concise positive vision that is articulated throughout the organization.
- Fosters the view of the organization as a knowledge-based organization.
- Identifies knowledge gaps and develops processes to close these gaps.
- Champions innovation and strategically aligns knowledge management activities with organizational performance and goals.
- Creates the right context to foster dialogue and communication across job functions.
- Recognizes and advocates environmental boundary spanning.
- Develops and champions a reward system that recognizes and rewards information sharing and discourages information hoarding.

Culture

- An atmosphere of trust permeates the organization.
- Ethical behavior is the norm and expected at all costs.

Copyright © 2004, Idea Group Inc. Copying or distributing in print or electronic forms without written permission of Idea Group Inc. is prohibited.

- Experimentation and risk-taking are encouraged and openly supported.
- Mistakes are considered opportunities for learning and improvement, are openly discussed and solutions are shared.
- Diversity is fostered, including diversity in learning styles, and is exemplified in core competency training.
- Customer input at all stages is encouraged and solicited.
- Periodic assessments are done within the organization to assess its capability to foster innovation and knowledge creation.

Knowledge Creators

- White spaces – competence based opportunities are explored (Hamel & Prahalad, 1994).
- Creativity, experimentation, flexibility, and curiosity are qualities desired in knowledge creators.
- Employees possess the necessary technical skills, experience and expertise.
- Opportunities for socialization, collaboration and team-building are ubiquitous.

Technology & Communication

- Opportunities for individual dialogue across the organization are identified and facilitated using technology.
- The physical environment and technical resources encourage information sharing, collaboration and virtual communities.
- Information flows are multi-directional.
- Technology is user friendly, flexible and open.
- Recognition of diversity is supported in language translation tools and communication methods.

Copyright © 2004, Idea Group Inc. Copying or distributing in print or electronic forms without written permission of Idea Group Inc. is prohibited.

Implications for the Future

The technological playing field will become more level as technologies become cheaper to purchase, so organizations will have to invest their resources in the development of new core competencies. E-commerce will continue to support organizational restructuring of core competencies, the creation of new ones and boundary expansion. The development of a strong knowledge strategy as a key component of corporate strategy will become fundamental to the process of knowledge creation and competitive advantage (Zack, 2003). Organizations will need to identify the specific knowledge strategies that will contribute to their organizational goals. Continual innovation will be the motto for those organizations desiring to remain competitive; those who do not or who cannot marshal their internal resources effectively to enhance their performance will not survive.

Conclusion

Knowledge creation doe not occur by chance; it must be carefully orchestrated. Organizations wishing to improve their knowledge creating ability must value the factors that support innovation and place less reliance on technology to resolve problems or create opportunities. Organizations must develop the characteristics necessary to become a learning organization and remain in a perpetual state of learning: from the external forces that influence its operations and from the internal forces, which shape who listens to whom and what. Organizations need to develop the leadership characteristics, culture, and technology that will support an innovative organizational personality and employ individuals with the experience and expertise needed to enable the desired state to become a reality. Moreover, they must identify the constraints to organizational innovation and develop methods for overcoming them. Organizations must continually reassess their intellectual bandwidth for knowledge creation.

Copyright © 2004, Idea Group Inc. Copying or distributing in print or electronic forms without written permission of Idea Group Inc. is prohibited.

References

Alavi, M., & Leidner, D.E. (2001). Knowledge management and knowledge and knowledge management systems: Conceptual foundations and research issues. *MIS Quarterly, 25*(1), 107-136.

Baum, G.C., Ittner, D.L., Low, T.S., & Malone, M.S. (2000, April 3). Introducing the new value creation index. *Forbes ASAP*.

Belardo, S. (2001). *Learning organizations and knowledge management: A conventional and alternate view*. Lecture slides. Albany.

Belardo, S., & Belardo, A.W. (2002). *Innovation through learning*. Albany: Whitston Publishing Company, Inc.

Bhatt, G.D. (2000). Information dynamics, learning and knowledge creation in organizations. *The Learning Organization, 7*(2), 89-90.

Brown, J.S., & Duguid, P. (2001). Knowledge and organization: A social-practice perspective. *Organization Science, 12*(2), 198-227.

Cohen, W.M., & Levinthal, D.A. (1990). Absorptive capacity: A new perspective on learning and innovation. *Administrative Science Quarterly, 35*, 128-152.

Davenport, T.H., & Prusak, L. (1998). *Working knowledge*. Boston: Harvard Business School Press.

Davis, F.D. (1989). Perceived usefulness, perceived ease of use, and user acceptance of information technology. *MIS Quarterly, 13*(3).

DeLong, D., & Fahey, L. (2000). Diagnosing cultural barriers to knowledge management. *The Academy of Management Executive, 14*(4), 113-127.

Drucker, P.F. (1988). The coming of the new organization. *Harvard Business Review, 66*(45), 49. Boston: Harvard Business School Press.

Drucker, P.F. (1994). The age of social transformation. *Atlantic Monthly, 274*(5), 53-80.

Grover, V., & Davenport, T.H. (2001). General perspectives on knowledge management: Fostering a research agenda. *Journal of Management Information Systems, 18*(1), 5-21.

Hamel, G., & Prahalad, C.K. (1994). Competing for the future. *Harvard Business Review, 72*(5), 64.

Copyright © 2004, Idea Group Inc. Copying or distributing in print or electronic forms without written permission of Idea Group Inc. is prohibited.

Huber, G. (1991). Organizational learning: The contributing processes in literature. *Organization Science, 2*, 88-115.

Kogut, B., & Zander, U. (1992). Knowledge of the firm, combinative capabilities, and the replication of technology. *Organization Science, 3*(3), 383-397.

Krasner, J. (2001, October 13). Tech icon Polaroid files for bankruptcy company slashes workers, benefits. *The Boston Globe,* A4.

Nestor-Baker, N.S., & Hoy, W.K. (2001). Tacit knowledge of school superintendents: Its nature, meaning and content. *Educational Administration Quarterly, 37*(1), 86-129.

Nevis, E.C., DiBella, A.J., & Gould, J.M. (1995). Understanding organizations as learning systems. *Sloan Management Review,* 73-85.

Nonaka, I., & Takeuchi, H. (1995). *The knowledge-creating company: How Japanese companies create the dynamics of innovation.* New York: Oxford University Press.

Nunamaker J.F., Briggs, R.O., & de Vreede, G.R. (2001). Value creation technology. In G.W. & G.D. Dickson (Eds.), *Information technology and the future enterprise: New models for managers* (pp. 102-124). New York: Prentice-Hall.

Polyani, M. (1998). The tacit dimension. In L. Prusak (Ed.), *Knowledge in organizations* (pp. 135-146). Boston: Butterworth-Heineman.

Porter, M. (1998). *Competitive advantage: Creating and sustaining superior performance.* The Free Press.

Resnick, P., & Varian, H.R. (1997). Recommender systems. *Communications of the ACM, 40*(3), 56-58.

Sambamurthy, V., Bharadwaj, A., & Grover, V. (2003). Shaping agility through digital options: Reconceptualizing the role of information technology in contemporary firms. *MIS Quarterly, 27*(2), 237-263.

Schein, E.H. (1999). *The corporate culture survival guide: Sense and nonsense about culture change.* San Francisco: Jossey-Bass.

Stenmark, D. (2001). Leveraging tacit knowledge. *Journal of Management Information Systems, 17*(3), 9-24.

Unknown. *Forbes Magazine.*

Von Krogh, G., Ichijo, K., & Nonaka, I. (2000). *Enabling knowledge creation.* New York: Oxford University Press.

Copyright © 2004, Idea Group Inc. Copying or distributing in print or electronic forms without written permission of Idea Group Inc. is prohibited.

Zack, M.H. (1999). Developing a knowledge strategy. *California Management Review, 41*(3), 125-145.

Zack, M.H. (2003). Rethinking the knowledge-based organization. *Sloan Management Review, 44*(4), 67-72.

Copyright © 2004, Idea Group Inc. Copying or distributing in print or electronic forms without written permission of Idea Group Inc. is prohibited.

Chapter XIV

Promoting Organizational Knowledge Sharing

Jack S. Cook
Rochester Institute of Technology, USA

Laura Cook
State University of New York at Geneseo, USA

Abstract

This chapter examines knowledge sharing and management within an organization. More importantly, it addresses what organizations can do to promote knowledge sharing in order to gain a competitive edge. Included are the results of a survey that explores employees' willingness to share knowledge. Today, more than ever, organizations must efficiently manage their knowledge assets in order to remain competitive. Some knowledge management (KM) initiatives have failed, while others have succeeded. A key factor associated with successfully managing knowledge is creating an environment that encourages individuals to share their knowledge.

Copyright © 2004, Idea Group Inc. Copying or distributing in print or electronic forms without written permission of Idea Group Inc. is prohibited.

Introduction

Knowledge management (KM) is critical to organizations today. Completely and effectively documenting knowledge lessens the chance that an organization will fail. Successful KM turns real-life work experiences, hidden practices, facts and know-how into an organizational resource. Peter Drucker first pointed out that the "U.S. had shifted from an economy of manufactured goods to a 'knowledge economy'" (Stewart et al., 2001, p. 41). He stated that, "knowledge is the most important resource – more important than labor, capital and land – and, indeed, the only meaningful resource today" (Gore & Gore, 1999, p. S555). James Quinn explains that "knowledge is the new power base of the modern corporation and that the value of most products and services depends primarily on how 'knowledge-based intangibles' – such as technological know-how, product design, marketing presentation, understanding of the customer, personal creativity and innovation – can be developed" (Gore & Gore, 1999, p. S555). If knowledge-based intangibles represent the greatest share of the value of most products and services, what are companies doing to promote sharing of knowledge? Realizing the growing importance of managing knowledge, progressive corporations proactively learn how to better capture knowledge. By identifying what knowledge is vital to securing and sustaining a competitive advantage, organizations can make the first step towards KM success.

This chapter explores how to take an organizational approach to knowledge sharing. Strategies to gain a competitive advantage through effective KM are given. A survey was administered to gauge employees' willingness to share knowledge and those results are discussed. In addition, strategies that promote knowledge sharing are given.

Solutions through Behavior versus Technology

Technology no longer provides a competitive advantage, since everyone has it and uses it. However, knowledge can continually bring an advantage if the knowledge base and knowledge activities are continuously maintained and enhanced (Awad & Ghaziri, 2004). Most knowledge management initiatives fall short of their goals (Desouza, 2003), largely due to taking a technologist perspective rather than a humanistic or balanced perspective (Desouza, 2003). Understanding how people are innately motivated to apply their personal

Copyright © 2004, Idea Group Inc. Copying or distributing in print or electronic forms without written permission of Idea Group Inc. is prohibited.

expertise is the key to avoiding the trap of building technology marvels no one uses (Tiwana, 2003). Technology alone, despite its power, flexibility and ability to transcend geographical and temporal barriers, rarely suffices to motivate employees to share knowledge. "Technology is merely one medium for knowledge transfer; it is not synonymous with knowledge transfer, and certainly not with knowledge acquisition. Acquisition is a loose but complex process that depends on messy human-related factors like motivation, commitment, hopes and rewards. Any attempt at knowledge transfer and acquisition that fails to account for human characteristics cannot succeed," states Hamilton Beazley, chairman of Strategic Leadership Group (Carey, 2003, p. 36). Employees must be given the time, space and opportunity to share knowledge.

In an ideal world, employees would document their knowledge. Any knowledge solution involves people, processes, and technology (Baker, Barker, Thorne & Dutnell, 1997). Too often, technology is the focus. However, experts estimate "three-quarters of all knowledge crucial to a company's efforts is transmitted verbally; virtually none of this knowledge has been captured for use" (Angus, 2003, p. 34). "Notwithstanding these opportunities, human behavior, not technology, represents the most daunting caveat. Unlike information sharing, knowledge sharing has a competitive dimension: The more valuable a nugget of knowledge is to an individual, the less likely he or she is to share it" (Tiwana, 2003, pp. 79-80).

Knowledge Evolution

One controversial issue surrounding the field is what constitutes knowledge. To clarify what constitutes knowledge, it is helpful to first distinguish between data, information, knowledge and wisdom. Words and numbers taken out of context represent data. Once context is added, data becomes information. Information applied by people based on their experience and judgment creates knowledge. For example, the number 15855551212 is data. When placed in a context, such as a phone number, it now has more meaning and can be construed as information. When a person recognizes that the number is how to call information in Rochester, NY, it becomes knowledge. "Wisdom is the highest level of abstraction, with vision, foresight, and the ability to see beyond the horizon. It is the summation of one's career experience in a specialized area of work" (Awad & Ghaziri, 2004, p. 40). Kirrane (1999, p. 34) defines wisdom as "understanding how to use knowledge to make sound judgments and decisions". Figure 1 demonstrates this evolution from data towards wisdom.

Copyright © 2004, Idea Group Inc. Copying or distributing in print or electronic forms without written permission of Idea Group Inc. is prohibited.

Figure 1. Knowledge evolution.

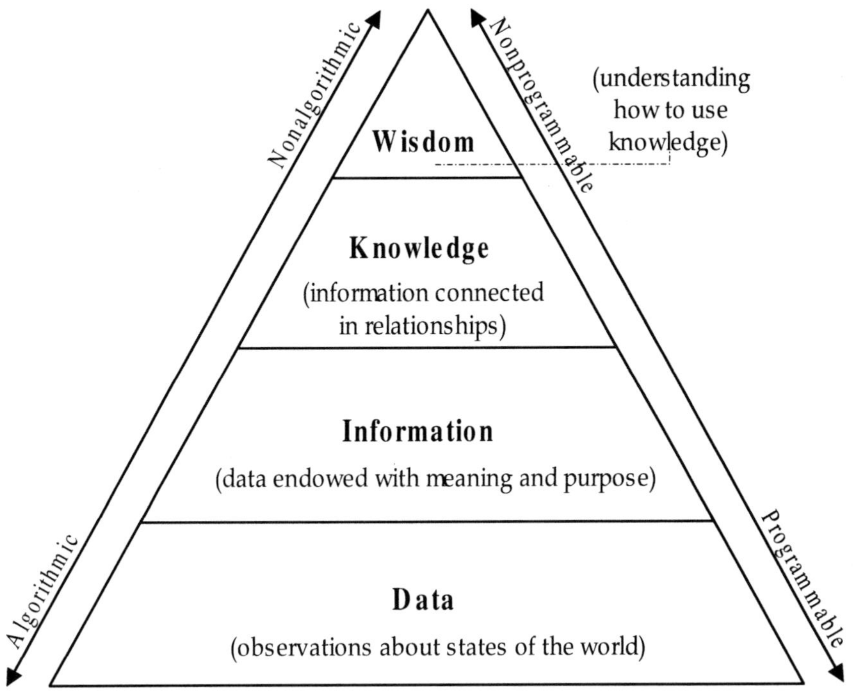

Source: Adapted from Awad and Ghaziri, 2004, p. 41. and Kirrane, 1999, p. 34.

A further distinguishing feature between data, information and knowledge is the method of transfer. Data and information can be transferred through information technologies, but knowledge requires human involvement in addition to information technology both in the development of new knowledge and modifying existing knowledge (Grover & Davenport, 2001). As shown in Figure 1, as one moves closer to wisdom, the information becomes nonprogrammable and nonalgorithmic; hence the use of technology is reduced or eliminated.

Distinguishing knowledge from data and information allows it to be studied as a separate entity. Alavi and Leidner (2001) define knowledge from five perspectives: (1) a state of mind – knowledge from experience, (2) an object – something to be stored and utilized, (3) a process – knowing resulting in action, (4) a condition to access information – ease of access to retrieve information, and (5) a capability – ability to influence upcoming action. Which perspective is taken changes with how one views knowledge.

Copyright © 2004, Idea Group Inc. Copying or distributing in print or electronic forms without written permission of Idea Group Inc. is prohibited.

How is Corporate Knowledge Lost?

The loss of employees' knowledge is attributable to any number of factors. Employees are transferred or fired, often unwillingly, or they may simply retire, become ill or die. Although such events are not pleasant to discuss, not planning for the inevitable does not make such events less likely to occur. On average, 275,000 jobs were cut per month last year in the U.S. (Carey, 2003, p. 31). With respect to retirement, the Bureau of Labor Statistics estimates 19% of those holding executive, administrative, and managerial positions will retire within the next five years in the U.S. (Carey, 2003, p. 32). The public sector is even worse off. By 2005, more than half of the 1.8 million U.S. federal government employees will be eligible for retirement, including 71% of those within the senior ranks (Carey, 2003, p. 32). Delphi group estimates that 70% of organizational knowledge resides in the minds of employees, while 30% is in externalized forms (Carey, 2003, p. 33). The knowledge and experience that reside in these individuals must be captured; otherwise, the loss will decrease productivity and possibly cripple the economy. In addition, companies must recognize and minimize ghost work. Ghost work refers to assigning the responsibilities of those who left to those who remain. It is "very demoralizing because people are expected to do more – without a pay raise or the knowledge to handle the additional tasks," says Hamilton Beazley, chairman of Strategic Leadership Group, an Arlington, VA-based consulting firm (Carey, 2003, p. 31). Employees need to document two types of knowledge – explicit and tacit, as discussed next.

Tacit and Explicit Knowledge

Explicit and implicit (i.e., tacit) knowledge must interact with each other for efficient knowledge creation and exchange. Explicit knowledge can be easily shared among people once codified or stored in a central location, making it accessible to most anyone. It is structured and contained within such items as policies, procedures, patents, trademarks, research and trade skills. Hence, it is found in processes or routines that follow some predetermined set of logical guidelines.

Tacit knowledge is embedded in an individual's thinking, making it difficult to capture and equally challenging to transform into useful information. It is an

Copyright © 2004, Idea Group Inc. Copying or distributing in print or electronic forms without written permission of Idea Group Inc. is prohibited.

outcome of individual and group social activity (Alavi & Leidner, 2001). Another way to look at it is that it is an individual's know-how and the context added through experience and interaction. For example, the knowledge of how to best approach a particular customer (using flattery, a hard sell, or a no-nonsense approach) represents tacit knowledge (Alavi & Leidner, 2001, p. 109). It can be further broken down into technical (personal skills) and cognitive (beliefs, values, and ideals) (Nonaka & Konno, 1998). It also includes creativity, insight and innovation.

Some examples of explicit and implicit knowledge are provided in Table 1. In order to encourage documentation of both types of knowledge, the mechanisms that motivate employees to document knowledge will be explored later in this chapter. Converting tacit knowledge into explicit knowledge within an organizational context is difficult at best. The next section provides insight into the organizational knowledge transfer process.

Knowledge acquisition based on experience takes time. Tacit knowledge underpins classic expert behavior – the uncharted, unpredictable combination of skill, information, expertise, experience, and judgment that work together in a seemingly ad hoc way in the minds and actions of an expert surgeon, lawyer, executive, architect, designer, navigator, writer, consultant, or programmer (May & Taylor, 2003, p. 97). Hence, context-specific tacit knowledge tends to be unique and difficult to imitate. It is not easily purchased. Tacit knowledge can be transformed into explicit knowledge by documenting it through patterns. A pattern can express tacit knowledge, "in written language, where it may be described at various levels of granularity and generality, depending on how well the pattern author can express the pattern's context, problem, forces, and solution" (May & Taylor, 2003, p. 97). Stories, metaphors, and analogies are other methods for documenting knowledge. Stories help disseminate experi-

Table 1. Examples of implicit versus explicit knowledge.

Implicit Knowledge	**Explicit Knowledge**
o Personal skills	o Trade skills
o Beliefs	o Policies
o Values	o Procedures
o Ideals	o Patents
o Creativity	o Trademarks
o Insight	o Research
o Innovation	

Copyright © 2004, Idea Group Inc. Copying or distributing in print or electronic forms without written permission of Idea Group Inc. is prohibited.

ences and lessons learned, metaphors combine ideas into expressive imagery, and analogies help form new ideas by comparing them with familiar ones (May & Taylor, 2003).

Knowledge Conversion in the Workplace

Table 2 summarizes the processes by which knowledge is transformed between its tacit and explicit forms (Marwick, 2001). None of these processes occur in isolation, but naturally occur in a working environment. Tacit to tacit knowledge produces socialization where individuals discuss and collaborate. Tacit knowledge converges to explicit knowledge through answering questions, explaining models, and other similar forms of team communication. Explicit knowledge to tacit knowledge produces internalization where a person creates his or her own tacit knowledge through learning from documents and others and synthesizing this material into his or her own knowledge. Finally, conversion from explicit to explicit knowledge happens through e-mails, reports, databases, and other types of information sharing.

Currently, organizational projects designed to capture knowledge often focus primarily on explicit information. A problem arises when knowledge is viewed

Table 2. Conversion of knowledge.

From Tacit to Tacit produces: **Socialization** Examples: team meetings and discussions, collaboration	From Tacit to Explicit produces: **Externalization** Examples: dialog with team, answer questions, models, metaphors, stories
From Explicit to Tacit produces: **Internalization** Examples: learn from a report, read from many sources and create new knowledge from combining existing tacit knowledge with knowledge gained from others	From Explicit to Explicit produces: **Combination** Examples: share a report or document, training, shared database of information

Source: Adapted from Marwick, A.D. (2001). Knowledge management technology. IBM Systems Journal, 40(4), 815.

Copyright © 2004, Idea Group Inc. Copying or distributing in print or electronic forms without written permission of Idea Group Inc. is prohibited.

as an object that resides outside of individuals. Organizations frequently minimize the significance of the fact that knowledge is useless without a "knower," the individual who, through thought and incorporation of new stimuli, shapes knowledge (Fahey & Prusak, 1998). Projects that neglect the "knower" while focusing on new and complex technological solutions are destined to fail. So how can companies address this problem? The answer lies in knowledge management.

Knowledge Management

Knowledge is vital to creating and sustaining a competitive advantage. Knowledge management (KM) is the process of adding value to the know-how and experience within and, in many cases, between organizations (Ruggles, 1998). It is concerned with the creation, capture, integration, and utilization of knowledge within the context of an organizational setting (Schulz, 2001). KM will not "fix" a poorly run business. Major KM activities include (1) creating knowledge, (2) discovering knowledge, (3) borrowing or buying knowledge, (4) capturing knowledge, (5) distributing knowledge, (6) adding value to knowledge, information, or data, (7) retrieving knowledge, information, or data, and (8) measuring and updating knowledge (Kirrane, 1999).

KM looks different to different companies. In health care, KM may be concerned with patient care (e.g., treatments, cure rates, length of hospital stays). In retail, KM may focus on customers (e.g., customer relationship management, sales trends, and quick response programs). In higher education, KM may concentrate on student graduation rates as a proxy to success (e.g., admission patterns, enrollment and retention enhancement, and assistance to students with disabilities). Since knowledge in each company is different, there is a tendency to focus on the common aspects of these KM projects, namely the technology. However, KM is more than project management and collaboration tools, Web publishing, Internet-based technologies (e.g., intranets, extranets, and portals), decision and predictive modeling, and instant messaging. Gupta and Govindarajan (2000) suggest building a social ecology. "Social ecology refers to the social system in which people operate. It drives an organization's formal and informal expectations of individuals, defines the types of people who will fit into the organization, shapes individuals' freedom to pursue actions without prior approval, and affects how people interact with

Copyright © 2004, Idea Group Inc. Copying or distributing in print or electronic forms without written permission of Idea Group Inc. is prohibited.

others both inside and outside of the organization" (Gupta & Govindarajan, 2000, p. 72). Gupta and Govindarajan (2000) state that social ecology is determined by organizational culture, structure, information systems, reward systems, processes, people, and leadership.

The main challenge of KM and KMS implementation is organizational acceptance. The truth is that KMSs are seldom enthusiastically received. Pillsbury Perkins attributes this phenomenon to the "Field of Dreams" syndrome – "Don't assume that if you build it, they will come" (Charles, 2001, p. 24). Typically, the technical aspects of KM account for only 20% of the problems encountered (Ruppel & Harrington, 2001). In order to gain a competitive advantage, companies must spend less time on technical implementation and more on the human, social and cultural issues that impede KM within the organization. "The emphasis on people is deliberate because technology itself cannot deliver benefits. Technology only enables people to work better, and it is new ways of working that deliver the benefits" (Murray, 2002, p. 74).

Gaining a Competitive Advantage Using Knowledge

As the new economy continues evolving, organizations must adapt by better managing their knowledge assets. The competitive game has changed. Companies now share a common set of explicit knowledge and technologies. For example, many large companies use systems from the same technology providers (e.g., Oracle or SAP). Hence, how a company leverages its knowledge sources to gain a competitive edge is very important since the technologies themselves are neither proprietary nor unique.

Competitive pressures in the market are fostering an environment in which companies review their knowledge assets, looking for ways they can create value for the firm. However, many existing projects are no more than undertakings that compile information, but do not provide any innovation (Gold, Malhotra & Segars, 2001). The key to gaining a competitive advantage is best stated by Gold, Malhotra and Segars: "Contributions [of knowledge management] include improved ability to innovate, improved coordination of efforts, ...responsiveness to market change, and reduced redundancy of information/knowledge" (Gold, Malhotra & Segars, 2001).

Copyright © 2004, Idea Group Inc. Copying or distributing in print or electronic forms without written permission of Idea Group Inc. is prohibited.

Competing based on knowledge management requires a company to analyze not only its data, but its culture and structure as well. Management must create an organizational infrastructure that will leverage existing knowledge in the marketplace, while developing new knowledge to sustain their position (Gold, Malhotra & Segars, 2001). This ability to compete using knowledge stems from the growth in IT and resources such as the Internet, as well as from the desire to gain value from organizational information (Grover & Davenport, 2001).

Organizations must determine what type of knowledge is best suited for their needs. Firms can derive significant benefits from proactively managing their knowledge. This requires aligning a firm's resources and capabilities with its knowledge strategy (Zack, 1999). The knowledge strategy will be largely dependent upon the type of business. Knowledge is now such a key source of competitive advantage, influencing the ways that businesses are run, that business can no longer afford to ignore it (Schaefer, Cook & Barrett, 2002).

Willingness to Share Knowledge

Cook, Hunt, McCullor and Szymanski (2003) surveyed 75 business professionals to gauge why employees are unwilling to share knowledge and to determine what would entice or encourage them to share knowledge with others. The survey instrument contained questions concerning the degree to which respondents currently share knowledge, their willingness to share knowledge, management enforcement of knowledge sharing and the effect of incentives, recognition and rewards on knowledge sharing.

Of those surveyed, most people were "very willing" to share knowledge within their organization (73%), while 23% were "somewhat willing" to share knowledge. Only one person was neutral and two people were "somewhat unwilling". While the survey did not explore what knowledge is shared, 71% indicated they share knowledge often, while 28% shared knowledge only occasionally. Only one person reported rarely sharing knowledge within his/her organization.

Employees share information with others in their organization for many reasons. Sixty percent of those surveyed reported a high level of importance that management share knowledge with others. Some people feel obligated to share knowledge, while others feel it is necessary to complete their job to the best of

Copyright © 2004, Idea Group Inc. Copying or distributing in print or electronic forms without written permission of Idea Group Inc. is prohibited.

their ability. More than half of those surveyed responded that they are not evaluated based on willingness to share knowledge. For the most part, people willingly share knowledge on their own, without formal recognition. The majority (75%) said knowledge sharing does not negatively impact performance evaluations, but many workers feel obligated to share knowledge due to perceived importance by management. Eighty-nine percent felt it necessary to share knowledge with co-workers. Not one person felt sharing knowledge was unnecessary. What must be explored is why, even though the majority of professionals surveyed felt that sharing knowledge with other co-workers is important, some people are hesitant to share knowledge.

Reluctance to Share Knowledge

Employees are reluctant to share knowledge for many reasons. "What's in it for me?" and the "knowledge is power" syndrome drives some employee behavior. Viewing knowledge as a source of power encourages hording it, which negatively affects an organization. It provides those employees that possess certain types of knowledge an advantage over employees who cannot create it or do not have the opportunity to rediscover it. If a person has knowledge that others do not, he or she may feel more important and be more important than others who do not possess that knowledge. By being one of the few people that have knowledge of something important to others, one may be reluctant to share this information. The organization's responsibility is to encourage employees to share knowledge despite employees' natural reluctance to not share their knowledge. Jan Duffy defines knowledge management as an anti-hording set of principles: "KM describes a set of business practices and technologies used to assist an organization to obtain maximum advantage from one of its most important assets – knowledge" (Duffy, 2000, p. 62).

Employees also will be reluctant to share knowledge if it impacts their job security. If a person has knowledge essential to performing daily tasks and routines and he or she alone possesses that knowledge, he or she may be unwilling to share their knowledge. They may rightly believe that once others capture the knowledge they possess, they are not as valuable anymore and can easily be replaced. When sharing knowledge threatens a person's job, understandably, he or she will resist. Additionally, employees may be unwilling to share knowledge if there is little incentive to do so. Approximately half of those surveyed would be increasingly willing to share knowledge if employers offered

Copyright © 2004, Idea Group Inc. Copying or distributing in print or electronic forms without written permission of Idea Group Inc. is prohibited.

incentives for sharing. This compensation could range from simple recognition to financial incentives or compensation time. When asked if they are currently compensated in any way for sharing knowledge, 92% of the respondents replied they were not. Since most people are not already recognized or rewarded, they may feel that some type of incentive would be nice for the knowledge they already share with others.

Unwillingness to share knowledge can be explained because many corporate cultures and their corresponding value systems do not encourage it. However, job positions, level of responsibility, and general personality types also play a role. A majority of those surveyed said that management does not encourage knowledge sharing in any meaningful way. While the majority felt management thinks it is very important to share knowledge, they do not have any means of making it mandatory within an organization and it is often difficult to quantify and reward knowledge sharing. Management may wish to consider using a rubric or scale to evaluate knowledge shared as part of a person's job performance evaluation. A final reason why people may be unwilling to share knowledge with others is the value system they subscribe to, which may not encourage such behavior.

Motivating Knowledge Sharing

Everyone has a value system; some are intrinsic while others are extrinsic. Individuals with intrinsic value systems tend to naturally share knowledge and help others simply for the sake of helping them. They do it openly and willingly. They do not need rewards, incentives, recognition, encouragement, or persuasion. If they believe their knowledge will benefit others and help the greater good, they will not hesitate to share. They get pride and satisfaction out of knowing that the knowledge they share will help others complete their job more efficiently and effectively. They do not need any type of encouragement or persuasion in order to share what they have. Extrinsic people, however, are not as willing to share information with others without some type of incentive. These types of people are motivated by awards and recognition and are not as open to sharing knowledge freely. If they have something that is of value to others, they will give it to them but they expect something in return for it. As long as they are given something of value in return for the knowledge they share, they are happy. Otherwise, they are not very willing to share knowledge just for the sake of sharing it or for the personal satisfaction of helping others.

Copyright © 2004, Idea Group Inc. Copying or distributing in print or electronic forms without written permission of Idea Group Inc. is prohibited.

Figure 2. Motivation for sharing knowledge with others.

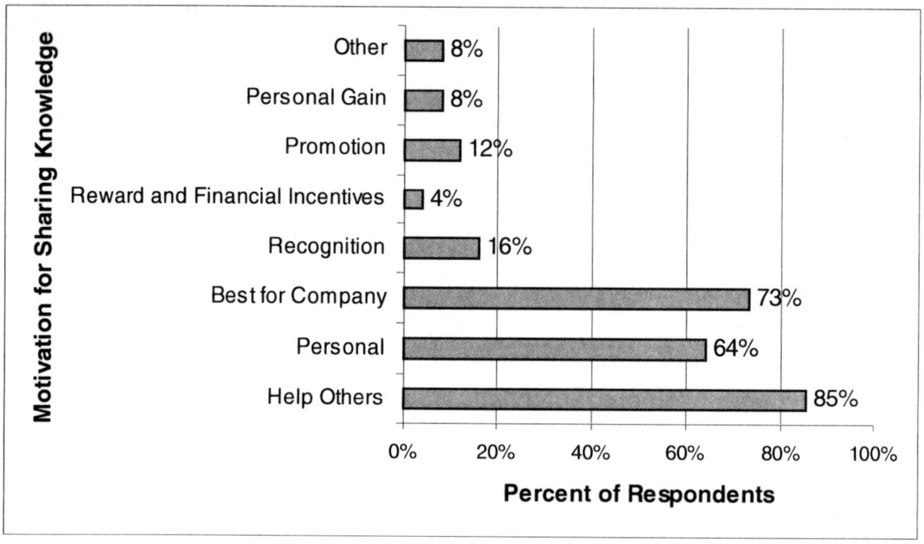

Beyond the intrinsic belief in sharing knowledge and the encouragement by incentive, a few other reasons explain why people share knowledge. When asked what motivates them to share knowledge, the majority of the responses were to help others in the organization, for personal satisfaction, and because it is best for the company (see Figure 2). Since those who actively share knowledge think that it is best for the company, those who do not share knowledge may begin if the company recognizes the importance of knowledge sharing to the organization and thereby rewards those who share. While very few people surveyed said their motivation primarily stems from recognition, rewards or promotions, this type of incentive system should not be discounted (Cook, Hunt, McCullor & Szymanski, 2003, p. 80).

Knowledge Stewards, Consumers, and Lurkers

Communities of Practice (CoPs) consist of three generic categories of participants shown in Figure 3 – knowledge stewards, consumers and lurkers (Brazelton & Gorry, 2003). Stewards possess an active curiosity and genuine desire to share ideas with others and do so by creating, organizing and distributing knowledge to their CoP (Brazelton & Gorry, 2003). Consumers are the second largest group. During the process of consuming (i.e., applying)

Copyright © 2004, Idea Group Inc. Copying or distributing in print or electronic forms without written permission of Idea Group Inc. is prohibited.

Figure 3. Knowledge stewards, consumers and lurkers and their role in sharing knowledge.

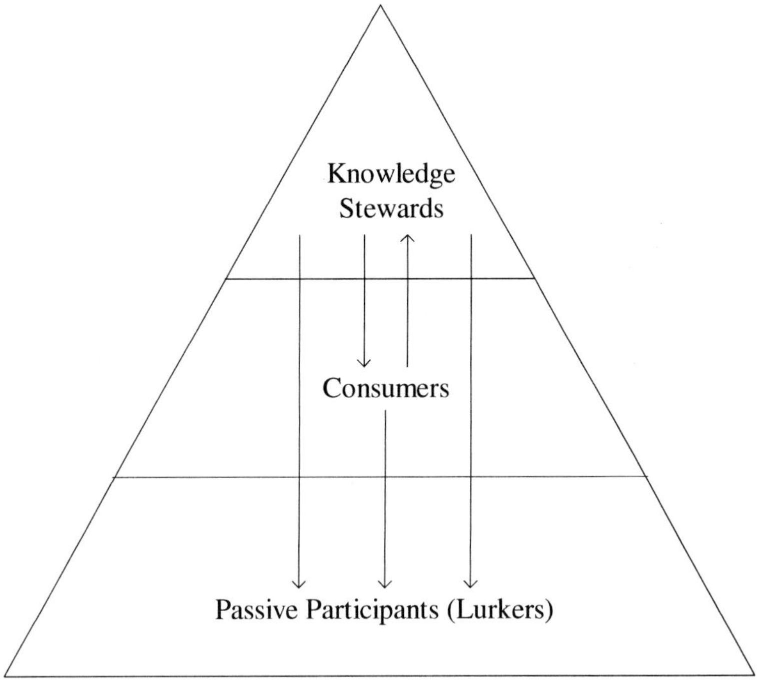

knowledge, individuals within this group may experience valuable insight useful in generating additional knowledge. Lurkers, the largest group in the CoP, do not contribute knowledge but must glean some value from the community since system logs verify they regularly log in (Brazelton & Gorry, 2003). Managers must ensure that stewards are properly and adequately rewarded since they are vital to successful knowledge documentation and use.

Promoting Knowledge Sharing

"For knowledge management efforts to bear fruit, they must contain large doses of attention to organizational culture, performance measurements and rewards, decision making processes, human resource policies, and communication styles" (Lubit, 2001, p. 173). There are many ways for organizations to

Copyright © 2004, Idea Group Inc. Copying or distributing in print or electronic forms without written permission of Idea Group Inc. is prohibited.

promote knowledge sharing. Three main sources of encouragement include team-based rewards and recognition, the physical layout, and technology support.

Team-Based Rewards and Recognition

Team-based rewards must be consistent with team dynamics in order for rewards to properly motivate. Consistent rewards provide proper recognition for high performance teams. Organizations that have team-based rewards along with merit systems based upon an individual's team contribution will be more productive and motivated. The transition from individual work and rewards to a team-based work environment can be complex and difficult to manage.

Employees must feel valuable before they will be comfortable sharing their knowledge. An employee who fears being laid off or replaced is unlikely to share his or her valuable knowledge. Reward systems are necessary, particularly in organizations with an individualistic culture. These reward and incentive programs are intended to compensate employees for the power they lose by sharing knowledge.

Rewards must be timely. If a team performs commendably, increasing profitability or efficiency, recognize the team immediately to encourage repeat behavior. At Xerox, recognition is a driving factor among photocopier maintenance engineers who perform "fix-its, work-arounds, patches, and so on" (Earl, 2001, p. 219). Xerox handles tricky repairs by having engineers submit a possible solution to a panel of peer assessors who evaluate the solution while taking into consideration the novelty, worthiness, and practicality of the proposed solution. If the solution is approved, it is added to the knowledge base of the company and the engineer is rewarded with the prestige of finding a solution to a unique problem that others may use in the future (Earl, 2001).

Physical Layout

Our environment directly influences the openness and ease with which employees communicate. Physical structures are often excellent representations of the company's beliefs and values. A company headquartered in a featureless rectangular building forty stories tall will promote a hierarchical style of communication and bureaucratic values. A flatter structure with rounded

Copyright © 2004, Idea Group Inc. Copying or distributing in print or electronic forms without written permission of Idea Group Inc. is prohibited.

curves and giant windows promotes a sense of openness and simplicity. Open space encourages more collaboration than space divided into cubicles. Free-flowing shapes incorporated into lounges and cafeterias are often useful in promoting an atmosphere where friendly interaction among employees is possible. Open dialogue can commence at a moment's notice instead of through a scheduled meeting where people are late or unable to attend due to scheduling difficulties. Dialogue sets the groundwork for new ideas, and consequently the possibility of knowledge (Gold, Malhotra & Segars, 2001, p. 189).

Technology

Keep in mind that not all knowledge shared is beneficial. The "garbage in, garbage out" syndrome is all too common when units are asked to upload best practices into a shared database (Gupta & Govindarajan, 2000). In addition, effective and efficient communication channels will vary with the different types of knowledge. For example, by now most people understand what type of knowledge transfer should occur over e-mail or instant messaging, and what types of knowledge are best communicated face-to-face.

An intranet is sometimes thought of as a "quick fix" that will automatically boost productivity. Unfortunately, this is not the case. Cultures that reward their members for innovative thinking and continual learning are supportive of intranets (Ruppel & Harrington, 2001). The culture of an organization must actively encourage KM and intranet use for it to be efficient (Ruppel & Harrington, 2001). A contribution-based work culture will utilize an intranet in a more efficient manner than a company that simply implements an intranet to solve problems quickly. However, it is quite difficult to put into practice a knowledge management culture if it does not already exist (Ruppel & Harrington, 2001). Hence, intranets are a valuable tool in the implementation of KMSs if employees are accustomed to openly sharing ideas (Cook, Hunt, McCullor & Szymanski, 2003).

Challenges of Knowledge Management

Investments in knowledge management are not always beneficial. John Seely Brown, director of Xerox Parc, notes that U.S. industry had realized little

Copyright © 2004, Idea Group Inc. Copying or distributing in print or electronic forms without written permission of Idea Group Inc. is prohibited.

improvement in the value obtained from its knowledge workers, despite an investment in technology exceeding $1 trillion (Malhotra, 2000). Some knowledge management challenges include: employee participation, constantly updating the KMS, and sorting useful from useless information (Santosus & Surmacz, 2001). In order for knowledge management to be successful, all employees must understand that they are an integral part of the life cycle.

Identifying and disseminating knowledge is not easy. Location to location transfer is only one issue. On average, it takes over two years from identification to installation of a best practice (O'Dell & Grayson, 1998). While these challenges may cause reluctance to implement, there are more persuasive reasons to transfer tacit knowledge. A further issue that can hinder success of knowledge management is when an organization's true purpose of their knowledge management activities is not focused. When questioning corporate executives, less than 15% felt that their company was addressing all the areas set by objectives within their current initiatives (Ruggles, 1998). The knowledge management endeavor is generally commenced to formulate solutions that will aid in future decision making, yet currently, most information is only used to understand the past and present and not to forecast the future (Fahey & Prusak, 1998). This may be due to the comfort level in reviewing past data, the tendency to not risk future projections and a lack of desire to analyze various future uses.

Knowledge continuously changes. As with physical assets, the value of knowledge erodes over time. "Like product development, marketing and R&D, knowledge management is a constantly evolving business practice" (Santosus & Surmacz, 2001, p. 3). The contents of a KMS must be regularly updated. If not, knowledge in overwhelming quantities creates information overload. Knowledge must be properly classified so that an employee is not overwhelmed. Just as the supply of knowledge is infinite, so is the supply of useless information. The Internet is one example of this tragedy. Although the Internet can be an excellent source of information, it can be difficult to find, in a simple search, exactly what one is looking for. The challenge is finding the needle in the knowledge haystack. Barriers created by functional silos and management levels also hinder knowledge management.

Creating a successful project hinges on management's perception of success. The challenge with knowledge management is that the success of a project may not be something that is easily measurable. A key concept of knowledge is as an intangible asset, which focuses on the difficulty of assigning a value to

Copyright © 2004, Idea Group Inc. Copying or distributing in print or electronic forms without written permission of Idea Group Inc. is prohibited.

knowledge (Grover & Davenport, 2001). The success of knowledge management initiatives may be measured, albeit not easily. The success of both identifying and implementing processes should be measured, but this measurement is still in the development stages. Measurement devices such as cycle time and efficiency benchmarks can be used as a starting point (O'Dell & Grayson, 1998).

While management frequently seeks to quantify project success, this is not the best approach to knowledge management. Organizations tend to focus too much attention on the metrics (# of databases, hits on the Web site, etc.), rather than the output and consequences of the knowledge management activities (Fahey & Prusak, 1998). These metric activities do not provide a feel of actual performance and again ignore the human factor. The use of metrics overlooks efficiencies, reduced stress, improved effectiveness and many other benefits achieved through knowledge management.

The biggest challenge is still the initial stages and implementation. Using benchmarking can create the momentum. Begin with a project that will have a

Table 3. Benefits and challenges of knowledge management.

Benefits of KM	Challenges of KM
• Fosters innovation • Improves efficiency • Improves coordination of efforts • Encourages free flow of ideas • Improves response time • Rewards employees • Improves market time • Responsive to market changes • Reduces costs • Enhances customer and employee satisfaction • Connects geographically dispersed people (e.g., customers, employees, suppliers, and consultants) • Fosters collaboration • Improves information access • Expertise location	• KM projects are not always successful in terms of increased profit margins and reduced costs • Requires full employee participation • Requires constant updating • Must sort useful knowledge from useless information

Copyright © 2004, Idea Group Inc. Copying or distributing in print or electronic forms without written permission of Idea Group Inc. is prohibited.

high pay-off in line with corporate goals to gain further support (O'Dell & Grayson, 1998). Companies must make sure that each activity has the resources available for implementation and does not let competition impede progress. A reward system that encourages open transfer of knowledge and the encouragement of those in leadership positions are key components, as well as technology to support network exchanges (O'Dell & Grayson, 1998). Management must show consistent support of the initiatives to maintain effectiveness. The key points of both the benefits and challenges of knowledge management are detailed in Table 3 (Schaefer, Cook & Barrett, 2002, p. 1117).

Conclusion

Knowledge enables organizations to develop and exploit resources, both tangible and intangible, even if those resources are not unique. Some companies begin KM initiatives by asking employees to document their knowledge. "What's obviously good for the enterprise, however, is not so obviously good for the individual, and therein lies the rub. Knowledge is power, and many people are (not surprisingly) reluctant to share that power. Somehow we've got to engineer environments in which sharing knowledge feels like an empowering behavior" (Udell, 2003, p. 34). Relying on employees to find the time and motivation to document is impractical. For one, many pieces of knowledge have such a small audience that there is little pressure to document, but that knowledge becomes critical once an employee is no longer with the company.

For an organization to fully utilize their employees' potential, employees must be encouraged to share knowledge. Management must promote and support the creation, sharing and use of knowledge among employees and discourage knowledge hoarding. Successful companies have employees who consistently collaborate, cooperate and communicate both formally and informally. As our pilot study showed, most individuals are willing to share their knowledge and just need to be encouraged to do so. The organization must take the initiative to change their environment to one that is conducive to sharing knowledge. This will create a more competitive and agile organization.

Copyright © 2004, Idea Group Inc. Copying or distributing in print or electronic forms without written permission of Idea Group Inc. is prohibited.

References

Alavi, M., & Leidner, D.E. (1999, February). Knowledge management systems: Issues, challenges and benefits. *Communications of the Association for Information Systems, 1*(7), 2-27.

Alavi, M., & Leidner, D.E. (2001, March). Knowledge management and knowledge management systems: Conceptual foundations and research issues. *MIS Quarterly, 25*(1), 107-136.

Angus, J. (2003, March 17). Knowledge managing. *InfoWorld, 25*(11), 1, 32-35.

Awad, E., & Ghaziri, H. (2004). *Knowledge management.* New Jersey: Prentice Hall.

Baker, M., Barker, M., Thorne, J., & Dutnell, M. (1997, September). Leveraging human capital. *The Journal of Knowledge Management, 1*(1), 63-74.

Carey, R. (2003, February). Fight the brain drain. *Successful Meetings, 52*(2), 31-36.

Charles, S. (2001, September). Lessons from the document management trenches. Global library and information services. Retrieved January 2003, from <http://www.hpl.hp.com/techreports/2001/HPL-2001-230.pdf

Cook, J., Hunt, C., McCullor, J., & Szymanski, A. (2003, May). An organizational approach to knowledge sharing. *Proceedings of the 2003 Information Resources Management Association International Conference*, 79-81.

Desouza, K. (2003, January). Barriers to effective use of knowledge management systems in software engineering. *Communications of the ACM, 46*(1), 99-101.

Desouza, K. (2003, June). Facilitating tacit knowledge exchange. *Communications of the ACM, 46*(6), 85-88.

Duffy, J. (2000, April). The KM technology infrastructure. *Information Management Journal, 34*(2), 62-66.

Earl, M. (2001, Summer). Knowledge management strategies: Toward a taxonomy. *Journal of Management Information Systems, 18*(1), 215-233.

Copyright © 2004, Idea Group Inc. Copying or distributing in print or electronic forms without written permission of Idea Group Inc. is prohibited.

Fahey, L., & Prusak, L. (1998, Spring). The eleven deadliest sins of knowledge management. *California Management Review, 40*(3), 265-276.

Gold, A., Malhotra, A., & Segars, A. (2001, Summer). Knowledge management: An organizational capabilities perspective. *Journal of Management Information Systems, 18*(1), 185-214.

Gore, C., & Gore, E. (1999, July). Knowledge management: The way forward. *Total Quality Management & Business Excellence, 10*(4/5), S554-S560.

Grover, V., & Davenport, T. (2001, Summer). General perspectives on knowledge management: Fostering a research agenda. *Journal of Management Information Systems, 18*(1), 5-22.

Gupta, A., & Govindarajan, V. (2000, Fall). Knowledge management's social dimension: Lessons from Nucor Steel. *Sloan Management Review*, 71-80.

Kirrane, D. (1999, August). Getting wise to knowledge management. *Association Management*, 31-39.

Lubit, R. (2001, Winter). Tacit knowledge and knowledge management: The keys to sustainable competitive advantage. *Organizational Dynamics, 29*(3), 164-178.

Malhotra, Y. (2000, Summer). Knowledge management for e-business performance: Advancing information strategy to 'Internet time'. *Information Strategy, 16*(4), 5-16.

Marwick, A.D. (2001). Knowledge management technology. *IBM Systems Journal, 40*(4), 814-830.

May, D., & Taylor, P. (2003, July). Knowledge management with patterns. *Communications of the ACM, 46*(7), 94-99.

Murray, P. (2002, March/April). Knowledge management as a sustained competitive advantage. *Ivey Business Journal, 66*(4), 71-76.

Nonaka, I., & Konno, N. (1998, Spring). The concept of "ba": Building a foundation for knowledge creation. *California Management Review, 40*(3), 40-54.

O'Dell, C., & Grayson, J. (1998, Spring). If we only knew what we know: Identification and transfer of internal best practices. *California Management Review, 40*(3), 154-174.

Ruggles, R. (1998, Spring). The state of the notion: Knowledge management in practice. *California Management Review, 40*(3), 80-89.

Copyright © 2004, Idea Group Inc. Copying or distributing in print or electronic forms without written permission of Idea Group Inc. is prohibited.

Ruppel, C., & Harrington, S. (2001, March). Sharing knowledge through Intranets: A study of organizational culture and intranet implementation. *IEEE Transactions on Professional Communication, 44*(1), 37-49.

Santosus, M., & Surmacz, J. (2001, May). The ABC's of knowledge management. *CIO Magazine,* 1-5.

Schaefer, M., Cook, S., & Barrett, J. (2002, November). Creating competitive advantage in large organizations using knowledge management. *Proceedings of the Decision Sciences Institute 2002 Annual Meeting*, San Diego, CA, 1113-1118.

Schulz, M. (2001, August). The uncertain relevance of newness: Organizational learning and knowledge flows. *Academy of Management Journal, 44*(4), 661-681.

Stewart, K., Baskerville, R., Storey, V., Senn, J., Raven, A., & Long, C. (2000, Fall). Confronting the assumptions underlying the management of knowledge: An agenda for understanding and investigating knowledge management. *The DATA BASE for Advances in Information Systems, 31*(4), 41-53.

Tiwana, A. (May 2003). Affinity to infinity in peer-to-peer knowledge platforms. *Communications of the ACM, 46*(5), 76-80.

Udell, J. (2003, March 17). Trends bode well for KM. *InfoWorld, 25*(11), 34-35.

Zack, M. (1999, Summer). Managing codified knowledge. *Sloan Management Review, 40*(4), 45-58.

Copyright © 2004, Idea Group Inc. Copying or distributing in print or electronic forms without written permission of Idea Group Inc. is prohibited.

Chapter XV

Value Creation through Customer Derived Revenue

Michael Hall
Nakamura Gakuen University, Japan

Abstract

This chapter presents a model that allows customer capital to be incorporated into a company's human capital in a way that is not now practiced. The model outlines the essential steps necessary to tap into the vast reservoir of a firm's customer tacit knowledge and this will increase the potential for greater revenues. Companies that take advantage of the advances in IT hardware and software can provide interested loyal customers with the opportunity to enter a company's inner circle of knowledge and offer innovative ideas, pose questions and provide answers to other customers' queries. This approach to knowledge acquisition in this chapter is called customer derived revenue (CDR). The essential company architecture necessary to successfully implement CDR is explained and case studies utilizing similar methods are presented to lend support for this new approach to customer capital to be adopted on a wider scale to extract more value for a firm.

Copyright © 2004, Idea Group Inc. Copying or distributing in print or electronic forms without written permission of Idea Group Inc. is prohibited.

Introduction

Innovation through knowledge transfer in most companies is treated as an internal matter and the customer is simply considered as an external revenue source. That approach has been redefined in this chapter to a new method that captures customers' innovations. The old-school method that focuses on listening carefully to what customers want and then responding with new products that meet or exceed their needs is what Miller and Morris (1999) referred to as: "'explicit' needs, that constitute only the visible tip of the iceberg, the part of need that is above the surface of awareness. By far the larger mass of need, the submerged part, is 'latent' need, and this will probably not be discovered, nor satisfied, in a practice that fragments critical knowledge" (p. 16). This fragmentation fails to meet the modern needs of knowledge-driven enterprises, exempts customers from financial measurements that add value to a firm and clarity to stakeholders, and finally, excludes customers' tacit knowledge that can be extracted at a minimal cost to a firm.

This chapter details how an organization can focus its vision, strategy and culture to open up channels to permit the CDR concept to maximize revenues. Robert Blattberg (2001) states that "the customer is a financial asset that companies and organizations should measure, manage, and maximize just like any other asset" (p. 3). Research shows that in some companies 80% of all innovations originate from customers rather than producers (Hippel, 1988). These data are more than a decade old, but they have not changed, which indicates a strong desire for knowledge sharing has existed and the need for a CDR model in organizations is long overdo in coming.

Background

One reason that it is important to treat customers as human capital assets within a firm is that it will provide a more accurate market value of that organization. The market value of a knowledge company as determined by the stock exchanges is calculated by multiplying the stock price by the number of shares of stock outstanding. This simple calculation provides the market's value of the company. Where the market value is greater than the value of the firm's total tangible assets, then the value in excess of this amount may be said to be the

Copyright © 2004, Idea Group Inc. Copying or distributing in print or electronic forms without written permission of Idea Group Inc. is prohibited.

premium the market places on two aspects of the firm's intellectual capital: its perception of the amount of intellectual capital held by the firm, as well as its perception of the firm's ability to leverage this intellectual capital in the business marketplace (Sullivan, 1998).

If a company incorporates the CDR model that extracts customers' untapped tacit knowledge and converts it into intellectual assets, the calculation of a firm's market value introduced by Sullivan will change. This occurs because there will be an increased perception of the amount of a firm's intellectual capital and an increase in its ability to leverage this intellectual capital. However, this is only possible if there is a strong alignment of the following three categories: vision and strategy, values and culture, leadership and management. When each of these overlaps each other, the degree of overlap indicates the level of values shared by members of an organization, and these shared values rarely change in comparison with group behavior norms. Edgar Schein called this the "performance trinity". There is strong evidence that shows strong cultures play an important role in success or failure of an organization to accomplish a strong alignment. The importance of these three categories will be discussed in detail later in this chapter.

The obvious drawback when dealing with tacit knowledge and intangible assets is that they are nearly impossible to measure, and current accounting standards prohibit accounting for the vast majority of intangible assets because they are viewed as too abstract and fluid. Current GAAP (Generally Accepted Accounting Principals) basically do not allow intangible assets to be accounted for. As will become more evident later in chapter, this creates misleading information on many companies' balance sheets, especially for knowledge-based firms.

The focus of this chapter is not on accounting, but intangible assets have taken on a significant role in the knowledge driven economy and must not be underestimated. Baruch Lev, the world's leading researcher on intangible assets, discovered that 70% of American investments in 1929 were in tangible assets and the other 30 were in intangibles, but by 1990 this figure had reversed. In response to this paradigm change, some Swedish firms like Celemi International have included information about their intangible assets as a supplement to their balance sheet to make their business potential and market value more transparent to their stakeholders. Edvinsson (2002) pointed out, "in America, the Intellectual Property Association has estimated that the creative sectors—chiefly communications, information, entertainment, science and technology—are already worth $360 billion a year" (p. 35).

Copyright © 2004, Idea Group Inc. Copying or distributing in print or electronic forms without written permission of Idea Group Inc. is prohibited.

Fitz-enz (2000) commented on the uphill battle faced by the accounting world when he wrote: "Granted the accounting establishment has not yet accepted human capital accounting. This is not surprising, since dramatic changes and new methods seldom come from within the establishment. None of the mainframe computer makers came up with the personal computer. None of the airlines or railroads originated next-day delivery of small packages. This is because institutions concentrate most of their energy on fighting a rearguard action to protect their assets" (p. 117). Investments in intangibles continue to rise; therefore, the debate on how to account for intangibles will grow and most likely force changes in the present accounting standards from external pressure.

Value Creation and Value Extraction Models

The following models all relate to turning hidden value into tangible value. Hubert Saint-Onge and Leif Edvinsson's value creation models, along with Patrick Sullivan's approach to value extraction, have influenced the model presented in this chapter. Hubert Saint-Onge, working for the Canadian Imperial Bank of Commerce (CIBC), and Leif Edvinsson, working at a Swedish insurance firm, Skandia, developed the Skandia/CIBC (1995) model of intellectual capital that they divided into three parts: human capital, structural capital, and customer capital. Stewart (1997a) outlines the advantages of the model, "each of the three elements—human, structural, and customer capital—can be measured and targeted for investment. Each is intangible—each reflects the knowledge assets of a company—and yet each describes things that managers and investors can get their arms around. Moreover, once you are thinking in categories like human, structural, and customer capital, it becomes possible to ask the questions that allow you to identify tacit as well as explicit knowledge" (p. 75).

Sullivan introduced his strategy development spectrum that covers: mission, vision, objectives, goals, issues, alternatives and decision to action plans. He then divided them into two groups: "strategic thinking" and "strategic planning," to show their value on a time scale. Sullivan (1998) states, "A strategic vision is a set of operationally meaningful statements describing the organization as it wishes to be in the future. It is more specific than a mission statement, which set forth objectives in broad business terms" (p. 31). Sullivan (1998) continues:

Copyright © 2004, Idea Group Inc. Copying or distributing in print or electronic forms without written permission of Idea Group Inc. is prohibited.

"This vision (as well as the firm's strategy for achieving it) may be used as the basis for measuring the utility or value of intangibles such as intellectual capital. If an intellectual asset such as an idea, a patent, or a process can assist the company in implementing its strategy or achieving its vision, then it has value to the firm. The amount of value depends on the degree to which the intellectual asset enables the strategy or vision" (p. 33).

Sullivan's ideas and the Skandia/CIBC model add value to a firm, but the CDR model in Figure 1 that has been plugged into the Matsuda and Hall (2001) model illustrates how this new approach adds an important link to customers' tacit knowledge that is missing from the Sullivan, Saint-Onge and Edvinsson models. The CDR model assimilates the customer into a firm's human capital to produce greater revenue potential. Human capital is significant because it is the source of innovation and renewal. Customer capital is the value of an organization's relationships with the people it does business with. Stewart (1997b) says that, "whether the relationship is upstream or downstream, its

Figure 1. Matsuda & Hall dynamic mechanism of value creation with customer derived revenue.

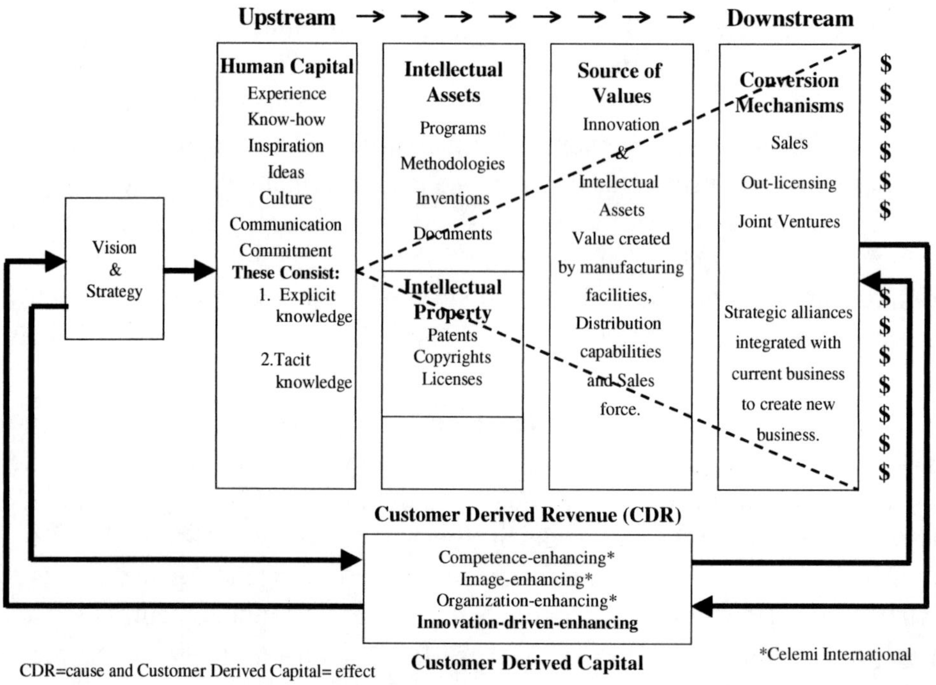

Copyright © 2004, Idea Group Inc. Copying or distributing in print or electronic forms without written permission of Idea Group Inc. is prohibited.

economics and dynamics are the same. It is here, in the relationships with customers, that intellectual capital turns into money" (p. 77).

This chapter presents the argument that customer capital is not only reserved for a downstream value-added component, but it is also a value-added component that feeds into a company's upstream flow and contributes to innovation and revenue creation for an enterprise. Customers have become empowered with knowledge from an ever-disclosing world driven by IT systems; therefore, companies must be more transparent in dealing with clients and customers in the present sharing generation. When knowledge is shared between clients, customers and competitors, positive tension to excel is drawn out and innovation thrives. In the beginning many wrote that knowledge management (KM) was a passing phase, but that was more than a decade ago and what we see is that KM has created a new paradigm that is evolving and is in need of appropriate strategies to increase a firm's value. The CDR theory seeks to expand the traditional approach of the sales representative bringing back innovative ideas derived from customers into a comprehensive knowledge acquisition and company-wide sharing. Miller and Morris (1999) state, "customer needs are rarely articulated. In fact, they may not be able to be articulated at all, and so the only effective way to understand future needs is for customers to participate in the innovation process" (p. 10). Loyal customers especially are willing to give feedback to a company that can lead to new innovation or improvement. The problem is that very few companies have a system that links its customers with the development staff.

Celemi International, a Swedish consulting firm, named the three areas listed in the box above in a 1995 company report. When the author's innovation-driven enhancing is included it completes the CDR mechanism. A customer can and often does add to more than one or can even contribute to all of these categories. Definition of the terms and examples are as follows: Competence-enhancing customers are those who bring projects challenging the competence of a company's employees. These customers are valuable because a company's employees learn from them. Image-enhancing comes from famous customers who speak well about the company or products it produces. This is a type of free advertising that adds value to an organization by reducing the high advertising cost necessary. Organization-enhancing comes from customers whose demands force a company to become more efficient or acquire new tangible or intangible assets.

Copyright © 2004, Idea Group Inc. Copying or distributing in print or electronic forms without written permission of Idea Group Inc. is prohibited.

Vision and Strategy

Sullivan's strategy development spectrum was introduced earlier as a method to develop an overall strategy for intellectual assets; however, we must examine it from a customer policy deployment view. There are similarities, but customer policy deployment, in particular, aims to move the entire organization to focus more on customers in order to increase their satisfaction and loyalty. The policy includes four major steps: mission and vision, goals, communication strategy and priority setting and implementation (Johnson, 2000). Mission and vision state the firm's philosophy; goals are the short and medium-term goals aligned with the vision; communication strategy conveys the vision and goals company-wide; priority setting and implementation align the incentives and priorities of the company to match the vision and goals and to implement quality improvement projects. The author adds a fifth step, "culture strategy," which involves internal culture building and external culture understanding of international markets.

When a company sets out to incorporate the CDR concept in its vision and goal, it is vital for those companies not to correlate customer satisfaction with loyalty, because data show 15% to 40% of customers who say they are satisfied change to a competitor. This defection rate broken down by age bracket reveals customers 65 and older have a 40% defection rate; with those 35 and older it rises to 60%; and the news grows worse for those in the 20 to 35 bracket, with an enormous 85% defection rate (Bhote, 2003 a). This proves that customer satisfaction and loyalty have little correlation; consequently, firms that focus their mission and vision only towards customer satisfaction will not maximize revenues. Bhote (2003 b) outlines six facts that point out the significance for developing customer loyalty, and the author added the seventh fact.

Fact 1: There is a very close correlation between customer loyalty and profitability.

Fact 2: A 5% reduction in customer defection can result in profit increases from 30% to 85%. (This includes companies from a wide range of industries.)

Fact 3: If customers increase their customer retention (the opposite of customer defection) by 2%, it is the equivalent of cutting their operating costs by 10%.

Fact 4: Loyal customers provide higher profits, more repeat business, higher market share, and more referrals than do "just satisfied" customers.

Copyright © 2004, Idea Group Inc. Copying or distributing in print or electronic forms without written permission of Idea Group Inc. is prohibited.

Fact 5: It costs five times more to find new customers than to retain customers.

Fact 6: One lifetime customer is worth more than $850,000 to a car company (p. 46). Fact 7 is an additional fact added by the author.

Fact 7: Innovation-driven enhancing loyal customers produce increased revenues in certain firms. One example is the $15 billion growth in 2001 in the custom-chip market (Thomke & Hippel, 2002).

To establish a successful communication strategy, an organization first needs to establish an environment that breeds trust company-wide; employ a democratic structure that fosters free exchange of ideas throughout the different levels of the organization; and reward an atmosphere of knowledge sharing in the organization that creates positive tension. That knowledge can stem from the individual or external sources such as customers or suppliers. The problem is that too often employees who share ideas suffer from a jealous backlash from fellow workers if the knowledge sharing leads to promotion or some significant benefit. This is where it is imperative that all employees understand the company's mission, vision and goals, and the leadership must trust employees and give them space to carry out the goals. An organization in today's knowledge-driven economy that fears to tear down the traditional vertical management and secretive policies will be left far behind by those companies that set priorities and implement a horizontally aligned flat structure with knowledge sharing channels that thrive on positive tension.

Culture strategy is the fifth part of the customer deployment policy. It has an internal and external role in a company. The internal cultural strategy is developed as part of the company vision and the external influence originates from international customers. Companies involved in international trade should at best, incorporate cultural understanding and, at the very least, a cultural awareness on a worldwide scale in order to realize the highest return from the CDR concept. Recent data show that in North America alone there are 197 million Internet users, an increase of 78.7% from 2000 to 2003. Contrast that to the three Asian powerhouses: China, Japan and South Korea, the three countries with a combined total of 152 million users (InternetWorldStats.com, 2003a). Even though the three countries together have fewer users than in North America, these are rapidly growing markets for Internet users: 202% increase from 2000 to 2003 in China, 38% in South Korea and 22% in Japan (InternetWorldStats.com, 2003b). A large misconception is that all Asian countries can be lumped together. Each country has its own unique culture and

Copyright © 2004, Idea Group Inc. Copying or distributing in print or electronic forms without written permission of Idea Group Inc. is prohibited.

Figure 2. Double rotary knowledge drivers.

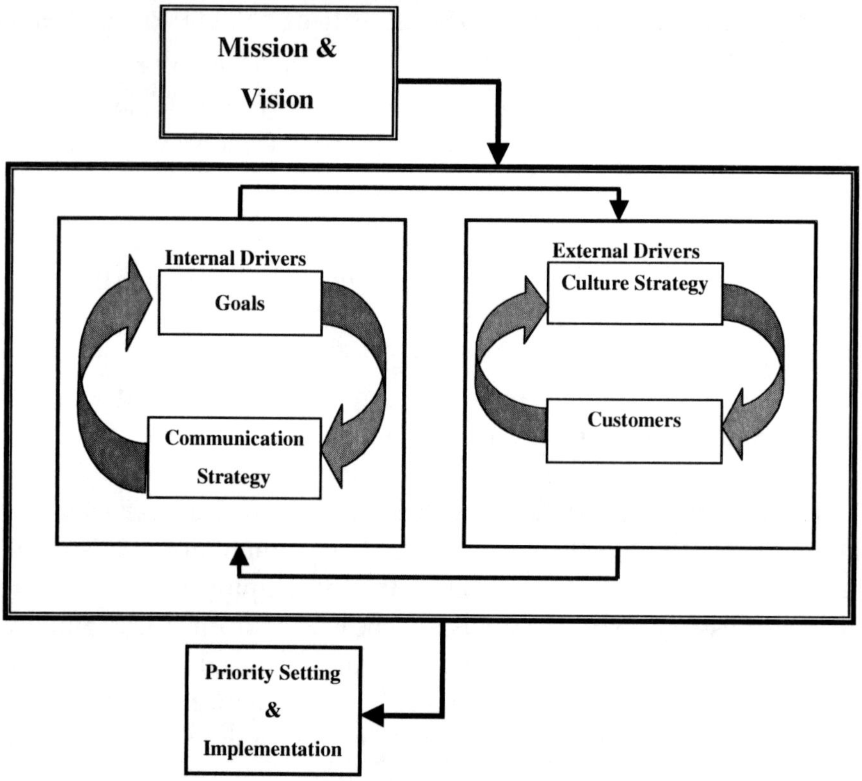

ideas and it would benefit companies dealing with or targeting these counties to provide a channel of knowledge sharing. This not only applies to Asian countries but to other non-western societies. This might entail expanding the role of the international department or creating a whole new department, but the addition of culture strategy in customer policy deployment will play a significant role in capturing a greater portion of CDR and magnify the human capital. Figure 2 illustrates the flow that exists within the strategy and vision box introduced in Figure 1.

Case Studies with Enhancing Factors

The alliance between Aluminum maker Alcoa and Audi Car Company that began in 1985 is a good example of how a relationship can take on the role as

Copyright © 2004, Idea Group Inc. Copying or distributing in print or electronic forms without written permission of Idea Group Inc. is prohibited.

a competence-enhancing, image-enhancing and organization-enhancing customer. Alcoa was looking to increase sales because its market had flattened out, so it targeted the huge car industry. At about the same time Audi was looking for new ways to expand its market in Europe. Two factors drew Audi to look at doing business with Alcoa: The European car market is heavily influenced by engineering prestige and German law requires that cars be recycled. An all-aluminum car has both the sleek image and a green marketing advantage in Europe. The problem was how to make a car from aluminum. It took Audi and Alcoa engineers nine years to roll out the first production model of an all-aluminum car. When the first cars rolled off the assembly line, Audi benefited from image-enhancing through Alcoa's environmentally friendly aluminum parts and it reached a new engineering height in the car industry.

Audi's demands forced Alcoa to find ways to produce aluminum that would be suitable enough to handle the excessive friction produced by the engine and the load to other parts. Audi's demands forced Alcoa to make engineering advances and because of those changes, the company underwent competence-enhancing as well as organization-enhancing. The organization-enhancing that took place at Alcoa became known as Alcoa Business System (ABS). The core principles of ABS are: make to use, eliminate waste and people linchpin the system. It has evolved since its first introduction in the 1990s from trying simply to meet customers' explicit needs to a customer-centric engineering management style and improved knowledge transfer between customers and employees. In addition to the positive and tangible financial outcomes, ABS provides a simple, consistent, powerful framework for decision-making, communication and people engagement (Alcoa News Letter, 2003). Even though sales dropped by 10% and net income was down for 2002, the company has strengthened itself in cost reductions, increasing productivity and strengthening connection with customers to meet the short-term challenges facing the company.

In another case, Cisco Systems implemented an innovation-enhancing system to relieve a bottleneck created after a new software package was released. The company was overwhelmed with queries and the need for support, so Cisco went straight to its existing strength—the Web. Lev (1999) describes what Cisco did was "to put as much of its support as possible online so that customers would be able to resolve most workaday problems on their own, leaving the engineers free to do the heavy lifting. It was almost instant success, becoming in Mrs. Bostrom's [head of Cisco's Internet Solutions Group] words, a 'self-inflating balloon of knowledge.' Cisco's customers did not just

Copyright © 2004, Idea Group Inc. Copying or distributing in print or electronic forms without written permission of Idea Group Inc. is prohibited.

go to the website to get information, they started using it to share their own experiences with both Cisco itself and other customers" (p. 25). Now the company's homepage is loaded with valuable links, including specific online forums, case studies and networking solutions. Cisco's bottleneck solution is a good illustration of the differences between innovation-driven enhancing and the other enhancers. Loyal customers are not merely pushing employees to new heights, adding brand value or forcing organizational changes; they become an unpaid, but potential revenue creating part of the value chain. The motivation for loyal customers to participate in such a scheme lies in improved products, improved service and if the customer is a shareholder he or she can realize profits from the improved market value. Any one or all of these motivators give a customer an actual stake in the company and make him or her feel a part of the organization.

Loyal Customers and Loyal Employees

Heskett (2003a) comments that "revenue enhancement occurs through the new product ideas proposed by loyal customers that can be filtered through the 'listening post' of a loyal employee" (p. 86). The significance of a satisfied customer compared to a loyal one was delineated early, but in this section the process and importance of selecting loyal customers and employees will be presented.

Frederick Reichheld (2001 a) cites the importance of choosing the right customers to become loyal customers. The costs associated with customer acquisition, retention and defection are significant; therefore he emphasizes companies must collect barnacles and resist luring butterflies. Barnacles will stay around for a long time, whereas butterflies get their fill and leave. He chose several forward thinking companies to support his argument that being particular can reduce costs. Dell narrowed its customer segment by focusing on the Internet as its primary consumer channel. Since only consumers who already had a computer could get online, these were almost certainly experienced users, who would be less expensive to serve. Another famous company that avoids certain types of customer is Enterprise Rent-A-Car. It refuses to cater to the large corporate-account, frequent-traveler segment because these rentals are detrimental to fleet utilization because of cyclical demand and short-term rentals. This inflates administrative costs with the national account billing system it requires.

Copyright © 2004, Idea Group Inc. Copying or distributing in print or electronic forms without written permission of Idea Group Inc. is prohibited.

Figure 3. What employees want, expressed in terms of the employee value equation.

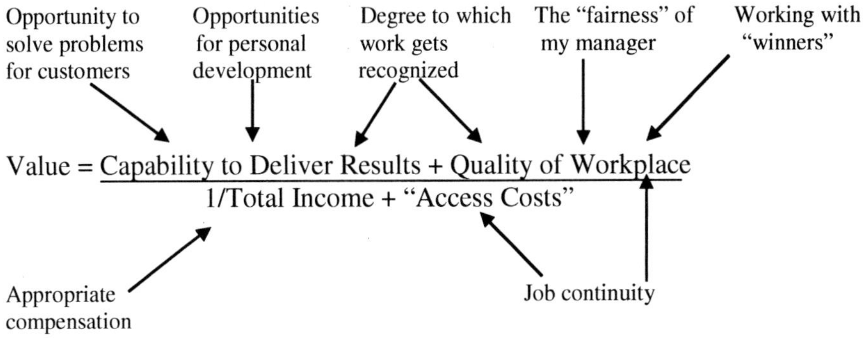

Many will argue loyal employees do not exist in the 21st century. Reichheld (2001b) gives four examples that refute this argument. The three most important are: Harley Davidson Motorcycle Company, Dell Computer and Chick-fil-A. All have excellent employee relations in relation to the average in their respective industry. They search for candidates who will dedicate themselves to the company for the long run and in return provide opportunities for advancement and unique compensation packages. It must be emphasized that loyalty cannot be bought; it comes about through a two-way commitment to trust, appreciation and sharing the same vision. The three companies mentioned have spent large amounts of money and time in order to choose the correct employees over the years, but when one considers the extremely low turn-over rates at 5% compared to 20 to 30% on average, the cost saved through fewer trainees needed annually and costs associated with disgruntled workers, the attained revenues far outweigh the selection costs. Heskett (2003b) developed a value equation in Figure 3 to show how loyal employees play a crucial role in maintaining the loyal customer base (p. 158).

Conclusion

Clearly, innovation is not unique to the current economic environment, but what is unique to the modern corporation is the urgency to innovate. Given the decreasing economies of scale (efficiency gains) from production, coupled with the ever-increasing competitive pressures, innovation has become a matter of

Copyright © 2004, Idea Group Inc. Copying or distributing in print or electronic forms without written permission of Idea Group Inc. is prohibited.

corporate survival (Lev, 2001). Companies must find a way to capitalize on their customer knowledge and more accurately account for it for their stakeholders and other interested parties. Miller and Morris (1999) argue that "what is now required is a business process focused on innovation rather than a business structure focused on R&D, technology development, and product/service development" (p. 24). However, many companies fail to comprehend that their present systems will be inhibited and some will even fail as the knowledge-driven economy gains momentum.

The three enhancing factors mentioned in this chapter that are used by some firms gives evidence that profits can be realized through customer innovation. The innovation-driven enhancing addition presented in the CDR model presently is still untested, but it is hoped that by presenting the arguments about the potential benefits that discussion will be forthcoming, and it will lead to a practical application and greater revenues for knowledge-driven firms. Arguments presented in this chapter brought out the importance of establishing a strong vision, goal, communication, commitment and culture, and that generating loyalty internally and externally plays a key role in the overall success of this model. As was pointed out, loyalty relies heavily on recognition of work completed, fairness and personal development. However, top management is often unable to recognize the significance in promoting both employee and customer loyalty. This obstacle, along with denial of the present paradigm shift, may prove to be a barrier in accepting the CDR concept. For those who deny there has been a paradigm shift, a quote from 19th century economic theory should help erase any doubt that times have changed.

"Only the investment of capital assets can increase the productivity of labor."

References

Aboody, D., & Lev, B. (1998). The value relevance of intangibles: The case of software capitalization. *Journal of Accounting Research* (supplement), *36,* 161-91.

Alcoa. (2003). *Annual company report.*

Bhote, K. (2003). *The power of ultimate six sigma.* New York: AMACOM.

Copyright © 2004, Idea Group Inc. Copying or distributing in print or electronic forms without written permission of Idea Group Inc. is prohibited.

Blattberg, T., Gary, G., & Thomas, J. (2001). *Customer equity.* Boston: Harvard University Press.

Celemi International. (1995). *Annual report.*

Edvinsson, L. (2002). *Corporate longitude: What you need to know to navigate the knowledge economy.* Prentice Hall.

Fitz-enz, J. (2000). *The ROI of human capital: Measuring the economic value of employee performance.* New York: AMACOM.

Heskett, J., Sasser, E., & Schlesinger, L. (2003). *The value of the profit chain.* New York: Simon & Schuster.

Hippel, E. von. (1988). *The sources of innovation.* New York: Oxford University Press.

Johnson, M. (2000). *Improving customer satisfaction, loyalty, and profit.* San Francisco: Jossey-Bass Inc.

Lev, B. (1999, June 26). *The Economist,* p. 12.

Lev, B. (2001). *Intangibles management, measurement, and reporting.* Washington DC: Brookings Institution Press.

Matsuda, J., & Hall, M. (2001). *A dynamic mechanism of value creation: A model for intangible assets.* 2002 IRMA Conference (International Resource Management Association) (pp. 261-62).

Miller, W., & Morris, L. (1999). *Fourth generation R&D.* New York: John Wiley & Sons, Inc.

Reichheld, F. (2001. *Loyalty rules!* Boston: Harvard Business School Press.

Saint-Onge, H., & Edvinsson, L. (1995, October 3.). *Intellectual capital as a business reality.* Presentation.

Stewart, Th. (1997). *Intellectual capital the wealth of organizations.* New York: Doubleday.

Sullivan, P. (1998). *Profiting from intellectual capital.* New York: John Wiley & Sons.

Thomke, S., & Hippel, E. von. (2002, April 1). Customers as innovators. *Harvard Business Review,* 74-81.

Copyright © 2004, Idea Group Inc. Copying or distributing in print or electronic forms without written permission of Idea Group Inc. is prohibited.

About the Editor

Bonnie Montano earned her PhD from the University of Pennsylvania in 1997, and she is currently an assistant professor of Management Information Systems with the McDonough School of Business, Georgetown University, Washington, DC. Dr. Montano has completed funded research for the U.S. Social Security Administration, the Health Care Financing Administration, and the Naval Postgraduate School. She has authored or coauthored papers in *Decision Support Systems, Communications of the ACM, ASCE Journal of Urban Planning and Development,* and *Information Knowledge Systems Management.* Her current research interests include the areas of intelligent decision support, knowledge management, and organizational learning.

Copyright © 2004, Idea Group Inc. Copying or distributing in print or electronic forms without written permission of Idea Group Inc. is prohibited.

About the Authors

Witold Abramowicz is currently the chair of Department of Information Systems at The Poznan University of Economics, Poland. His particular areas of interest are information filtering to MIS, information retrieval, and applications of knowledge discovery in MIS. He received his MSc from The Technical University of Poznan, Poland, PhD from The Wroclaw Technical University, Poland and habilitation from The Humboldt University Berlin, Germany. He worked for three universities in Switzerland and Germany for 12 years. He chaired eight scientific international conferences and was a member of the program committees of 81 other conferences. He is an editor or co-author of 14 books and 98 articles in various journals and conference proceedings.

Glenn Bewsell is currently an associate lecturer in the School of Information Systems, Technology and Management at The University of New South Wales in Sydney, Australia. His research interests are in the fields of knowledge management and trust.

N.A. Boraie is director of Triple Line Consulting, UK,president of Triple Line Consulting Inc., USA, and founder of House of Egypt Management Consultants, Egypt. She holds a BSc degree in Chemistry and an MBA in Knowledge Management from the University of Bradford (UK)/NIMBAS (NL). Nevert is a senior management consultant and a certified mediator. She has extensive experience in business and in the financial markets, and has consulted in the areas of business policy and strategy. Besides working as an upgrading manager for an EU financed private sector development programme, Nevert has worked extensively with SMEs in multi-cultural environments as well as

Copyright © 2004, Idea Group Inc. Copying or distributing in print or electronic forms without written permission of Idea Group Inc. is prohibited.

with the privatisation of public sector companies. She has served on the board of several international schools and trading companies.

Francisco Vilar Brasileiro received the bachelor's degree in Computing Science and MSc degree in Informatics from the Federal University of Paraíba, Brazil, in 1988 and 1989, respectively. He received the PhD degree in Computing Science in 1995 from the University of Newcastle upon Tyne, England, for his work on fail-controlled nodes and agreement protocols. In 1989, after a brief incursion in industry, he joined the Department of Systems and Computing of the Federal University of Paraíba, where he is currently a senior lecturer. His main research areas are in fault tolerance and distributed systems and protocols. Dr. Brasileiro is a member of the Brazilian Computing Society, the ACM, and the IEEE Computer Society.

Abdus Sattar Chaudhry is programme director of MSc (Knowledge Management) and Head of Division of Information Studies at the School of Communication and Information at Nanyang Technological University of Singapore. He has earlier held a variety of managerial and professional positions at different types of information organizations in the USA, Saudi Arabia, Pakistan, and Malaysia. Dr. Chaudhry holds a master's degree from University of Hawaii and a PhD from University of Illinois at Urbana-Champaign. His areas of teaching and research include organization and management of information and knowledge. He can be reached by e-mail at aschaudhry@ntu.edu.sg.

Jack S. Cook is a professor, speaker, author, and consultant. He is associate professor of Management Information Systems at the Rochester Institute of Technology (RIT) (USA). His areas of expertise include electronic commerce, information systems and production/operations management. Jack's extensive experience teaching and training over the last two decades includes over 90 conference presentations and numerous journal articles. He has an entertaining and engaging approach and is known for bringing theories to life. Dr. Cook is a certified fellow in Production and Inventory Management (CFPIM). His education includes a PhD in Business Administration, an MS in Computer Science, an MBA, an MA in Mathematics, and a BS in Computer Science. To learn more about Jack, visit his Web site at www.sizzlingsolutions.com.

Copyright © 2004, Idea Group Inc. Copying or distributing in print or electronic forms without written permission of Idea Group Inc. is prohibited.

Laura Cook works as a technology support professional for the Computing & Information Technology Department at the State University of New York at Geneseo (USA). She manages all technology support for seven departments. She has a bachelor's degree in Business Administration from Washington State University and a Master's of Science in Information Technology from the Rochester Institute of Technology (RIT). Laura is the Webmaster and on the board of directors for the Rochester, New York chapter of APICS.

Ana Maria R. Correia obtained her first degree in Chemical Engineering (1972), her PhD (Organic Chemistry) at the University of Liverpool, UK (1979) and her Agregação (equivalent to Habilitation) (Information Systems and Technology, area of Information Management) (1998) from the Universidade Nova de Lisboa. She is professora associada com Agregação at Universidade Nova de Lisboa (UNL) (Portugal)/ISEGI (Instituto Superior de Estatística e Gestão de Informação – Higher Institute of Statistics and Information Management). Since 1993, she has been Professor Associate at the Department of Information Studies at the University of Sheffield (United Kingdom). She lectures on knowledge management, information policies, information systems, research methodologies, information resources digital libraries.

Farhad Daneshgar is a senior lecturer at the School of Information Systems, Technology and Management at The University of New South Wales, Australia. His main areas of research interest are knowledge sharing, and analysis and design of collaboration support systems. His awareness framework has been widely regarded by both academic and industry communities for the purpose of identifying the awareness requirements of the actors in collaborative business processes. He has publications in 26 international conferences, journals and books. Farhad is also a member of the editorial board of the *Electronic Journal of Knowledge Management.*

Michael Hall is a full time instructor at the School of Business, Marketing and Distribution at Nakamura Gakuen University in Fukuoka, Japan. He teaches business English and America management practices and principles to his junior and senior seminar students. He is currently enrolled in a doctoral program at Kyushu University located in Fukuoka. His research interests lie in environmental management, in particular, recycling concrete and wood products and knowledge management. He received his BA from Augustana College in Illinois

Copyright © 2004, Idea Group Inc. Copying or distributing in print or electronic forms without written permission of Idea Group Inc. is prohibited.

and has lived and taught in Japan for 24 years. He participates in community volunteer activities to bring greater awareness about environmental problems and has his seminar students become involved in planning and executing environmental volunteer activities for the local community.

Meliha Handzic received her PhD in Information Systems from The University of New South Wales (Australia). She is currently senior lecturer and inaugural leader of the Knowledge Management Research Group (kmRg) in the School of Information Systems, Technology and Management. Her main research interests include knowledge management and decision support.

Tony Jewels, BBus *QIT,* MIT (Professional) *QUT,* CMACS (Project Management), MAIEx, is a lecturer within the School of Information Systems at Queensland University of Technology (Australia), teaching IT management and IT project management at undergraduate and postgraduate levels. He is currently completing a PhD with a theme of increasing IT project success through the application of knowledge management principles. An IT professional for over 30 years, he has worked in a variety of roles on many leading edge IT projects throughout the world, running his own IT consultancy company for over 10 years. He is a regular contributor to international IS conferences that include ECIS, ACIS, AMCIS, InSite and IRMA.

Pawel Jan Kalczynski is an assistant professor of Information Systems and works for the College of Business Administration at the University of Toledo (USA). He received his MIS (summa cum laude) and PhD degrees from The Poznan University of Economics in Poland. His primary research interests are in the area of knowledge management systems with the particular focus on the integration of structured and unstructured information. He is a co-author of the monograph *Filtering the Web to Feed Data Warehouses,* published by Springer Verlag, London.

Ching Lee is the president of Hyper Taiwan Technology Inc., Taipei, Taiwan. The company provides Qualification Services for wireless communication products. He has over twenty years of experience in Avionics system design and analysis, program management, avionics planning and integration. He has successfully led and managed Taiwan IDF and F-5 avionics upgrade program teams.

Copyright © 2004, Idea Group Inc. Copying or distributing in print or electronic forms without written permission of Idea Group Inc. is prohibited.

Maria Ruey-Yuan Lee is a department head and associate professor of the Information Management Department, Shih Chien University, Taipei, Taiwan. Her current research interests include ontology, wireless Internet and mobile commerce. She has published in several international conferences and journals and has been a referee, panelist, program committee member and organizer at a number of international conferences. She has also worked with CSIRO Mathematical and Information Sciences, Sydney, Australia for over 12 years, and led a group conducting research and development in applying artificial intelligence technologies to electronic business applications.

Albert C. K. Leung is assistant professor of Information Systems at Lingnan University in Hong Kong. He received his PhD in Information Systems from University of Manchester Institute of Science and Technology (UMIST). His research mainly focuses on instructional technology, training and learning effectiveness, and strategic issues of e-business development. His research has been published in *Journal of Computer Information Systems, Journal of Computer Assisted Learning, Educational Technology Review,* and *International Journal of Computer Integrated Manufacturing.*

Patricia C. Miller is a PhD candidate in Information Science at the University at Albany (USA). Her research interests are in knowledge management, interorganizational collaboration, innovation in government and business, and technology implementation. Ms. Miller works for a state agency as the Director of Information Services and is a lecturer in the School of Business at the University at Albany. To contact Ms. Miller: pmiller@albany.edu.

Francisco Milton Mendes Neto received a bachelor's degree in Computing Science from the State University of Ceará, Brazil (1997). He received an MSc in Informatics in 2000 from the Federal University of Paraíba, Brazil, for his work on environments to support web-based collaborative learning. Currently, he is receiving a PhD in Computing Science from the Federal University of Campina Grande, Brazil, for his work on knowledge management and computer-supported collaborative learning. In 1998, he joined the Superintendence of Corporate Systems of the Federal Service of Data Processing, where he is currently an adviser. Mendes Neto is a member of the Brazilian Computing Society and the Brazilian Knowledge Management Society.

Copyright © 2004, Idea Group Inc. Copying or distributing in print or electronic forms without written permission of Idea Group Inc. is prohibited.

Jonathan Pemberton, BSc (Hons), PhD, FSS, is a senior lecturer at Newcastle Business School, Northumbria University, UK, and is programme leader for the Faculty's Doctor of Business Administration (DBA). He lectures in a range of subjects including quantitative business research, forecasting, and strategic knowledge management. His research interests and publications cover socio-technological issues of knowledge management, knowledge management and competitive advantage, organisational and individual learning, technology initiatives and knowledge management in general practice.

Anabela Sarmento obtained her first degree in the management area, her Master in Science Education and her PhD in Technology and Information Systems, at University of Minho. She is a professor at Higher Institute of Administration and Accountancy (ISCAP)/Polytechnic School of Porto (Portugal). She lectures on business communication and information society. Her research areas are the impact of information systems on organisations and knowledge management (SMEs, intellectual capital and higher education).

George Stonehouse, BA (Hons), MA, M.Ed is associate dean for Undergraduate Programmes at Newcastle Business School, Northumbria University, UK, and specializes in strategic management, global and transnational business and organizational learning. He is visiting professor at a number of institutions in Russia and China. As well as publishing a number of texts in strategic management and global business, he has written several journal articles on organizational learning, knowledge management, strategic management and competitive advantage.

W. A. Taylor is associate dean of Research and full professor of Information Systems at the Bradford School of Management in England, where he teaches courses in information and knowledge management. He holds a BSc in Electronics and Computer Systems, an MSc in Industrial Engineering and a PhD in Knowledge Based Systems, all from The Queen's University of Belfast. Andrew spent several years working in manufacturing, public utilities and government agencies before returning to academia in 1984. He has published over 100 articles and books on his research interests in knowledge based systems, knowledge management, organizational information systems and performance improvement. He acts as a consultant to many multinational companies and government departments. He is a chartered engineer, and

Copyright © 2004, Idea Group Inc. Copying or distributing in print or electronic forms without written permission of Idea Group Inc. is prohibited.

fellow of the Institution of Electrical Engineers and the Institute of Quality Assurance.

Alan Underwood, BBus *QIT*, MS (MIS) *Texas Tech,* MBA *Qld,* PhD *QUT,* FACS, PCP, is head of school and associate professor in Information Systems in the Faculty of Information Technology at Queensland University of Technology in Brisbane, Australia. Professor Underwood is a past national president and vice president of the Australian Computer Society (ACS) and a past chairman of the ACS (Qld) Branch. In 1997 he stepped down as the national director of the ACS Professional Board, responsible, among other things, for the PCP and certification programmes offered by the ACS. Professor Underwood's contributions to the IT industry have been recognised with his election as Fellow of the Australian Computer Society in 1993 and Honorary Life Member in 1994. Current research interests include professional certification, management information systems, project management of virtual/meta teams, knowledge management and IT curricula and accreditation standards. It is likely that once any appropriate knowledge sharing strategy (formal or informal) is securely in place, the widespread adoption of any alternative strategy (formal or informal) will need not only to prove its own worth but also to prove itself more effective than any existing strategy, in order to take a preeminent position.

Krzysztof Wecel is currently working as a lecturer and research assistant in the Department of Management Information Systems at The Poznan University of Economics. He holds an MSc in Business Computing (2000, summa cum laude) and a PhD in Economics (in the area of Business Information Systems). His research areas includes ontologies, semantic Web, data warehousing, and knowledge management. He holds an internationally recognized certificate of SAS certified developer, and also participated in courses covering data warehouse technologies organized by SAS Institute. He is a co-author of the monograph *Filtering the Web to Feed Data Warehouses,* published by Springer-Verlag, London.

Katsutoshi Yada received the PhD from Kobe University of Commerce, Hyogo, Japan in 2002. From 1997-2000, he was an assistant professor in the Department of Business Administration, Osaka Industrial University, Osaka, Japan. He is currently an associate professor in the Faculty of Commerce,

Copyright © 2004, Idea Group Inc. Copying or distributing in print or electronic forms without written permission of Idea Group Inc. is prohibited.

Kansai University, Osaka, Japan. His research interests focus on information strategy concerning data mining and effects on organizations of information technology. He is a member of IEEE Computer Society, Organizational Science Society of Japan, Japan Business Management Society and Japan Society for Management Information.

Copyright © 2004, Idea Group Inc. Copying or distributing in print or electronic forms without written permission of Idea Group Inc. is prohibited.

Index

A

B

C

Copyright © 2004, Idea Group Inc. Copying or distributing in print or electronic forms without written permission of Idea Group Inc. is prohibited.

Copyright © 2004, Idea Group Inc. Copying or distributing in print or electronic forms without written permission of Idea Group Inc. is prohibited.

G

H

I

K

Copyright © 2004, Idea Group Inc. Copying or distributing in print or electronic forms without written permission of Idea Group Inc. is prohibited.

L

M

N

O

P

Copyright © 2004, Idea Group Inc. Copying or distributing in print or electronic forms without written permission of Idea Group Inc. is prohibited.

Q

R

S

T

Copyright © 2004, Idea Group Inc. Copying or distributing in print or electronic forms without written permission of Idea Group Inc. is prohibited.

U

V

W

X

Copyright © 2004, Idea Group Inc. Copying or distributing in print or electronic forms without written permission of Idea Group Inc. is prohibited.

Instant access to the latest offerings of Idea Group, Inc. in the fields of
INFORMATION SCIENCE, TECHNOLOGY AND MANAGEMENT!

InfoSci-Online Database

- BOOK CHAPTERS
- JOURNAL ARTICLES
- CONFERENCE PROCEEDINGS
- CASE STUDIES

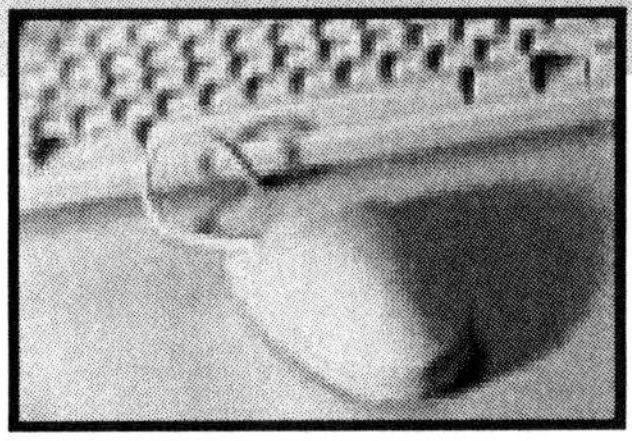

"The Bottom Line: With easy to use access to solid, current and in-demand information, InfoSci-Online, reasonably priced, is recommended for academic libraries."

- Excerpted with permission from Library Journal, July 2003 Issue, Page 140

Start exploring at www.infosci-online.com

The InfoSci-Online database is the most comprehensive collection of full-text literature published by Idea Group, Inc. in:

- Distance Learning
- Knowledge Management
- Global Information Technology
- Data Mining & Warehousing
- E-Commerce & E-Government
- IT Engineering & Modeling
- Human Side of IT
- Multimedia Networking
- IT Virtual Organizations

BENEFITS

- Instant Access
- Full-Text
- Affordable
- Continuously Updated
- Advanced Searching Capabilities

Recommend to your Library Today!

Complimentary 30-Day Trial Access Available!

A product of:
Information Science Publishing*
Enhancing knowledge through information science

*A company of Idea Group, Inc.
www.idea-group.com

NEW RELEASE

Beyond Knowledge Management

Brian Lehaney, PhD, University of Coventry, UK
Steve Clarke, PhD, University of Luton, UK
Elayne Coakes, PhD, University of Westminster, UK
Gillian Jack, PhD, University of Glamorgan, UK

Beyond Knowledge Management provides a balance of conceptual and practical aspects of knowledge management, offering the opportunity for students and practitioners to understand and effectively consider knowledge management approaches in their organizations. Everyday examples are used to lead the reader into the development of knowledge management, then further into a conceptual perspective, and finally to the practical application of knowledge management in organizations.

ISBN 1-59140-180-1 (h/c) • US$79.95 • *ISBN 1-59140-223-9 (s/c)* • US$64.95
• *280 pages* • *Copyright © 2004*

Beyond Knowledge Management *provides a balance of conceptual and practical aspects of Knowledge Management, offering the opportunity for students and practitioners to understand and effectively consider knowledge management approaches in their organizations.*

- Gillian Jack, University of Galmorgan, UK

It's Easy to Order! Order online at www.idea-group.com or call 717/533-8845 x10
Mon-Fri 8:30 am-5:00 pm (est) or fax 24 hours a day 717/533-8661

IGP **Idea Group Publishing**
Hershey • London • Melbourne • Singapore

An excellent addition to your library

IDEA GROUP PUBLISHING

Publisher of IT books, journals and cases since 1988

NEW RELEASE

Trust in Knowledge Management and Systems in Organizations

Maija Leena Huotari, Ph.D., University of Oulu, Finland
Mirja Iivonen, Ph.D., University of Tampere, Finland

Trust in Knowledge Management and Systems in Organizations aims at tying trust to knowledge management (KM). It highlights the complexity of the invisible phenomenon of trust challenged by the global economy. Fresh insights, novel theoretical frameworks, and empirical results and ideas for future research are presented that differ from those since the 1950s. The eleven chapters (whose authors represent information studies, economics, administrative scientists, mass communications, computer science and cognitive science) explore the multidisciplinary nature of the concepts of trust and KM. The concept of trust is analyzed by presenting its extensive description in relation to knowledge and information-intensive activities and systems for understanding the dynamics of knowledge-based production at the levels of individuals, information systems, organizations, networks and society. Systems are considered from the social or the socio-technological perspective.

ISBN 1-59140-126-7 (h/c) • US$79.95 • *ISBN 1-59140-220-4 (s/c)* • US$64.95
eISBN 1-59140-127-5 • 296 pages • Copyright © 2004

"Trust has a crucial role to play when organizations aim at innovation and successful operation. Although trust has been studied for decades in various disciplines, the importance of trust has probably never before been more significant than it is today both in theory and practice."

- Maija Leena Huotari, University of Oulu, Finland &
Mirja Iivonen, University of Tampere, Finland

It's Easy to Order! Order online at www.idea-group.com or call 717/533-8845 x10
Mon-Fri 8:30 am-5:00 pm (est) or fax 24 hours a day 717/533-8661

An excellent addition to your library!

IGP

I D E A G R O U P P U B L I S H I N G

Hershey
London
Melbourne
Singapore

Idea Group Publishing
701 E. Chocolate Ave.
Suite 200
Hershey, PA 17033,
USA
Tel: (717) 533-8845
Fax: (717) 533-8661
cust@idea-group.com
www.idea-group.com

Knowledge and Information Technology Management: Human and Social Perspectives

Angappa Gunasekaran, PhD
University of Massachusetts, USA

Omar Khalil, PhD
University of Massachusetts, USA

Syed Mahbubur Rahman
Minnesota State University, USA

The importance of knowledge and information technology management has been emphasized by researchers and practitioners in order for companies to compete in the global market. Now such technologies have become crucial in a sense that there is a need to understand the business and operations strategies, as well as how the development of IT would contribute to knowledge management and therefore increase competitiveness.

Knowledge and Information Technology Management: Human and Social Perspectives strives to explore the human resource and social dimensions of knowledge and IT management, to discuss the opportunities and major issues related to the management of people along the supply chain in Internet marketing, and to provide an understanding of how the human resource and the IT management should complement each other for improved communication and competitiveness.

ISBN 1-59140-032-5(h/c)
eISBN 1-59140-072-4
US$84.95
380 pages
Copyright © 2003

"Knowledge management initiatives are undertaken for the purpose of achieving better organisational efficiency and effectiveness, with the goal being able to achieve superior performance."

Angappa Gunasekaran, University of Massachusetts,
Omar Khalil, University of Massachusetts &
Syed Mahbubur Rahman, Minnesota State University

It's Easy to Order!
Call our Order Department at
717-533-8845 (Ext. 10)

Mon-Fri 8:30 am-5:00 pm (est) or
fax 24 hours a day
717/533-8661

For the latest information and news about IGP publications, please visit IGI's web site at http://www.idea-group.com

An excellent addition to your library!